# Queer Studies and Education

# Queer Studies and Education
*An International Reader*

Edited by Nelson M. Rodriguez
Robert C. Mizzi
Louisa Allen
*and*
Rob Cover

Oxford University Press is a department of the University of Oxford. It furthers
the University's objective of excellence in research, scholarship, and education
by publishing worldwide. Oxford is a registered trade mark of Oxford University
Press in the UK and certain other countries.

Published in the United States of America by Oxford University Press
198 Madison Avenue, New York, NY 10016, United States of America.

© Oxford University Press 2023

All rights reserved. No part of this publication may be reproduced, stored in
a retrieval system, or transmitted, in any form or by any means, without the
prior permission in writing of Oxford University Press, or as expressly permitted
by law, by license, or under terms agreed with the appropriate reproduction
rights organization. Inquiries concerning reproduction outside the scope of the
above should be sent to the Rights Department, Oxford University Press, at the
address above.

You must not circulate this work in any other form
and you must impose this same condition on any acquirer.

Library of Congress Cataloging-in-Publication Data
Names: Rodriguez, Nelson M., editor
Title: Queer studies and education : an international reader / [edited by]
  Nelson M. Rodriguez, Robert C. Mizzi, Louisa Allen, and Rob Cover.
Description: New York, NY : Oxford University Press, [2023] |
Includes bibliographical references and index. |
Identifiers: LCCN 2023017332 (print) | LCCN 2023017333 (ebook) |
ISBN 9780197687000 (hardback) | ISBN 9780197687024 (epub) |
ISBN 9780197687031
Subjects: LCSH: Gay and lesbian studies. | Homosexuality and education.
Classification: LCC HQ75.15 .Q484 2023 (print) | LCC HQ75.15 (ebook) |
DDC 306.76/607—dc23/eng/20230417
LC record available at https://lccn.loc.gov/2023017332
LC ebook record available at https://lccn.loc.gov/2023017333

DOI: 10.1093/oso/9780197687000.001.0001

Printed by Integrated Books International, United States of America

# CONTENTS

*Acknowledgments*    ix
*Editors' Biographies*    xi
*Contributors' List*    xiii
*Contributors' Biographies*    xvii

Introduction: Reading Queer Studies and/in Education:
International Contexts and Perspectives    1
*Nelson M. Rodriguez, Robert C. Mizzi, Louisa Allen, and Rob Cover*

1. Space, Place, and Queerness: The University of the West Indies,
Mona Campus' Queer Zoning    27
*Adwoa Onuora and Nadeen Spence*

2. A Queer Sexuality Education: The Possibilities and
Impossibilities of Knowing    47
*Naomi Rudoe*

3. Rupturing the "Cul-de-Sac": Queer(y)ing Graduate Education
Studies    65
*James Burford and Genine Hook*

4. Racism, Heteronormativity, and Educational Assemblage in
Germany    81
*María do Mar Castro Varela and Yener Bayramoğlu*

5. Queered Failure and Management Education    99
*Nick Rumens*

6. Navigating Personal and Professional Identities in the Higher
Education Workplace: A Facilitated Autoethnography    115
*Craig M. McGill, Tonette S. Rocco, Joshua C. Collins, Lorenzo Bowman,
Rod P. Githens, Holly M. Hutchins, Nathan Victoria, Saul Carliner,
Gisela P. Vega, Julie Gedro, and Thomas Nechodomu*

7. Shifting the Gaze: A Decolonial Queer Analysis of Photographs of the Canadian Indian Residential Schools    *138*
*Spy Dénommé-Welch and Robert C. Mizzi*

8. "No Queers, No Marching Bands": Schools, Social Recognition, and Gender Visibility on the Brazil–Bolivia Border    *156*
*Tiago Duque and Gustavo Moura*

9. Timely Interventions: Queer Activist Early Childhood Teaching in Aotearoa New Zealand    *175*
*Alexandra C. Gunn*

10. Beyond "Abstinence Only": The U.S. Christian Right's "Pro-Family" Countermovement against Comprehensive Sexuality Education and Sexual and Reproductive Rights in Eastern and Southern Africa    *195*
*Finn Reygan and Haley McEwen*

11. Queering School Sport and Physical Education    *217*
*Richard Pringle and Dillon Landi*

12. Queer Screen Pedagogies: Australian Queer Audiences and the Educational Value of LGBTQ Film and Television Stories    *234*
*Rob Cover*

13. The Possibilities and Futurities of LGBTQ Youth: Thinking From a Queer of Color Critique in Educational Research    *254*
*Andrea Vasquez and Cindy Cruz*

14. An Assimilation or Transgression of "Normativities": A Qualitative Sociological Exploration of the Experiences of Gay and Lesbian Students at a South African University    *270*
*Tshanduko Tshilongo and Jacques Rothmann*

15. Norm-Critical Pedagogy as Femo- and Homonationalism: Perspectives on Norm Critique in Swedish Research, Activism, and Educational Practice    *296*
*Eva Reimers*

16. "The Only Orange Park Bench": Using Photo Elicitation to Explore Campus Experiences of LGBTIQA+ Students    *311*
*John Fenaughty, Lucy Cowie, and Louisa Allen*

17. Trans Children in Primary Schools: Thinking Queerly About Happiness and Time    *333*
    *Aoife Neary*

18. Queer Love and Education    *350*
    *Nelson M. Rodriguez and William F. Pinar*

*Index    367*

# ACKNOWLEDGMENTS

The editors would like to thank all of the contributors for their excellent chapters. We are grateful for their time and intellectual energy in helping us to organize and reflect on international work in the field of queer studies and education. Many thanks are owed as well to our editors at Oxford University Press, Hayley Singer and Abby Gross, to project editor Lacey Harvey, as well as to editor Tim Allen for his initial interest in and encouragement of our proposal, and to the entire team at Oxford University Press for all of their assistance with, commitment to, and support in helping to bring this project to fruition.

# EDITORS' BIOGRAPHIES

**Nelson M. Rodriguez** is Associate Professor of Women's, Gender, and Sexuality Studies at The College of New Jersey, where he serves as Coordinator of the Sexuality and Queer Studies Program. His scholarship spans the fields of queer and gender studies, Foucault studies, critical pedagogy and cultural studies, and education. His recent publications include *Michel Foucault and Sexualities and Genders in Education: Friendship as Ascesis* (with David Lee Carlson, 2019); *Queer Pedagogies: Theory, Praxis, Politics* (with Cris Mayo, 2019); *Critical Concepts in Queer Studies and Education: An International Guide for the Twenty-First Century* (with Wayne J. Martino, Jennifer C. Ingrey, and Edward Brockenbrough, 2016); *Educators Queering Academia: Critical Memoirs* (with sj Miller, 2016); *Queer Masculinities: A Critical Reader in Education* (with John C. Landreau, 2012); and *Queering Straight Teachers: Discourse and Identity in Education* (with William F. Pinar, 2007).

**Robert C. Mizzi** is the Canada Research Chair in Queer, Community, and Diversity Education and Associate Professor in the Faculty of Education at the University of Manitoba, Canada. He has over 200 publications and presentations, including articles published in the *Journal of Homosexuality* and the *Journal of Studies in International Education*. He has also published five books, with the most recent being the *Handbook of Adult and Continuing Education* in 2020. He is President Emeritus of the Canadian Association of Adult Education and is Editor Emeritus of the *Canadian Journal for the Study of Adult Education*. Robert has been inducted into the International Adult and Continuing Education Hall of Fame and the Royal Society of Canada (College of New Scholars).

**Louisa Allen** is a Professor in the Faculty of Education and Social Work at the University of Auckland. Her scholarship spans the areas of gender, sexualities, sexuality, reproduction, and education. This work is informed by queer theory, feminist new materialism, feminist philosophy and sensory studies. To explore these areas, she employs innovative research methodologies such as visual and more recently sensory methods, including soundwalks and smellwalks. With her colleague Professor Mary Lou Rasmussen, she is currently Editor-in-Chief of the first *Encyclopedia of Sexuality Education*. Her most recent project is a Marsden Grant with Professor Katrina Roen, which explores experiences of shame and silence for intersex young people. In 2021, she published a sole-authored book, *Breathing Life Into Sexuality Education*, which disrupts existing ideas about the nature and purpose of this curriculum. It employs scholarship from disparate disciplinary fields, including feminist philosophy, education, sound studies, geography, and anthropology to imagine the possibilities of a sensuous sexuality education pedagogy.

**Rob Cover** is Professor of Digital Communication at RMIT University, Australia. He is Chief Investigator on an Australian Research Council Discovery project investigating the pedagogies of gender and sexual diversity in Australian screen media and on an ARC Linkage studying the well-being aspects of gender- and sexually diverse migration. The author of seven books and over 100 journal articles and chapters, his recent books include *Queer Youth Suicide, Culture and Identity: Unliveable Lives?* (2016); *Digital Identities: Creating and Communicating the Online Self* (2016); *Flirting in the Era of #MeToo* (with A. Bartlett and K. Clarke, 2019); *Emergent Identities: New Sexualities, Gender and Relationships in a Digital Era* (2019); and *Fake News in Digital Cultures* (with J. Thompson and A. Haw, 2022).

# CONTRIBUTORS' LIST

**Louisa Allen**, Professor in the Faculty of Education and Social Work, The University of Auckland

**Yener Bayramoğlu**, Guest Professor of Gender and Queer Studies, Alice Salomon University

**Lorenzo Bowman**, Professor of Business and Management, DeVry University/Keller Graduate School of Management

**James Burford**, Lecturer in Research Education and Development, Graduate Research School at La Trobe University

**Saul Carliner**, Professor of Education, Concordia University

**María do Mar Castro Varela**, Professor of Pedagogy and Social Work, Alice Salomon University

**Joshua C. Collins**, Associate Professor and Graduate Program Coordinator of Human Resource Development, University of Minnesota–Twin Cities

**Rob Cover**, Professor of Digital Communication, RMIT University

**Lucy Cowie**, completing a Doctor of Clinical Psychology, University of Auckland

**Cindy Cruz**, Associate Professor in the Department of Teaching, Learning, and Sociocultural Studies, University of Arizona

**Spy Dénommé-Welch**, Associate Professor and Canada Research Chair in Indigenous Arts, Knowledge Systems and Education, Western University

**Tiago Duque**, Professor of Sociology, Federal University of Mato Grosso do Sul (UFMS)

**John Fenaughty**, Lecturer in the Faculty of Education and Social Work, University of Auckland

**Julie Gedro**, Dean of the School of Business, SUNY Empire State College

**Rod P. Githens**, Alexandra Greene Ottesen Endowed Chair and Associate Professor in Leadership and Organization Development, Benerd College, University of the Pacific

**Alexandra C. Gunn**, Associate Professor, University of Otago

**Genine Hook**, Adjunct Lecturer in Sociology, University of New England

**Holly M. Hutchins**, Vice Provost of Faculty Success and Professor (Counseling and Higher Education), University of North Texas

**Dillon Landi**, Lecturer, School of Education, University of Strathclyde

**Haley McEwen**, Postdoctoral Researcher, Department of Political Science, Gothenburg University and affiliated Research Associate, Wits Centre for Diversity Studies, University of the Witwatersand

**Craig M. McGill**, Assistant Professor in the Department of Special Education, Counseling and Student Affairs, Kansas State University

**Robert C. Mizzi**, Canada Research Chair in Queer, Community and Diversity Education and Associate Professor in the Faculty of Education, University of Manitoba

**Gustavo Moura**, PhD candidate in Education, University of Manitoba

**Aoife Neary**, Lecturer in Sociology of Education, University of Limerick (UL)

**Thomas Nechodomu**, independent scholar in Education, University of Minnesota

**Adwoa Onuora**, Senior Lecturer/Associate Professor, at The Institute for Gender and Development Studies, The University of the West Indies

**William F. Pinar**, Tetsuo Aoki Professor in Curriculum Studies, University of British Columbia

**Richard Pringle**, Professor of Socio-Cultural Studies of Sport, Genders/Sexualities, and Human Movement, Monash University

**Eva Reimers**, Professor of Educational Practices, University of Gothenburg

**Finn Reygan**, Research Director in the Human and Social Capabilities (HSC) Division, Human Sciences Research Council (HSRC) in South Africa, and Extraordinary Associate Professor in Educational Psychology, University of the Western Cape

**Tonette S. Rocco**, Professor in Adult Education and Human Resource Development, Florida International University

**Nelson M. Rodriguez**, Associate Professor of Women's, Gender, and Sexuality Studies, The College of New Jersey

**Jacques Rothmann**, Senior Lecturer in Sociology, North-West University

**Naomi Rudoe**, Senior Lecturer in Sociology, University of Westminster

**Nick Rumens,** Professor of Business and Management, Oxford Brookes University

**Nadeen Spence,** student affairs, The University of the West Indies

**Tshanduko Tshilongo,** Master of Arts in Sociology Graduate and PhD candidate, North-West University, Potchefstroom Campus

**Andrea Vasquez,** studying education anthropology, University of California

**Gisela P. Vega,** Director of the LGBTQ Center and Adjunct Faculty in Gender and Sexuality Studies, University of Miami

**Nathan Victoria,** father, husband, and radical activist scholar-practitioner

# CONTRIBUTORS' BIOGRAPHIES

**Louisa Allen** is Professor in the Faculty of Education and Social Work at The University of Auckland. Her scholarship spans the areas of gender, sexualities, sexuality, reproduction, and education. This work is informed by queer theory, feminist new materialism, feminist philosophy, and sensory studies. To explore these areas, she employs innovative research methodologies such as visual and more recently sensory methods, including soundwalks and smellwalks. With her colleague Professor Mary Lou Rasmussen, she is currently Editor-in-Chief of the first *Encyclopedia of Sexuality Education*. Her most recent project is a Marsden Grant with Professor Katrina Roen, which explores experiences of shame and silence for intersex young people. In 2021, she published a sole-authored book, *Breathing Life Into Sexuality Education*, which disrupts existing ideas about the nature and purpose of this curriculum. It employs scholarship from disparate disciplinary fields, including feminist philosophy, education, sound studies, geography, and anthropology to imagine the possibilities of a sensuous sexuality education pedagogy.

**Yener Bayramoğlu** is a media and communication scholar whose work focuses on queer theory, migration, temporalities, and social inequality. Bayramoğlu studied communication in Istanbul and received his PhD from the Free University of Berlin. He was a visiting scholar at the University of Salzburg and postdoc fellow at the FU Berlin. His work was published in several journals, including *Ethnic & Racial Studies*. His first monograph, *Queere (Un-)sichtbarkeiten*, was published in Germany in 2018. He is the co-author of *Post/pandemisches Leben*, published in 2021. He is currently Guest Professor of Gender and Queer Studies at the Alice Salomon University in Berlin.

**Lorenzo Bowman**, JD, PhD, is Professor of Business and Management at DeVry University/Keller Graduate School of Management.

**James Burford** is Lecturer in Research Education and Development in the Graduate Research School, La Trobe University, Melbourne, Australia. James is a critical university studies researcher, and he is particularly interested in space, place, affect, and politics in the academic profession and doctoral education. James's doctoral thesis received the 2017 NZARE Sutton-Smith Award. James has taught in the areas of comparative education, educational equity, and academic literacies. His recent projects have focused on academic mobilities (both short and longer term), as well as the spatialities of graduate education. With Emily Henderson, James edits *Conference Inference*, an academic blog on conferences.

**Saul Carliner** is Professor of Education at Concordia University in Montreal whose research focuses on the design of materials for communication and training, the management of groups that produce them, and related issues of policy and professionalism. Also an industry consultant, he conducts analyses and evaluations for corporations, nonprofits, and government agencies. Among his publications are *Career Anxiety: Guidance for Tough Times* (with Margaret Driscoll and Yvonne Thayer); *An Overview of Training and Development* (with Margaret Driscoll); *Informal Learning Basics*; and *Training Design Basics.* He is President of the Canadian Network for Innovation in Education; board member of the International Board of Standards in Training and Performance Improvement; a Fellow and past board member of the Institute for Performance and Learning; past Research Fellow of the Association for Talent Development; and a Fellow and past international president of the Society for Technical Communication.

**María do Mar Castro Varela** is Professor of Pedagogy and Social Work at the Alice Salomon University in Berlin. She holds degrees in psychology and pedagogy and a PhD in political science. Her research interests lie in postcolonial theory, queer studies, critical migration studies, critical (adult) education, trauma studies, and conspiracy theories. Recently, she was awarded the Ustinov Visiting Professorship at the University of Vienna. María do Mar Castro Varela is the founder of the bildungsLab* in Berlin (https://www.bildungslab.net) and chair of the Berlin Institute for Contrapunctual Social Analysis (BIKA).

**Joshua C. Collins**, EdD, is Associate Professor and Graduate Program Coordinator of Human Resource Development at the University of Minnesota–Twin Cities. He is also graduate and affiliate faculty in Gender, Women, and Sexuality Studies. Dr. Collins is the recipient of the AHRD Early Career Scholar Award and the University Council for Workforce and Human Resource Education Assistant Professor Award. His research focuses on issues of learning and work for racial, ethnic, gender, and sexual minorities.

**Rob Cover** is Professor of Digital Communication at RMIT University, Australia. He is Chief Investigator on an Australian Research Council Discovery project investigating the pedagogies of gender and sexual diversity in Australian screen media, and on an ARC Linkage studying the well-being aspects of gender- and sexually diverse migration. The author of seven books and over 100 journal articles and chapters, his recent books include *Queer Youth Suicide, Culture and Identity: Unliveable Lives?* (2016); *Digital Identities: Creating and Communicating the Online Self* (2016); *Flirting in the Era of #MeToo* (with A. Bartlett and K. Clarke, 2019); *Emergent Identities: New Sexualities, Gender and Relationships in a Digital Era* (2019); and *Fake News in Digital Cultures* (with J. Thompson and A. Haw, 2022).

**Lucy Cowie** is currently completing a Doctor of Clinical Psychology at the University of Auckland. She is particularly interested in how people navigate and challenge inequity, with a focus on the intersection between psychological distress and power. Her doctoral research explores queer and gender-diverse young people's understandings of psychological distress, with a focus on improving outcomes for queer and gender diverse young people.

**Cindy Cruz** is Associate Professor in the Department of Teaching, Learning, and Sociocultural Studies at the University of Arizona. She is a critical ethnographer and youth researcher, and her work with LGBTQ street youth is grounded by her use of decolonial and U.S. women of color feminisms, resistance and infrapolitical theory, and critical pedagogy. Cindy is the recipient of the 2021 Body of Work Award from the Queer Studies in Education SIG of the American Educational Research Association. Her publications can be found in the *International Journal of Qualitative Studies in Education, Anthropology & Education Quarterly, Excellence & Equity in Education, Theory Into Practice, Curriculum Inquiry, Chicana/Latina Education in Everyday Life*, and *Youth Resistance Research and Theories of Change* and *Latinos and Education: A Critical Reader*. She was an associate editor with the Frontiers Journal Collective from 2016 to 2020, and most recently, co-edited with Jose Aguilar-Hernandez a 2020 Special Issue on Chican@/Latin@ Queer and Trans* Pedagogies in Education for the *Association of Mexican American Educators (AMAE) Journal*.

**Spy Dénommé-Welch** (Algonquin-Anishnaabe) is an interdisciplinary scholar, artist (composer and librettist/playwright), and educator. His research focuses on Indigenous arts, music, performance, and education. He

*Contributors' Biographies* [xix]

is an Associate Professor and Canada Research Chair in Indigenous Arts, Knowledge Systems, and Education in the Faculty of Education at Western University.

**Tiago Duque** is Professor of Sociology at the Federal University of Mato Grosso do Sul (UFMS), Brazil. He holds a PhD in social sciences from the State University of Campinas (UNICAMP), Brazil. Duque's program of research deals with education, body, border, health, gender, sexuality in a perspective of queer theory. He is the coordinator of Working Group 23 (Gender, Sexuality and Education) of the Association for Research and Postgraduate Studies in Education (ANPED) in the Midwest region. He is the leader of *Impróprias—Research* Group on Gender, Sexuality and Differences (UFMS).

**John Fenaughty** is Lecturer in the Faculty of Education and Social Work at the University of Auckland. John's disciplinary background in community psychology pivots around youth well-being, particularly as impacted by harassment and/or cisheteronormativity. He has over two decades of experience in queer community activism, research, and action. His research interests vary from queer youth experiences in schools, queer community organization, and queer teacher experiences, through to how men who have sex with men understand, experience, and enact sexual consent. He draws from a range of methodologies, including mixed methods, and is often informed by feminist and Foucauldian approaches. Having developed a norm-critical teaching resource via codesign methodologies, he is also exploring the opportunities and limits of norm-critical pedagogies in sexuality education in schools and youth work settings.

**Julie Gedro** is Dean of the School of Business at SUNY Empire State College, where she is also a tenured Full Professor. Dr. Gedro holds a BA from the College of William and Mary, an MBA from Kennesaw State University, and a Doctorate of Education (EdD) from the University of Georgia. Dr. Gedro is a Society of Human Resource Management Senior Certified Professional (SHRM-SCP). Dr. Gedro is a recipient of several awards, including the State University of New York Chancellor's Award for Excellence in Scholarship and Creative Activities; the Susan H. Turben Award for Excellence in Scholarship; the Jane Altes Prize for Exemplary Community Service; and the Arthur Imperatore Fellowship.

**Rod P. Githens** serves as the Alexandra Greene Ottesen Endowed Chair and Associate Professor in Leadership and Organization Development at Benerd College, University of the Pacific. He focuses on developing human and organizational potential through innovation processes, strategy

[xx]    *Contributors' Biographies*

development, group facilitation, and user-centered program development. In addition to his faculty role, Rod has worked as a consultant, human resources leader, academic program leader, assistant dean, and associate dean.

**Alexandra C. Gunn** is a former early childhood teacher who now works as an Associate Professor at the University of Otago, Dunedin, where she teaches and conducts research into early childhood education, teacher education, inclusion, genders, sexualities, and educational assessment.

**Genine Hook** completed her PhD from the Faculty of Education at Monash University in May 2015. Her research explored the experiences of sole parents at universities in Australia, and her thesis was awarded the Vice-Chancellor's Commendation for Thesis Excellence in 2015. Genine's first book was published by Palgrave Macmillan (United Kingdom) in July 2016, *Sole Parent Students and Higher Education: Gender, Policy and Widening Participation*. Dr. Hook now works as an Adjunct Lecturer in Sociology at the University of New England. Her research focuses on gender performativity, higher education, family-based violence, familial norms, feminist pedagogy, and social policy.

**Holly M. Hutchins**, PhD, is Vice Provost of Faculty Success and Professor (Counseling and Higher Education) at the University of North Texas. Dr. Hutchins's research expertise is in faculty development, training transfer, and leadership development. Her award-winning research has been published in numerous U.S. and international peer-reviewed and high-impact journals and featured in media outlets, notably National Public Radio, *Psychology Today*, BBC, and in a TEDX talk (Sugar Land, TX).

**Dillon Landi** is Lecturer in the School of Education at the University of Strathclyde (Glasgow, U.K.). He is a sociologist of health, physical activity, and education with expertise in qualitative methods, critical theory, and gender/sexuality. He received his PhD in education from the University of Auckland (New Zealand), where he also served as a faculty member in the School of Curriculum and Pedagogy. Prior to Auckland, Dillon received two postgraduate degrees from Columbia University (New York, NY, USA) while serving as a public school teacher and district supervisor.

**Haley McEwen** is a Postdoctoral Researcher in the Department of Political Science at Gothenburg University. She is also an affiliated Research Associate of the Wits Centre for Diversity Studies at the University of the Witwatersrand, Johannesburg.

She holds a PhD in sociology from the University of the Witwatersrand, Johannesburg. Her research focuses on "antigender" movements against LGBTIQ+ rights, reproductive justice, gender studies, and comprehensive sexuality education in African contexts. Haley is a nationally rated researcher in South Africa and holds a Senior Fellowship at the Center for Analysis of the Radical Right. Haley is Associate Editor of the *International Journal of Critical Diversity Studies*.

**Craig M. McGill** is Assistant Professor in the Department of Special Education, Counseling, and Student Affairs at Kansas State University. He teaches primarily for the master's and doctoral degree programs in Academic Advising. Dr. McGill holds master's degrees in music theory (University of Nebraska–Lincoln) and academic advising (Kansas State University) and a doctorate in adult education and human resource development (Florida International University). Prior to his arrival at Kansas State University (in summer 2020), he was a primary role academic advisor for nearly a decade at the University of Nebraska–Lincoln (2009–2012) and Florida International University (2012–2018) and then transitioned to a postdoctoral research fellowship at the University of South Dakota. He is a qualitative researcher with an emphasis on professional identity, professionalization, feminist, queer and sexuality studies, and social justice.

**Robert C. Mizzi** is the Canada Research Chair in Queer, Community, and Diversity Education and Associate Professor in the Faculty of Education at the University of Manitoba, Canada. He has over 200 publications and presentations, including articles published in the *Journal of Homosexuality* and the *Journal of Studies in International Education*. He has also published five books, with the most recent being the *Handbook of Adult and Continuing Education* in 2020. He is President Emeritus of the Canadian Association of Adult Education and is Editor Emeritus of the *Canadian Journal for the Study of Adult Education*. Robert has been inducted into the International Adult and Continuing Education Hall of Fame and the Royal Society of Canada (College of New Scholars).

**Gustavo Moura** is a PhD candidate in education at the University of Manitoba, where his dissertation focused on unpacking Western LGBTQ+ teachers' identities using English as a medium of instruction. Originally from Brazil, he has had teaching and research experiences in his home country as well as Canada and Cuba. Gustavo's academic experiences include English as a second language/English as an additional language (ESL/EAL) language teacher education, intercultural teacher development, LGBTQ+ teacher education, teacher identity, technologies in education, online and remote learning, and intersectionality in education.

**Aoife Neary** is Lecturer in Sociology of Education at the School of Education, University of Limerick (UL), Ireland. Drawing on feminist, queer, and affect

[xxii]   *Contributors' Biographies*

theory, her research explores the politics of gender and sexuality in education. She held an Irish Research Council (IRC) Doctoral Scholar award (2011–2014) and IRC New Foundations awards in 2013, 2014, 2015, and 2016. Most recently, she was Primary Investigator/Academic Mentor on an IRC/Marie Curie cofunded project, "Achieving Equality for Trans and Gender Diverse Youth in Schools" (2018–2020). She leads and teaches teacher education modules that explore equality and diversity from a sociological perspective.

**Thomas Nechodomu** is an independent scholar with an MA in education from the University of Minnesota. He has over two decades of experience in the field of learning and development and has consulted and taught in corporate, nonprofit, and higher education institutions. He most recently opened his own research-based bakery, Behind the Breadbox, where he has excitedly taken on the title "Experimental Baker and Owner."

**Adwoa Onuora** is Senior Lecturer/Associate Professor at The Institute for Gender and Development Studies at The University of the West Indies, Mona Campus. She is the author of *Anansesem: Telling Stories and Storytelling African Maternal Pedagogies* and co-editor with Anna Kasafi Perkins and Ajamu Nangwaya of *Rough Riding: Tanya Stephens and the Power of Music to Transform Society* (UWI Press, 2020).

**William F. Pinar** is the Tetsuo Aoki Professor in Curriculum Studies and former two-term Canada Research Chair at the University of British Columbia in Vancouver, Canada. Pinar has also served as the St. Bernard Parish Alumni Endowed Professor at Louisiana State University (LSU), the Frank Talbott Professor at the University of Virginia, and the A. Lindsay O'Connor Professor of American Institutions at Colgate University. He has lectured widely, including at Harvard University, McGill University, the University of Wisconsin–Madison, as well as the Universities of Chicago, Helsinski, Oslo, and Tokyo. The former President of the International Association for the Advancement of Curriculum Studies and the founder of its U.S. affiliate, the American Association for the Advancement of Curriculum Studies, in 2000 Pinar received the LSU Distinguished Faculty Award and a Lifetime Achievement Award from the American Educational Research Association; in 2004, he received an American Educational Association Outstanding Book Award for *What Is Curriculum Theory?*, the third edition of which was published in 2019. Pinar is also the author of the recently published *Moving Images of Eternity: George Grant's Critique of Time, Teaching, and Technology*.

**Richard Pringle** is Professor of Socio-Cultural Studies of Sport, Genders/Sexualities, and Human Movement at Monash University, Melbourne. He is the coauthor of *Foucault, Sport and Exercise* (2006) (with Pirkko Markula) and *Sport and the Social Significance of Pleasure* (2015) (with Bob Rinehart and Jayne Caudwell) and co-editor of *Examining Sport Histories: Power, Paradigms and Reflexivity* (with Murray Phillips) and *Critical Research in Sport, Health and Physical Education* (2018) (with Håkan Larsson and Göran Gerdin).

**Eva Reimers** is Professor of Educational Practices at the University of Gothenburg, Sweden. Her research focus is on norms and diversity in education. She is co-editor of several books, including *School in Norms [Skola i normer]* (Martinsson and Reimers, 2009), with new extended editions published in 2014 and 2020; *Norm-Struggles* (Martinsson and Reimers, 2010); and *Norms at Work* (Martinsson and Reimers, 2007). Other publications include "Homonationalism in Teacher Education" (Reimers, 2017), "Disruptions of Desexualised Heteronormativity—Queer Identifications as Pedagogical Resources" (Reimers, 2019), and *Education and Political Subjectivities in Neoliberal Times and Places. Emergences of Norms and Possibilities* (Reimers and Martinsson, 2017).

**Finn Reygan** is Research Director in the Human and Social Capabilities (HSC) Division at the Human Sciences Research Council (HSRC) in South Africa and Extraordinary Associate Professor in Educational Psychology at the University of the Western Cape. He leads multiyear, multicountry projects across Africa focused on supporting the broad development agenda, particularly as this relates to education, gender, youth, and sexual and reproductive health and rights (SRHR).

**Tonette S. Rocco** is Professor in Adult Education and Human Resource Development at Florida International University in Miami, Florida. She is a Houle Scholar, a member of the 2016 class of the International Adult and Continuing Education Hall of Fame, 2016 Outstanding HRD Scholar, and recipient of more than 35 awards for scholarship, mentoring, and service. She is Editor-in-Chief of *New Horizons in Adult Education and Human Resource Development* (Wiley) and serves on a dozen editorial boards. She is a founding board member for the *Journal of Mixed Methods Research*; *Dialogues in Social Justice: An Adult Education Journal*; *Journal of Global Education and Research*; *New Directions in Adult and Continuing Education*; and *Nursing & Health Sciences Research Journal*. She publishes work on continuing professional education; equity and privilege (specifically in terms of race/critical race theory, sexual minorities/LGBT, disability, and age);

[xxiv] *Contributors' Biographies*

employability/career development; fostering student research and professional writing; and qualitative methods. Her current projects include *The Routledge Handbook of LGBTQ Identity in Organizations and Society* (with Gedro) and "Doing Transgender: Gender Minorities in the Organization" [Special Issue] of *Gender, Work, and Organization* (with McFadden, Crowley-Henry, Rumens, and Collins).

**Nelson M. Rodriguez** is Associate Professor of Women's, Gender, and Sexuality Studies at The College of New Jersey, where he serves as Coordinator of the Sexuality and Queer Studies Program. His scholarship spans the fields of queer and gender studies, Foucault studies, critical pedagogy and cultural studies, and education. His recent publications include *Michel Foucault and Sexualities and Genders in Education: Friendship as Ascesis*; *Queer Pedagogies: Theory, Praxis, Politics*; *Critical Concepts in Queer Studies and Education: An International Guide for the Twenty-First Century*; *Educators Queering Academia: Critical Memoirs*; *Queer Masculinities: A Critical Reader in Education*; and *Queering Straight Teachers: Discourse and Identity in Education*. Rodriguez's forthcoming books include *LGBTQ+ Studies in Education: Theoretical Interventions in Curriculum and Pedagogy* and *Foucauldian Philosophy and Implications for Educational Research: Michel Foucault's Lectures at the Collège de France*.

**Jacques Rothmann** is Senior Lecturer in Sociology at the North-West University, Potchefstroom Campus. His research interests include Gender Studies, Lesbian and Gay Studies, and Queer Theory. He has served as convener for the South African Sociological Association's Lesbian, Gay, and Queer Studies working group. He published articles and book reviews in national and international academic journals on themes concerning gender and sexuality. He obtained the Y-Rating from the National Research Foundation (NRF) in 2019.

**Naomi Rudoe** is Senior Lecturer in Sociology at the University of Westminster, U.K. Her research interests are in the sociology of education and education policy, with particular focus on sexuality education, parents and sex education, and early years education.

**Nick Rumens** is Professor of Business and Management at Oxford Brookes University, United Kingdom. His main research interests are lesbian, gay, bisexual, transgender, and queer+ (LGBTQ+) sexualities and genders in organizations, workplace friendships, and queer theories. He has published on these topics in journals, including *Human Relations, Organization Studies, British Journal of Management, Organization, Journal of Personal and Social Relationships*, and *Gender, Work & Organization*. Single-authored books include *Queer Company: Friendship in the Work Lives of Gay Men* (Ashgate, 2011) and *Queer Business: Queering Organisation Sexualities* (Routledge, 2018).

**Nadeen Spence** works in student affairs at The University of the West Indies, Mona Campus, where much of her work centers on women's development as well as students' leadership development in higher education. She is a political and social commentator who has shared her opinions on political and social life in the Caribbean on a number of radio and television programs throughout the Caribbean and Latin American region. Her doctoral dissertation focuses on women's leadership identity and transformational pedagogies in higher education.

**Tshanduko Tshilongo** is a Master of Arts in sociology graduate and a PhD candidate at the North-West University, Potchefstroom Campus. Her research interests include gender studies, lesbian and gay studies and industrial sociology.

**Andrea Vasquez** is an education anthropologist studying at the University of California, Santa Cruz. A finalist for the Miriam Jiménez Román Fellowship from the Latinx Project at New York University, her work locates the everyday mechanisms of geographies of anti-Blackness and how they shape the lives of Black and Latinx youth in Mexican/Chicanx Californian communities. Her areas of expertise include ethnography, anti-Blackness/Blackness, liberal statecraft, multiracial coalition, U.S. women of color theorizing, and the anthropology of education. You can read her work in the *Association of Mexican American Educators (AMAE) Journal* and follow her on Twitter at @_LaVazquez_.

**Gisela P. Vega** is Director of the LGBTQ Center and Adjunct Faculty in Gender and Sexuality Studies at the University of Miami. Previously she served as the inaugural LGBTQ professional at Florida International University (FIU) and as a professor with Women's and Gender Studies, assisting in the establishment of their Queer Studies Certificate. In 2019 she received the National LGBTQ Task Force's Eddy McIntyre Service Award. She holds her doctorate in higher education leadership from FIU, a master's in education instructional leadership, two BFAs in art education and in graphic design from the University of Illinois at Chicago.

**Nathan Victoria** is a father, husband, and a radical activist scholar–practitioner. Featured as the "Exec of the Future: Change Agent" by ASAE's *Associations Now* and recognized as one of the *Association Forum's* 2018 Class of Forty Under 40 award winners, he is the inaugural Executive

Director for the Society for Personality Assessment. He is also a doctoral candidate in the Executive Leaders Program, Human and Organizational Learning, at the George Washington University, where he is challenging the concept of "objective" research through his dissertation, which examines how minoritized volunteer leaders navigate Whiteness within their professional associations.

# Introduction

## Reading Queer Studies and/in Education:
## International Contexts and Perspectives

NELSON M. RODRIGUEZ, ROBERT C. MIZZI,
LOUISA ALLEN, AND ROB COVER

*Queer Studies and Education: An International Reader* explores how the category queer, as a critical stance or set of perspectives, contributes to opportunities individually and collectively for advancing queer social justice.[1] Our collection takes up this general goal by presenting a cross section of international perspectives on queer studies in education to demonstrate commonalities, differences, uncertainties, or pluralities across a range of national contexts and topics, drawing a heightened awareness of heterodominance and heteropatriarchy, and to conceptualize nonnormative and nonessentialist imaginings for more inclusive educational environments. Indeed, in a world that continues to be rife with conflict and oppression, including reactionary backlash to sociocultural and political advances made by any number of marginalized groups, there is good reason to consider how researchers and activists position or queer their educational work in this current climate. This work is achieved via diverse theories of critique as researchers, scholars, educators, activists, and other cultural workers labor across any number of sites that now constitute places where people engage in processes of teaching and learning: for example, polytechnics, workplaces, human services agencies,

---

Nelson M. Rodriguez, Robert C. Mizzi, Louisa Allen, and Rob Cover, *Introduction* In: *Queer Studies and Education*.
Edited by: Nelson M. Rodriguez, Robert C. Mizzi, Louisa Allen, and Rob Cover, Oxford University Press.
© Oxford University Press 2023. DOI: 10.1093/oso/9780197687000.003.0001

training programs, primary and secondary education and university classrooms, (social) media, streetscapes, and many other sites of education. Queer critique in these locations is always a matter of where we begin and is always caught in a complex web of heteronormative discourses that we may want to challenge as we are also caught up in reproducing them. The route to unraveling these discourses, and the perpetual reification of them, will remain a long road, and yet, the work needs to be done.

Critiques of heteronormativity and normativity more generally have endured within queer studies scholarship since queer theory emerged in academe in the late 1980s and early 1990s (Berlant & Warner, 1998; Butler, 1990, 2013; Foucault, 1978; Jagose, 1996, 2015; McCann & Monaghan, 2020; Morgensen, 2021; Rubin, 1993; Sedgwick, 1990; Spargo, 1999; Warner, 1991, 1993).[2] Highlighting, while also contributing to, debates about "the constitutive limitations of institutionalized identity-based fields of study" (Amin, 2020, p. 18), including the perceived limitations associated with the study of foundational identities within the field of gay and lesbian studies,[3] queer theorists reframed the questions they would pursue, asking, as Salamon (2021) explained:

Not *where are the queer subjects?*, but rather *how do we become subjects in the first place? Into what regimes of gender and sexuality are we conscripted, and through what means?* In posing these questions, queer theorists share certain presuppositions: that sexuality is constructed rather than natural, that queer as a descriptor offers significant resistance to referentiality, that attention to the workings of power and its relation to recognition and legibility is of crucial importance in understanding sexuality. As Berlant and Warner put it: "without forgetting the importance of the hetero-homo distinction of object choice in modern culture, queer work wants to address the full range of power-ridden normativities of sex." (p. 507, original italics)

Recalibrating the focus on a critical analysis of the construction between normative and nonnormative discursive formations has been impactful in terms of the way scholars in queer studies have approached their work across the humanities and social sciences; in this context, the work of deploying the concept of heteronormativity "situates queerness in a perpetually slant relation to the norm," thus laying "bare the regulatory forces and norms that inevitably underlie gender and sexuality" (Salamon, 2021, p. 507). Through what processes and with what effects and consequences has sexuality become legible in the modern world?

In the field of queer studies in education, a critical engagement with heteronormativity and normativity is no less visible and can be discerned

[2]    *Rodriguez et al.*

across a broad swath of its scholarship. For example, positioned mainly in North America, there is a body of literature provided by scholars that "queers" education (bringing to light the dominance of heteronormativity in school systems and envisioning different ways in which to organize—that is, queer—education, including queering educational research) (see, e.g., Letts & Sears, 1999; Pinar, 1998; Rasmussen, 2006; Renn, 2010; Rodriguez & Pinar, 2007; Rofes, 2005; Talburt & Steinberg, 2000; Taylor & Coia, 2014; Tierney, 1997). These texts offer a queer epistemology by way of critiquing schools or universities and highlighting (1) the difficult experiences of queer educators and learners, (2) the dominance of sexual politics and exclusive policies in educational settings, and (3) the practice of panicking about, policing, and regulating sexualities in education. There is also a body of literature that describes the politics and goals of queer activism, internal and external to educational systems, and suggests a queer pedagogy that "troubles" (hetero)normative assumptions in education; confronts or teaches against heteronormativity; problematizes the containment of gender and sexuality through everyday social norms, institutions, and policies; raises awareness about queer oppression; and argues for nonnormative teaching and leadership approaches (see, e.g., Britzman, 1995; Bryson & DeCastell, 1993; Kaufman & Powell, 2014; Kumashiro, 1999, 2002; Luhmann, 1998; Martinsson & Reimers, 2010; Mayo & Rodriguez, 2019; Meyer, 2019; Quinlivan & Town, 1999; Rottmann, 2006; Walton, 2014). In addition, there is a body of literature that extends concepts situated within queer theory, gender and sexuality studies, as well as studies of intersectionalities, and extrapolates them to analyses of the queer context in education (see, e.g., Carlson & Rodriguez, 2019; Harris & Gray, 2014; Landreau & Rodriguez, 2012; Mayo, 2022; Rodriguez, 2016, 2019; Rodriguez et al., 2016; Strunk & Shelton, 2021). These concepts range from notions of masculinity and femininity, performativity, in/visibility, and locations of difference to the problem of "truth," resistances and resist-stances, and hegemony, among many others. Such concepts have been useful in understanding the unfolding dynamics and persistence of (hetero)normativity in specific political, historical, and sociocultural contexts associated with schooling and education.

As an object of critique, heteronormativity features prominently across the 18 chapters assembled in *Queer Studies and Education*. The first set of chapters, for instance, provides perspectives from Jamaica, England, Aotearoa New Zealand, Australia, Germany, and the United States and Canada and adds to the body of literature in the area of international perspectives on queer studies and education (see, e.g., Francis et al., 2020; Kjaran & Sauntson, 2019).[4] Despite clear differences in national and political contexts among these chapters, which can vary internally to the country, there are some common threads, such as the pervasiveness of heteronormativity and its negative influence on queerness and queer identities. However, as these initial six chapters in the collection demonstrate, heteronormativity is not a uniform concept, and therefore ameliorative approaches and reading practices will vary.[5]

A broad view of this first cluster of chapters suggests heteronormativity forms a political spectrum depending on the conservative, liberal, and moderate contexts that surround queerness and queer identities. First, there are conservative contexts that entrench heteronormativity with deep fervor and clearly rebuke any social movement working toward alleviating the deleterious effects of heteronormativity. The first chapter on Jamaica can be read as an example of this conservative context, where queer people become objects of scorn and contempt as part of heteronormativity. Second, there are liberal contexts, where conversations about heteronormativity are indeed possible, but are largely contained to a knowledge periphery. The chapters situated within England, Aotearoa New Zealand, Australia, and the United States and Canada are examples of "liberal heteronormativity." Openly challenging heteronormative policies and practices may lead to some awareness and change, but these efforts often produce liminal impact. Third, the chapter from Germany presents an interesting moderate view of this political spectrum. The political context may permit conversations that address heteronormativity, but only within cases rendered acceptable to discourses of nation-building and citizenship.[6] The transnational experience, such as the case of queer migrant students in the chapter, demonstrates how heteronormativity racializes educational spaces. Racialization creates multiple systems of domination, which limits queer agency and development (Brockenbrough, 2016).

In addition to troubling heteronormative assumptions in education, these chapters compare and analyze the similarities and differences across various educational spaces; determine ongoing disconnects with hierarchy, structure, and experience; and contribute to a growing discussion about the utility of queer studies in education. Some chapters work at the intersections of identity, resistance, and practice, which can be pretty queer by nature of this complex, uncertain, and fluid effort. Collectively, this first set of chapters offers a useful road map toward deciphering heteronormativity as a political spectrum, with the readers' interpretations of the chapters forming the compass for which to arrive at fresh insights as well as forms of queer critical praxis.

Opening the volume with work situated at The University of the West Indies (Kingston campus) in Jamaica, Adwoa Onuora and Nadeen Spence examine, in "Space, Place, and Queerness: The University of the West Indies, Mona Campus', Queer Zoning," the systemic zoning of queerness that is a part of a culture of exclusion. Onuora and Spence point out that safer spaces exist for queer people, but only within particular social and geographic spaces as a form of social control. Drawing on Fanon's (1967) zone of nonbeing and their empirical research involving queer students on campus residences, they explore the material consequences of the gendering and sexualization of spaces. As Onuora and Spence demonstrate, laws are made ambiguous so that they can be applied to anyone fitting outside a status quo and therefore considered to be in the wrong space. The impact can be queer people being marked as "sexual deviants" or as noncitizens on campus and in the broader Jamaican society, reifying a heterosexual and hypermasculine leadership. Onuora and Spence conclude that this political context results in dichotomous experiences with fetishization and affirmation of queer leaders.

Attempts aimed at zoning, containing, or delimiting queerness in education, including those aimed at rendering invisible, or limiting the parameters of exposure to, queer knowledge formations unfold in various ways and encompass any number of practices, including those related to curriculum, pedagogy, and educational policy. The next chapter by Naomi Rudoe can be read in part as a critical examination of the politics of what can be known about queerness within the context of relationships and sex education. In "A Queer Sexuality Education: The Possibilities and Impossibilities of Knowing," Rudoe, for example, takes up the topic of a queer sexuality education in England, helping readers understand the limits of policy around sex/uality education, arguing that adults determine "appropriate" content for children. Determining appropriateness is problematic, as it often means sustaining a heteronormative logic system, such as forbidding local authority to promote homosexuality or to determine when to introduce LGBTQ (lesbian, gay, bisexual, transgender, queer/questioning) topics. It also positions the child as innocent, non-sexual, or queer. Rudoe calls for a deeper analysis into antihomophobic education and questions if homophobia is so easily identifiable and held responsible for queer exclusion. It is clear that English teachers need to know what the effect of their teaching choices and practices are and how to generate this awareness. According to Rudoe, a queer sex/uality education may be a useful space for exploration, which consists of a multidimensional understanding of sex/uality, questions of un/happiness in relationships, or in the future, and affirmation of uncertainty and complexity.

Also engaging with the limits and possibilities of thinking queerly in education, James Burford and Genine Hook, in their chapter "Rupturing the

'Cul-de-Sac': Queer(y)ing Graduate Education Studies," focus their work on queer aspects of graduate education studies, inviting queer researchers to deeply consider why they adhere to certain subjects and objects within their research projects. In this way, their work pushes us to broaden our thinking about what accounts for queer studies' proper objects of analysis and research (Berlant & Warner, 1995), encouraging us "not to presume ahead of time what methods or objects might constitute a queer project" (Somerville, 2020, p. 6). Drawing on their own experiences as doctoral students in Aotearoa New Zealand and Australia, Burford and Hook exemplify how queer concepts can function as disruptive and nonidentitarian tools across graduate education. Burford's experience suggests that the affective-politics of doctoral research sheds light on how "strong" emotions (e.g., hope, anger) were attributed to political agency, and "weak" emotions (e.g., depression, anxiety) became liabilities. In Burford's experience, a queer analysis of these politics reveals a governable and compliant subject. While "success" has deep and sometimes painful roots in education research, Burford suggests that "failure" produces alternative feelings (e.g., joy, satisfaction), thus allowing emotions to teach about the possibilities and constraints for educational research. In comparison, Hook's experience in Australia while researching the lives of single-parent graduate students produced a series of heteronormative and partner-normative barriers. Drawing on Butler's (1990) notion of performativity, Hook unsettles norms around gendered parenting, and how thinking queerly presents fresh alternatives in settings not normally considered queer. Both authors conclude that queer concepts can travel across research settings and, in doing so, develop a rich potential that advances forms of queer research and politics within graduate education.

As with Burford and Hook's work, the next chapter by María do Mar Castro Varela and Yener Bayramoğlu is attentive to the politics of educational assemblages, offering a compelling case of transnationalism in education through the lens of queer migrant students in Germany. In "Racism, Heteronormativity, and Educational Assemblage in Germany," the authors analyze how heteronormativity and racism continue to dominate German schools, and this dominance reproduces oppressive experiences that lead to feelings of shame among the students. Through their participants' voices, Castro Varela and Bayramoğlu argue that education is an assemblage of a larger power structure, which injures subjects as they interact with this structure. The application of an assemblage perspective, queer of color critique, and critical life course analysis through a migration lens can shed light on and possibly disrupt stratification and violence in schools. Migration can proffer analyses of epistemologies of sexualized and racialized differences and bring awareness to colonialism and the categorization of identity. The authors conclude the chapter with questioning why educational institutions function to stabilize the nation state and produce a hegemonic citizenry. Being aware of an educational assemblage that is shaped by eurocentrism and white supremacy can help realize the emotional impact of experiences of racism.

While work in queer studies has arguably become normalized in some settings in academia (Halperin, 2003), rounding out the first cluster of essays are two chapters that share a commitment to queering higher education in an area that both readings highlight as lacking in queer research: namely, the study of (and teaching about) LGBTQ+ (LGBTQ and other identities [except heterosexual]) minorities in the workplace. In "Queered Failure and Management Education," Nick Rumens, for example, notes the paucity of queer theorizing in the field of management education and across business schools in general due to an unexamined pervasiveness of heteronormativity in these settings, leading to not only the limited presence of classroom discussions of LGBT+ topics in business courses but also limited ways of framing the dialogue about the types of LGBT+ inclusivity possible in the workplace. Striving to incorporate a more humanistic management education that utilizes a queer analytic, Rumens draws on Halberstam's (2011) work on queer failure to consider the complexities and contradictions involved in attempts at rupturing heteronormativity in management education.[7] That is, Rumens leverages the insights gleaned from critically reflecting on what he describes as "failing to fail queerly" while teaching an undergraduate module on human resource development situated in the United Kingdom. In this way, his chapter thoughtfully and self-reflexively challenges a discourse of diversity management that normalizes and makes legible, within the context of conforming to heteronormativity, only certain types of LGBT+ subjects in management education and in workplace environments. Also committed to closing the research gap in the study of sexual minority workers, Craig M. McGill and colleagues, in "Navigating Personal and Professional Identities in the Higher Education Workplace: A Facilitated Autoethnography," examine the experiences of gay and lesbian professionals working in academe in the United States and in Canada. More specifically, grounding their work philosophically in a queer theoretical perspective, while utilizing a facilitated autoethnography methodology, they explore how gay and lesbian higher education personnel manage the coconstruction of the complex intersections of their personal (i.e., sexual minority) and professional identities against a backdrop of the ways in which occupational norms are controlled and reinforced in part by entrenched heteronormative discourses. In centering queer voices in the "(re)telling of what it means to be a queer professional in higher education," McGill and colleagues illuminate the constitutive identity fluidity involved as gay and lesbian professionals, navigating their intersecting identities, as they move across space and time within higher education settings.

The second set of chapters in *Queer Studies and Education*, drawn from Canada, Brazil, Aotearoa New Zealand, Eastern and Southern Africa, and Australia can also be framed, like the first cluster of essays, as engaging in a "relational analysis of marginal and normalized" sexualities and genders by way of interrogating the operation of heteronormativity across various educational sites (Morgensen, 2021, p. 111). These chapters focus on the way educational institutions work to reproduce certain sexualities, gender identities, and expressions of gender as "legitimate" and "normal" and others as not. One way to read this second cluster of essays is in how they help illustrate the various and contradictory ways that heteronormativity operates not only within the official curriculum but also in the unofficial curricula of education, which includes archival educational photographs (Dénommé-Welch and Mizzi); extracurricular activities such as "marching bands" (Duque and Moura); children's play in early childhood centers (Gunn); parental reactions to curriculum content on WhatsApp (Reygan and McEwen); physical education (PE) and sport (Pringle and Landi); and film and television as cultural pedagogy (Cover). Through their work, these authors extend, while also at times directly and indirectly problematize, the now-established idea that educational spaces are heteronormative. They do this by concentrating on the minutiae of discourses and practices by which heteronormativities are enacted, thus providing illuminating details of their configuration in diverse global locations. Despite the geographical distance, for instance, between countries like Brazil, Aotearoa New Zealand, and South Africa, the authors demonstrate that heteronormativity functions in educational arenas to regulate, denigrate, and dismiss identities and knowledge formations that do not conform to normative conceptualizations; yet, at the same time, as readers we are invited to consider how heteronormativity is far from homogeneous, sometimes unfolding queerly and in contradictory ways, across various educational contexts, thus pushing us to move beyond conceptualizing the dynamics of heteronormativity in overly simplistic, singular, and totalizing ways (Cohen, 2013; Jagose, 2015; Wiegman & Wilson, 2015).

Also connecting the work of these authors is their commitment to challenging, in addition to illuminating, heteronormativities in educational settings. One of the early critiques of queer theory was that it lacked an activist politics due to its radical deconstructive "critique of settled identities" (Amin, 2020, p. 18). While some articulations of queer theory might profess that an anti-identitarian approach does not pursue social/sexual justice for LGBTIQA+ (LGBT, intersex, queer/questioning, asexual [or allies], and other identities) people, it is recognized that most work in the field cannot untether itself from this desire (even if it wanted to). From this perspective, each of the authors below is committed to thinking deeply and complexly about meaningful ways to attain the goal of creating and sustaining more equitable, inclusive, and socially just forms of education for various marginalized groups and identities, including for diverse gender and sexual identities.

For example, Spy Dénommé-Welch and Robert C. Mizzi, in "Shifting the Gaze: A Decolonial Queer Analysis of Photographs of the Canadian Indian Residential Schools," explore archival photographs and historical images taken of Indian residential schools throughout Canada. The authors examine these images to illuminate how heteronormativity and binary gender systems were instituted within the architecture and design of these schooling spaces. Decolonial queer theory is employed to draw attention to how Two-Spirit and Indigenous people are regulated by heteronormative thinking and histories around race, gender, and sexuality with harmful effects for their cultural expression (Gomes Pereira, 2019). Through their analysis, the authors identify the way Indian residential schools incorporated heteronormative expressions of gender by regulating the bodies of Indigenous students and their white teachers within heteronormative logics. Some examples include the arrangement and configuration of people and space so that display of Indigenous culture is absent in photographs. Similarly, photos portray a rigid binary of masculine/feminine gender expression, where girls are photographed in sewing rooms or kitchens and boys in agriculture, machine, or carpentry classrooms. Despite this, these images also offer moments of resistance to Western depictions of school productivity, modernity, and the colonial gaze. These are evident in photographs that reveal a turned head, smile, or frown, that interrupt the otherwise regimented conformity of rows of students. The authors argue that these photographs capture a colonial legacy that continues to shape how Two-Spirit and queer identities are viewed in Canada's posttruth and reconciliation context. In this way, Dénommé-Welch and Mizzi's research provides important historical knowledge and theoretical tools and insights for challenging the persistence of this legacy in the present across considerations of curriculum development, pedagogy, and educational administration and policy.

Further reflecting a commitment to social justice education within the context and concerns of cultivating transformative forms of queer diversity and inclusion, Tiago Duque and Gustavo Moura's chapter, "'No Queers, No Marching Bands': Schools, Social Recognition, and Gender Visibility on the Brazil–Bolivia Border," examines the experience of gender among young queers from the Brazilian city of Corumbá. Marching bands are an integral part of school culture in Corumbá, with students practicing regularly to perform in them at the city's anniversary parade. Duque and Moura's ethnographic research reveals how some young queers achieve social recognition for the talent they display in the performances of these marching bands. These performances are heralded by school and city inhabitants as an example of the "acceptance of queers" by heterosexual inhabitants in the city of Corumbá. The "happy coexistence" of queers and heterosexuals at these performances is subsequently often cited as an example of how homophobia does not exist in this city. Yet, as Duque and Moura demonstrate, queer students are confined to particular roles within the bands, such as "cymbal players" and exclusively effeminate expressions of queerness. While these young queers receive a level of gender visibility and are often "praised" for their performance, such restrictions highlight the limits of queer inclusion. Duque and Moura argue that until queer youth receive social recognition for their diverse participation in these bands, they will form part of the myriad educational practices that remain oppressive for this group.

While Duque and Moura's work, drawing inspiration from Kumashiro (2002), argues for the importance of antioppressive approaches in education, Alexandra C. Gunn's chapter, "Timely Interventions: Queer Activist Early Childhood Teaching in Aotearoa New Zealand," explores how "thinking and practicing queerly" can improve the quality of early childhood education and provision. Her account is situated within the historical specificities of Aotearoa New Zealand, where changes to family and child law, as well as new curriculum developments and educational theories, have opened spaces to ask queer questions of the world and to live as queer subjects within it. Gunn argues that early childhood is replete with normative discourses about gender, sexuality, and the family that also saturate learning contexts like early childhood centers. Subsequently, paying attention to how early childhood education works to construe heteronormative concepts of child, parent, gender, sexuality, teacher, and family are imperative for thinking and practicing queerly. For Gunn, thinking queerly in early childhood education involves identifying when heteronormative understandings are present and how they serve to privilege and marginalize particular groups. Thinking queerly also involves attempting to disrupt such heteronormative patterns by understanding phenomena differently and pushing beyond the normative. She suggests that one way this might

[10]   *Rodriguez et al.*

be operationalized is by listening closely to children and their "working theories" of gender, sexuality, family, and others as expressed during moments of play. Teachers might capitalize on instances when children position themselves and others outside heteronormative understandings, by engaging them in exploring different ways of knowing and being. Gunn proposes that by drawing attention to how early childhood teachers think about, practice, and understand potential impacts of a "more queer teaching practice," transformation in this sector, and the education system more broadly, may be supported.

As the work of Dénommé-Welch and Mizzi, Duque and Moura, and Gunn demonstrates, to disrupt heteronormativity in our thinking and practice in education we need to work at multiple levels, such as early childhood and secondary schooling, and in and out of schooling contexts. The authors' work in the next three essays similarly remind us it is only by working with an expansive conceptualization of education and recognizing its complexities and nuances that our thinking and practice might exceed the heteronorm. In this regard, Finn Reygan and Haley McEwen's chapter, "Beyond 'Abstinence-Only': The U.S. Christian Right's 'Pro-Family' Countermovement Against Comprehensive Sexuality Education and Sexual and Reproductive Rights in Eastern and Southern Africa," examines how the "pro-family" movement in Eastern and Southern Africa has advanced a campaign against the implementation of comprehensive sexuality education and the provision of sexual and reproductive health and rights for young people. The authors note an intensification and increased coordination of this movement in the last 5 years, which they attribute to transnational politics and financial support from pro-family organizations in the United States and Eastern and Western Europe. To demonstrate how the pro-family movement mobilizes its opposition, they employ desktop studies of academic literature as well as document analysis of online articles and government policy and statements. These methods identify strategies and discourses employed by the pro-family movement, such as the belief that foreign powers are imposing comprehensive sexuality education and ideas about LGBTIQ+ rights. This particular discourse is mobilized to exploit existing anxieties exhibited by citizens about coloniality and Western hegemony. Such discourses reinscribe cisnormative and heteropatriarchal constructions of gender and sexuality that protect forms of power and privilege that queer and feminist advocacy and scholarship have been challenging for the past 50 years. Reygan and McEwen utilize a decolonial queer critique of heterosexuality and the nuclear family model to interrogate the ideological work of the pro-family movement as a site where hegemonic forms of power intersect to maintain heteropatriarchal and geopolitics of power. Their chapter highlights the importance of students' right to comprehensive sexuality education and the way in which this is too easily undermined by the increasingly coordinated and well-funded efforts of global-reaching conservative groups.

Further adding to our conceptualization of the broad range of sites where processes of education take place, completing this second cluster of essays are two chapters focusing on the sites of school sport/PE and on popular culture. These two chapters remind us of a now long-standing critical insight associated with queer theorizing that has informed and animated numerous scholarly discussions since its earliest articulations: that subjectivity is discursively constituted and made to cohere or stabilize in its endless citational practices of (identity) norms specific to a given culture, or, drawing from Butler's (1990) poststructuralist formulation, that identity is performative. This long-standing insight has been taken up by critical and queer theorists across a host of topics or concepts of concern, stretching from complicated conversations about the meaning and practice of agency, resistance, and subversion to explorations of the "complexities and productive contradictions that arise when considering sexual practices that seem at odds with the claiming of particular sexual identities" (Rodriguez, 2019, p. 140). In their chapter, "Queering School Sport and Physical Education," Richard Pringle and Dillon Landi utilize deconstructionist insights regarding notions of the contingency or queerness of identity formations as a theoretical intervention for critically examining approaches to research on sexualities and genders in the field of school sport and PE. Their review of research in PE, including across different national contexts, highlights, on the one hand, that the dominant approach to research in this field of study remains one that is "identity bound." On the other hand, their review demonstrates that queer(er) approaches to knowledge production are not only possible but also desirable in challenging the limitations of research that frames PE spaces by default as purely homophobic and heteronormative; in this way, Pringle and Landi invite researchers to critically engage with the normative framework that guides the study of sexualities and genders in PE research in ways that potentially reify static understandings of identities and PE spaces. From this perspective, the authors conclude their chapter by presenting research from a project situated in Aotearoa New Zealand that explores PE spaces, in light of the "messiness" of identities and the queerness of desire, as potentially "always already queer," and that an understanding of these spaces as such opens up opportunities for pursuing research trajectories that may provide more utopian visions for queer inclusiveness in school sport and PE settings.

In his chapter "Queer Screen Pedagogies: Australian Queer Audiences and the Educational Value of LGBTQ Film and Television Stories," Rob Cover also engages with the notion that identities are always in the process of formation as they are constituted, that is, formed and re-formed, in their encounters with myriad discourses, including in their encounters with the discourses of screen media texts. Presenting a cross section of findings from a project funded by the Australian Research Council, the *AusQueerScreen* (Australian Queer Screen) study, Cover's research explores the ways in which his participants positioned their relationship to or encounters with Australian queer screen media in ways that highlighted its pedagogical possibilities or dimensions. As such, his work situates screen media in general as part of a broader and interconnected constellation or matrix of pedagogies, calling attention to the ways in which "education as a cultural pedagogical practice takes place across multiple sites as it signals how, within diverse contexts, education makes us subjects of and subject to relations of power" (Giroux, 2001, p. 13). That is, rather than engaging in a textual analysis or examination of the meanings in LGBTQ+ film and television texts, his work instead explores how creative stakeholders (e.g., producers, scriptwriters, and actors) and audience members alike across various regions of Australia frame queer screen media in pedagogical terms, including accounts of the complex pedagogical processes involved in the constitution or performativity of gender- and sexually diverse subjectivity. In this way, Cover presents a chapter that importantly contributes queer theoretical and (cultural) pedagogical perspectives to media theories of reception situated within a critical project exploring views on the production and reception of queer screen pedagogies that provide a way to reflect on the significance of moving beyond "the primacy of signification over power" and on an examination of how "cultural texts work within the material and institutional contexts that structure everyday life" (Giroux, 2001, p. 14).

Concluding *Queer Studies and Education* with work that spans the United States, South Africa, Sweden, Aotearoa New Zealand, and Ireland, the final set of chapters broadly examines the persistence of various kinds of enactments of normativity, including as part of the wider and now long-recognized pitfall of liberalism and neoliberalism as the frameworks through which "achievable" social change and belonging are fostered (e.g., through policy and organizational initiative), particularly in educational settings. Situated as such, the tenaciousness of entrenched and recurring normativities often unwittingly reinforce older stereotypes and exclusionary practices as an element of the package of policy or intervention on behalf of LGBTQ+ students or educators and often seemingly articulate new ways of being and being together that fall short of genuine social change and practices of belonging. This is not, of course, a new phenomenon. While there are many wonderful examples of alternative practices of producing resilient, engaged, and relational social change toward genuine and transformative inclusivity, (neo)liberal models, by contrast, tend to do two things: first, they focus on the figure of the individual as the key agent of change and the object of inclusivity, such that the failing of inclusivity is understood as the failing of those who have not stepped up to the mark, rather than a problem of the wider cultural structures that could potentially operationalize the emergence of new, more accepting ways of performing engagement across communities of difference (Williams, 1977). As a political ideology dating back to the 1980s that encompasses both economic and social/cultural aspects, McCann and Monaghan (2020) explained the cultural dimensions of neoliberalism as follows:

> We might say that on a cultural level, neoliberalism represents a move against the feminist slogan of the 1970s "the personal is political," towards "the personal is privatized." In terms of activism, neoliberal ideology has encouraged a turn away from structural accounts of oppression, towards individual and depoliticised accounts. (p. 155)

The second pitfall of (neo)liberal approaches is the tendency to demarcate by bordering, bounding, and then counting a minority group and applying policy contingent on the size of the group (Savin-Williams, 2016, p. 42) in ways that not only exclude but also elide the possibility of recognizing intersectional experiences (Jagose, 2015) and changing self-identities across new and emerging practices of multiplicity, microminoritization, and fluidity (Cover, 2019). While categorizations and community border policing can, at times, be understood to disempower the monolithic dominance of individualism, they also often present the clustering of a group as being responsible for their own resilience rather than as being both actors in and subject for social change; this is primarily because such change is not in the interests of capital and other dominant structures that demand the persistence of survival conditions of precarity (Skeggs, 2011).

Indeed, even as the projects of liberalism and neoliberalism are regularly called out as global failures (Shinko, 2010), not least for the ways in which they exacerbate rather than address socioeconomic inequalities of health, identity, and belonging (Chandler, 2020), chapters in this book point to the way in which they are retained as the "go-to" solutions for addressing LGBTQ+ educational inequalities and related issues. As many of these chapters explain or suggest, the opportunity to utilize gender- and sexually diverse subjectivities themselves as mechanisms for the critique of the wider structures of oppression, suppression, marginalization, and health and education inequities is there, but not often taken up.

Andrea Vasquez and Cindy Cruz, for example, in "The Possibilities and Futurities of LGBTQ Youth: Thinking From a Queer of Color Critique in Educational Research," cogently demonstrate the way in which antihomophobia and antiheterosexism campaigns, and their inclusion in education policy and diversity scholarship, may not be as effective at promoting genuine agency, belonging, and healthy social relationships as intended because they sustain the positioning of LGBTQ young people as "other." Belonging and social participation are, of course, not produced through tolerance frameworks that categorize and demarcate different groups and then expect them to get along through convivial participation in shared spaces such as schools and social networks (Georgiou, 2017). Rather, there is a need—as Angela McRobbie (2020) has shown elsewhere—to be careful what we mean by a sense of belonging and whether what is measured as belonging is actually a fantasy to protect the status quo. As Vasquez and Cruz demonstrate in their study of two decades of scholarship on antihomophobia and heterosexualism in education settings, a more genuine form of resistance that might promote a framework for critical belonging may well be found in the intersectionalities that critique liberal norms; these include the identity multiplicities that emerge among queer students of color, "as subjects marked by standing in a densely trafficked intersection" (Nash, 2021, p. 130), and the discourses through which they find a sense of agency (see, e.g., Van Asselt, 2019).[8]

In "An Assimilation or Transgression of 'Normativities': A Qualitative Sociological Exploration of the Experiences of Gay and Lesbian Students at a South African University," Tshanduko Tshilongo and Jacques Rothmann also critically explore the meanings and practices of inclusion and belonging, with their work focusing on gay and lesbian student experiences across campus cultures at a South African university. Their study is situated against a backdrop of an incongruity between a national constitution that protects the rights of sexual minorities and the realities on the ground of the continued marginalization of gays and lesbians in civil society, including within educational settings. The authors note that a variation of this incongruity can be further identified within university statements and policy documents that make a commitment to diversity and diversification within academic settings across the categories of race, gender, and disability while downplaying sexual orientation or sexual minorities within discussions of equity, inclusion, and change. In this context, contrary to

INTRODUCTION    [15]

celebrationist accounts of diversity on university campuses, Tshilongo and Rothmann identify a widespread and deep-seated practice in which students regularly assimilate into heteronormative or homonormative campus cultures in order to curtail the possibility or risk of homophobia. In this way, their study highlights a continuum or fluidity of sexual identity formations based on whether students are conforming to heteronormativity and/or homonormativity as they move across time and interact with various spaces and contexts, as well as experience concerns or feelings of (un)safety (including within so-called safe spaces), at the university where the authors carried out their qualitative exploration. Importantly, however, Tshilongo and Rothmann also recognize and analyze the powerful antinormative transgressions that are at play among some students and the power of such transgressions to undermine processes of normalization or forms of normalizing power that reproduce normative practices that encourage, among other things, the alignment of behavior with exclusionary practices such as various forms of bullying. When considering the issue of queer inclusion and belonging within higher education settings, from the academic curriculum and participation in student organizations to the creation of policies that address legal concerns and safety issues, Tshilongo and Rothmann's study and findings importantly remind us not to homogenize the experiences and identities of LGBTQ+ students. This insight is especially useful to consider in light of the complexities of navigating the dynamics of heteronormativity and homonormativity as well as negotiating the "simultaneity of multiple structures of domination" (Nash, 2021, p. 128) associated with the lived realities of intersectional identities.

In the next chapter, "Norm-Critical Pedagogy as Femo- and Homonationalism: Perspectives on Norm Critique in Swedish Research, Activism, and Educational Practice," Eva Reimers also engages with the ways in which norms function as vectors for practices of inclusion and exclusion by pushing us to critically theorize their intersections. She takes up this work by engaging with the intersections between and among theoretical perspectives and concepts as a methodological approach for critically analyzing and disrupting the ongoing production of networks of intersecting regulatory norms, specifically within the context of discussions regarding the development and normalization of norm-critical theory and norm-critical pedagogy within Swedish educational research and practice. For example, according to Reimers, norm critique can be framed as an extension of queer theory that not only includes a critical examination of the heterosexual norm (which includes an interrogation of dominant gender and sexuality norms), but also encompasses or casts a wider net of analysis

[16]   *Rodriguez et al.*

on the production and effects of all regulatory norms. Thus, norm critique as a framework of analysis is potentially able to leverage an array of critical theoretical perspectives and concepts (e.g., queer theory, intersectionality, and homonationalism) and deploy these in intersecting ways to critically explore the intersections of "governing" or hegemonic norms that produce conditions of exclusion, marginalization, and forms of othering across a broad range of (intersecting) social categories, including sexuality, gender, race, ethnicity, class, nation -state, and religion, among others. However, in part resulting from studies (that utilize a norm-critical perspective) of norm-critical pedagogy, Reimers considers how, in normalizing a critique of heteronormative and patriarchal norms as part of the official Swedish national curriculum and by way of educational theory and practice, such a critique can inadvertently become part of the process of constructing and stabilizing new "we/them" norms. Reimers is specifically concerned with the construction of national identity formations that produce femo- and homonationalism (Puar, 2007)—that is, a binary construction between a queer-friendly (i.e., homotolerant) and gender equal Swedish nation and an intolerant, homophobic, and misogynistic set of otherized cultures and nation states, the latter often associated with the Global South and encompassing or targeting the categories of race, ethnicity, and religion. Reimers concludes her chapter with a set of reflections on the importance of maintaining the subversive force of the category queer and of norm-critique and norm-critical pedagogy, not only by continuously illuminating and subverting the formation of new hegemonic norms that replace previous ones but also by politicizing or queering norms that have become normalized or taken for granted (i.e., depoliticized) in their deployment across (neo)liberal education and nationalistic discourses and practices.

The next chapter by John Fenaughty, Lucy Cowie, and Louisa Allen also takes up questions of identity, belonging, and sociality related to enactments of normativities by way of liberal policy frameworks. In "'The Only Orange Park Bench': Using Photo-Elicitation to Explore Campus Experiences of LGBTIQA+ Students," the authors present a photo methodology study of student life on a university campus in Aotearoa New Zealand, focusing on the extent to which reported declining rates of homophobia in education might herald new and more equitable ways of belonging or, conversely, obscure the persistence of cisheteronormativity. Indeed, their key finding is that homophobia, transphobia, and biphobia have not been eradicated—while students find that limited institutional tolerance for discrimination removes the blatancy of abuse, various discriminations and exclusions operate in the more implicit but equally insidious forms of the absence of queer spaces and nonbinary gender lavatories. Here, again, is a case of the persistence of normativities despite—or, indeed, hidden by—the practices of liberal policies that claim to achieve equity through banning certain kinds of behavior while leaving the underlying discrimination intact. This is a case of what Sara Ahmed (2011) identified as the operations of diversity claims that are actually in place to protect the dominant or mainstream group. While these often apply to the protection of whiteness by outlawing *personalized* racist abuse while leaving intact the structures of discrimination, the critique of problematic diversity claims by pointing to antidiscrimination rules is equally applicable to helping us understand the kinds of exclusions that operate for the "minorities within minorities." For example, gender-diverse students are often tacked on somewhere in the middle of the acronym LGBTQ+, and students' intersectional identities are not as easily protected from discrimination because they are potentially not equipped or empowered to claim "offense" at discriminatory language or practices. From this perspective, intersectionality as a framework formulated as an analytic "of structures of power and modes of social organization" (HoSang, 2020, p. 144) can offer a valuable critical resource for analyzing and responding to ongoing relations of power enacted through various forms of normativity that persist in part via their deployment within (neo)liberal policies and practices across a broad range of educational contexts. An engagement with normativities and their vehicles of transmission as such, may be especially useful and timely in fostering dialogue on the production of a constellation of discourses and initiatives on "diversity, equity, and inclusion" within higher education today.

The final two chapters of this third cluster of essays, the first by Aoife Neary and the second by Nelson M. Rodriguez and William F. Pinar, closes out *Queer Studies and Education* with work that further affords us opportunities to critically engage with the repetition of normativities, particularly as this work "offers methods of critiques to mark the repetitions of normalcy as a structure and as a pedagogy" (Britzman, 1995, p. 153). One way, among others, to consider the pedagogical dimensions of these repetitions is by drawing from the theoretical insights associated with queer theory's engagement with temporality, particularly in ways that critically highlight how dominant temporal logics work as forms of teaching and learning in terms of orienting (Ahmed, 2006) our conceptualizations and lived experiences of concepts and things in (cis)(hetero)normative directions. For instance, one approach to reading Aoife Neary's chapter, "Trans Children in Primary Schools: Thinking Queerly About Happiness and Time," is by focusing on the ways her study provides us with opportunities to critically reflect on how everyday practices in and out of school contexts function as forms of pedagogy that compel us along pathways and timelines toward gender normativity. More specifically, Neary's research project, conducted in collaboration with the Transgender Equality Network of Ireland, presents interview data from parents and educators of trans and gender-diverse children that explore how perceptions of time (e.g., in relation to gender in childhood development) and emotions (e.g., happiness) overlap in ways that are deeply invested in cisheteronormative notions of what constitutes "the normatively gendered body." In this way, temporalities can be understood, within the context of Neary's study, as representing a contested political and pedagogical site or terrain of struggle, a politics of temporally organizing gendered bodies, between (cis)normative linear constructions of time that unfold across life narratives associated with gender normativity and queer or nonlinear temporalities that, in potentially disrupting the repetitions of the normative logics associated with gender, time, and childhood development, open up the possibility to cultivate alternative or queer life narratives or trajectories of gender embodiment and legibility that function as a counterhegemonic practice or set of counterpublics to "cis (and straight) time."

As with Neary's essay, the final chapter by Rodriguez and Pinar can be read across intersections of the categories of normativity, education, and temporality. In "Queer Love and Education," Rodriguez and Pinar situate their chapter as contributing to ongoing knowledge production on the topic of queer love through a set of critical analyses and reflections on its meanings and practices within education. More specifically, they examine recent work generated within the North American academic context on the concept of queer love, demonstrating that normativities and their repetitions encompass a range of practices. From this perspective, knowledge production across two narratives is presented: Drawing on Halberstam's (2011) notion of queer failure, Rodriguez argues that queer love can be formulated as a productive example of queer failure, thus offering ways of teaching and learning about "subjugated knowledges" or "knowledges from below" (Foucault, 2003, p. 7) within the context of sexuality studies that can highlight and potentially disrupt how love and desire are oriented and configured temporally in heteronormative ways. Pinar's narrative critically engages with Halperin's (2019) formulation of queer love, that is, with the repetitions of normative thought it potentially induces, by locating his reflections in relation to different moments in time related to (queer) knowledge production, queer history, as well as his own queer biography. The chapters by Neary and by Rodriguez and Pinar, along with all the other chapters in *Queer Studies and Education*, remind us that queer's potential lies not only as a critical analytic of past and present

INTRODUCTION [19]

hegemonies and forms of normative power, but also as a future-oriented potentiality, a queer there that is out there, yet remains one step ahead of present forms of queer critical praxis. From this perspective, in the words of Jose Esteban Muñoz (2009, p. 1): "We are not yet queer."

## NOTES

1. Somerville (2020) highlighted two distinct ways that the category queer has circulated in "productive tension over the past few decades" (p. 2). First, as an umbrella term, queer signals a broad range of nonnormative sexual and gender identities, and second, queer registers a critical stance that is "skeptical of existing identity categories and more interested in understanding the production of normativity and its queer companion, nonnormativity, than in delineating any particular population" (p. 2). Both uses of the term can be located in the essays in *Queer Studies and Education*. Beyond this interrelated sense, however, we do not further delineate queer with any specificity; rather, we encourage readers to generate their own meanings as they engage with the term in its deployment across the numerous contexts and topics presented in the chapter essays assembled in this reader.

2. Although the theoretical work of certain scholars (e.g., Michel Foucault, Judith Butler, and Eve Kosofsky Sedgwick) has been repeatedly positioned as central to the formation of the field of queer theory/studies, Amin (2020) urged researchers and scholars to seek out alternate founding genealogies and provided, among other examples, Love's (2015) work on midcentury deviance studies (see also Love, 2021), as well as work in queer of color critique. Seeking out "alternative intellectual roots for the field," noted Amin (2020), not only "reveals the element of chance that allowed certain theoretical schools to become central to the field," but also creates the conditions for the claiming of "new founding figures, largely in a bid to center racialized populations and/or geopolitical spaces outside Europe and North America" (p. 17). We would add that seeking out alternate founding genealogies or theoretical precursors could bring into view a new constellation of concepts, perspectives and insights, and methodologies that could significantly (re)shape future research trajectories in queer studies across any number of fields, including within the field of queer studies in education. The point is not to replace one set of founding theoretical schools with another, but rather, as Amin (2020) noted, to work toward a "genuinely interdisciplinary field" by "multiply[ing] its theoretical genealogies" (p. 26).

3. Queer theory's "paradoxically identitarian anti-identitarianism" remains a source of theoretical and political contradiction/tension within contemporary queer studies (see, e.g., Hall & Jagose, 2013). That is, to date, it continues to offer illuminating critiques of identity knowledges and identity politics yet remains "one of the major sites for the study of (homo)sexuality and gender transgression in the U.S. academy" (Amin, 2020, p. 18). One way to engage with the essays in this volume is to read them alongside this continued tension.

4. We decided to forgo creating thematic sections in the hope that this will free readers to creatively imagine their own themes in relation to the broad range of

topics presented across the chapter essays. In addition, although the chapters are organized into several cluster groups, we encourage readers to reorganize the order of the chapters based on their interests and needs (e.g., for teaching purposes).

5. The ways in which any number of concepts, including the concept of heteronormativity, can be taken up or deployed as a critical analytic within the contextual specificities of marginalized struggles and forms of resistance that constitute differing national cultures and political histories are a source of ongoing productive discussion and debate. See, for example, Morgensen's (2021) reflections on the importance of narrating the construction of modern sexuality discourses, including accounts of heteronormativity, as imbricated in, and thus conditioned by, the dynamics of "race, colonialism, capital, or empire" that are specific to different national contexts (p. 112). "To invoke heteronormativity in gender and sexuality studies," Morgensen stated, "we must take an interest in the modern violences that condition it" (2021, p. 112).

6. One example of the way queer has been critically mobilized to challenge or disrupt exclusionary discourses of nation-building and citizenship, as relates to localized same-sex formations, is in the efforts of diasporic and Global South activists to "demarginalize 'nonnormative' local and vernacular sexualities restrictively incorporated by the postcolonial state or heteropatriarchal histories" (Reddy, 2021, p. 173). In this context, Reddy (2021) explained, queer diaspora, as a critical formulation, "signals a challenge to statist and postcolonial nationalist efforts to control the lives and meaning of local instances of sexual 'nonnormativity' in ways that do not disturb national norms" (p. 173).

7. Regarding the production of discourses on queer negativity, of which queer failure is an example, Halberstam (IPAK Centar, 2014) explained his own work as "very deliberately setting out to name a subject position, a political agenda, and a form of critique that is radically dissenting, grounded in refusal, and explicitly queer." In this way, Halberstam differentiated his own work on queer negativity from accounts that may be characterized as lacking or withdrawing from a transformative project. From this perspective, Halberstam (IPAK Centar, 2014) offered a set of critical reflections on Edelman's (2004) formulation and embrace of queer failure, which was inspired by Bersani's (1987) influential antisocial thesis that impacted subsequent queer theorizing and critique. Muñoz's (2009) queer utopian work, which can be situated more broadly as part of the temporal turn in queer studies, constitutes a critical response to Edelman's "no future" formulation of queer negativity by positioning queerness as a "horizon imbued with potentiality" (p. 1), hence why McCann and Monaghan (2020, p. 229) described Muñoz's (2009) work as a project of "critical hopefulness." For a wide-ranging study of various discourses on queer negativity and their impact on ethical theory and practice, see Ruti (2017).

8. It may be useful to distinguish between two conceptualizations of intersectional work, particularly as these understandings impact knowledge production in queer studies. First, intersectionality as a critical analytic of the ways in which multiple social categories (e.g., race and gender) imbricate to produce multiple forms of domination that impact "the experiences of the multiply rather than the singly marginalized" (Nash, 2021, p. 129) can be situated within Black feminist thought, practice, and organizing. Coined by legal scholar Kimberlé Williams Crenshaw (1989, 1991) in the late 1980s as part of a broader body of scholarship known as critical race theory, Crenshaw's work

"mapped the legal invisibility of Black women in multiple doctrinal contexts, including antidiscrimination, domestic violence, and rape laws" (Nash, 2021, p. 129). From this perspective, as HoSang (2020) explained, intersectionality "disrupts 'single-axis' conceptualizations of domination that are a hallmark of liberal legal thought" (p. 142). Pre-dating Crenshaw's work and coining of the term, intersectional praxis can be located within earlier traditions of Black feminist thought (see, e.g., Carastathis's 2016 discussions of the Combahee River Collective and Nash's 2021 explorations of intersectional genealogies). In contemporary work today, including within gender and sexuality studies, intersectionality remains a highly useful framework for theorizing and addressing intersecting forms of domination experienced across different marginalized groups. A second conceptualization of intersectional work can "refer to instances where one theoretical frame meets another" (McCann & Monaghan, 2020, p. 188). These intersections may or may not foreground theoretically and methodologically the framework of intersectionality as discussed above. Within queer studies, "confluences" (Somerville, 2020, p. 7) between theoretical perspectives have generated the production of new knowledge formations, that is, "distinct areas of inquiry in their right" (Somerville, 2020, p. 7), including "work between queer theory and Critical Race Studies which produced Black Queer Studies and queer analyses of race; queer theory's geopolitical turn, focused on issues including migration and diaspora; queer Indigenous studies; queer theory's ontological turn, focused on issues including materiality, affect, and a turn away from representation; intersections between Marxism and queer theory; and deployments of disability studies with queer theory," among other intersections (McCann & Monaghan, 2020, p. 188). In calling attention to these two conceptualizations of intersectional theory and practice, we wish to highlight that researchers, scholars, educators, activists, and other cultural and knowledge workers may approach, understand, or locate their intersectional work differently based on different meanings and practices of intersectionality.

## REFERENCES

Ahmed, S. (2006). *Queer phenomenology: Orientations, objects, others*. Duke University Press.

Ahmed, S. (2011). Problematic proximities: Or why critiques of gay imperialism matter. *Feminist Legal Studies, 19*(2), 119–132. https://doi.org/10.1007/s10 691-011-9180-7

Amin, K. (2020). Genealogies of queer theory. In S. Somerville (Ed.), *The Cambridge companion to queer studies* (pp. 17–29). Cambridge University Press.

Berlant, L., & Warner, M. (1995). What does queer theory teach us about *X? PMLA, 110*(3), 343–349. http://www.jstor.org/stable/462930

Berlant, L., & Warner, M. (1998). Sex in public. *Critical Inquiry, 24*(2), 547–566. https://doi.org/10.1086/448884

Bersani, L. (1987). Is the rectum a grave? *October, 43*, 197–222. https://doi.org/ 10.2307/3397574

Britzman, D. (1995). Is there a queer pedagogy? Or, stop reading straight. *Educational Theory, 45*(2), 151–165. https://doi.org/10.1111/j.1741-5446.1995.00151.x

Brockenbrough, E. (2016). Queer of color critique. In N. M. Rodriguez, W. J. Martino, J. C. Ingrey, & E. Brockenbrough (Eds.), *Critical concepts in queer studies and education: An international guide for the twenty-first century* (pp. 285–297). Palgrave Macmillan. https://doi.org/10.1057/978-1-137-55425-3_28

Bryson, M., & De Castell, S. (1993). Queer pedagogy: Praxis makes im/perfect. *Canadian Journal of Education, 18*(3), 285–305. https://journals.sfu.ca/cje/index.php/cje-rce/article/view/2661

Butler, J. (1990). *Gender trouble: Feminism and the subversion of identity*. Routledge.

Butler, J. (2013). Critically queer. In D. E. Hall, A. Jagose, A. Bebell, & S. Potter (Eds.), *The Routledge queer studies reader* (pp. 18–31). Routledge.

Carastathis, A. (2016). Interlocking systems of oppression. In N. M. Rodriguez, W. Martino, J. Ingrey, & E. Brockenbrough (Eds.), *Critical concepts in queer studies and education: An international guide for the twenty-first century* (pp. 161–171). Palgrave Macmillan. https://doi.org/10.1057/978-1-137-55425-3_17

Carlson, D. L., & Rodriguez, N. M. (Eds.). (2019). *Michel Foucault and sexualities and genders in education: Friendship as ascesis*. Palgrave Macmillan. https://doi.org/10.1007/978-3-030-31737-9

Chandler, A. (2020). Socioeconomic inequalities of suicide: Sociological and psychological intersections. *European Journal of Social Theory, 23*(1), 33–51. https://doi.org/10.1177/1368431018804154

Cohen, C. J. (2013). Punks, bulldaggers, and welfare queens: The radical potential of queer politics? In D. E. Hall, A. Jagose, A. Bebell, & S. Potter (Eds.), *The Routledge queer studies reader* (pp. 74–95). Routledge.

Cover, R. (2019). *Emergent identities: New sexualities, gender and relationships in a digital era*. Routledge.

Crenshaw, K. W. (1989). Demarginalizing the intersection of race and sex: A black feminist critique of antidiscrimination doctrine, feminist theory and antiracist politics. *University of Chicago Legal Forum, 1*, 139–167. http://chicagounbound.uchicago.edu/uclf/vol1989/iss1/8

Crenshaw, K. W. (1991). Mapping the margins: Intersectionality, identity politics, and violence against women of color. (Women of Color at the Center: Selections from the Third National Conference on Women of Color and the Law.) *Stanford Law Review, 43*(6), 1299. https://doi.org/10.2307/1229039

Edelman, L. (2004). *No future: Queer theory and the death drive*. Duke University Press.

Fanon, F. (1967). *Black skin, white masks*. Grove Press.

Foucault, M. (1978). *The history of sexuality, volume 1: An introduction* (R. Hurley, Trans.). Penguin Books.

Foucault, M. (2003). *Society must be defended: Lectures at the Collège de France, 1975–1976* (D. Macey, Trans.). Picador.

Francis, D. A., Kjaran, J. I., & Lehtonen, J. (Eds.). (2020). *Queer social movements and outreach work in schools: A global perspective*. Palgrave Macmillan. https://doi.org/10.1007/978-3-030-41610-2

Georgiou, M. (2017). Conviviality is not enough: A communication perspective to the city of difference. *Communication, Culture and Critique, 10*(2), 261–279. https://doi.org/10.1111/cccr.12154

Giroux, H. A. (2001). Cultural studies as performative politics. *Cultural Studies ↔ Critical Methodologies, 1*(1), 5–23. https://doi.org/10.1177/153270860100100102

Gomes Pereira, P. P. (2019). Reflecting on decolonial queer. *GLQ: A Journal of Lesbian and Gay Studies, 25*(3), 403–429. https://doi.org/10.1215/10642684-7551112

Halberstam, J. (2011). *The queer art of failure*. Duke University Press.

Hall, D. E., & Jagose, A. (2013). Introduction. In D. E. Hall, A. Jagose, A. Bebell, & S. Potter, (Eds.), *The Routledge queer studies reader* (pp. xiv–xx). Routledge.

Halperin, D. M. (2003). The normalization of queer theory. *Journal of Homosexuality, 45*(2–4), 339–343. https://doi.org/10.1300/J082v45n02_17

Halperin, D. M. (2019). Queer love. *Critical Inquiry, 45*, 396–419. https://doi.org/10.1086/700993

Harris, A., & Gray, E. M. (Eds.). (2014). *Queer teachers, identity and performativity*. Palgrave Pivot.

HoSang, D. M. (2020). Intersectionality. In K. W. Tompkins, A. Z. Aizura, A. Bahng, K. R. Chavez, M. Goeman, & A. J. Musser (Eds.), *Keywords for gender and sexuality studies* (pp. 142–145). New York University Press.

IPAK Centar. (2014, September 5). *Jack Halberstam on queer failure, silly archives and the wild* [Video]. YouTube. https://www.youtube.com/watch?v=iKDEil7m1j8

Jagose, A. (1996). *Queer theory: An introduction*. New York University Press.

Jagose, A. (2015). The trouble with antinormativity. *differences: A Journal of Feminist Cultural Studies, 26*(1), 26–47. https://doi.org/10.1215/10407391-2880591

Kaufman, J. S., & Powell, D. A. (Eds.). (2014). *The meaning of sexual identity in the twenty-first century*. Cambridge Scholars Publishing.

Kjaran, J. I., & Sauntson, H. (Eds.). (2019). *Schools as queer transformative spaces: Global narratives on sexualities and genders*. Routledge.

Kumashiro, K. (1999). Reading queer Asian American masculinities and sexualities in elementary school. In W. J. Letts & J. T. Sears (Eds.), *Queering elementary education: Advancing the dialogue about sexualities and schooling* (pp. 61–70). Rowman & Littlefield.

Kumashiro, K. (2002). *Troubling education: Queer activism and antioppressive pedagogy*. Routledge.

Landreau, J. C., & Rodriguez, N. M. (Eds.). (2012). *Queer masculinities: A critical reader in education*. Springer Dordrecht. https://doi.org/10.1007/978-94-007-2552-2

Letts, W. J. IV., & Sears, J. T. (Eds.). (1999). *Queering elementary education. Advancing the dialogue about sexualities and schooling*. Rowman and Littlefield.

Love, H. (2015). Doing being deviant: Deviance studies, description, and the queer ordinary. *differences: A Journal of Feminist Cultural Studies, 26*(1), 74–95. https://doi.org/10.1215/10407391-2880609

Love, H. (2021). *Underdogs: Social deviance and queer theory*. University of Chicago Press.

Luhmann, S. (1998). Queering/querying pedagogy? Or, pedagogy is a pretty queer thing. In W. Pinar (Ed.), *Queer theory in education* (pp. 1–15). Lawrence Erlbaum Associates.

Martinsson, L., & Reimers, E. (Eds.). (2010). *Norm-struggles: Sexualities in contentions*. Cambridge Scholars Publishing.

Mayo, C. (Ed.). (2022). *The Oxford encyclopedia of gender and sexuality in education*. Oxford University Press.

Mayo, C., & Rodriguez, N. M. (2019). Wanting more: Queer theory and education. In C. Mayo & N. M. Rodriguez (Eds.), *Queer pedagogies: Theory, praxis, politics* (pp. 1–8). Springer.

McCann, H., & Monaghan, W. (2020). *Queer theory now: From foundations to futures*. Red Globe Press.

McRobbie, A. (2020). *Feminism and the politics of resilience: Essays on gender, media and the end of welfare*. Polity Press.

Meyer, E. (2019). Ending bullying and harassment: The case for a queer pedagogy. In C. Mayo & N. M. Rodriguez (Eds.), *Queer pedagogies: Theory, praxis, politics* (pp. 41–57). Springer. https://doi.org/10.1007/978-3-030-27066-7_4

Morgensen, S. L. (2021). Heteronormativity. In K. W. Tompkins, A. Z. Aizura, A. Bahng, K. R. Chavez, M. Goeman, & A. J. Musser (Eds.), *Keywords for gender and sexuality studies* (pp. 111–113). New York University Press.

Muñoz, J. E. (2009). *Cruising utopia: The then and there of queer futurity.* New York University Press.

Nash, J. C. (2021). Intersectionality. In K. W. Tompkins, A. Z. Aizura, A. Bahng, K. R. Chavez, M. Goeman, & A. J. Musser (Eds.), *Keywords for gender and sexuality studies* (pp. 129–133). New York University Press.

Pinar, W. (1998). *Queer theory in education.* Lawrence Erlbaum Associates.

Puar, J. K. (2007). *Terrorist assemblages: Homonationalism in queer times.* Duke University Press.

Quinlivan, K., & Town, S. (1999). Queer as fuck? Exploring the potential of queer pedagogies in researching school experiences of lesbian and gay youth. In D. Epstein & J. T. Sears (Eds.), *A dangerous knowing: Sexuality, pedagogy and popular culture* (pp. 242–256). Cassell.

Rasmussen, M. (2006). *Becoming subjects: Sexualities and secondary schooling.* Routledge.

Reddy, C. (2021). Queer. In K. W. Tompkins, A. Z. Aizura, A. Bahng, K. R. Chavez, M. Goeman, & A. J. Musser (Eds.), *Keywords for gender and sexuality studies* (pp. 172–177). New York University Press.

Renn, K. A. (2010). LGBT and queer research in higher education: The state and status of the field. *Educational Researcher, 39*(2), 132–141. https://doi.org/10.3102/0013189X10362579

Rofes, E. (2005). *A radical rethinking of sexuality and schooling: Status quo or status queer?* Rowman & Littlefield.

Rodriguez, N. M. (2016). Trans generosity. In N. M. Rodriguez, W. J. Martino, J. C. Ingrey, & E. Brockenbrough (Eds.), *Critical concepts in queer studies and education: An international guide for the twenty-first century* (pp. 407–420). Palgrave Macmillan. https://doi.org/10.1057/978-1-137-55425-3_39

Rodriguez, N. M. (2019). Michel Foucault and queer ascesis: Toward a pedagogy and politics of subversive friendships. In D. L. Carlson & N. M. Rodriguez (Eds.), *Michel Foucault and sexualities and genders in education: Friendship as ascesis* (pp. 139–153). Palgrave Macmillan. https://doi.org/10.1007/978-3-030-31737-9_10

Rodriguez, N. M., Martino, W. J., Ingrey, J. C., Brockenbrough, E. (Eds.). (2016). *Critical concepts in queer studies and education: An international guide for the twenty-first century.* Palgrave Macmillan. https://doi.org/10.1057/978-1-137-55425-3

Rodriguez, N. M., & Pinar, W. F. (Eds.). (2007). *Queering straight teachers: Discourse and identity in education.* Peter Lang.

Rottmann, C. (2006). Queering educational leadership from the inside out. *International Journal of Leadership in Education, 9*(1), 1–20. https://doi.org/10.1080/13603120500389507

Rubin, G. S. (1993). Thinking sex: Notes for a radical theory of the politics of sexuality. In H. Abelove, M. A. Barale, & D. H. Halperin (Eds.), *The lesbian and gay studies reader* (pp. 3–44). Routledge.

Ruti, M. (2017). *The ethics of opting out: Queer theory's defiant subjects.* Columbia University Press.

Salamon, G. (2021). Queer theory. In K. Q. Hall & Ásta (Eds.), *The Oxford handbook of feminist philosophy* (pp. 506–516). Oxford University Press.

Savin-Williams, R. C. (2016). Sexual orientation: Categories or continuum? *Psychological Science in the Public Interest, 17*(2), 37–44. https://doi.org/10.1177/1529100616637618

Sedgwick, E. K. (1990). *Epistemology of the closet.* University of California Press.

Shinko, R. E. (2010). Ethics after liberalism: Why (autonomous) bodies matter. *Millennium: Journal of International Studies, 38*(3), 723–745. https://doi.org/10.1177/0305829810366474

Skeggs, B. (2011). Imagining personhood differently: Person value and autonomist working-class value practices. *Sociological Review, 59*(3), 496–513. https://doi.org/10.1111/j.1467-954X.2011.02018.x

Somerville, S. B. (2020). Introduction. In S. Somerville (Ed.), *The Cambridge companion to queer studies* (pp. 1–13). Cambridge University Press.

Spargo, T. (1999). *Foucault and queer theory.* Totem Books.

Strunk, K. K., & Shelton, S. A. (Eds.). (2021). *Encyclopedia of queer studies in education.* Brill.

Talburt, S., & Steinberg, S. (Eds.). (2000). *Thinking queer: Sexuality, culture and education.* Peter Lang.

Taylor, M., & Coia, L. (Eds.). (2014). *Gender, feminism, and queer theory in the self-study of teacher education practices.* Sense Publishers.

Tierney, W. G. (1997). *Academic outlaws: Queer theory and cultural studies in the academy.* Sage Publications.

Van Asselt, B. (2019). Imagining otherwise: Transgender and queer youth of color who contest standardized futures in secondary schools. *TSQ: Transgender Studies Quarterly, 6*(4), 608–619. https://doi.org/10.1215/23289252-7771765

Walton, G. (Ed.). (2014). *The gay agenda: Claiming space, identity, and justice.* Peter Lang.

Warner, M. (1991). Introduction: Fear of a queer planet. *Social Text, 29,* 3–17. http://www.jstor.org/stable/466295

Warner, M. (Ed.). (1993). *Fear of a queer planet: Queer politics and social theory.* University of Minnesota Press.

Wiegman, R., & Wilson, E. A. (2015). Introduction: Antinormativity's queer conventions. *differences: A Journal of Feminist Cultural Studies, 26*(1), 1–25. https://doi.org/10.1215/10407391-2880582

Williams, R. (1977). *Marxism and literature.* Oxford University Press.

CHAPTER 1

# Space, Place, and Queerness

*The University of the West Indies, Mona Campus'*

*Queer Zoning*

ADWOA ONUORA AND NADEEN SPENCE

As queer students demand visibility on The University of the West Indies (UWI), Mona Campus, they are seen by some members of the university community as an affront to the heteropatriarchal gender order.[1] This has resulted in the systemic zoning of queerness on the campus. This zoning is most pronounced on the traditional halls of residence built between the 1950s and 1960s. In these halls, a phallocentric brand of leadership prevails, and difference is sometimes violently rejected. While on the surface, learning spaces present as hospitable places that are open, inviting, free, and trustworthy (Palmer & Zajonc, 2010); for queer students this is an imagined ideal. In reality, a culture of exclusion permeates the campus, which allows the general student body to develop their own organizing principles and establishing rules around who lives and goes where. In this queer landscaping, "safe spaces" exist for queer students; however, their safety is only guaranteed if they remain in their "rightful" places.

The UWI is a regional university, a colonial creation built on the remains of two plantations in St. Andrew, Jamaica. It has campuses in Trinidad, Barbados, and Jamaica—its oldest campus. There is also an Open Campus offering online and distance education programs. More recently, a fourth

Adwoa Onuora and Nadeen Spence, *Space, Place, and Queerness* In: *Queer Studies and Education.*
Edited by: Nelson M. Rodriguez, Robert C. Mizzi, Louisa Allen, and Rob Cover, Oxford University Press.
© Oxford University Press 2023. DOI: 10.1093/oso/9780197687000.003.0002

landed campus was approved for Antigua and Barbuda, called the Five Islands Campus (*Jamaica Observer*, 2019).

The first campus at Mona in Jamaica began in 1948 with 33 medical students drawn from the countries of the British Caribbean. The campus, in its original manifestation, was entirely residential. The first hall of residence was in fact an old building used to house refugees from Malta and Gibraltar who had sought asylum in Jamaica through Britain. Irvine Hall was later built in 1950 and was named after Sir James Irvine, who was asked to chair the 1944 Committee, which recommended the establishment of The University College of the West Indies. Taylor Hall was built in 1952, Chancellor Hall in 1955, and Mary Seacole Hall in 1957. No other hall was built at The UWI until the Aston Preston Hall in the 1995–1996 academic year when the hall was opened (The University of the West Indies, n.d.-b).

For a number of years, the sex composition of the first halls vacillated between single-sex to coeducational housing arrangements. Taylor Hall was single sexed from 1952 and welcomed its first women in residence in 1965—some 13 years later. Irvine Hall was constructed as a coed hall initially, then transitioned to becoming an all-female hall between 1952 and 1957. After 1957, it returned to being coed, the same year Mary Seacole Hall began to operate as an all-female hall. Chancellor Hall was opened as an all-male hall in 1955. Since then, it has consistently offered accommodations for male students, though ironically it was named in honor of the first chancellor of the University College of the West Indies, the Countess of Athlone Princess Alice. Interestingly, Princess Alice was the first woman anywhere in the world to have been inaugurated as chancellor of a university (Massiah et al., 2016).

Gender and sex (or some relationship between the two) are the main organizing principles around which the zoning of students' residences at The UWI Mona Campus takes place. The term *sex* is based on the binary categorization of male and female and refers to the biological arrangement of persons based on their genitalia at birth. *Gender*, on the other hand, is a social categorization that facilitates the ascription of roles and characteristics to a person based on genitalia. The latter is used when referencing the socially defined behaviors regarded as appropriate for individuals based on their sex (Lindsey & Christy, 1997). Individuals assigned male at birth are generally expected to be "devoid of emotions," "strong," "aggressive," and "default leaders" in society, whereas those assigned the sex categorization female are framed as always and already "emotional," "weak," "soft," "followers," and "helpmates" to their male counterparts.

Both terms are often conflated; however, the above conceptual distinction is key to understanding the material consequences of the gendering and sexualization of space at The UWI. The rules of residential engagement within the halls of residence are heavily predicated on the maintenance of normative gendered roles, roles that are assigned to persons based on a two-sex binary categorization. It is the presumed immutability of gender that results in the policing and confinement of nonbinary persons to particular spaces. Any transgression of the gendered scripts based on biological sex carries with it negative sanctions not only inside The UWI, but also within the wider Jamaican society. This historically constituted gendering defines how persons of diverse gender identities relate to each other within these spaces. The gender order also has contemporary implications in that it guides the leadership aspirations of students while at The UWI. Importantly, the gender order also shapes the standards, expectations, and ideals of leadership in Jamaican society. In Jamaica, the quintessential leader is understood to be male, heterosexual, Christian, and a person who has access to material and social capital.

## FANON'S ZONE OF NONBEING

One way of understanding the zoning of students' residences on the UWI Mona Campus is by drawing on the insights of postcolonial theory, a body of thought that examines the social, cultural, economic, and political effects of European colonization on postindependent societies (Ashcroft et al., 2000). Because of its preoccupation with highlighting the consequences of colonial domination on peoples of formerly colonized spaces, the theoretical insights are useful to any discussion of the contemporary gendered, racist, and classist dynamics that influence the identity politics and lived realities of people located in former colonies like Jamaica. To this end, Martiniquan revolutionary psychologist Frantz Fanon's articulation of spaces as zones of nonbeing opens up possibilities for thinking through the ways in which colonial ideas of sexual and gender respectability are reproduced in and through the policing of space on the campus.

In *Black Skin, White Masks* (1967), Fanon used the concept zone of nonbeing to foreground the workings of the masculinist, classist, patriarchal body politic in the era of flag independence. For Fanon, the zone of nonbeing signifies the attachment of values of "nothingness" to the existence of working-class Blacks under the rulership of the Black political elite (Fanon, as cited in Thame, 2011). It refers to a social order that solidifies the "thingification" (Césaire, 2000, p. 42) or dehumanization of those located within sites of difference. The zoning of humans as nonbeings denotes a racialized hierarchy, a categorizing of bodies based on notions of personhood and subpersonhood (Thomas, 2016). This zoning, to quote Ahmed (2000), systematically renders identifiable, "bodies out of place" (p. 56); bodies whose lives do not bear value outside of the prism of extraction; bodies who do not count and therefore do not have the power to determine what matters. In Fanon's estimation, the relegation of the racialized other to confined zones of nothingness is tantamount to rendering those so marked as disposable objects. In this regard, zoning also becomes a necessary tool of social control. It serves as a way for members of the petite bourgeoisie class to assert power over and manage dissent within the ranks of the working class trapped in these designated zones. This exercise of power by the ruling elite is activated through oppressive and sometimes violent suppression of disruptions to the established social order.

It is important to understand that zones of nonbeing can also be constructed outside of racialized forms of oppression (Grosfoguel, 2011). Thus, Fanon's conceptualization of racialized zones of nonbeing provides room for an understanding of how similar hierarchies of oppression and domination are maintained through other social identity markers. When we examine closely the formation of Caribbean nation states today, for instance, no formerly colonized state or institutions therein have been shielded from the classist, religious, linguistic, sexual, and gender hierarchies fashioned by the colonial heteropatriarchal capitalist system (Grosfoguel, 2007, 2011, 2016). It is for this reason that, in this chapter, we underscore the simultaneity of our colonial past and present (Thomas, 2016) by focusing on the implications of the reproduction of colonial hierarchies as evidenced in the zoning of queerness. We recognize that a central feature of postcolonial politics, nation-building (and by extension institution building) within the Caribbean region is "the creation of alienating experiences determined by questions of who belongs . . . to whom the nation belongs and therefore, who gets rights and privileges within it" (Thame, 2011, p. 76). This was further underscored by Sheller (2012), who shared:

> Histories of sexual citizenship have shown how state policies, welfare systems, and legal systems have all served to constitute a heteronormative national citizenship that excludes those with same-sex and other non-normative sexual orientations from the rights and protections of citizenship. Many Caribbean feminists have also pointed out the pressure to perform reproductive heterosexuality as a form of national citizenship, with the state (and the church) in many cases violently policing same-sex intimate relations. Thus, the language of the family and its interpersonal intimacies can be read in primary texts as evidence of larger biopolitical processes. (p. 239)

Although Fanon spoke of racialized spaces as zones of nonbeing in referring to the anti-African racism perpetuated vis-à-vis the White supremacist colonial project, we submit that his ideas can be extended to contemporary analyses of patriarchal systems of domination within institutions of higher learning. We suggest further that, just as colonial racialization catapulted bodies marked as Black into zones of nothingness, a similar process occurs in and through the zoning of bodies marked as gender and sexual dissidents on The UWI Mona campus. Through processes such as sex segregation, gender policing, the formal regulation of sexual morality, and the maintenance of the classist respectability politics of the colonial era, queer bodies located in areas deemed queer on campus are framed as "deviant," "disruptive," and "abnormal." Thus, sex segregation through zoning becomes a mechanism for excluding those who defy neocolonial gender and sexual respectability.

While this line of reasoning might appear at odds with postcolonial analyses, we see validity in asserting that queer spatialization is but a mere offshoot of colonial racialization because, as Grosfoguel (2016) reminded us, "when the colonizer and the colonized share the same skin color, the marker of superiority/inferiority along the line of the human has to be constructed with a different marker beyond color racism" (p. 11). In this chapter, we attempt to demonstrate the parallel by turning our attention to how campus residential spaces instantiate this colonial racializing process through the "coding of spaces" (Maliepaard, 2015, p. 156). We draw on the narratives of student leaders to illustrate how they are affected by the "institutionalized normative sexual and gender hegemony" (Onuora & Nangwaya, 2020, p. 199) that, like the colonial racialization of Black bodies, marks queer students for epistemic violence (Spivak, 1988). We examine how the zoning of space impacts the identification of queer students and underscores the challenges and possibilities they face negotiating and accessing leadership spaces as perceived "gender traitors" (Hope, 2006, p. 80). Ultimately, we aspire to offer an assessment of the extent to which queer zones on campus (as neocolonial zones of nonbeing) also afford queer students access to liberation, allowing them to construct autonomous selfhoods outside the confines of heteropatriarchy. Thus, what we are offering in this chapter is a nuancing that sees queer zones on the campus as not simply spaces of abjection.

We would be remiss to overlook a critique of Fanon's work, what Walcott (2006) described as a "disturbing" footnote for racialized queer folks in Fanon's (1967) text *Black Skin, White Masks*. In this book, Fanon located homosexuality within the context of prostitution, which could be seen as him reinforcing a "homohegemony"[2] (Moore, 2020, p. 182), a Westernized

SPACE, PLACE, AND QUEERNESS [31]

framing of queerness that flattens racialized queer folks' dynamic experiences locating them strictly within the confines of the sex economy (Walcott, 2020). Nevertheless, we concur with Crath (2010) that Fanon's insights on decolonization offers space for a "rethinking of how [racialized queer people's] experiences of gender and sexuality are understood and practiced (p. 125)" in the neocolonial moment because of his emphasis on decolonization as transformation.

When used in this chapter, then, queerness is understood as a radical political tool. It is, for us, a commitment to challenging and confronting various social practices and hierarchies fashioned by global coloniality (Grosfoguel, 2007). Consistent with queer of color scholars (Crath, 2010; Moore, 2020; Walcott, 2006), we proffer an understanding of queerness that, like Fanon's decolonial process, locates it as a site of resistance and liberation. However, whereas Fanon was concerned with queerness as the articulation of sex and sexual desires, our intellectual and political project is one that aims to unmask various social practices (outside of, but not limited to, sex and gender) that sustain othering.

While for Fanon queerness may have been thought of as a European import, we understand queerness as the way in which queer-identified persons perform and embody Black femininity because Black women's bodies were originally the site upon which queerness was enacted, defined, and initially framed even before Euro-Western liberal paradigms began to influence dominant understandings of sexual queerness (Moore, 2020). Moore (2020) reminded us that Blackness in general, and Black femininity in particular, is synonymous with nonsexual queerness. We are clear that racist Africanist tropes were scripted unto our bodies (specifically our buttocks, wide hips, large clitoris, full lips and breasts) in an attempt to frame us as fetish objects not deserving of the full menu of rights and dignity afforded to White men and some White women (Mama, 1995; Mazama, 1998; Parkinson, 2016). Euro-Western queer culture has and continues to rely on the articulation of Black femininity and the presence of our physical bodies for its re/production and the simultaneous in/visibility of queerness. Thus, queerness, for us, is first understood in its broadest sense, in a political (nonsexual) sense, as a site of defiance made manifest in and through the physical presence of our racialized queer bodies. We understand that, as Black women, our bodies were historically constructed as sites for re/gendering under the plantation system, sites for the colonial scripting of deviant masculinity and femininity juxtaposed against respectable White masculinity and femininity (Beckles, 2011), and sites that facilitated a colonial framing that pre-dates the homohegemonic notions of queerness that have been thrusted on racialized queers in the neocolonial moment. Like

Crath (2010), therefore, in this chapter, we embrace and reclaim queerness as politics because for us it is a space of critique, a platform from which we are able to resist the "normalizing [tendencies] of state and other social institutions" (Crath, p. 124).

## THE LIVED EXPERIENCES OF QUEER STUDENTS ON CAMPUS

The exclusion of queer students from halls deemed "traditionally straight" has significant epistemic and material consequences (Grosfoguel, 2011). Students, through their zoning of space as either straight or queer, become complicit in a body politic that perpetuates epistemic heterosexism. The very knowledge they produce about gender and sexual variance specifically, and difference generally, reinforces harmful stereotypes about queer bodies located within halls of residence. Halls constructed as queer are also framed within the institutional imagination as threats to the hegemonic gender order characterized by domesticity, chastity, wifehood, motherhood, and caregiving for female students, compared to domestic freedom, fathering, aggression, promiscuity, access to and the provisioning of material resources, leadership/authority, and compulsory heterosexuality for male students (Chevannes, 2001; Reddock, 2004). These stereotypes, though shrouded in unwritten rules, fuel pre-existing antiqueer animus within the wider student population.

Antiqueer sentiments on residential halls often spill over into the wider university community, where homophobic violence is even further institutionalized. In April 2017, for instance, nine trans-identified persons were arrested and charged under Section 6 of The University of the West Indies (Mona Campus) Security Act after attending a movie night to mark the International Day Against Transphobia and Biphobia (IDAHOT) at Mary Seacole Hall—a known queer-friendly all-female hall on the campus. Section 6 of the act allows for the criminalization of persons who enter or remain in a "restricted area" on the campus unless they are a member of staff who works in the area, a security officer on duty, or a person authorized by the campus security committee to be in the restricted area. According to a *Jamaica Observer* report on the incident, the group of nine trans women were invited to an event that ended at about 11:30 p.m. One member of the group recounted in the newspaper report that they had challenges getting a cab after the event ended. Consequently, they waited in a well-lit area under a gazebo on the campus (Mundle, 2017).

An April 10, 2017, letter captioned, "Request for Information for the Benefit of the Kingston Parish Court—Weekly Staging of Trans-Gender

Event at the Mary Seacole Hall on Friday Nights," from the director of campus security at the time and addressed to the student services development manager of Mary Seacole Hall (one of the authors of this chapter), corroborated aspects of the newspaper report and further outlined the campus security's "concerns" about "the possible fall-out that could accompany the staging of such event and the need for additional security to maintain law and order":

> On Saturday the 1st of April 2017 at 1:30 a.m. a group of men of no-fixed address, some of them armed with offensive weapons including knives and scissors were arrested by the Campus Police when they were found loitering in the area of the Mona School of Business and Management.
>
> The nine (9) appeared before the Kingston Parish Court on Monday April 10, 2017 to answer to charges of Being Found in a Restricted Area on the Mona Campus and Being Armed with Offensive Weapons contrary to the Offensive Weapons Act.

The letter above gives insight into what campus security saw as "threatening" and "deviant." It is the body with "no fixed address," the "loitering" body, the body armed with "offensive weapons." It implies that Mary Seacole Hall, by virtue of being a queer-friendly space, knowingly harbors bodies deemed a dangerous threat to The UWI and society as a whole. Besides the epistemological violence meted out against the nine queer persons by the director of security and later, the arresting officer, through the discursive negation of their trans identity evidenced in references to them as "men", the incident showed the consequences of the toxic mix of institutionalized patriarchy, heterosexism, and transphobia. It also highlighted just how certain bodies (in this case feminine-presenting males) become targeted and criminalized through legislative frameworks housed within the institution.

One of the trans women, a student at the institution, shared her experience:

> The UWI Security Act is used by the campus police and security to discriminate against LGBT students and persons who use the space. The University of the West Indies claims to be a space that is diverse and inclusive and welcomes all once they meet the criteria, which is academic excellence and nothing else. However, as a [queer] student, I feel unsafe and targeted by members of the campus police and security who constantly harass not just me, but anyone they deem to be from the community. . . . The UWI securities Act of 2002 was developed to guide the protection of the university which includes the students, staff,

and anyone who is lawfully using the space. This very ambiguous document is used to harass . . . students who are members of the [queer] community on the campus, of which I have been a victim.

Her account illustrates that the April 2017 incident was not an isolated one. She continued:

The most recent incident being this past Saturday night May 12, 2019. While on campus with friends we were approached by two officers, both attached to the office of the Director of Securities. Both officers were not only rude but clearly discriminatory citing the act as justification to forcibly remove persons from a general public area without proper cause, only stating that the area was restricted for non-students. Similar incidents took place last year where members of the trans community were arrested under the Act. . . . Unsurprisingly, only members of the [queer] community have ever been arrested and charged under this act, and given the increased number of robberies and sexual abuse that's been happening on campus by non-students and non-LGBTQ people, you would think the [institution] and those being paid to ensure its protection would spend more time trying to find those persons who are actually committing crimes on campus instead of harassing persons lawfully using the space. As a student, I should not have to feel like I'm being targeted by members of the security and campus police because of my sexual orientation and gender identity.

Based on this student's narrative, it is clear that members of the group in the April 2017 incident were already known to security personnel on the campus from previous run-ins where they attended Pride JA and other events hosted by queer rights advocacy groups on the campus. This incident was therefore not unique and instead reflected a general trend of surveillance of queer persons who are thought to have been "let loose" on the "respectable" campus.

The section of the act under which they were charged is worded in such a way that, when applied, allows for certain individuals to be criminalized for unknowingly being in the wrong place on the campus even if they have a legitimate reason to be there. The very broad provision within the act has far reaching implications because, Section 6, left up to the interpretation and discretion of security personnel on the campus, can be implemented in a way that allows bias to color the decision to arrest. The vagueness of the section also gives campus security latitude to perform their duties in a predatory manner. The section, in effect, allows campus security tremendous freedom to target individuals and groups based on unchecked prejudices they hold against individuals who are gender nonconforming or who are affiliated with halls known to provide space for members of the queer community.

It is clear from the above incident that campus security attached connotations of criminality to queer bodies. The causality for their arrest was, arguably, their gender appearance coupled with the belief that some of the individuals arrested were affiliated with the infamous Gully Queens (homeless queers) located in the New Kingston area.[3] Gender identity or perceived sexual orientation give rise to the predatory policing of bodies located within or associated with queer zones on campus. For many, the mere presence of queers on campus justifies surveillance because queerness disturbs the "sanctity" and "civility" of the established hegemonic masculinity and femininity so central to the heteronationalism around which Jamaican-ness and Jamaican masculinity is formed.

Lewis and Carr (2009) gave context to the exclusionary phallocentrism at the heart of the Jamaican national identity and nation-building project when they stated:

> At the dawn of the 21st century, patriarchal and gendered identity constructions, with their resultant antipathy toward minority sexualities have become central themes in the struggle to define an authentic . . . Jamaican national identity. . . . The racial and religious parameters of Jamaican national identity, characterized by vocal denunciations of overt manifestations of non-normative sexualities, have permeated the public space in unexpected ways, reinforcing a dynamic of exclusion which, despite its claim to indigeneity, marks a continuity of the exclusionary practices of slave society. (n.p.)

The above quotation underscores how the practice of mapping boundaries onto racialized bodies under colonization, a practice used as a way of determining the distribution of rights and freedoms within the nation state (Sheller, 2012), is similarly deployed in the spatial bifurcation of queer and straight sexual subjects into zones on campus. It is in and through this spatialization, or zoning, that a person is marked as a sexual citizen or noncitizen—one who either belongs or does not belong to the university and, by extension, the Jamaican society. The ramifications of spatialization are even more pronounced when we consider the fact that, as Sheller (2012) pointed out, the sexualization of citizens effectively safeguards "normative performances of masculinity and femininity" (p. 241) within the nation state today.

The UWI is a microcosm of the wider society. The articulation of a national identity based on the exclusionary practices spoken of by Lewis and Carr (2009) played out on campus in a similar manner, through zoning of

[36]  *Adwoa Onuora and Nadeen Spence*

queerness both on halls and in spaces of leadership. The UWI students and student leaders are part and parcel of the nation-building project, as it is a Caribbean regional think tank that Jamaica and other Caribbean states turn for its next generation of political elites. The UWI is, essentially, a training ground for those who aspire to later take up the mantle of leadership in society. UWI Vice-Chancellor Sir Hilary Beckles stated that 24 graduates of the UWI have, since its founding in 1948, become national leaders and prime ministers. He stated on UWI TV in 2018 that: "No university in any place in the world can claim ten (10) sitting political leaders among its alumni." When Bruce Golding, then prime minister of Jamaica, declared in a 2008 interview with BBC's *HardTalk* that he did not want any gays to serve in his cabinet (Goddess's Spiritual Lessons, 2018), he was continuing a tradition of exclusionary leadership honed and solidified in the UWI's Chancellor Hall, a space where he, as a student, lived while an undergraduate student at The UWI Mona.

Chancellor Hall, for instance, is regarded by chancellorites (the moniker given to male-identified persons living in this traditionally all male hall) as "the last bastion of masculinity" on the university campus. Since Jamaica's independence in 1962, it has elected seven prime ministers. Three of the seven prime ministers were residents of Chancellor Hall while they attended the university. One participant noted the relationship that this particular hall has to national leadership said:

> Chancellor Hall gets some help from prevailing philosophy in society about . . . the fact that men ought to be leaders; leaders of homes, leaders of business, [and] in all social spheres. But what struck me when I went there would have been how much of an effort is put into training men to take on leadership roles. Within their own systems, within their own cliques, there is an understanding of identifying talent and seeking to hone those [leadership] talents.

Superficially, this might seem a noble project; however, there is a corresponding attitude that this sentiment encourages toward women-identified persons. In many cases, women find themselves at risk physically if they find that their leadership ambitions cannot be developed or explored; this is because they are regarded as assuming a privilege that is reserved exclusively for men, as highlighted in the statement below by another student participant:

> We have seen unfortunate areas over the course of Chancellor Hall and other traditional halls too, where there is generally—it reveals itself in terms of extreme violence against the opposite sex, that may have started a long time ago

and gone unchecked. We would have known even in our own minds leaders and their public relationship with women over time, and how it was dealt with. Some people still recall the stories with laughter. When in truth, it was a criminal offense. But as it relates to issues of misogyny, one of the things that the university in general I think suffers from, is the fact that [it] does not lead, it follows. The sort of belief and . . . culture that exists in Chancellor [Hall] would be the culture that would have existed among any group of men in [Jamaican] society.

Worthy of note here is that male identity in this residential hall space has been contoured around a particular brand of masculinity, one that is consistent with the nationalist leadership of the past. The members of the hall are also invested in preserving that status quo for future generations. Chancellor Hall therefore becomes central to defining and defending the patriarchy of nationalist predecessors through the construction of the hall as necessarily heterosexual—a defining feature of that brand of masculinity to which these men hold dear. Other halls of residences are zoned as queer based on the extent to which they approximate Chancellor Hall's heteropatriarchal gender order. The hall therefore becomes a barometer through which other residential spaces (and students located within) are zoned as straight or genderqueer. Those who are genderqueer are usually regarded as not worthy of engagement in the leadership enterprise. In this case, it is not only that leadership is male identified, but also, as previously mentioned, leadership is heterosexual, hypermasculine, and decidedly antiwoman and antiqueer.

In underscoring the importance of the heteromasculinist[4] project to Chancellor Hall's identity and the general perception about whether individuals are fit to take up leadership on the Guild of Students, one respondent had this to say:

> I think it [the masculinist project] has worked for the dominance of the hall. I think other halls, other newer Halls, have a different philosophy. Their philosophy is if you want to serve, serve. You shouldn't be blocked out of it. You should put yourself up, and you should express yourself through the democratic processes and people will either vote for you or not. . . . Sometimes this may divide a hall [and] may divide support. And so, I think that has contributed largely to Chancellor Hall's dominance [which] has continued even 'till now where Chancellor Hall boasts . . . a strong presence on the [Guild's] executive again this year. And that's a pride for them because of the strategy they would have employed.

In this respondent's mind, Chancellor Hall's success is mostly attributed to their leadership ambition and their willingness to make sacrifices and do the hard work of winning leadership positions. Their strategy is a deliberate and targeted preparation of their students for leadership. There is an expectation, according to this student, that the young men will lead and therefore should be prepared for leadership. They therefore engage in careful selection and grooming of leaders from the moment a student first enters the hall. But, even before that, young boys grow up with notions of men's right to lead (Chevannes, 2001). In this regard, Chancellor Hall perpetuates the male-centered, heteronormative leadership culture that sees cisheterosexual men as leaders and cisgender women and genderqueers as followers.

Mary Seacole Hall is regarded as the sister hall to Chancellor Hall. The women students of Mary Seacole Hall are expected to support "their brothers" in Chancellor Hall as they pursue their ambitions for dominance in sports and in student leadership. Interestingly, but perhaps unsurprisingly, a Chancellor Hall student has served as the head of the Guild of Students[5] for over 50 years, while Mary Seacole Hall has had a Seacolite at the head of the guild for just 6 years. Even as Chancellor Hall commands its expectations of leadership, it engages in practices that are said to be critical to the survival of its brotherhood. Practices such as the maintenance of a "panty tree" symbolizing sexual conquest of women on the campus, where women's panties are flown, and "poo songs" (which speak of the sexual prowess of Chancellor men) are sung as a way of ushering the young men who reside in the hall into the cult of male-dominated leadership. The culture of the hall is such that the hall environment gives them the freedom to engage in practices that openly declare it a heterosexual space. Other traditional fraternity-like practices include those that reinforce the defining features of heterosexual masculinity as necessary for character building.

Seacolites, on the other hand, are expected to support their brothers in their quest to pursue their leadership and other ambitions. When Seacole women resist the patriarchy of Chancellor Hall, they are labeled as stereotypical "bra-burning lesbians" who simply hate men. They therefore run the risk of being demonized, labeled feminists, and ostracized. They can only truly own womanhood by supporting their brothers. Any dissent on their part could lead to questioning of their legitimacy as sisters and as heterosexual women. When Seacole women challenge the norms of sexuality or the patriarchal leadership culture, they face potential male backlash[6] because Seacolites are always expected to support Chancellorites as brother and sister halls.

SPACE, PLACE, AND QUEERNESS [39]

Taylor Hall was opened in 1952 and accepted women in 1965, but as one participant noted, the structure of the residential facilities for women and for men are vastly different and sends a strong message about how women are valued in the space. Up to the 2019 academic year election cycle, Taylor Hall made it clear that it would not welcome women in a leadership role in its student body. The hall tradition boasts an unwillingness to accept women in the leadership of the student body. Their insistence that they do not want any "panty government" speaks to not only an undermining of women's leadership capacity but also their refusal to accept women in any powerful leadership position. In the 2019 academic year, for the first time, two women contested the leadership position for Taylor Hall. This was monumental in the history of this hall of residence.

The spaces occupied by men and women within "traditional halls" are carefully policed to maintain the gendered division of labor and hetero-sexual hierarchies. Women are expected to "know their place" and not to challenge traditional gender norms. Where gender norms are transgressed, women pay a heavy price. While neither woman won the leadership, the fact that they ran was in and of itself a huge challenge to the accepted pa-triarchal dictates of life in Taylor Hall. The popularly articulated assertion "no panty government" highlights the unwillingness to accept the idea that women can be competent leaders. It is through bodies located in these spaces that the alienating experience of exclusion is activated. Sexual and gender dissidents in halls are a representation of the disruption of the het-erosexual patriarchal order necessary to reproduce and lead the nation.

As has been mentioned before, nontraditional understandings and definitions of masculinity and femininity are not accepted and are in fact publicly frowned on in traditional halls of residence on The UWI Mona Campus. Male gender and sexual identity are sites of contestation. And in spaces where a "real man" is judged and honored as heterosexual, he must be careful not to undermine his status by associating with one of the halls where masculinity is called into question.

In the early 2000s, two young undergraduate women were labeled as lesbians in one of the traditional halls. Their transgression was seen as un-forgivable by both the students and the hall's administration, so much so that they were asked to leave the hall immediately. The hall manager at the time informed both young women that he could not guarantee their safety and would not tolerate their "behavior" in the hall. They had to find housing in "other" spaces on the campus. Labeled and ostracized, they bore the brunt of verbal attacks and slurs as they navigated the campus.

Some 9 years later, one young woman from Rex Nettleford Hall de-cided to run for a position on the Guild of Students. She shared that she was openly queer, and that she enjoyed acceptance among her peers on her hall of residence. When her candidacy was announced, she recognized how complex the decision to run as a masculine-presenting queer woman was. Campaigning was a challenge because her sexuality became the central focus despite her best efforts. She recounted how unnerving it was to have complete strangers walk up to her and ask her if "she was the lesbian girl":

> I can't say I know the guy to have personally said anything against me, but I know people close to him have. So, if they're campaigning for their friend and they woulda seh [say]: yu know de gyal a lesbian weh him a run against [the girl is a lesbian that he is up against]? Yu nuh [you know], plainly say it, yu nuh. I remember passing the humanities and seeing one of my posters marked with the words dutty lesbian gyal, don't vote fi ar, that kinda thing, yu nuh [dirty lesbian girl, don't vote for her]. I remember a friend or somebody [saying] they saw one of my posters and it was [defaced] with some terrible things. They didn't tell me exactly what it was but they said they just took it down, and so I should replace it, where they took it down from. So every time you go to somebody to campaign that's the first thing they meet you with, "A chuu sey yaa lesbian [Is it true that you are a lesbian]"? Like that's just what they meet you with, yu nuh. But I must say, I think the unintentional good side to that was that a lot of queer people could identify me. So people would anti-campaign me to queer people that they didn't even know [were] queer, and when I go to talk to a girl and, dem a sey, oh, a yu mi a vote fah eno; mi know yaa family, that kinda thing [Oh, I am voting for you, because you are family].

Heteronormativity (the belief that being heterosexual is the "normal" way to articulate one's sexual orientation) imposes a default heterosexual identity on all human beings. This student recognized that persons who sought to confirm whether she was a lesbian had previously assumed that she was heterosexual. In many ways, we are "born straight" until proven otherwise. In this case, the student recognized that her very body presented a challenge to the status quo expectation that someone running for a leadership position should not be openly queer and instead should hide this part of their identity. Her experience is not without nuance. It also showed that being a queer candidate was also affirming not only for her, but also for other queer-identifying student voters who saw themselves represented in her candidacy. Her assertion of her queer identity in answering the question, "Are you the lesbian girl running for the External Affairs Chairperson position?" in the affirmative, we suggest, signals her politicization of queerness. This act is meaningful in that it signifies for us a transgressive body politic, a resistance to any attempt at amputating to paraphrase Fanon (1967), her embodied queerness from the sphere of leadership. This same student discussed how vulnerable she was during the campaign as well as how her queer body was fetishized in a way that was simultaneously traumatizing and affirming. In conversations with her, she recounted that on the day of the electoral debates, she decided to make a political statement by wearing a tuxedo typically associated with the male gender. We interpret this as her attempt at challenging the neocolonial framings of queerness through a redefinition of queerness as "sartorial excess" (Moore, 2020, p. 169).

One other story shared by a participant was that of a male student who offered himself for the position of secretary. At The UWI Mona, the student body has elected 69 presidents of the Guild Council. Of that number, nine have been women. The student body has also elected over 60 students to serve as secretary of the guild. Since its founding, it has elected just about eight males as guild secretary. No man has been elected as guild secretary since the 1980s. A young man who served as hall chair for The UWI's oldest hall decided to contest the position of secretary. His contestation of the position was seen as a betrayal of acceptable standards of masculinity in his hall. The act of offering himself for the position cemented in the minds of male students in this hall that he was not "a real man." His leadership ambitions were thought of as damaging to the hall's reputation. His actions "tainted" the hypermasculine identity of the hall, placing it at risk of being labeled a queer space. In the minds of many on the hall, the leadership choice of secretary marked him as a "batty man" (gay man).

## THE QUEER BODY THAT QUESTIONS

We began this chapter as a foray into Fanon's decolonial/anticolonial theorizing around racialized zones. We believe that notwithstanding critiques about his limited framing of queerness, Fanon has much to offer in terms of broadening our understanding of the embodied experiences of queer students navigating spaces of learning. Therefore, it is only fitting that we return to Fanon in this, our conclusion.

In his magnum opus, Fanon ended with a final prayer: "O my body, make of me always a [body] who questions!" (Fanon, 1967, p. 232). This is, for us, a queer calling of sorts, a declaration that, in our minds, locates queerness as corporeal resistance. The queer body, as evidenced in the experiences of student leaders, is the body that activates an emancipatory decolonial queer praxis. It is the body that challenges marginalization wrought by the demarcation of space. Thus, for us, queer zones on campus are spaces of possibility, spaces that in the words of Walcott (2020) "signify more complex articulations of queerness" (p. 244) that move beyond the negation of queer selfhood. Viewed in this way, the queer spatialization on campus, like the process of decolonization, is as Dei (2020) suggested: "a violent but [simultaneously] creative necessity" (p. XVIII). In a way, the process of zoning and its accompanying violence, creates space for queer students to assume this questioning role of which Fanon spoke by pushing back against individual and institutionalized attempts at plunging them into nihilism.

While we do not wish to gloss over the potentially deleterious consequences the zoning of queerness has on their ability to negotiate power within the context of a patriarchal body politic, we also see where they, through their very presence, actively reject the neocolonial script that says (albeit implicitly) that leadership does not reside in queer subjectivities. Based on our conversations with students, queer zoning offers possibilities for affirmation, reclamation, community building, organizing, as well as opportunities for reconfiguring realities outside of compulsory heteronormativity (Konrad, 2014). At the same time, creating queernormative realities within "queer-friendly zones" on campus poses risks because doing so singles queer students out. These zones paradoxically mark queer students as visible, even as the process of zoning invisibilizes them.

## NOTES

1. Here we are referring to a social order where primacy is given to heterosexual males over persons who are gender queer and nonheterosexual.
2. Moore (2020) defined homohegemony as "the contemporary iteration of white, middle-class, male, Northern out-of-the closet queerness that holds great cultural currency and is presently being deployed as the 'right way' to be queer" (p. 182).
3. The case was later dismissed as the presiding judge ruled that the law was too vague and needed to be re-formed. The judge concluded that for the institution to designate an area as restricted, there needed to be clear signposts indicating which areas were restricted in advance.
4. When used here, this term denotes the way in which society constructs masculinity as necessarily tied to heterosexuality. In other words, masculinity and heterosexuality are deemed inseparable. It is therefore used to refer to a cultural context where some men feel compelled to authenticate a particular brand of masculinity through heterosexuality.
5. The Guild of Students is the official student government organizing body at University of the West Indies.

6. Male backlash, according to Guarnieri and Rainer (2018), holds that women's economic empowerment makes things worse. They argued that when gender roles and the relations of power are redefined or challenged, men will resort to violence to reassert the culturally prescribed norm of male dominance and female subordination.

## REFERENCES

Ahmed, S. (2000). *Strange encounters: Embodied others in post-coloniality.* Psychology Press.

Ashcroft, B., Griffiths, G., & Tiffin, H. (2000). *Post-colonial studies: The key concepts* (2nd ed.). Routledge.

Beckles, H. (2011). Sex and gender in the historiography of Caribbean slavery. In V. Shepherd (Ed.), *Engendering Caribbean history* (pp. 38–48). Ian Randle Publishers.

Césaire, A. (2000). *Discourse on colonialism.* Monthly Review Press.

Chevannes, B. (2001). *Learning to be a man: Culture, socialization, and gender identity in five Caribbean communities.* University of the West Indies Press.

Crath, R. (2010). Reading Fanon in "homosexual territory": Towards the queering of a queer pedagogy. In G. Dei & M. Simmons (Eds.), *Fanon and education: Thinking through pedagogical possibilities* (pp. 125–146). Peter Lang.

Dei, G. (2020). Rereading Fanon for his pedagogy and implications for schooling and education. In G. Dei & M. Simmons (Eds.), *Fanon and education: Thinking through pedagogical possibilities* (pp. 1–27). Peter Lang.

Fanon, F. (1967). *Black skin, white masks.* Grove Press.

Goddess's Spiritual Lessons. (2018, June 29). *No gays says Jamaica's Prime Minister on BBC's hard talk* [Video]. YouTube. https://www.youtube.com/watch?v=YeVy5Sp6xyw&t=135s&ab_channel=GODDESS%27SSpiritualLessons

Grosfoguel, R. (2007). The epistemic colonial turn: Beyond political-economy paradigms. *Cultural Studies, 21*(2), 211–223. https://doi.org/10.1080/09502380601162514

Grosfoguel, R. (2011). Decolonizing post-colonial studies and paradigms of political-economy: Transmodernity, decolonial thinking and global coloniality. *Transmodernity: Journal of Peripheral Cultural Production of the Luso-Hispanic World, 1*(1), 1–38. https://escholarship.org/uc/item/21k6t3fq

Grosfoguel, R. (2016). What is racism? *Journal of World-Systems Research, 22*(1), 9–15. https://doi.org/10.5195/jwsr.2016.609

Guarnieri, E., & Rainer, H. (2018). Female empowerment and male backlash. CESifo Working Paper, No. 7009, Center for Economic Studies and ifo Institute (CESifo), Munich. CESifo. https://www.cesifo.org/en/publications/2018/working-paper/female-empowerment-and-male-backlash

Hope, D. P. (2006). *Inna di dancehall: Popular culture and the politics of identity in Jamaica.* University of the West Indies Press.

Jamaica Observer. (2019, June 18). Antigua gets UWI Campus. https://www.pressreader.com/jamaica/daily-observer-jamaica/20190618/281586652118263

Konrad, C. (2014). This is where we live: Queering poor urban spaces in literature of black gay men. *Gender, Place and Culture: A Journal of Feminist Geography, 21*(3), 337–352. https://doi.org/10.1080/0966369X.2013.781014

Lewis, R. A., & Carr, R. (2009). Gender, sexuality and exclusion: Sketching the outlines of the Jamaican popular nationalist project. *Caribbean Review of Gender Studies: A Journal of Caribbean Perspectives on Gender and Feminism, 3*. https://sta.uwi.edu/crgs/november2009/index.asp

Lindsey, L., & Christy, S. (1997). *Gender roles: A sociological perspective* (3rd ed.). Prentice Hall.

Maliepaard, E. (2015). Bisexuals in space and geography: More than queer? *Fennia, 193*(1), 148–159. https://fennia.journal.fi/article/view/46303/14643

Mama, A. (1995). *Beyond the masks: Race, gender, and subjectivity*. Routledge.

Massiah, J., Leo-Rhynie, E., & Bailey, B. (2016). *The UWI gender journey: Recollections and reflections*. University of the West Indies Press.

Mazama, A. (1998). The Eurocentric discourse on writing: An exercise in self-glorification. *Journal of Black Studies, 29*(1), 3–16. https://doi.org/10.1177/002 193479802900101

Mundle, T. (2017, April 16). *Transgender men offer defence for being on UWI female hall*. Jamaica Observer. https://www.jamaicaobserver.com/news/transgender-men-offer-defence-for-being-on-uwi-female-only-hall/

Moore, C. (2020). Brave "battymen" and the (im)possibilities of a straight dancehall. In E. McLeod & M. Anderson (Eds.), *Beyond homophobia: Centring LGBTQ experiences in the anglophone Caribbean* (pp. 167–186). University of the West Indies Press.

Onuora, A.N., & Nangwaya, A. (2020). Toward a working-class queer agenda and leadership in Jamaica. In E. McLeod & M. Anderson (Eds.), *Beyond homophobia: Centring LGBTQ experiences in the anglophone Caribbean* (pp. 191–213). University of the West Indies Press.

Palmer, P. J., & Zajonc, A. (2010). *The heart of higher education: A call to renewal: Transforming the academy through collegial conversations*. Jossey-Bass.

Parkinson, J. (2016, January 7). The significance of Sarah Bartman. *BBC News Magazine*. https://www.bbc.com/news/magazine-35240987

Reddock, R. (2004). Interrogating Caribbean masculinities: An introduction. In R. Reddock (Ed.), *Interrogating Caribbean masculinities: Theoretical and empirical analyses* (pp. xiii–xxxiv). University of the West Indies Press.

Sheller, M. (2012). *Citizenship from below: Erotic agency and Caribbean freedom*. Duke University Press.

Spivak, G. C. (1988). Can the subaltern speak? *Die Philosophin, 14*(27), 42–58.

Thame, M. (2011). Reading violence and postcolonial decolonization through Fanon: The case of Jamaica. *Journal of Pan-African Studies, 4*(7), 75–93. http://www.jpanafrican.org/docs/vol4no7/4.7-6Reading.pdf

Thomas, D. A. (2016). Time and the otherwise: Plantations, garrisons and being human in the Caribbean. *Anthropological Theory, 16*(2–3), 177–200. https://doi.org/10.1177/1463499616636269

The University of the West Indies. (n.d.-a). *About the University of the West Indies Five Islands*. https://fiveislands.uwi.edu

The University of the West Indies. (n.d.-b). *History*. https://www.mona.uwi.edu/uwimona-history

UWI TV. (2018, November 9). *UWI tribute to Caribbean leaders* [Video]. YouTube. https://www.youtube.com/watch?v=l0593qeewG8&feature=youtu.be&list=PLwn3me5yK4YbjtKmTjVKsrG8T_19e

Walcott, R. (2006). Black men in frocks: Sexing race in a gay ghetto (Toronto). In C. Teelucksingh (Ed.), *Claiming space: Racialization in Canadian cities* (pp. 121–133). Wilfred Laurier University Press.

Walcott, R. (2020). Queer life beyond and against homophobia. In E. McLeod & M. Anderson (Eds.), *Beyond homophobia: Centring LGBTQ experiences in the anglophone Caribbean* (pp. 237–250). University of the West Indies Press.

CHAPTER 2

# A Queer Sexuality Education

## The Possibilities and Impossibilities of Knowing

NAOMI RUDOE

Queer theory has been extremely valuable in developing a pedagogy, as it engages with the parameters of the (im)possibilities of knowing.
—Haywood & Mac an Ghaill (2016, p. 57)

This chapter involves an exploration of how queer theoretical ideas can be thought about in relation to English school policy and practice in relationships and sex education (RSE). It examines how thinking queerly and with queer theory can contribute to a more research-/scholarship-informed policy and practice around sex/uality education in schools. England has recently reached a point in 2020, after many years of lobbying and political shifting, where schools provide compulsory RSE. How "successful" this education will be, given the amount of teacher training and curriculum space and resourcing that is needed, is a separate issue. The teaching will be given a level of accountability through the school inspection system by consideration of pupils' personal development, behavior and welfare, and spiritual, moral, social, and cultural development. In this chapter, I critically examine the content of government policy guidance for schools in relation to sexuality and provide some thoughts about how queer theory might usefully inform practice in relation to teaching about sexuality.

I first set out the policy context with an analysis of how this new guidance engages with sexuality and teaching young people about sexuality.

Naomi Rudoe, *A Queer Sexuality Education* In: *Queer Studies and Education*. Edited by: Nelson M. Rodriguez, Robert C. Mizzi, Louisa Allen, and Rob Cover, Oxford University Press. © Oxford University Press 2023.
DOI: 10.1093/oso/9780197687000.003.0003

I then explore the notion of childhood innocence as a way to explain and discuss the limits of what many adults perceive as being "appropriate" for children to learn about sex/uality. As children learn what it means to be a sexual being from the sociocultural discourses that surround them, much of which comes from their peers (Robinson & Davies, 2019), one issue that becomes apparent is the sense of "catching up" that teachers and parents do in terms of young people's lived experiences and knowledge. As Whittington and Thomson (2018) noted: "Curriculum discourses appear to be out of sync with lived cultures—which themselves may be marginalised within institutional contexts" (p. 52). I engage with the notion of childhood innocence as reinforcing "heteronormative logics of growing up" (Neary & Rasmussen, 2020, p. 901), linking to the element of fantasy invested in this idea of children as innocent. Using the work of Rasmussen (2013), I then examine the notion of antihomophobic education (identifying prejudice and tackling it) as a solution to homophobia, questioning whether it is possible always to identify someone/thing as "homophobic," and where the responsibility for antihomophobic education may lie. In all this I repeatedly meet the question of what it is possible to know (about oneself or others), in the present or future, and whether it is possible for educators to know they are teaching the "right thing." Finally, I address some ideas that could inform a queer sexuality education.

Queer theory opens up a powerful realm of meaning for sexuality educators. "Queer" rejects binary gender and heterosexuality as pregiven and dominant state; it disturbs, shakes up, and renders fictitious and yet can also fix, settle, and make true. As Sedgwick (1993) wrote:

> "Queer" can refer to: the open mesh of possibilities, gaps, overlaps, dissonances and resonances, lapses and excesses of meaning when the constituent elements of anyone's gender, of anyone's sexuality aren't made (or *can't be* made) to signify monolithically. (p. 8)

Queer troubles certainty: the certainty of any stable sexual or gender identity, and I would suggest, the certainty of knowing what is "appropriate" for a sexuality education curriculum. Queer operates as a noun to define identity, an adjective to modify theory, and a verb that unsettles something (Greteman, 2014). Queer theory sees sexuality as a social construction and identification as unstable and fluid, although this is not to deny that many people experience their sexuality and gender identity as a fixed and innate part of themselves, dictated by biology. The term *queer* is reflective of an increasing diversity and fluidity to young people's sexual and gender identifications: One in two young British people describe themselves as "not

[48]  *Naomi Rudoe*

exclusively heterosexual" according to a 2015 YouGov survey (Dahlgreen & Shakespeare, 2015). Bragg et al.'s (2018) study of 12- to 14-year-olds in England found participants using 23 different terms for gender identity, and young people "confidently exploring identities such as 'gender fluid', 'agender', 'gay', 'lesbian or bisexual' or 'pansexual'" (p. 425). This diversity and fluidity, which I symbolize here as queer, particularly among young people, may present a challenge to educators in considering the meanings of identity categories that are less "straightforward" than "lesbian" or "gay." Queer seeks to move away from fixed identity categories while, ironically, forming its own category, albeit a more complex one. A sexuality education that is informed by queer theory, though, can allow young people a space in which to consider more complex understandings of sexuality and identity.

Writing over 20 years ago, Berlant and Warner (1998) referred to "the changed possibilities of identity, intelligibility, publics, culture, and sex that appear when the heterosexual couple is no longer the referent or the privileged example of sexual culture" (p. 548). Same-sex-attracted people in the United Kingdom now enjoy the same age of consent as heterosexuals, may now marry, and are even beginning to be seen in TV advertisements (!), but it would be hard to argue that straight couples have been displaced from a dominant discourse. Much has been written about the heteronormativity of the school as an institution (DePalma & Atkinson, 2009; Epstein et al., 2003); homophobic, biphobic, and transphobic (HBT) bullying remain an issue, though schools are increasingly addressing this by, for example, making use of the U.K. charity training-based program Educate & Celebrate, which includes embedding LGBTQ people and issues in the curriculum. The term *queer* "challenges educators to attend to the ongoing processes of normalization and the continued violence enacted against bodies deemed different" (Greteman, 2017, p. 197). As I show, queer theoretical ideas can assist with developing a more inclusive sexuality education in schools that builds on the new policy guidance for teaching RSE.

## RELATIONSHIPS AND SEX EDUCATION POLICY: PREPARING YOUNG PEOPLE "FOR LIFE IN MODERN BRITAIN"[1]

After many years of political battles over the status and content of sex and relationships education in England, in 2017 the Conservative government announced there would be compulsory relationships education in all primary schools and RSE in all secondary schools in England (which began in 2020), and in 2018 issued initial draft statutory RSE guidance for consultation, providing advice on what schools should do and setting out legal duties with which they must comply. Following the consultation period, in 2019 the government issued updated draft statutory guidance, which then passed through both houses of Parliament and was made final. This guidance replaced the last (New Labour) government-issued Sex and Relationship Education (SRE) guidance dating from 2000. That document contains the "ambiguous" wording that "there should be no direct promotion of sexual orientation" (Department for Education and Employment [DfEE], 2000, p. 13) in schools, echoing the Conservative implementation of Section 28 of the Local Government Act 1988, that forbade local authorities from "promoting homosexuality" or "the teaching in any maintained school of the acceptability of homosexuality as a pretended family relationship," that was not repealed in England until 2003.

The final statutory RSE guidance contains this advice for all schools in relation to developing a policy for RSE, under the section "Lesbian, Gay, Bisexual and Transgender":

> Schools should ensure that all of their teaching is sensitive and age appropriate in approach and content. At the point at which schools consider it appropriate to teach their pupils about LGBT, they should ensure that this content is fully integrated into their programmes of study for this area of the curriculum rather than delivered as a stand-alone unit or lesson. Schools are free to determine how they do this, and we expect all pupils to have been taught LGBT content at a timely point as part of this area of the curriculum. (Department for Education [DfE], 2019a, p. 15)

Under Secondary RSE, the guidance states:

> Pupils should be taught the facts and the law about sex, sexuality, sexual health and gender identity in an age-appropriate and inclusive way. All pupils should feel that the content is relevant to them and their developing sexuality. Sexual orientation and gender identity should be explored at a timely point and in a clear, sensitive and respectful manner. When teaching about these topics, it must be recognised that young people may be discovering or understanding their sexual orientation or gender identity. There should be an equal opportunity to explore the features of stable and healthy same-sex relationships. (DfE, 2019a, p. 20)

Between the initial and the final guidance, some language was altered: The initial guidance referred to "discovering or *coming to terms with* their sexual orientation or gender identity" (emphasis added). This was replaced with "discovering or *understanding*," thus avoiding the suggestion that (nonnormative) sexual orientation or gender identity may cause traumatic experience and that being same-sex attracted or identifying as gender nonconforming is not "normal." Schools are, however, left to decide on how and where to address "LGBT content" and secondary schools left to decide what is "age appropriate and inclusive" and a "timely point" to learn about sexual orientation and gender identity. This equivocal language is reflective of the fact that, as the DfE stated in its response to the initial guidance, a "large proportion" of the responses disagreed with the position on teaching LGBT in the guidance:

> Some respondents felt primary children, or all children and young people, are too young to be taught about LGBT, while others felt it was important for children to be aware of LGBT content and that this could be appropriately delivered in secondary or in both primary and secondary schools. (DfE, 2019b, p. 8)

The government holds firm in a view that pupils need to understand that some people are LGBT and they are afforded protections and rights within the law. Following disruptions over LGBT content already being taught in some primary schools, in early 2019, the government was forced to publish on its website in FAQs about RSE that: "Primary schools are strongly encouraged and enabled to cover LGBT content when teaching about different types of families" (GOV.UK, 2019, para. 25).

The final guidance makes allowance for faith schools as follows:

> Schools with a religious character may teach the distinctive faith perspective on relationships, and balanced debate may take place about issues that are seen as contentious. (DfE, 2019a, p. 12)

Faith schools, which as of 2019 constituted 34% of the total of state-funded mainstream schools in England (House of Commons Library, 2019), are given flexibility to teach according to their faith, while being required to adhere to the Equality Act 2010. There is no doubt that some religious teachings are at odds with teaching children about the flexibility of sexual orientation and gender identity. At the time of writing the first draft of this chapter (2019), a Catholic secondary school in England stated in its SRE policy that the "sexual activity of homosexual people" is "unacceptable" (I retain the schools' anonymity in this chapter). Another secondary school's policy cited Paragraph 2358 from the catechism of the Catholic Church, which states that "homosexual tendencies" are "objectively disordered." An English primary school's SRE policy contained the following sentence reminiscent of Section 28: "Teachers take care not to advocate homosexual behaviour, present it as the norm, or encourage homosexual experimentation"; a number of primary schools' policies stated: "Under no circumstance do we use sex education as a means of promoting any form of sexual orientation." These statements, however, can be contrasted with extracts from other, inclusive, primary schools' policies: "SRE aims to: . . . Provide knowledge of loving relationships including same sex relationships," and "An understanding of human difference, including sexuality, is an important aspect of education and will be addressed as appropriate through the curriculum."

It is evidently easier to change the law to reflect the facts about—and young people's lived experiences of—sex, sexuality, sexual health, and gender identity than it is to change people's beliefs. It took from 1835, the date of the last execution for homosexuality in England, to 1967 for homosexuality to be partially decriminalized, to 2003 for the sexual offense of gross indecency (used to criminalize gay men) to be repealed. Around 20% of Britons in the National Survey of Attitudes and Lifestyles (known commonly as Natsal) in 2010 reported their belief that same sex relationships are always wrong, although this represents a shift from around 50% holding that belief in 1990 (Watt & Elliot, 2017). It is also evidently easier for teachers to reflect the law around the rights of sexual minorities and to defend LGBTQ pupils from discrimination and bullying than it is to teach from perspectives informed by queer theory and to challenge heteronormativity, but it is clearly possible.

## THE CHILD AS INNOCENT/QUEER

I move now to examine queer theoretical perspectives on the notion of childhood innocence. Much sociological, psychological, and queer theoretical work questioning the notion of childhood innocence has sought to demonstrate children as sexual beings, whether this be through a Freudian understanding of children's sexuality as innate or through a Foucauldian analysis of sexuality as produced in discourse (Britzman, 2019). The notion of childhood innocence, as I discuss in an examination of the ways in which parents attempt to uphold or protect this idea, seems to be imagined as children being nonsexual (as a result of being ignorant of sexual relations), "uncorrupt," or "pure," or as childhood being a period that should be kept this way. Sexuality is generally represented as beginning at puberty, even though Freud's theories of infantile sexuality challenged the idea that children's sexual development begins at puberty (Robinson & Davies, 2019). In fact, by the start of the twentieth century, children's sexuality was considered by many psychological disciplines as

[52]  *Naomi Rudoe*

part of "normal" development, though disagreement lay in the meanings that could be attached to child as opposed to adult sexuality (Sauerteig, 2012). In 1983, the World Health Organization stated that "every person has a right to receive sexual information and to consider accepting sexual relationships for pleasure as well as for procreation. Sexuality starts at birth.... Masturbation and sexual play in children are normal and healthy" (as cited in Zimmerman, 2015, p. 100). Children *are* sexual, Lamb et al. (2019) plainly stated, and they made a case for the child not as innocent, but as *vulnerable*, and in this respect, in need of protection from harms already a problem in the adult world: "abuse, degrading porn, stereotypes, compulsive behaviours, lack of privacy, heteronormativity, disregard for bodies, objectification, and more" (p. 29).

The notion of childhood innocence can be conceived of as "an adult ideal, something which adults would like childhood to be" (Kehily & Montgomery, 2009, p. 85). Jacqueline Rose (1984/1992) brought our attention to *Peter Pan* as the fantasy of the myth of the eternal child; the story was not originally intended for children, and, as Rose argued, it "shows innocence not as a property of childhood but as a portion of adult desire" (p. xii). Taking up this theme, Owen (2010) noted how little can be really known about the child (or indeed about any other person), and that the child as filled with adult desire or projection, in itself, renders it impossible to know the child.

Kathryn Bond Stockton (2009) outlined childhood—including the concept of childhood innocence, typified by the White, middle-class child—as somehow essentially strange (using the concept of "queer" as "strange"). In relation to queer identity, Stockton (2009) wrote that the (sexualized) identity of "gay child" can only be applied retrospectively ("I *was* a gay child")—though noting in later writing that the gay child is becoming "ever more discussed" and "belief in its existence daily grows" (Stockton, 2016, p. 507). Stockton (2016) wrote that children's "innocence" must be "protected," as adults "walk the line—the *impossible* [emphasis added] line—of keeping the child at once what it is (what adults are not) and leading it toward what it cannot (at least, as itself) ever be (what adults are)" (pp. 513–514). This *is* a difficult process and one that the parent can never completely control. A parent is in the unsettling position of not always being able to know what a child does or does not know, what sexual feelings or knowledge (or indeed experience) a child may possess or desire, and yet they hold a responsibility for raising the child toward adulthood. Stockton (2009) complicated any route of innocence to knowledge as a linear process: "One does not 'grow up' from innocence to the adult position of protecting it. This view of innocence—the growing up view—leaves one open to its particular dangers" (p. 12). Stockton posited that in its delay—the child's enforced distance from adulthood—the child "grows sideways" or "to the side of cultural ideals" (p. 13), rather than up, a notion that suggests that growth is not limited to one direction, (st)age or developmental end point, but is a lifelong process.

Adult/parental fear of children's "loss" of innocence, of their "growing up too soon," Stockton (2009) noted, revolves around particular fears of children's sexualization, sexual activity and desires, their aggression, the "gay child," of gender identity transition, of child as consumer. Stockton here alluded to both the child with money and the child as consumer of candy, ending the book with a queer reading of *Charlie and the Chocolate Factory*. The particular irony of the feared phenomenon of the child with money or children's "robust consumer wishes that lessen our control" (Stockton, 2009, p. 126) grows ever stronger in times of neoliberal austerity and crises over children's well-being. As Gill-Peterson et al. (2016) pointed out, the "modern fantasies of the child-figure have simply become unconvincing in the face of the material conditions of contemporary life" (p. 497), with children needing to work at earlier ages in order to lessen debt, and being in an apparent grip of mental health disorders.

Studies examining parents' talk with their children about sex and sexuality continue to demonstrate an immensely strong cleavage to the notion of childhood innocence. A major barrier to parent–child communication, McGinn et al. (2016) argued, is precisely a desire to protect childhood innocence, manifested in, for example, false accounts of where babies come from. Parents of 4- to 7-year-olds in this study conceptualized innocence as "lesser knowledge" and as "nonsexual," although there was considerable uncertainty about how to define innocence and how to conceptualize the difference between innocence and noninnocence. A study conducted by Bennett et al. (2017) that interviewed eight fathers about their discussions with their 10-year-old children about sex and relationships also demonstrated their beliefs that their children did not need, or were not ready, for this kind of information or discussion. When fathers in this study were asked whether they had discussed any aspect of puberty, sex, or relationships with their children, their responses included the following:

> He really doesn't need to know yet. It's not relevant to him. Perhaps when he's going to secondary school but not now, he's more into playing than all that stuff.

> I'm not sure that she is ready yet, she still likes her dolls and stuff like that.

> He's ten so a bit early, but he's showing an interest in girls now and I don't think he's equipped to deal with that. . . . I am terrified that his innocence is going to be taken away. (Bennett et al., 2017, pp. 1368–1369)

These responses suggest a protectionist notion of children as not being equipped or "ready" for things that are "not relevant" and a confusion about an age-appropriate way of educating their children—indeed a confusion about when children need to know about bodily changes since puberty, according to the National Health Service, can begin at any point from the ages of 8 to 14, with an average of 11 for girls and 12 for boys. This study did not engage with any mothers of these children; as Robinson and Davies (2019) commented, mothers are usually considered more responsible than fathers for educating their children about sex. The DfE recommends schools teaching about puberty in Year 5 (when children are 9–10 years old), so parental reluctance about their children's readiness for this may in fact be superseded by school education or that of peers or siblings.

It is possible to read into these parental responses, as I have suggested, and as Dyer (2019) argued, an adult investment in a fantasy of childhood innocence, an anxious adult transference of complex relationships to their own childhoods onto debates about an "appropriate" sex education for children. Dyer suggested that there is an inherent uncertainty around the developmental appropriateness of teaching children about sex, and that "we should all be implicated in the impossibility of knowing what is best for the child" (p. 12). This sense that it is impossible to make a blanket statement about what is age appropriate for all children, or young people, is reflected in the issue of whether a young person is ready to consent to sex at the age of 16. Englishlaw actually works so that no one under the age of 13 can ever legally give consent for sex and to protect those under 16 from sex with older people and those under 18 from sex with anyone in a position of trust. Data from Natsal showed that the median age at first heterosexual intercourse is 17, and 30% of those aged 16–24 reported sexual intercourse before age 16 years (Mercer et al., 2013). The law recognizes that young people do have sex before they are 16; whether or not a young person is "ready" to have sex at 13, 14, or 15 is another matter.

Teaching young people about safe, consensual sex, and indeed about sexual activity that does not involve "having sex," rather than being seen as disturbing their innocence, is important to equip them with the critical skills to help them to navigate their sexuality; to understand that there is a variety of choices that they can make, including to delay sex; and to help them to avoid harm. As is the case with teaching about puberty, there is actually little uncertainty in the national curriculum for science in terms of the age appropriateness of equipping children with knowledge about sex (or at least sex for reproductive purposes): Children should learn about human reproduction at Key Stage 3 (Years 7–9, when young people are aged 11–14), although the RSE guidance recommends that children should learn about how a baby is conceived by the end of primary school, in the context of the human life cycle as set out in the science curriculum.

What is clear here is that there is solid guidance that involves teaching related to heterosexual, biological processes. What is on less solid ground, and subject to notions of age or developmental appropriateness, is discussion of same-sex desire and sexual pleasure, as well as "artificial" methods of conception. An engagement with queer theory can entail a deeper understanding both of the concept of children as sexual beings and of experiencing both opposite and same-sex attraction; queer theory can disrupt these "heteronormative logics of growing up" (Neary & Rasmussen, 2020, p. 901).

## MOVING AWAY FROM AN ANTIDISCRIMINATION/ VICTIM PARADIGM

Queer thinking is instructive in terms of the ways in which schools tackle homophobia. LGBTQ equality in schools has traditionally been addressed primarily through an approach of clamping down on homophobic bullying (or what in policy terms is now called HBT bullying). There is a slow shift in U.K. schools in beginning to move from an approach that focuses solely on preventing homophobic bullying and from reproducing discourses of queer youth as victims, toward one that more broadly challenges heteronormativity and seeks to embed a culture of embracing LGBTQ people—as I discussed previously in relation to programs such as Educate and Celebrate. A balance has to be sought in recognizing the real effects of homophobia on queer youth and not reinforcing a "victim" paradigm; discourses of "at-risk" LGBTQ youth are in danger of remarginalizing them (Harris & Farrington, 2014; Marston, 2015). "School policy and practice . . . can lead (albeit inadvertently) to an assumption that to be young and LGBT means facing adversity" (Formby, 2015, p. 636), as I stressed in relation to the initial RSE guidance, which was suggestive of an inevitable difficulty or trauma resulting from a young person realizing they are gay. Cover (2016) pointed out that queer youth are "neither all victims and vulnerable, nor are they all self-reliant and resilient" (p. 351). Each young person will have a different experience.

Identifying and addressing homophobia are not necessarily straightforward issues. For example, homophobia can operate in contexts where it is not an individual's intent or directed at a queer-identified subject (Allen, 2018). Rasmussen (2013) questioned the notion that there can be agreement on what constitutes homophobia and how it is understood, and thus that there is a "right way" to respond to it, and that people who are commonly and stereotypically understood as being homophobic (e.g., religious people who believe being gay is sinful) will change their beliefs following antihomophobic education. The RSE guidance perhaps nods to this concept with its reference to religious teaching and flexibility for faith schools, as discussed previously: Schools "may teach the distinctive faith perspective on relationships"—though establishing one distinctive religious perspective on homosexuality will not be straightforward.

In a study with 13- and 14-year-olds in Australia and New Zealand, Rasmussen et al. (2017) presented a scenario of a boy, Jo, being teased by his peers for wearing makeup and hanging out with girls, to their participants and asked them what advice they would give Jo about being teased. The young people cited in the article advised him to "fix it" or ignore it. Rasmussen et al. pointed out that both these options place responsibility on Jo in a way that seems unsatisfactory. They went on to elaborate other scenarios relating to homophobia and transphobia and stressed the impossibility of knowing "what responding well looks like" (p. 41). They argued that bullying is embedded in complex sets of power relations, that there may be a lack of awareness of what underpins homophobia, and that responsibility lies in a context that is wider than an individual. Gilbert (2014) echoed this in the reminder that "an engagement with queerness must risk the failure of a certain dream of education—that prejudice can be educated and identifications anticipated" (pp. 92–93). This is not an argument for an acceptance of homophobia; rather, it highlights the need for a more holistic approach, as I discuss in the following material.

In a study conducted by Carlile and Paechter (2018) with LGBTQI-parented families, primary school children with same-sex parents reported dealing with questions from peers about how they were conceived. One boy stated:

> Like still year 5 and 6 people come up to you who you don't really know and say "wait, so how are you alive if you only have two mums?" And I have to explain to them. (cited in Carlile and Paechter, 2018, p. 122)

This scenario highlights the difficulty a 10-year-old might have in gauging a depth of response for the questioner in detailing nonnormative methods of conception in the context of same-sex relationships, an issue that again brings up the impossibility of knowing how best to respond and the problems with placing individual responsibility on the child. Judith Butler (2004) asked in relation to this issue:

> How do children who are . . . born through . . . donor insemination under-
> stand their origins? . . . Must the story . . . that will no doubt be subject to
> many retellings, conform to a single story about how the human comes into
> being? . . . How must we revise our understanding of the need for a narrative un-
> derstanding of a self that a child may have that includes a consideration of how
> those narratives are revised and interrupted in time? (p. 128)

Any notion of 10-year-olds being too young for "LGBT content," then, will lead to an omission of any more complex conception stories in formal education contexts and thus to an erasure of possibilities and to a knowledge gap. It will also mean that peer sex education—the 10-year-old with same-sex parents might just inform the questioners how they were conceived—will take on more weight.

Moving away from an antidiscrimination/victim paradigm, then, entails an approach that attempts to disrupt the heteronormative culture of the school rather than one that simply attempts to attend to homophobic incidents. Schools need to work—and in some cases to navigate in difficult contexts—to both represent and embrace sexual and gender diversity *and* challenge heteronormativity and homonormativity (Carlile & Paechter, 2018; Cumming-Potvin & Martino, 2014), thus reducing the onus on individual children to "fix" homophobia or educate their peers. As I implied, this may be a challenge for educators: It is easier for them to combat homophobia in line with legal duties than to grapple with strategies to unsettle dominant paradigms of heterosexuality and binary identity categories. However, an interrogation of heteronormativity can be realized, for example, simply through introduction and discussion of LGBTQ-themed texts or picture books (Martino & Cumming-Potvin, 2016), as well as through more comprehensive school-wide culture change. Schools need to commit to a holistic approach that challenges the limits of binary thinking, challenges narrow conceptions of what is "normal," and raises the status of a marginalized sexuality education. This last is difficult to achieve in the context of England's neoliberal education system, but becomes ever more possible with the introduction of compulsory RSE.

## A QUEER SEXUALITY EDUCATION: POSSIBILITIES

A queer theory of childhood education should not be invested in predicting the child's future identity, but rather attend to the child's present curiosity about sexual difference.
—Dyer (2017, p. 299

I have been operating in this chapter with some of the poststructural limits of queer theory, embracing its tenets of instability and uncertainty. However, sitting with the impossibilities of knowing offers new possibilities for sexuality education. Psychological research suggests the impossibility of predicting future sexual or gender identity: these identities are

> ongoing productions of dynamic and sometimes unpredictable person-environment interactions. . . . There is no single point in time at which they are definitively "finished" and/or fixed . . . although individuals may be born with a predisposition for same-sex, other-sex, or bisexual attractions, environmental experiences play a fundamental role in shaping how these predispositions develop into phenomenology. (Diamond, 2019, pp. 102–104)

A recognition that sexuality should be understood as biopsychosocial—therefore these elements are impossible to separate out in terms of causal explanation (Barker, 2018)—is useful for thinking about how to teach young people about sexuality. A queer sexuality education would also pay more attention to the multidimensionality of sexuality: the idea that human sexuality is more than simply about gender (of oneself and one's partner[s]), but also encompasses elements of physical attraction beyond gender, such as the nature and amount of desire, roles people play, or being attracted to a particular personality type (Barker, 2018). These kinds of understandings play an important role in decentering heterosexuality as a norm and in expanding possibilities for a wider range of identifications encompassing "not knowing" and fluidity.

A queer sexuality education would do well to question the idea of happiness as an end point (Ahmed, 2010) and to question the meanings of "happiness" and "unhappiness" in relation to life trajectories and, for that matter, the possibility of any certain knowing about what would make one happy or unhappy, particularly in the future. The "queer life is already constructed as an unhappy life, as a life without the 'things' that make you happy, or as a life that is depressed as it lacks certain things: 'a husband, children'" (Ahmed, 2010, p. 93). Ahmed (2017) suggested: "In some parental responses to a child coming out, this unhappiness is expressed not so much as being unhappy about the child being queer, but as being unhappy about the child being unhappy" (p. 51). Again, an assumption here of difficulties on the part of the queer child (or indeed an assumption that a queer person would not marry or have children) is unhelpful. Another assumption that is worth challenging is the idea that people need to be in a relationship in order to be happy: As Wilkinson (2014) pointed out, it is useful to think about the single person as a potentially queer subject and how heteronormativity excludes people who are not part of a couple, no matter how they identify in terms of sexual orientation.

Jen Gilbert (2014) suggested that it is the development of children's capacity to think that is most important, and that adults can model this thinking:

> A thoughtful sex education would be less organized by what to think and how to act than by developing the capacity to think for one's self: "I am thinking about you, and in this thinking I am offering to you my own capacity for thoughtfulness." And through this conversation that asks teachers and adults to risk their own sense of expertise, to remember their own feelings of helplessness, we could come to tolerate the ways sexuality obscures clarity, surfaces through negotiations and other symptoms, and troubles the barely concealed wish for omnipotence that structures sex education. (p. 74)

This philosophy can be applied to what is laid out in the RSE guidance; although the guidance document contains three pages of bullet points of what pupils should know by the end of primary and another three pages of what they should know by the end of secondary school, it also clearly states that pupils should be equipped with the ability to make their own decisions.

The child has a right to understand difference, and as Butler argued, opening up different spaces for children is a way of reducing harm and extending them permission in their difference:

> Teaching gender equality and sexual diversity calls into question the repressive dogma that has cast so many gender and sexual lives into the shadows. . . . The struggle for gender equality and sexual freedom seeks to alleviate suffering and to recognise the diverse embodied and cultural lives that we live. Teaching gender is not indoctrination: it does not tell a person how to live; it opens up the possibility for young people to find their own way in a world that often confronts them with narrow and cruel social norms. . . . It affirms human complexity and creates a space for people to find their own way within this complexity. (Butler, 2019, para. 14–15)

A queer sexuality education, I suggest, will affirm uncertainty and complexity and offer this up within a context of possibility. Queer theory, as I have briefly explored some aspects of it, can usefully inform practice here; the educator can hold on to a sense of "not knowing" for, or in relation to, the child, while offering an understanding, without prejudice or fear, of the diversities of sexuality and gender identity. Sexuality education infused with queer thinking can encourage nonbinary thinking and can consider how identity categories can exclude and regulate (Allen, 2010). It can hold on to a critical consideration of childhood innocence and of heteronormativity.

These ways of thinking and teaching about sexuality *are* possible within the parameters of the new policy guidance. Questions about sexuality and sexual diversity may be easier to answer if the child is considered as a sexual being with a right to information and also protection from harm; these harms may include heteronormative assumptions or expectations. Questions about what is age appropriate, while important to consider that this will vary by context or developmental stage, will always be answered differently, and an overanxious focus on this may obscure a focus on providing an understanding of diversity and difference, which is crucial for all young people's self-expression.

## NOTE

1. From the DfE's policy statement introducing statutory RSE in 2017.

## REFERENCES

Ahmed, S. (2010). *The promise of happiness*. Duke University Press.

Ahmed, S. (2017). *Living a feminist life*. Duke University Press.

Allen, L. (2010). Queer(y)ing the straight researcher: The relationship(?) between researcher identity and anti-normative knowledge. *Feminism & Psychology, 20*(2), 147–165. https://doi.org/10.1177/0959353509355146

Allen, L. (2018). Reconceptualising homophobia: By leaving "those kids" alone. *Discourse: Studies in the Cultural Politics of Education, 41*(3), 441–453. https://doi.org/10.1080/01596306.2018.1495617

Barker, M. J. (2018). *The psychology of sex*. Routledge.

Bennett, C., Harden, J., & Anstey, S. (2017). The silencing effects of the childhood innocence ideal: The perceptions and practices of fathers in educating their children about sexuality. *Sociology of Health & Illness, 39*(8), 1365–1380. https://doi.org/10.1111/1467-9566.12591

Berlant, L., & Warner, M. (1998). Sex in public. *Critical Inquiry, 24*(2), 547–566.

Bragg, S., Renold, E., Ringrose, J., & Jackson, C. (2018). "More than boy, girl, male, female": Exploring young people's views on gender diversity within and beyond school contexts. *Sex Education, 18*(4), 420–434. https://doi.org/10.1080/14681811.2018.1439373

Britzman, D. P. (2019). Difficulties in the study, research, and pedagogy of sexuality. In S. Lamb & J. Gilbert (Eds.), *The Cambridge handbook of sexual development: Childhood and adolescence* (pp. 315–335). Cambridge University Press.

Butler, J. (2004). *Undoing gender*. Routledge.

Butler, J. (2019, January 21). Judith Butler: The backlash against "gender ideology" must stop. *New Statesman*. https://www.newstatesman.com/2019/01/judith-butler-backlash-against-gender-ideology-must-stop

Carlile, A., & Paechter, C. (2018). *LGBTQI parented families and schools: Visibility, representation, and pride*. Routledge.

Cover, R. (2016). Resilience. In N. M. Rodriguez, W. J. Martino, J. C. Ingrey, & E. Brockenbrough (Eds.), *Critical concepts in queer studies and education: An international guide for the twenty-first century* (pp. 351–360). Palgrave Macmillan. https://doi.org/10.1057/978-1-137-55425-3_34

Cumming-Potvin, W., & Martino, W. (2014). Teaching about queer families: Surveillance, censorship, and the schooling of sexualities. *Teaching Education, 25*(3), 309–333. https://doi.org/10.1080/10476210.2014.889672

Dahlgreen, W., & Shakespeare, A. (2015, August 16). 1 in 2 young people say they are not 100% heterosexual. YouGov. https://yougov.co.uk/topics/lifestyle/articles-reports/2015/08/16/half-young-not-heterosexual

DePalma, R., & Atkinson, E. (2009). *Interrogating heteronormativity in primary schools*. Trentham Books Ltd.

Department for Education (DfE). (2019a). *Relationships education, relationships and sex education (RSE) and health education: Statutory guidance for governing bodies, proprietors, head teachers, principals, senior leadership teams, teachers*. DfE.

Department for Education (DfE). (2019b). *Relationships education, relationships and sex education, and health education in England. Government consultation response*. DfE.

Department for Education and Employment (DfEE). (2000). *Sex and relationships education guidance*.

Diamond, L. M. (2019). The dynamic expression of sexual-minority and gender-minority experience during childhood and adolescence. In S. Lamb & J. Gilbert (Eds.), *The Cambridge handbook of sexual development: Childhood and adolescence* (pp. 94–112). Cambridge University Press.

Dyer, H. (2017). Queer futurity and childhood innocence: Beyond the injury of development. *Global Studies of Childhood, 7*(3), 290–302. https://doi.org/10.1177/2043610616671056

Dyer, H. (2019). The contested design of children's sexual education: Queer growth and epistemic uncertainty. *Gender and Education, 31*(6), 742–755. https://doi.org/10.1080/09540253.2017.1380171

Epstein, D., O'Flynn, S., & Telford, D. (2003). *Silenced sexualities in schools and universities*. Trentham.

Formby, E. (2015). Limitations of focussing on homophobic, biphobic and transphobic "bullying" to understand and address LGBT young people's experiences within and beyond school. *Sex Education, 15*(6), 626–640. https://doi.org/10.1080/14681811.2015.1054024

Gilbert, J. (2014). *Sexuality in school: The limits of education*. University of Minnesota Press.

Gill-Peterson, J., Sheldon, R., & Stockton, K. B. (2016). What is the now, even of then? *GLQ: A Journal of Lesbian and Gay Studies, 22*(4), 495–503. https://doi.org/10.1215/10642684-3603078

GOV.UK. (2019). Relationships education, relationships and sex education (RSE) and health education: FAQs. https://www.gov.uk/government/news/relationships-education-relationships-and-sex-education-rse-and-health-education-faqs

Greteman, A. (2014). Dissenting with queer theory: Reading Ranciere queerly. *Discourse: Studies in the Cultural Politics of Education, 35*(3), 419–432. https://doi.org/10.1080/01596306.2014.888845

Greteman, A. (2017). Helping kids turn out queer: Queer theory in art education. *Studies in Art Education, 58*(3), 195–205. https://doi.org/10.1080/00393541.2017.1331089

Harris, A., & Farrington, D. (2014). "It gets narrower": Creative strategies for re-broadening queer peer education. *Sex Education, 14*(2), 144–158. https://doi.org/10.1080/14681811.2013.854203

Haywood, C., & Mac an Ghaill, M. (2016). Containment. In N. M. Rodriguez, W. J. Martino, J. C. Ingrey, & E. Brockenbrough (Eds.), *Critical concepts in queer studies and education: An international guide for the twenty-first century* (pp. 57–66). Palgrave Macmillan. https://doi.org/10.1057/978-1-137-55425-3_7

House of Commons Library. (2019). Faith schools in England: FAQs. Briefing paper no. 06972, 20 December 2019. https://researchbriefings.files.parliament.uk/documents/SN06972/SN06972.pdf

Kehily, M. J., & Montgomery, H. (2009). Innocence and experience. In M. J. Kehily (Ed.), *An introduction to childhood studies*. Open University Press.

Lamb, S., White, L., & Plocha, A. (2019). Are children sexual? Who, what, where, when, and how? In S. Lamb & J. Gilbert (Eds.), *The Cambridge handbook of sexual development: Childhood and adolescence* (pp. 17–34). Cambridge University Press.

Marston, K. (2015). Beyond bullying: The limitations of homophobic and transphobic bullying interventions for affirming lesbian, gay, bisexual and trans (LGBT) equality in education. *Pastoral Care in Education, 33*(3), 161–168. https://doi.org/10.1080/02643944.2015.1074266

Martino, W., & Cumming-Potvin, W. (2016). Teaching about sexual minorities and "princess boys": A queer and trans-infused approach to investigating LGBTQ-themed texts in the elementary school classroom. *Discourse: Studies in the Cultural Politics of Education, 37*(6), 807–827. https://doi.org/10.1080/01596306.2014.940239

McGinn, L., Stone, N., Ingham, R., & Bengry-Howell, A. (2016). Parental interpretations of "childhood innocence": Implications for early sexuality education. *Health Education, 116*(6), 580–594. https://doi.org/10.1108/HE-10-2015-0029

Mercer, C. H., Tanton, C., Prah, P., Erens, B., Sonnenberg, P., Clifton, S., & Johnson, A. M. (2013). Changes in sexual attitudes and lifestyles in Britain through the life course and over time: Findings from the National Surveys of Sexual Attitudes and Lifestyles (Natsal). *Lancet, 382*(9907), 1781–1794. https://doi.org/10.1016/s0140-6736(13)62035-8

Neary, A., & Rasmussen, M. L. (2020). Marriage equality time: Entanglements of sexual progress and childhood innocence in Irish primary schools. *Sexualities, 23*(5–6), 898–916. https://doi.org/10.1177/1363460719861819

Owen, G. (2010). Queer theory wrestles the "real" child: Impossibility, identity, and language in Jacqueline Rose's *The Case of Peter Pan. Children's Literature Association Quarterly, 35*(3), 255–273. https://doi.org/10.1353/chq.2010.0007

Rasmussen, M. L. (2013). Taking homophobia's measure. *Confero: Essays on Education, 1*(2), 16–45. https://doi.org/10.3384/confero.2001-4562.13v1i21a

Rasmussen, M. L., Sanjakdar, F., Allen, L., Quinlivan, K., & Bromdal, A. (2017). Homophobia, transphobia, young people and the question of responsibility. *Discourse: Studies in the Cultural Politics of Education, 38*(1), 30–42. https://doi.org/10.1080/01596306.2015.1104850

Robinson, K., & Davies, C. (2019). A sociological exploration of childhood sexuality: A discursive analysis of parents' and children's perspectives. In S. Lamb & J. Gilbert (Eds.), *The Cambridge handbook of sexual development: Childhood and adolescence* (pp. 54–75). Cambridge University Press.

Rose, J. (1992). *The case of Peter Pan or the impossibility of children's fiction.* University of Philadelphia Press. (Original work published 1984)

Sauerteig, L. D. H. (2012). Loss of innocence: Albert Moll, Sigmund Freud and the invention of childhood sexuality around 1900. *Medical History, 56*(2), 156–183. https://doi.org/10.1017/mdh.2011.31

Sedgwick, E. K. (1993). *Tendencies.* Duke University Press.

Stockton, K. B. (2009). *The queer child or growing sideways in the twentieth century.* Duke University Press.

Stockton, K. B. (2016). The queer child now and its paradoxical global effects. *GLQ: A Journal of Lesbian and Gay Studies, 22*(4), 505–539. https://doi.org/10.1215/10642684-3603186

Watt, L., & Elliot, M. (2017). Continuity and change in sexual attitudes: A cross-time comparison of tolerance towards non-traditional relationships. *Sociological Review, 65*(4), 832–849. https://doi.org/10.1177/0038026116674887

Whittington, E., & Thomson, R. (2018). Educating for consent: Beyond the binary. In F. Sanjakdar & A. Yip (Eds.), *Critical pedagogy, sexuality education and young people: Issues about democracy and active citizenry.* Peter Lang.

Wilkinson, E. (2014). Single people's geographies of home: Intimacy and friendship beyond "the family." *Environment and Planning A, 46*(10), 2452–2468. https://doi.org/10.1068/a130069p

Zimmerman, J. (2015). *Too hot to handle: A global history of sex education.* Princeton University Press.

# CHAPTER 3

# Rupturing the "Cul-de-Sac"

## Queer(y)ing Graduate Education Studies

JAMES BURFORD AND GENINE HOOK

> queer concepts ≠ queer subjects/objects
> —Rasmussen and Allen, 2014, p. 434

In a 2014 article, Mary Lou Rasmussen and Louisa Allen encouraged education researchers working with queer theory to consider the following question: *What can a concept do?* The authors' were quick to clarify that their invitation to *think more* about what might be done with "queer" is not simple advocacy for using the concept *more often* in gender, sex, and sexuality education, as "this is surely where concepts associated with queer assemblages are thought to belong" (p. 433). Instead, they invited queer researchers to consider why it is that they habitually adhere themselves to "certain sexual subjects, and objects, of investigation" (p. 433) and unleash their research energies in pursuit of "particular identities, politics and programs" (p. 433). While Rasmussen and Allen (2014) acknowledged that they themselves had been a part of a wave of scholars who have used queer concepts in sexuality and gender education research, they advocated for a fresh look at *nondescriptive* deployments of queer theory. That is, uses of queer theory that take queer not as a noun, but as a verb that might be applied to a wider zone of inquiry. The vision Rasmussen and Allen (2014)

James Burford and Genine Hook, *Rupturing the "Cul-de-Sac"* In: *Queer Studies and Education.* Edited by:
Nelson M. Rodriguez, Robert C. Mizzi, Louisa Allen, and Rob Cover, Oxford University Press.
© Oxford University Press 2023. DOI: 10.1093/oso/9780197687000.003.0004

sketched is for a more expansive use of queer—a form of use that takes it as an open and "continuously changing assemblage of ideas that can mutate, renew, and be replaced" (p. 433).

In asking what queer can *do*, Rasmussen and Allen are inviting educational researchers to reflect on the ways in which queer conceptual borders are usually marked and policed. Rasmussen and Allen's (2014) view was that there is an impulse to contain queer concepts "within the cul de sac of studies of sexuality and gender" (p. 434). By speaking of a cul-de-sac here, Rasmussen and Allen were referring to a tendency that sticks queer concepts to the bodies of particular researchers or subjects. While it appears that some concepts (e.g., Ranciere's democracy or Foucault's biopolitics) frequently inspire educational research, Rasmussen and Allen wondered why it is that queer concepts such as Butler's performativity (J. Butler, 2009; J. P. Butler, 2005), Halberstam's *Queer Art of Failure* (2011), and Berlant's *Cruel Optimism* (2011) are not deployed as frequently. Rather than "corral queer theory" (p. 434), Rasmussen and Allen (2014) were curious to see what might happen if such concepts were allowed to roam more widely across the education assemblage. As doctoral students, we (James and Genine) found ourselves interested in queer theory and writing in the wake of Rasmussen and Allen's (2014) call to interrogate the corralling of queer theory in education research. A further layer to our interest was that Genine's doctoral research was supervised by Mary Lou and James's research was supervised by Louisa. So, it is fair to say that we were likely to be aware of this call!

In this chapter, we demonstrate how we have used Rasmussen and Allen's (2014) thinking about nondescriptive uses of queer theory in education research. We share how we animated three of the queer conceptual lenses identified by Rasmussen and Allen (2014) in our own doctoral studies on postgraduate education in Australia and Aotearoa New Zealand. James outlines the research he did to unsettle habits of thinking about the political value of affect in doctoral education studies via an engagement with the thinking of Halberstam (2011), Berlant (2011), and Jagose (2010); and Genine reflects on the queer work she did with Butler's thinking (J. Butler, 2008, 2009, 2013; J. P. Butler, 2005) to unsettle gendered assumptions about sole-parent graduate students. What links our two studies together is our mutual interest in testing how far queer concepts might "travel" (Gowlett & Rasmussen, 2014, p. 333) within graduate education studies, with a particular concern with how they may be applied to objects/subjects that do not immediately seem a "fit." In so doing, we contribute to active conversations about the production of normalcy (Allen, 2015) in queer higher education (HE) research.

[66]  *James Burford and Genine Hook*

## USING QUEER THEORY IN HIGHER EDUCATION AND POSTGRADUATE EDUCATION RESEARCH

We understand the concept of "queer" as a spongy term, given its capacity to soak up multiple meanings simultaneously. The sponginess of queer has led various researchers to track the ways in which the term is used by different researchers and the various arrivals of queer to national contexts (see Davis & Kollias, 2012). For example, in their 2019 chapter "Starting with Queer," Burford and Allen drew on Duggan's (2015) articulation of three broad, and potentially overlapping, categories of use: *queer as identity*, *queer as practice*, and *queer as politics*. As they noted: "Each of these ways of understanding 'queer' has a different kind of motivation, and opens onto different possibilities" (p. 129). Those who use queer as an identity category tend to assert it as a label that exceeds the binary of heterosexuality/homosexuality. By this understanding, language such as "I identify as queer" may be used. In addition to its use as a personal identity label, queer is also often deployed as an umbrella term for a wider community of people who deviate from sex, sexual, and gender norms (i.e., the "queer community"). In both of these forms of use, queer has a similar kind of logic to LGBT+ (lesbian, gay, bisexual, transgender, and other minoritized sexual and gender identities) studies approaches, often taking up a minority rights discourse and concerning itself with questions of institutional and social equity.

Another form of use configures queer as a practice. When queer is configured in this way, it is usually taken as a "broad umbrella term for dissenting sexual practices and gender expressions" (Duggan, 2015, para. 1). In this form of use, researchers might identify normative and nonnormative sexual and gender practices (e.g., sadomasochism and drag), which are then identified "as resistant practices with the potential to subvert and unsettle normative cultures" (Burford & Allen, 2019, p. 130).

In the third form of use identified by Duggan (2015), queer is viewed as a form of politics similar to other political movements, such as feminism. In this form of use, queer need not be tied to an analyst's sexual or gender identity or practices. Instead, "queer as politics" focuses on what analysts *do* to identify and unsettle norms and the intellectual commitments that lead them to these actions. While each of these ways of understanding queer leads to different research pathways, they need not be configured as in opposition. Indeed, as Duggan (2015) noted, one person may deploy each of these uses at different moments.

Given the multiple ways in which queer might be used, we would like to turn our attention to consider how queer has been applied in research on postgraduate education to date. As has been noted elsewhere (Allen, 2015; Burford & Allen, 2019; Renn, 2010), the use of queer concepts across HE studies has been expanding, with multiple articles, journal special issues, and book chapters in circulation.[1] However, studies that apply queer concepts to postgraduate education remain thin on the ground, and existing work tends to configure queer in particular ways. In our reading across the field, we have observed various terms in circulation, such as "queer graduate students" (Burgess, 2005); "queer postgraduates" (Burford, 2012); "black queer men" (Blockett, 2017); "white, queer, doctoral students" (Mizzi & Stebbins, 2010); and "queer minority candidates" (Ings, 2013). Other pieces appear to use queer as broadly interchangeable with associated concepts, such as gay or LGBT+ (Endo & Reece-Miller, 2010). Queer as an identity label appears to be the most prevalent form of use in the literature on postgraduate education studies. By our reading of the literature to date, there have been few studies that have animated the nondescriptive possibilities of queer that we describe above.

Our chapter lands in the middle of these debates about the use of queer concepts. In writing the chapter, we hoped to illustrate how queer concepts might be used in disruptive and nonidentitarian ways in postgraduate education research. Writing in turn, we (James Burford and Genine Hook) report on nondescriptive uses of queer concepts in our own doctoral research projects about postgraduate students in Aotearoa New Zealand and Australia. Our mode is primarily one of exemplification, and we hope that by showing our own workings we might illuminate a path for future researchers who may wish to pursue similar queer projects in the future.

## JAMES'S RESEARCH: QUEERYING THE AFFECTIVE-POLITICS OF DOCTORAL EDUCATION IN AOTEAORA NEW ZEALAND

James's interest in the affective-political landscape of doctoral education emerged in a rather circuitous way. He had been a master's student who had struggled to write his thesis and had some big feelings about that struggle. As a sexuality researcher working in the field of development studies, James had undertaken difficult overseas fieldwork with LGBT+ community organizations. While collecting data James was attacked by a research participant, and very soon thereafter he left his fieldwork site and returned home. On returning home James, struggled to write. In part, his writing troubles were related to this attack and his need to recover from it. And yet another significant impediment to his writing progress involved questions about how to become a knower in a field (and immediate

[68]   *James Burford and Genine Hook*

department) that was riddled with homophobic discourse. Ultimately, James wrote a master's thesis that simultaneously offered a queer examination of the agency of LGBT+ community organizations to negotiate with their funders, as well as a queer critique of the conventions of presenting "a thesis" in development studies via the inclusion of some norm-bending genres of writing. When he commenced his doctoral studies, James intended to examine the affective dimensions of academic writing for "queer doctoral students" (i.e., students who identified with nonnormative sexual identities, like him). However, during his first year of candidature, his interest in queering doctoral education led him down an unexpected path.

During his first doctoral year, James read across scholarship concerned with how political transformations to the contemporary university such as neoliberalism (Barcan, 2013); audit culture (Grant & Elizabeth, 2014); and managerialism (White, 2013) increasingly shape the felt experience of academic work. A growing number of HE researchers have identified that *something* had changed in the academy: "One can observe it all around; a deep, affective, somatic crisis threatens to overwhelm us" (Burrows, 2012, p. 355). According to Gill (2010), academia is brimming with bad feelings, such as "exhaustion, stress, overload . . . anxiety, shame, aggression, hurt, guilt" (p. 229), and there have been calls to examine the injurious impacts these feelings have on academic workers.

At the same time, a body of research has investigated the increasingly pressurized practice of doctoral education. Scholars have tracked the impacts of increasing national and institutional regulation and surveillance, as well as shrinking doctoral completion times (Green & Usher, 2003), expanding expectations for writing outputs (Aitchison & Mowbray, 2015), and a widespread debate about there being too many PhDs and not enough academic jobs (McKenna, 2016). Arguably, all of these changes work together to shape how students think about themselves and their projects and also how they *feel* as they make their way through their doctoral degrees. James became interested in thinking about how the felt experience of doctoral education might be connected to wider political transformations to the university, similar to the research on academic labor described above.

In his reading across accounts of the affective-politics of academic labor and doctoral study, James began to notice that HE scholarship reproduced certain habits of thinking about the political utility of emotions. In the writing of a number of critical HE scholars, "strong" feelings such as hope, anger, and frustration were often associated with political agency, whereas "weak" feelings such as depression, numbness, and anxiety tended to be cast as political liabilities (Burford, 2017b). In response to these observations James began searching for some new tools to think with. He started engaging with a strain of queer and feminist cultural theory interested in questioning the norms associated with critical readings of emotion and affect. In particular, he was interested in work that explored the political possibilities of negative affects such as shame, failure, and depression (Blackman, 2015; Cvetkovich, 2012; Halberstam, 2011; Wiegman, 2014) and the political constraints of feelings that are usually coded as positive, such as love, happiness, and optimism (Ahmed, 2010; Berlant, 2011; Halberstam, 2011; Kipnis, 2004). Queer and feminist scholars had been advocating for a nonpathologizing approach to "bad feelings," arguing that so-called bad feelings might offer "productive possibilities for political practice and social transformation" (Blackman, 2015, p. 25; Wiegman, 2014). James wondered what it might mean to use these concepts to interrogate commonsense understandings of a dichotomy of politically "useful" and "useless" feelings of doctoral students. In recognition of the above concerns, his thesis was designed to address the following research aims: (1) to understand the implications of recognizing doctoral education as an affective-political practice and (2) to explore what queer concepts can do when applied to the affective-political scene of doctoral education.

In response to these questions, James organized his research as a series of case studies. Part of his research involved engagements with 10 doctoral students in faculties of arts and education at a university in Aotearoa New Zealand. He invited students to write diaries, conducted semistructured interviews, and held a writing retreat away from campus; at the retreat, students wrote, made creative artifacts, and engaged in discussion (Burford, 2016b). Another part of his study involved an examination of cultural texts generated on a public online photo blog (Burford, 2015a) and autoethnographic texts generated by his own self-reflective writing practice (Burford, 2014, 2016a). James organized his thesis as a series of chapters where different queer concepts were engaged to understand these data. While the limits of space preclude a full summary, what follows is a taste of James's use of queer concepts.

In one chapter (Burford, 2015b), James offered a queer analysis of the case of a doctoral student, "Catherine," who tightly controlled her emotions in order to facilitate writing productivity. James offered two readings of these data. His first reading of the case was built on existing critical studies about doctoral learning, academic identity, and anxiety and took quite a pessimistic view of Catherine "managing" anxiety in order to "keep calm and carry on" writing. In his first reading, he identified the "emotion manager" as an affective subject position likely to render doctoral students complicit and governable and unlikely to disrupt politics as usual. In his second approach to the case, James drew on queer theoretical work, including Jagose's (2010) consideration of complex agency, to subvert and extend critical readings of the politics of affect. He suspended his earlier impulse to associate anxiety with political irrelevance in order to explore how anxious affective configurations may also offer possibilities. Following the queer thinking of Jagose (2010), James proposed that affective phenomena that are coded "negative" and seemingly politically unhelpful—such as anxiety and calm self-management—might open twisted routes to agency. Such an understanding points toward the need to more closely consider the question of what counts as "political" in HE thought and to explore available political modes that may be routinely discounted. While these less recognizable modes of agency may not provide a clear pathway forward for political activism, accounts of agency that can understand it as an "activity of maintenance, not making" (Berlant, 2007, p. 759) may offer examples of how to recognize political engagement within the constraints of doctoral education's precarious present.

Another of his chapters (Burford, 2017a) explored queer readings of failure in order to reconsider the affective scene of guilt about (not) writing in a context where doctoral students are often on normalized timelines, which encourage them to "write early and write often" (Lee & Aitchison, 2009, p. 94). Following Halberstam's (2011) critique of conventional notions of heteronormative and neoliberal "success," James offered a case of a first-year student, "Ricki," who described their motivation for doing a doctorate as pursuing a "creative intellectual project." As a result of this framing, Ricki identified alternative terms for learning and writing than those typically seen in the doctoral education literature, as well as not writing much during their first doctoral year. After closely reading Ricki's interview transcript, James positioned "giving zero fucks" as a possible subject position vis-à-vis doctoral writing, and normative notions of doctoral "success." James suggested that such a mode of being may offer creative opportunities to rethink the doctorate outside of the reductive and technicist rationalities that tend to frame many HE debates. He also reconsidered failure's feelings. Despite being frequently associated with affective practices of guilt, shame, and disappointment, James suggested that failure might also open onto alternative feelings, such as relief, joy, and satisfaction. Ultimately, the chapter contends that queer concepts might assist HE researchers to interrogate normative framings of failure and to glimpse alternative possibilities for living the doctorate otherwise.

In the final chapter of his thesis (Burford, 2018), James drew on verbal and visual data from across his study to critically examine an affective practice that is often assumed to be positive for political transformation: aspiration.

Drawing on Berlant's (2011) idea of "cruel optimism," James argued that optimistic attachments to an "academic good life" can bind doctoral subjects to precarious modes of living in the present. In order to explain the endurance of such fantasies, James unpacked the difficult choices many students have to make between retaining an attachment to the doctorate despite not having access to the future that it was expected to promise, or detaching, and experiencing the loss of the fantasy associated with the PhD. James suggested that the practice of writing, and publication in particular, may be interpreted as a mode of "adjustment" that keeps students tethered to the organizing fantasy of the academic good life. He ended the chapter with a call to imagine new, and it is hoped less cruel, kinds of doctoral aspiration.

James's analyses within his thesis signal a commitment to a different kind of doctoral education scholarship—one that sees the doctoral experience as a messy, complex, and politically and emotionally engaged practice. The significance of this understanding is that researchers might supplement existing research that seeks to "improve" doctoral practice or "resolve" the emotions of students who undertake it, with studies concerned with what doctoral emotions can teach us about the possibilities and constraints for action in the present. James's contributed to knowledge that was not confined to the field of doctoral education. By using "queer insights to interrogate seemingly non-queer subjects" (Allen, 2015, p. 683), he also sought to rupture the "cul-de-sac" that constrains the possibilities of using queer concepts in postgraduate education studies.

## GENINE'S RESEARCH: QUEERLY DESTABILIZING PARENTAL BINARIES THROUGH SOLE PARENTING AS A POSTGRADUATE IN AUSTRALIA

Like James, Genine's interest in her doctoral project emerged from personal experience. Her initial interest in the topic of sole-parent postgraduates emerged during her own transition into an honors program. Genine found that previous positive sentiment toward her vocationally orientated bachelor degree studies began to evaporate as her continuing postgraduate studies were regarded by some members of her family and university policies and practices (e.g., via the timetabling of night classes) as a luxury that a sole parent (like Genine) ought not afford. This shift in sentiment prompted Genine to think more about *who* was able to access postgraduate education in Australia and the conditions within which they did so. Genine wondered if other sole parents were having similar experiences as her, and if so, how they negotiated and maintained continuing engagement with postgraduate education. As such, Genine developed an interest in recognition, or more specifically who can be recognized as a postgraduate candidate, and how sole parenting might enable and/or constrain the process of recognizability.

Genine's doctoral research was a collective case study, which involved 10 sole-parent postgraduates in Australian universities (Hook, 2015, 2016). This research explored how gender is constructed in the Australian HE context. More particularly, the project examined how gender is reinscribed in parental binaries and how this reinscription influences engagement with HE. To provide a detailed investigation of gendered parental constructs in universities, Genine focused on how sole parents traverse the gendered binary of motherhood and fatherhood. The aim of her project was to open up possibilities for disrupting gendered parenting norms that tend to naturalize the care of children as a feminine act. Genine felt that research focused on postgraduate education was a key entry and access point because postgraduate study is a gateway into the academy.

The queer intellectual resources Genine drew on included Judith Butler's theory of gender performativity. Genine used Butler's work to unsettle norms that surround gendered parenting as they are experienced by sole parents in Australian universities. Butler's thinking on performativity was useful because it destabilizes gendered norms through a critique of the repetitive acts that regulate how a subject is constituted:

> The theory of gender performativity presupposes that norms are acting on us before we have a chance to act at all, and that when we do act, we recapitulate the norms that act upon us, perhaps in new or unexpected ways, but still in relation to norms that precede us and exceed us. (J. Butler, 2009, p. xi)

Performativity allows an analyst to interrogate how the normative foundations of gender operate, considering how gender "gets done" within "discourse, power relations, historical experiences, cultural practices and material conditions" (Jackson & Mazzei, 2012, p. 72). For Genine, this was useful because it enabled her to consider how the apparently fixed connection between motherhood, femininity, and child care is continually maintained in social discourse and practice, including within HE in Australia. Genine also wondered if sole parenting outside hetero- and partner-normative structures is conducive to recrafting gender constructs that constitute mothering and fathering. The paradoxical conditions of sole parenting and postgraduate study set "the stage for the subject's self-crafting, one that takes place always in relation to an imposed set of norms" (J. Butler, 2008, p. 28). Thus, Butler's work helped Genine see that it is within and through these repetitive acts that instability can be revealed, which opens the potential for alternatives and change to take place.

Genine's research explored the instability of sole parents in postgraduate education and sought to reveal possibilities of doing parental care work queerly, beyond the scope of heterofamilial norms. She argued that sole parents rework the binaries attached to mothers or fathers and are, to some extent, traversing this gendered boundary. Hook's research focused on self-crafting of postgraduate education as an investment and opportunity for sole parents within the imposed set of norms in relation to both how universities construct postgraduate education and how society shapes heterofamilial norms.

Drawing on queer theory enabled Genine to offer an examination beyond "access" and "participation" of nontraditional students in HE to explore the permeability of gendered parenting and familial constructions. Familial structures become hierarchical because "marriage sanctifies some couples at the expense of others. It is selective legitimacy . . . if you don't have it, you and your relations are less worthy" (Warner, 1999, p. 82). Queering the "familial" in Hook's research extended an understanding of queer families in line with Newman's comments:

> When I say queer families, I'm not just talking about same-sex parented families, but also about what family means, how it is defined and made, among all people of diverse sexualities and gender. (Newman, 2019, p. 353)

This queering of the family, by including experiences of sole-parent families in joyful productive ways, refuses and reworks the narrative of deficit and "woundedness" (Rasmussen, 2004) that is often attached to sole parenting.

Thinking queerly also enabled a questioning of the assumption about gendered parental norms, particularly in relation to postgraduate students and university expectations of unencumbered, single-minded students. Butler's (J. Butler, 2009; J. P. Butler, 2005) theory of gender performativity provided a framework to destabilize gendered norms through critiquing the repetitive acts that attempt to regulate how a subject is constituted. In this case, the repetitive acts of parental care work are disrupted by sole parents within the constraining heteronorms of "the family." Genine suggests that sole-parent postgraduates mobilized the rules of motherhood to read parenthood to suit their sole-parenting conditions within HE.

A sole-parent family may be "queer in its reorganization of family and affinity and in the way it interrupts and disrupts more conventional romantic bonds" (Halberstam, 2011, p. 45). This contesting of heteropatriarchal expectations and norms of "the family" seeks to not only queer the patriarchal familial stronghold of heterocoupled families but also illustrate how queer theory is useful and productive. Queer resistance by sole parents opens up the potential to transform the familial. Recognizing queer families is critical because "queer families can help us question our assumptions about gender and sexuality norms" (Newman, 2019, p. 356). Ahmed reminded us that "the norm can be repressive and oppressive, but also strangely, even disturbingly generative" (Ahmed, 2016, p. 3). Genine's research demonstrated that for many sole parents it is precisely within their singleness, and because they are a sole parent, that queer alternatives and joyful and generative possibilities come into view. The majority of participants in Genine's study remarked that they would not have continued or resumed postgraduate study if they had still been married, that it was *because* they were the familial decision-makers that their educational and family conditions were shaped to enable postgraduate studies to be possible and successful.

## IN CLOSING: WHAT CAN QUEER CONCEPTS DO IN POSTGRADUATE EDUCATION STUDIES?

This chapter has built on the critique offered by Rasmussen and Allen (2014) that the use of queer concepts has been constrained in the wider field of educational research. Across our reading of the specific literature that links "queer" and "postgraduate education," we observed similar kinds of constraints. We found that there was a tendency for researchers to animate queer as an identity label, and that other forms of use were mostly absent from the literature. While inspired by Rasmussen and Allen's (2014) work and informed by our reading of published studies, our desire to think about where queer concepts might or might not "travel" (Gowlett & Rasmussen, 2014, p. 333) is also personal; it emerges out of policing practices that we have experienced as researchers working within the field. After giving presentations of our work, audience members have sometimes assumed that what makes our work "queer" is our sexual identities. Other times, we have been asked to justify our use of queer concepts when the foci of our projects are the feelings of doctoral students or sole-parent postgraduates. Some audience members have argued strongly that to detach queer concepts from queer subjects/objects is to dilute the concept's political utility. While we welcome the opportunities we have had to engage in these conceptual contestations, we believe that many of these questions function to "corral queer theory" (Rasmussen & Allen, 2014, p. 434), keeping it tethered to "particular identities, politics and programs" (Rasmussen & Allen, 2014, p. 433). Our chapter speaks back to these concerns and represents an attempt to disrupt these practices. Across this chapter, we have demonstrated how queer concepts can be fruitfully deployed otherwise within postgraduate education studies.

In sum, this chapter has explored two research projects that undertook disruptive queer work. James animated queer concepts associated with the work of Berlant (2011), Halberstam (2011), and Jagose (2010) in order to trouble normative framings of affective-politics in postgraduate education. He argued that commonsense readings of "bad feelings" as being bad for politics constrain analysts' possibilities for imagining political agency. Genine used Butler's queer concept of performativity (J. Butler, 2009) to trouble familial norms in relation to sole-parent postgraduates. Rather than viewing sole parents as a deficit, her queer reading enabled the alternatives and generative possibilities of being a sole parent to come into view. By linking our two studies and revealing the ways in which queer concepts have traveled through our work, we have demonstrated that "queer" can be used productively in a disruptive and nonidentitarian sense as well as to advance LGBT identity politics within postgraduate education studies.

In closing, we want to identify some possible openings for researchers who are working in the field of queer postgraduate education studies. Bearing in mind that our chapter has sought to disrupt queer gatekeeping practices, our goal here is not to close down alternatives or to institute a new norm. Instead, we offer these ideas because we hope such lines of inquiry may be interesting and productive. Perhaps future researchers might use queer concepts to unsettle a host of normativities that often go unchallenged, such as those surrounding "success" and "failure" within postgraduate education. Additionally, there may be rich potential to consider queer conceptualizations of temporality in order to trouble prevailing expectations that surround timeliness, completion, and career progression. Research supervision may be a rich scene to investigate queerly, as might enduring ideals such as the "autonomous postgraduate." For example, scholarship like Stockton's (2009) *The Queer Child* could be used to explore ways of progressing and developing that deviate away from expected postgraduate trajectories, or Puar's *Terrorist Assemblages* (2007) could be used to think through how postgraduate students may be impacted by increasing securitization and counterterrorism. Equally, postgraduate education researchers might explore the rich resources of Muñoz's (2009) ideas on futures and utopia, Ahmed's (2006) thinking on queer phenomenology, Sedgwick's (2003) work on reparative reading, or Barad's (2007) thinking on posthumanist performativity. Indeed, we hope that future postgraduate research might build on this wealth of queer conceptual frameworks, particularly to continue to link queer thinking to critiques of neoliberalism,

[76]   *James Burford and Genine Hook*

racism, colonization, and capitalism. We see these ideas as just one beginning, among many. Given queer's need to shift in opposition to new norms, we understand that researchers may explore in directions that we cannot anticipate. We look forward to seeing where queer concepts might travel next, and encourage our colleagues working in postgraduate education studies to play with their possibilities for thinking otherwise.

## NOTE

1. For example, queer concepts have been the focus of journal special issues, such as issue one of *International Journal of Qualitative Studies in Education* (2010), issue three of *Discourse: Studies in the Cultural Politics of Education* (2014), and issue four of *Higher Education Research & Development* (2015). The collection *Starting with Gender in Higher Education Research*, has chapters on "LGBT" as well as "queer."

## REFERENCES

Ahmed, S. (2006). *Queer phenomenology: Orientations, objects, others*. Duke University Press.

Ahmed, S. (2010). *The promise of happiness*. Duke University Press.

Ahmed, S. (2016). Interview with Judith Butler. *Sexualities, 19*(4), 482–492. https://doi.org/10.1177/1363460716629607

Aitchison, C., & Mowbray, S. (2015). Doctoral writing markets: Exploring the grey zone. In T. Bretag (Ed.), *Handbook of academic integrity* (pp. 1–12). Springer.

Allen, L. (2015). Queering the academy: New directions in LGBT research in higher education. *Higher Education Research & Development, 34*(4), 681–684. https://doi.org/10.1080/07294360.2015.1055052

Barad, K. (2007). *Meeting the universe halfway: Quantum physics and the entanglement of matter and meaning* (2nd ed.). Duke University Press.

Barcan, R. (2013). *Academic life and labour in the new university: Hope and other choices*. Routledge.

Berlant, L. (2007). Slow death (sovereignty, obesity, lateral agency). *Critical Inquiry, 33*(4), 754–780. https://doi.org/10.1086/521568

Berlant, L. (2011). *Cruel optimism*. Duke University Press.

Blackman, L. (2015). Affective politics, debility and hearing voices: Towards a feminist politics of ordinary suffering. *Feminist Review, 111*(1), 25–41. https://doi.org/10.1057/fr.2015.24

Blockett, R. A. (2017). "I think it's very much placed on us": Black queer men laboring to forge community at a predominantly White and (hetero)cisnormative research institution. *International Journal of Qualitative Studies in Education, 30*(8), 800–816. https://doi.org/10.1080/09518398.2017.1350296

Burford, J. (2012). A Queeresearch journey in nine poems. *Cultural Studies ↔ Critical Methodologies, 12*(1), 51–54. https://doi.org/10.1177/1532708611430488

Burford, J. (2014). A meditation on the poetics of doctoral writing. *Higher Education Research & Development*, *33*(6), 1232–1235. https://doi.org/10.1080/07294 360.2014.932040

Burford, J. (2015a). "Dear obese PhD applications": Twitter, Tumblr and the contested affective politics of fat doctoral embodiment. *M/C Journal*, *18*(3). https://doi.org/10.5204/mcj.969

Burford, J. (2015b). Queerying the affective politics of doctoral education: Toward complex visions of agency and affect. *Higher Education Research & Development*, *34*(4), 776–787. https://doi.org/10.1080/07294360.2015.1051005

Burford, J. (2016a). Doctoral induction day: An ethnographic fiction on doctoral emotions. In J. Smith, J. Rattray, T. Peseta, & D. Loads (Eds.), *Identity-work in the contemporary university: Exploring an uneasy profession* (pp. 117–128). Sense Publishers.

Burford, J. (2016b). *Uneasy feelings: Queer(y)ing the affective-politics of doctoral education* [Unpublished doctoral dissertation]. University of Auckland. https:// researchspace.auckland.ac.nz/handle/2292/31268?show=full

Burford, J. (2017a). Not writing, and giving "zero-f**ks" about it: Queer(y)ing doctoral "failure." *Discourse: Studies in the Cultural Politics of Education*, *38*(4), 473–484. https://doi.org/10.1080/01596306.2015.1105788

Burford, J. (2017b). What might "bad feelings" be good for? Some queer-feminist thoughts on academic activism. *Australian Universities' Review*, *59*(2), 2017.

Burford, J. (2018). The trouble with doctoral aspiration now. *International Journal of Qualitative Studies in Education*, *31*(6), 487–503. https://doi.org/10.1080/09518 398.2017.1422287

Burford, J., & Allen, L. (2019). Starting with queer: An enigmatic concept for higher education research and practice. In E. Henderson & Z. Nicolazzo (Eds.), *Starting with gender in international higher education research: Conceptual debates and methodological considerations* (pp. 126–143). Routledge.

Burgess, A. (2005). Queering heterosexual spaces: Positive space campaigns disrupting campus heteronormativity. *Canadian Woman Studies*, *24*(2–3), 27–30.

Burrows, R. (2012). Living with the H-Index? Metric assemblages in the contemporary academy. *The Sociological Review*, *60*(2), 355–372. https://doi. org/10.1111/j.1467-954x.2012.02077.x

Butler, J. (2008). An account of oneself. In B. Davies (Ed.), *Judith Butler in conversation: Analyzing the texts and talk of everyday life* (pp. 19–38). Routledge.

Butler, J. (2009). Performativity, precarity and sexual politics. *AIBR. Revista de Antropología Iberoamericana*, *04*(03), I–XIII. https://doi.org/10.11156/ aibr.040303e

Butler, J. (2013). Critically queer. In D. E. Hall & A. Jagose (Eds.), *The Routledge queer studies reader* (pp. 18–31). Routledge.

Butler, J. P. (2005). *Giving an account of oneself*. Fordham University Press.

Cvetkovich, A. (2012). *Depression: A public feeling* (Illustrated ed.). Duke University Press.

Davis, O., & Kollias, H. (2012). Editors' introduction: Queer theory's return to France. *Paragraph*, *35*(2), 139–143.

Duggan, L. (2015, September 22). Queer complacency without empire. *Bully Bloggers*. https://bullybloggers.wordpress.com/2015/09/22/queer-complacency-with out-empire/

Endo, H., & Reece-Miller, P. (2010). Retracing queer moments: Drawing a comparison between past and present LGBTQ issues. *International Journal of Critical Pedagogy, 3*(1), 134–147.

Gill, R. (2010). Breaking the silence: The hidden injuries of the neoliberal university. In R. Ryan-Flood & R. Gill (Eds.), *Secrecy and silence in the research process: Feminist reflections* (pp. 228–244). Routledge.

Gowlett, C., & Rasmussen, M. L. (2014). The cultural politics of queer theory in education research. *Discourse: Studies in the Cultural Politics of Education, 35*(3), 331–334. https://doi.org/10.1080/01596306.2014.888838

Grant, B. M., & Elizabeth, V. (2014). Unpredictable feelings: Academic women under research audit. *British Educational Research Journal, 41*(2), 287–302. https://doi.org/10.1002/berj.3145

Green, P., & Usher, R. (2003). Fast supervision: Changing supervisory practice in changing times. *Studies in Continuing Education, 25*(1), 37–50. https://doi.org/10.1080/01580370309281

Halberstam, J. (2011). *The queer art of failure*. Duke University Press.

Hook, G. A. (2015). Performatively queer: Sole parent postgraduates in the Australian academy. *Higher Education Research & Development, 34*(4), 788–800. https://doi.org/10.1080/07294360.2015.1051006

Hook, G. A. (2016). *Sole parent students and higher education: Gender, policy and widening participation*. Palgrave Macmillan.

Ings, W. (2013). Queer as a two-bob watch: The implications of cultural framing and self-declaration. In A. Engels-Schwarzpaul & M. Peters (Eds.), *Of other thoughts: Non-traditional ways to the doctorate: A guidebook for candidates and supervisors* (pp. 131–146). Sense Publishers.

Jackson, A. Y., & Mazzei, L. A. (2012). *Thinking with theory in qualitative research*. Routledge.

Jagose, A. (2010). Counterfeit pleasures: Fake orgasm and queer agency. *Textual Practice, 24*(3), 517–539. https://doi.org/10.1080/09502361003690849

Kipnis, L. (2004). *Against love: A polemic*. Vintage.

Lee, A., & Aitchison, C. (2009). Writing for the doctorate and beyond. In D. Boud & A. Lee (Eds.), *Changing practices of doctoral education* (pp. 87–99). Routledge.

McKenna, L. (2016, April 21). The ever-tightening job market for Ph.D.s. *The Atlantic*. https://www.theatlantic.com/education/archive/2016/04/bad-job-market-phds/479205/

Mizzi, R., & Stebbins, A. (2010). Walking a thin line: White, queer, (auto) ethnographic entanglements in educational research. *New Horizons in Adult Education & Human Resource Development, 24*(2–4), 19–29. https://doi.org/10.1002/nha3.10382

Muñoz, J. E. (2009). *Cruising utopia: The then and there of queer futurity*. NYU Press.

Newman, C. E. (2019). Queer families: Valuing stories of adversity, diversity and belonging. *Culture, Health & Sexuality, 21*(3), 352–359. https://doi.org/10.1080/13691058.2018.1468032

Puar, J. (2007). *Terrorist assemblages: Homonationalism in queer times*. Duke University Press.

Rasmussen, M. L. (2004). Wounded identities, sex and pleasure: "Doing it" at school. NOT! *Discourse: Studies in the Cultural Politics of Education, 25*(4), 445–458. https://doi.org/10.1080/0159630042000290946

Rasmussen, M. L., & Allen, L. (2014). What can a concept do? Rethinking education's queer assemblages. *Discourse: Studies in the Cultural Politics of Education, 35*(3), 433–443. https://doi.org/10.1080/01596306.2014.888846

Renn, K. A. (2010). LGBT and queer research in higher education. *Educational Researcher, 39*(2), 132–141. https://doi.org/10.3102/0013189x10362579

Sedgwick, E. K. (2003). *Touching feeling: Affect, pedagogy, performativity.* Duke University Press.

Stockton, K. B. (2009). *The queer child, or growing sideways in the twentieth century.* Duke University Press.

Warner, M. (1999). *The trouble with normal: Sex, politics, and the ethics of queer life.* Harvard University Press.

Wiegman, R. (2014). The times we're in: Queer feminist criticism and the reparative "turn." *Feminist Theory, 15*(1), 4–25. https://doi.org/10.1177/1464700113 513081a

White, J. (2013). Doctoral Education and new managerialism. In M. Vicars & T. McKenna (Eds.), *Discourse, power, and resistance down under* (pp. 187–194). Sense Publishers.

CHAPTER 4

# Racism, Heteronormativity, and Educational Assemblage in Germany

MARÍA DO MAR CASTRO VARELA AND
YENER BAYRAMOĞLU

Schools are powerful institutions and widely seen as the gatekeepers of future success. From the outset, attending school involves conforming to an often-unstated set of social and behavioral norms, which is assumed to set students on the path toward a successful life—or limit their potential if they struggle to comply. A number of studies, mostly conducted in the United States, have explored the multiple inequalities experienced by queer migrants and queer of color students in educational institutions, employing intersectionality and queer of color critique as their guiding frameworks (Blockett, 2017; Rodriguez et al., 2016). In this chapter, we assess the potentialities of further frameworks, such as assemblage and life course theory, to supplement an educational queer of color critique and extend our understanding of the multifaceted inequalities experienced by queers of color and migrant students in educational institutions. As we discuss in the following pages, the complex narratives of queer of color and queer migrant students in German schools point to an array of disturbing affective interactions within educational institutions. To better understand these adverse micropolitics, a range of theoretical tools are put to use.

It is often the *fear* of being bullied, the *anger* caused by racist practices, that *sticks* to the bodies of migrant and queer of color bodies (Ahmed, 2004). These emotions mark the experiences made in school as stories of injury. Queer of color and migrant students in Germany often describe

María do Mar Castro Varela and Yener Bayramoğlu, *Racism, Heteronormativity, and Educational Assemblage in Germany*
In: *Queer Studies and Education*. Edited by: Nelson M. Rodriguez, Robert C. Mizzi, Louisa Allen, and Rob Cover,
Oxford University Press. © Oxford University Press 2023. DOI: 10.1093/oso/9780197687000.003.0005

educational institutions as overflowing with experiences of discrimination, marginalization, and stigmatization (see bildungsLab*, 2021). Feelings associated with these experiences are a general sense of never being good enough, never being right, or always being too slow, which can be translated as being "backward."

Educational institutions are usually the very first institutions encountered during a person's life course. In Germany, attending state-approved schools is compulsory, and succeeding in school is seen as a key step toward a productive, fulfilling life by families and education stakeholders. Following a Marxist reading, schools can be described as a foundational part of civil society (Gramsci, 2005): Students are trained to not only read, write, and do arithmetic, but also learn what is seen as acceptable or unacceptable social behavior and, perhaps more significantly, which social groups are dominant and which students belong to the group of the *other*. Schools thus play an important role in forming classed subjects. The formative phase of schooling imparts a sense of belonging or nonbelonging to emergent citizens. Repression experienced by working-class students in school can be subtle and sometimes also blatant. But with compliance paramount for the civilizing mission, not only working-class students feel rejected, but also all students who do not belong to the hegemonic group do (see Mayo, 2016), including queer students, students of color, migrant students, and students with disabilities. Critical pedagogy has highlighted the important role schools play in stabilizing hegemonic state structures and producing the working power necessary to serve the dominant classes (see bell hooks, 1994).

If we view education as an assemblage (DeLanda, 2006; Deleuze & Guattari, 1980), we can perceive conflicting subject positions, such as diverse students, teachers, and staff, moving within structures of power with their own subconscious motivations. Educational materials, such as textbooks and equipment, as well as classrooms and a school's architecture, are part of the network that constitutes the educational assemblage, thus allowing us to analyze interactions between subjects. Some interactions between subjects may inflict injury, and those between subjects and objects may cause long-term harm. Queer migrant and queer of color students, our focus here, create strategies to navigate through heteronormative and racist educational assemblages. If we focus on the relations and interactions, emotions, and affects that emerge and take place when certain marginalized bodies enter hegemonic educational institutions and become visible in educational assemblages—a constellation that Gayatri Chakravorty Spivak (1993) described as *outside in the teaching machine*—we might be able to understand experiences of queer migrant and queer of color students as *outside in* the educational apparatus. In this chapter, we analyze interrelations of marginalization, but including assemblages will allow us to also recognize practices and structures of resistance. Furthermore, this perspective focuses on not only subjects, but also structures and objects.

## A POLYPHONIC APPROACH: ASSEMBLAGE AND QUEER OF COLOR LIFE COURSE

An important contribution to the scholarship on how different inequalities and experiences intersect within institutional contexts, such as schools, emerges from the concept of a *queer of color critique*. The concept was introduced by scholars such as Roderick A. Ferguson (2004), who explored how race, class, gender, and sexuality intersect in culture and society, describing racialization and heteronormativity as intertwined macrosystems. One particularly well-explored topic related to the experiences of queers of color in educational institutions is the specific difficulties they face during their coming out process. Studies have shown, for example, how queer of color students adapt to normativities in order to "hide" their identities from the outside world (Duran, 2019, p. 391). As Edward Brockenbrough (2015) argued, such studies mark the bodies of queer of color youth and queer migrant students with difference and risk producing a solely victimizing discourse that fails to grasp the potential for an epistemological shift that queer of color experiences could bring to studies of education. To counter this, Brockenbrough advocated tracing strategies of resistance, political and subjective contestations, cultural practices, and identity constructions employed by queer of color and migrant students to create new pathways toward their desired social futures in order to shift the discourses away from victimization to knowledge production and agency. In a similar vein, Martin Manalansan (2018) discussed how queer of color critique can render visible how queers and queerness are awash in the flow of everyday normativities. Rather than heralding queerness as a heroic rejection of normativities, a queer of color analysis reflects the messiness of everyday contestations between norm and queerness: "The norm and queer are not easily indexed or separable but constantly colliding, clashing, intersecting and reconstituting" (Manalansan, 2018, p. 1288). José Esteban Muñoz (1999), another prominent queer of color scholar, coined the term *disidentification* to explore how queers of color do not simply reject normativities completely, but instead create alternative coping strategies that adapt and transform normative perceptions of identities in order to navigate through life in heteronormative and racist societies.

The body of work on queer of color critique builds substantially on feminist scholarship by authors such as Gloria Anzaldúa (1987) and Kimberlé Crenshaw (1989). Crenshaw's concept of intersectionality offers a particularly useful analytical perspective, focusing on concrete social situations in which two or more social categories, identifications, and experiences intersect to produce new forms of vulnerabilities, marginalization, and exclusions. While there is no doubt that this is a very helpful tool for analyzing the social inequalities encountered by queer migrants and queers of color, an intersectional approach tends to limit its understanding of difference to the level of representation, language, and discourse. Furthermore, subject positions marked with difference and inequalities tend to appear rather static, and the concept rarely takes into account how inequalities can change with changing bodies, objects, and contexts (Dhawan & Castro Varela, 2018). Put differently, intersectionality attempts to describe identities at the intersection of different inequalities, an idea that was initially revolutionary in sparking a shift away from single-issue politics to recognize the effects of multiple forms of discrimination. On the other hand, intersectionality does not go so well with queer theory's critical engagement with the notion of identity as such. Whereas an intersectional approach necessarily characterizes identities as clear cut and constant, queer theory shows them to be ephemeral, constantly changing, and unstable categories (Duran, 2019, p. 396). If intersectionality is used as a tool operating with rather fixed categories, it runs the risk of overlooking the dynamic interactions that position different subjects in relation to one another in social situations. To overcome this risk, we have chosen to mobilize an assemblage perspective rather than an intersectionality approach in our queer of color analysis of educational institutions and practices for this chapter.

In their groundbreaking book, *A Thousand Plateaus*, Gilles Deleuze and Félix Guattari (1980) coined the concept *assemblage* after rereading psychoanalysis and critiquing its shortcomings. When different bodies or bodies and objects come together, they interact and affect each other, and things start happening. Assemblages focus less on identities and individual agency and more on interactions as well as affects in a given space. In a similar way, Spivak (1996) argued that when talking about subalternity we need to shift our attention away from concepts such as identity and voice to the concept of space. Spivak explained that it is space that allows us to discern the shifting meanings and position of identities within constellations of power relations in a given context. In that sense,

[84]   *María do Mar Castro Varela and Yener Bayramoğlu*

looking at spaces can help us to analyze what assemblages do to bodies and what subject positions they create and how these are in constant flow. To illustrate this with an example, we can consider a migrant queer of color professor teaching at a university. The classroom, as an educational assemblage, presents the migrant queer of color body as a professor and thereby attributes the body certain privileges. As Robert Mizzi (2013) argued, being a queer migrant educator in a classroom is a position of power, even when at other times they experience inequalities and discrimination from border regimes and racism. Once such an educator leaves the building, walks through the streets, and takes public transportation, they might no longer be perceived as an educator, but the affects between the passengers might turn the educator into a racialized and othered subject. Social assemblage (DeLanda, 2006; Puar, 2012) thus allows us to follow such dynamics and recognize the ever-changing positionalities in and beyond educational institutions.

Last, but not least, we supplement a queer of color analysis with a critical life course analysis, which permits us to look into a terrain that neither intersectionality nor assemblage theory is able to map. Life course approach not only traces individuals' biographies but also argues that each phase in life should be explored as a moment that is conditioned by steps taken in the past: School prepares an individual for work, work prepares them for retirement, and so on (Elder et al., 2003). This does not mean that such narratives have to reduce life to a dull story of linear progress, obscuring potential alternative routes like detours, retours, and zigzags. Sociologists and anthropologists in the early 20th century were particularly interested in the question of how industrialization had affected citizens' life spans. The groundbreaking research of William Thomas and Florian Znaniecki (1920/1996) on Polish immigrants to the United States showed how migrants had adapted to new cultural and temporal norms after arriving there. Later, in the 1970s, analyses of the impacts of important historical fractures dominated research, which looked at topics such as the effects of the Great Depression in the United States on the labor market, marriage rates and choices, and birth rates (Elder, 1994). This diachronic research focus led, among others, to an understanding of how post-Fordism had resulted in less standardized, more self-directed biographies. Today, life course studies are an established field with studies spanning a wide range of diverse topics, including queer studies (Bayramoğlu & Castro Varela, 2021). The lens of the life course can help us comprehend how experiences of discrimination at one time of life affect the next, in this case, how inequalities experienced early in educational institutions continue to haunt queer migrants and queers of color in their later lives. Furthermore, we recognize how specific experiences made during an individual's life are linked to the discourses, policies, and practices of migration politics. We do not approach migration as a tragedy, but as a potentiality that is shaped by the political, societal, and cultural context—or assemblage—within which it takes place. Migration infuses life with possibilities and predicaments—as do the different gender routes a person might follow. While intersectionality characterizes subjects in relation to normative, supposedly stable categories, assemblage concentrates on interrelated dynamics and unstable road maps. Meanwhile, life course research approaches biographies as a series of phases that can be analyzed in terms of their flows, breaks, and stops—termed as *turning points* in life course studies. Orchestrating these different approaches allows us to zoom in and out in order to examine subject formations and political practices as well as intersubjectivities.

### Shame and Knowledge

As part of a European Union–funded research project on intersectional inequalities during different life phases with a special focus on turning points, CILIA-LGBTQI+[1] carried out 43 in-depth interviews across Germany from 2019 to 2021. Participants were from different age groups (ranging from 18 to 70). Among 43 participants, who all self-identified as LGBTQI+, 12 had experienced migration and/or asylum processes and/or had been subject to racism. Focusing on three interviews selected from this pool, we explored how racialized LGBTQI+ students experience mainstream educational institutions—from early childhood to higher and further education. We were guided by qualitative content analysis (Mayring, 2004), which helped us to identify central themes across the interviews. Focusing on parts of the narratives that addressed education, we analyzed the statements drawing on queer of color critique, assemblage, and critical life course perspectives. As we sketch out in detail, our analyses led us to conclude that inequalities in educational assemblages produce a sociopolitical phenomenon that may be described as *fragmented citizenship* (Castro Varela, 2012). Here the subject position is characterized by having multiple layers of vulnerabilities, which neither allow the subject to completely reject democratic structures nor let them desire to fully participate in democratic society. Responding to a life characterized by experiences of exclusion, the fragmented citizen rejects a normative citizenship position. The consequences of this are rather ambivalent: While the problematization of normative citizenship is—in our

[86] *María do Mar Castro Varela and Yener Bayramoğlu*

view—a positive move, the fragmented citizen is not motivated to intervene into hegemonic structures. To put it differently: There is resistance *and* resignation.

### Complexities and the Trans Migrant

> I was afraid of being bullied by classmates [for being queer] and that was much more significant than my fear of being bullied by teachers. I experienced more racism from teachers in middle school. I was in a comprehensive school, and I had good grades and I wanted to take the A course for German. The pupils were divided into A, B and C courses from the 7th or 8th grade on. And I wanted to take the German A course, but because I once made a spelling mistake in a dictation, I was told that my German wasn't good enough. And I told my mother about it, and she was right to get angry, wrote a letter, went there and then I joined the A course. But then I noticed that I was being discriminated against, especially on the basis of racism. So, it might not be visible that I am queer, but I am racially discriminated against. And that there is always this subconscious, that teachers also . . . subconsciously discriminate against you. Maybe they don't always do it directly. But they do it unconsciously by simply saying that you don't deserve to take an A course because you have a migrant background. (Samet, 26, December 2, 2019)

The above quotation from an interview inspired us to recalibrate the intersection of critical race studies, queer studies, and pedagogy. Whereas existing research on LGBTQI+ and pedagogy focuses predominantly on hetero- and cissexism in educational institutions (see Kosciw et al., 2016; Pearson & Wilkinson, 2009) or critiques heteronormative school curricula and harmful sex and gender education (Jones et al., 2019), Samet's narrative pointed to a more complex story. What comes to the fore in this excerpt are experiences with racism, which to some extent turn "being queer" into an unmarked position. Put differently, being a migrant of color marks Samet as the *other,* with race becoming the salient marker. But what is perhaps even more noteworthy is that the fear of being shamed, bullied, and discriminated against is felt in a versatile space, which is unstable. The perceived threats are flexible and seem to constantly shift in character. They are dynamic and vigorous, never allowing the subject a moment of respite. In our particular example, the *fear* of getting bullied by the classmates for having a body that does not seem to conform to normative gender regimes is sometimes partly overshadowed by teachers' racist practices, which follow an almost classic racist script. This brings to our attention racist hate speech acts and the affects that accompany them in the context of education (Joseph et al., 2016). Samet's academic competence is overlooked by a teacher who sees only his racialized body—as justification for denying Samet access to the German literature A course. The mother gets *angry* on behalf of Samet and refuses to accept the teacher's discriminatory decision. Caught in between, Samet's narrative is shaped by his *cool-headed* interpretation ("it's *subconscious racism*") and his *rational* understanding of his mother's anger ("*she was right*"), as he works through his *injuries*. Although being queer becomes a less prominent field of vulnerability in this memory, it is our claim that the queer body nevertheless plays an important role in how the student reads, resists, and endures being shamed in the educational institution.

At the time of the interview, Samet was in his late 20s and defined himself as a Muslim trans person of color. His parents had migrated from Turkey to Germany as *Gastarbeiter* "guest workers." He grew up in a family that experienced not only anti-Muslim racism, but also classism. Employing Manuel DeLanda's (2006) theory on social assemblage enables us to recognize connections between social micro and macro levels (e.g., microaggressions in school and trans-exclusionary school structures operating simultaneously with an exploitative migrant labor system that was devoid of any measures to include migrants within mainstream German society). Samet faced racism from his early school years on, but neither his early experiences of racial prejudice nor his later encounters with cisnormativity should be seen as individual instances of interpersonal interaction. On the contrary, they are part of the history of the German nation state and the particular discourses, structures, and everyday practices that constitute it, which are woven into the educational system as a whole. Hence, the racist bias of one teacher has to be explored in relation to the entire web of inclusionary and exclusionary policies, practices, interactions, and contestations that feature across the part-to-whole (micro-to-macro) spectrum. Furthermore, categories such as race, gender, class, or sexuality are not simply entities or attributes of subjects, but arise through actions, relations, movements, and affects between bodies (Puar, 2012, p. 58). As becomes apparent in Samet's interview, it is through different relations and constellations of bodies that intersectional exclusions are experienced and structured by class-specific hierarchies and racist "knowledge." In combination, these produced the idea that Samet could not truly belong within the school system and would never be a successful student. If Samet—or any other student from a guest worker family—achieved better grades than expected, that would be perceived as exceptional or presumed to be due to some kind of mistake.

## Identifying Differences

I didn't know the terminology for it before, but already in kindergarten I said that I was a boy, and was also completely convinced of it. So, no matter what kind of body I had and so on. But then . . . from middle school and from puberty onwards I noticed, something is different about me. And I didn't really have any terms for it. And I didn't have such strong dysphoria back then either. That only came with . . . after I turned 20, it became stronger and stronger. I started with it . . . in my early 20s. (Samet, 26, December 2, 2019)

When Samet talked about his transition, he divided the process into stages that corresponded to his level of education at the time. In his memories, kindergarten stands out as a phase when he felt relatively comfortable with himself and his body as it was. He was able to express his gender identity with confidence. This reminds us of analogies drawn between childhood and queerness, as reflected in the works of Stockton (2009) and Halberstam (1998). These scholars noted that heteronormativity is less all-pervasive during childhood, a time in which the playful exploration of gender expressions and identities tends not to be (harshly) punished. Arguably, such claims risk romanticizing childhood by ignoring the violence that some children are exposed to—or even inflict on others. Indeed, our participants experienced mobbing, humiliation, and lack of respect from their peers from early childhood onward. What makes Samet's memories from the time he went to kindergarten striking is not that he felt that nonnormative gender identities were accepted by others, but that he himself was confident to assert the gender he felt. As he remembers, it wasn't until middle school that he entered a phase in which his body no longer seemed to correspond to his identity. His own body became a disturbance (e.g., "I noticed, something is different about me"). There is another important detail in his narrative: As he progressed through the different phases of schooling, he had no words for his feelings and thoughts about his body and identity. He remarked that he "really didn't have any terms for it." The lack of knowledge about trans lives intertwined with a body that was transforming in uncontrollable ways ultimately led to dysphoria. While Samet was going through such very confusing phases in life, the schools he attended did not equip him with knowledge about queer lives, but instead functioned as disciplinary forces.

Needless to say, education plays an important role when it comes to learning and internalizing hegemonic structures, exclusionary practices, and stereotypes. As prior research in Germany has demonstrated (Castro Varela, 2012, 2015), German schools cultivate narrow and normative concepts of gender, sexuality, and citizenship. Not only the curriculum, but also the routines and practices of school life are simply not oriented toward the White cis- and heterosexual bourgeois student, but produce it. In the 1970s and 1980s, critical pedagogic studies coined the term *hidden curriculum* to describe the types of social knowledge imparted implicitly in school education: how to behave in specific settings. Studies that made this hidden curriculum visible revealed the normative assumptions and ideas about appropriate behavior that shaped teachers' expectations and ways of addressing students. Research showed why and how educational institutions privileged students from a bourgeois class background (Apple & King, 1983). We would like to build on critical pedagogy's main arguments to add that the hidden curriculum not only privileges students from a certain class, but also camouflages heteronormativity and renders invisible hegemonic ideas about citizenship. We have to ask, for example, which language serves as the medium of communication? Which religion and religious practices are accepted? Why is Islam portrayed as dangerous? Furthermore, which clothes are seen as "normal" when worn by which gendered subject? How are needs and desires to be articulated? Accordingly, we argue, what Samet experienced in middle school was caused by the hidden curriculum of a hegemonic national culture in which full citizenship is a privilege only available to White bourgeois Germans who conform to hetero- and cisnormativities. Those who are unable to follow the rules set by the hidden curriculum will be excluded and marked by shame. Having learned that they cannot expect inclusion from educational institutions, they are unlikely to expect better from the social institutions that they experience in later life.

An overview of LGBTQI+ research in Germany highlighted a range of problematic issues in education, for example, verbal abuse and bullying as part of everyday life in schools (Biechele, 2004), teachers' failures to condemn heterosexist and/or transphobic jokes (Krell & Oldemeier, 2017), and a lack of queer-friendly content in sexual and gender education, with heteronormativity left unmentioned (Roth, 2015). Studies documented the difficulties of coming out in school (Krell & Oldemeier, 2017) and drew attention to the wanting ways in which educational institutions adopt perspectives from queer theory (Hartmann et al., 2017). However, the literature has been remarkably silent when it comes to queers of color in education. Most studies concerned with queer experiences in the classroom tend to imagine LGBTQI+ people as White and German. Racism is also constantly underemphasized in teachers' training and education (Shure, 2021). Strikingly, the existence of queers of color in educational settings tends to only be mentioned when heterosexism and transphobia in migrant communities is the issue. The main conclusion of the literature we reviewed was that young LGBTQI+ people whose parents have migrated from countries "in which non-heteronormative lifestyles are stigmatized and criminalized" tend to be more fearful of coming out than others (Krell & Oldemeier, 2017, p. 80). Some studies even uncritically reproduced racist and essentialist discourses. In seeking an explanation for why heterosexism and transphobia are still common in schools, migrants and/or refugees are brought into the frame. Migrant students and their families are thus blamed for the prevalence of heterosexism and transphobia in schools (LSVD, 2007[2]; MGEPA NRW, 2015[3]). Such discourse renders queer migrants and queer of color students and their experiences invisible. Rarely are their voices attended to. To overcome such problematic approaches, the focus of queer educational research must urgently shift to take account of underrepresented lives, while remaining wary of romanticizing or victimizing narratives.

### Excluded Knowledge

Shifting the attention to queer of color students' experiences in and with educational institutions spells out not only which knowledge is excluded from the curriculum, but also how hidden curricula force queer of color students to create new coping strategies. Käthe, who was born and grew up in a Syrian Orthodox family in Germany, remarked during his interview:

> Hmm, I think I already have a stigma consciousness. I've always had a bit of a slight fear of the expectation that I won't be recognized because of my origin or my ethnic origin or because I'm gay. But that's what I'm really trained to do, isn't it? So, I'm programmed [to fear]. Why? Because I've known since I was four years old or so that I'm different. (Käthe, 30, August 2, 2019)

Käthe described his fear of being discriminated against as *stigma consciousness*, which he had gained through experiencing intersectional inequalities throughout his life. The process started early and affected Käthe's entire biography, including experiences made in different educational spaces. Educational assemblages, in which teachers, school curricula, students, books, and the architecture of classrooms and school buildings work together to build a complex web of exclusionary processes, *train* and *program* queer of color students to live at the margins. Students of color and migrant students sense their *otherness* as soon as they enter the school doors. In many schools they are not allowed to communicate in the language they speak at home, as German is compulsory even during breaks. In textbooks, representations of nonhegemonic bodies are either completely absent or reduced to mere caricatures (see Feierstein, 2010; Marmer et al., 2011). Käthe talked about a "programming": He learned to be the other, and he became anxious of being read as only as other. Misrepresentation becomes the default position. Furthermore, instead of offering heterogeneous knowledge and diverse ways to understand the world, educational institutions limit students' imaginations. As Käthe powerfully testified, through such exclusionary processes, people who inhabit a space marked by intersectional discrimination from an early age experience *anxieties* that shape their life. Anxieties become simply part of everyday life.

Emotions and affects play an important role in experiencing inequalities and discrimination. For example, shame "is an affect that crosses many different orders of body" (Probyn, 2010, p. 82). Shame emerges through affects produced between bodies and sticks to the shamed body (Ahmed, 2004). Feeling shame emotionally expresses the lived experiences of injuries, violence, and exclusions inscribed on the body.

> In elementary school, a teacher said, I should not consider it so bad, if . . . there are these sweets *Negerküsse*[4] and said, I should not find it so bad, so I have a nice tasty skin, which reminds her of chocolate. That was such an essential experience for me, where I somehow started relatively early on not to see teachers as allies. And—and then also things like that, that teachers in, I think it was in the ninth grade, the teacher grabbed at my hair, and said that my hair was as soft as sheep's wool. So it was like comparing humans and animals . . . so, "your hair is soft like wool," where I just somehow think to myself: What the fuck? And these were of course things that make you feel uncomfortable, but for which you have no vocabulary at all. (Amin, 31, March 18, 2020)

When the interviewees talked about their experiences in educational institutions, they often mentioned particularly memorable affective moments caused by the remarks or actions of other students or teachers, in the playground or in the classroom, such as use of the N-word or derogatory terms for gays. The racist and heteronormative roots of such words and practices, deeply embedded in language and "culture," overpowered any potential alternative imaginations, and resistance was made all the more difficult as microaggressions were usually backed up by the authority of the teacher. The humiliating experiences were deterritorializing (DeLanda, 2006). As they recounted their experiences, several queers of color recalled being taken aback and stopped short by the bluntness of the everyday aggression that they encountered in educational institutions.

With everyone else present apparently taking for granted that such behavior was normal, objecting to it would inevitably shine a harsh spotlight on the—"not normal"—person objecting. This produced a constant feeling of nonbelonging throughout the educational phase of life. Queer of color and migrant students were confronted by—more or less overt—racism in the classroom. This was generally mentioned when interviewees recalled classroom discussions and interactions between teachers and students in lessons. On the other hand, heterosexism and cisviolence was inflicted directly in mobbing practices and hate speech. And then there was the most tedious phenomenon: a sense of *hate just being in the air*. Hate permeates everywhere, yet it is never graspable—and, as Amin put it, it leaves the subject behind speechless. Migration and race continue to function as part of a violent exclusionary network of educational policies, structures, discourses, and practices. Affects produced by those assemblages affect the injured and shamed body. Samet talked about his body being exposed to discriminatory violent acts in educational institutions, while Amin (31, student), a Black, nonbinary person, recounted how their body became the object of hate speech. It seems that heterosexist and racist assemblages force students to juggle their identities, choosing one over another according to the situation at hand. Being repeatedly subjected to multiple discriminations and violent everyday experiences taught Amin and Samet to observe closely which identity they could (and should) perform in any given situation. Amin, for example, remarked that although they liked to wear high heels at home, they would never wear them to university. As Black, indigenous, and people of color (BIPOC), they do not want to be read as queer in public—racism is already enough to have to deal with:

> And sexuality, gender identity, that's something I think with me, something where I realize also just like being Black, that's something where I'm very fragile and also very vulnerable and I just don't want to offer anyone a surface to attack. (Amin, 31, March 18, 2020)

*Home*, which Amin shares with another queer of color roommate, is a space full of potentialities, where they can freely express their gender identity without the fear of being attacked. University, on the contrary, is an educational assemblage that does not guarantee such a safe space. Indeed, with the threat of racism always lurking, the educational environment obliges Amin to show just one aspect of their identity. Their multifaceted self is forcibly fragmented: queer and Black at home, Black at university. The educational assemblage splits subject positions and plays different belongings out against each other—threatening to tear the subject apart.

This might be one explanation why queer of color students often recount experiences of racism in poignant detail, whereas their memories of discrimination suffered for being queer are often more fuzzy. Another explanation could be that queer of color students challenge educational institutions by their mere existence. Racism is after all a structural part of European educational institutions.

## CONCLUSION

As our analysis of the interview excerpts demonstrate, assemblages modulate specific affects and subject positions. The complex and multiple sources of injuries show the changing, dynamic character of subject positionings and throw light on the array of normative violence and hate speech that is experienced. It is the figure of the teacher that stands out as the main source of racist practice. Heteronormativity and heterosexism as well as cisnormativity appear to be all pervasive and hence more difficult to pin down to specific moments. One of the reasons why queers of color and migrants remember the figure of the teacher as *the* source of racism (but not as a source of heterosexism and transphobia) might be that educational institutions are not simply a part of civil society: They function to secure the stability of the nation state. Schools, it seems to us, operate as powerful producers of hegemonic citizens. While LGBTQI+ activism in Germany has led to more recognition of nonnormative genders and sexualities in schools and curricula, heterosexism and transphobia remain prevalent in classrooms. Nevertheless, such kinds of discrimination do not seem to have produced as many painful memories for BIPOC and migrant interviewees as racism did. Racism was felt as an overwhelming omnipresence, articulated in everyday hate speech and institutionally sanctioned by teachers who lacked the sensitivity or commitment—or both—to recognize it and hold perpetrators to account. We are confronted with an assemblage, which is connected to security discourses, migration policies, and structural racism—an assemblage that is configured by Eurocentrism and, ultimately, White supremacy.

The process of formal education placed Amin, Käthe, and Samet at the intersections of race, gender, sexuality, and class. Their complex positioning produced a dynamic assortment of affects, reactions, contestations, and interpretations as they developed strategies to endure the violence they experienced in educational institutions. Taking a life course perspective, we have been able to analyze not only the students' different shifts and maneuvers, but also how shame stuck to the bodies and continued to affect our interviewees even long after they had left the educational institutions. The assemblage approach enriches the life course perspective by pointing to the density and fluidity of the interactions within the teaching machine. In an era in which Germany has approved numerous pro-queer legislations, and popular media and politics represent queer subjects as likable and congenial, the educational assemblage is perceived by queer of color students as less hostile toward nonnormative gender performance than it is to non-Whites.

At the same time, racist discourses, antimigration politics, and the unrelenting public debate on the officially still nonaccepted colonial responsibility of Germany usher into an educational dispositive, in which teachers do not feel free to use racist words and even slurs. In reaction, queer students of color and migrant students learn to incorporate—bodily—a sense of shame as outsiders who can never belong to the White European hegemonic group. They feel that their right to be simply present in Germany is persistently questioned, with populist politicians proclaiming that their skin color or their non-Christian religion are irreconcilable with "Germanness." They are portrayed as a threat to the White hegemonic group. Focusing on the lives of queer students of color and queer migrant students inside the teaching machine presents us with insights into how these macrodynamics are experienced by individual persons in everyday situations—or assemblages—that dynamically bring forth injuries and resistance.

## NOTES

1. Comparing Intersectional Life-course Inequalities Among LGBTQI+ Citizens in Four European Countries (England, Germany, Portugal and Scotland).
2. Lesbian and Gay Federation in Germany.
3. Ministry for Health, Equalities, Care and Ageing of the State of North Rhine-Westphalia.
4. A German confectionery that contains the N-word in its name.

## REFERENCES

Ahmed, S. (2004). *The cultural politics of emotion*. Routledge.
Anzaldúa, G. (1987). *Borderlands—La frontera. The new mestiza*. Aunt Lute Books.
Apple, M., & King, N. (1983). What do schools teach? In H. Giroux & D. Purpel (Eds.), *The hidden curriculum and moral education* (pp. 82–99). McCutchan Publishing.

Bayramoğlu, Y., & Castro Varela, M. (2021). Post/pandemisches Leben. Eine neue Theorie der Fragilität. Transcript.

Biechele, U. (2004). *Identitätsentwicklung schwuler Jugendlicher. Eine Befragung deutschsprachiger junger Schwuler in der schwulen Szene und Internet* [Unpublished doctoral dissertation]. University of Basel. http://edoc.unibas.ch/diss/DissB_6970

bildungsLab*. (Ed.). (2021). *Bildung. Ein postkoloniales Manifest.* Unrast.

Blockett, R. A. (2017). "I think it's very much placed on us": Black queer men laboring to forge community at a predominantly White and (hetero)cisnormative research institution. *International Journal of Qualitative Studies in Education, 30*(8), 800–816. https://doi.org/10.1080/09518398.2017.1350296

Brockenbrough, E. (2015). Queer of color agency in educational contexts: Analytical frameworks from a queer of color critique. *Educational Studies, 51*(1), 28–44. https://doi.org/10.1080/00131946.2014.979929

Castro Varela, M. (2012). Einleitung: Traurige Forschung. In LesMigraS e.v. (Ed.), *Nicht so greifbar doch real. Eine qualitative und quantitative Studie zu Gewalt- und (Mehrfach-)Diskriminierungserfahrungen von lesbischen, bisexuellen Frauen und Trans\* in Deutschland* (pp. 9–19). LesMigraS.

Castro Varela, M. (2015). "Klassenapartheid." Postkoloniale Perspektiven auf Klassenherrschaft. Kurswechsel. *Zeitschrift für gesellschafts-, wirtschafts- und umweltpolitische Alternativen, 4*, 18–24.

Crenshaw, K. (1989). Demarginalizing the intersection of race and sex: A black feminist critique of antidiscrimination doctrine, feminist theory and antiracist politics. *University of Chicago Legal Forum, 1*, 139–167.

DeLanda, M. (2006). *A new philosophy of society. Assemblage theory and social complexity.* Bloomsbury.

Deleuze, G., & Guattari, F. (1980). *A thousand plateaus. Capitalism and schizophrenia.* University of Minnesota Press.

Dhawan, N., & Castro Varela, M. (2018). What difference does difference make?: Diversity, intersectionality and transnational feminist politics. *Tijdschrift voor Genderstudies* (TvG), *21*(1), 45–68.

Duran, A. (2019). Queer and of color: A systemic literature review of queer students of color in higher education scholarship. *Journal of Diversity in Higher Education, 12*(4), 390–400. https://doi.org/10.1037/dhe0000084

Elder, G. H. (1994). Time, human agency, and social change: Perspectives on the life course. *Social Psychology Quarterly, 57*(1), 4–15. https://doi.org/10.2307/2786971

Elder, G. H., Johnson, M. K., & Crosnoe, R. (2003) The emergence and development of life course theory. In J. T. Mortimer & M. J. Shanahan (Eds.), *Handbook of the life course* (pp. 3–19). Springer.

Feierstein, L. (2010). *Von Schwelle zu Schwelle: Einblicke in den didaktisch-historischen Umgang mit dem Anderen aus der Perspektive jüdischen Denkens.* Edition lumière.

Ferguson, R. A. (2004). *Aberrations in black: Toward a queer of color critique.* University of Minnesota Press.

Gramsci, A. (2005). *Selections from the prison notebooks.* Lawrence & Wishart.

Halberstam, J. (1998). *Female masculinity.* Duke University Press.

Hartmann, J., Messerschmidt, A., & Thon, C. (Eds.). (2017). *Jahrbuch Frauen und Geschlechterforschung in der Erziehungswissenschaft. Queertheoretische Perspektiven auf Bildung-Pädagogische Kritik der Heteronormativität.* Barbara Budrich.

hooks, b. (1994). *Teaching to transgress: Education as the practice of freedom.* Routledge.

Jones, T., Coll, L., van Leent, L., & Taylor, Y. (Eds.). (2019). *Uplifting gender and sexuality education research.* Palgrave Macmillan.

Joseph, N., Viesca, K. M., & Bianco, M. (2016). Black female adolescents and racism in schools: Experiences in a colorblind society. *High School Journal, 100*(1), 4–25. https://muse.jhu.edu/article/634277

Kosciw, J., Greytak, E., Giga, N., Villenas, C., & Danischewski, D. (2016). *The 2015 national school climate survey: The experiences of lesbian, gay, bisexual, transgender, and queer youth in our nation's schools.* GLSEN.

Krell, C., & Oldemeier, K. (2017). *Coming-out und dann . . . ?! Coming-Out-Verläufe und Diskriminierungserfahrungen von lesbischen, schwulen, bisexuellen, trans\* und queeren Jugendlichen und jungen Erwachsenen in Deutschland.* Barbara Budrich.

LSVD. (2007). *Einstellungen zur Homosexualität bei Jugendlichen mit und ohne Migrationshintergrund.* https://berlin.lsvd.de/wp-content/uploads/2017/01/Studie_Simon_2007.pdf

Manalansan, M. F. (2018). Messing up sex: The promises and possibilities of queer of color critique. *Sexualities, 21*(8), 1287–1290. https://doi.org/10.1177/13634 60718794646

Marmer, E., Marmer, D., Hitomi, L., & Sow, P. (2011). Racism and the image of Africa in German schools and textbooks. *International Journal of Diversity in Organizations, 10*(5), 1–12. https://doi.org/10.18848/1447-9532/CGP/v10 i05/38927

Mayo, P. (2016). *Hegemony and education under neoliberalism: Insights from Gramsci.* Routledge.

Mayring, P. (2004). Qualitative content analysis. In U. Flick, E. von Kardoff, & I. Steincke (Eds.), *A companion to qualitative research* (pp. 159–176). Sage.

MGEPA NRW. (2015). *Abwertung gleichgeschlechtlich liebender Menschen in Nordrhein-Westfalen. Aktualisierung zur Homophobie.* https://www.landtag.nrw.de/portal/WWW/dokumentenarchiv/Dokument/MMI16-299.pdf

Mizzi, R. C. (2013). Sexiles in the classroom: Understanding intersectionalities of sexuality, immigration, and education. https://digitalcommons.fiu.edu/

Muñoz, J. E. (1999). *Disidentifications: Queers of color and the performance of politics.* University of Minnesota Press.

Pearson, J., & Wilkinson, L. (2009). School culture and the well-being of same-sex attracted youth. *Gender & Society, 23*(4), 542–568. https://doi.org/10.1177/0891243209339913

Probyn, E. (2010). Writing shame. In M. Gregg & G. J. Seigworth (Eds.), *The affect theory reader* (pp. 71–92). Duke University Press.

Puar, J. (2012). I would rather be a cyborg than a goddess: Becoming intersectional in assemblage theory. *philoSOPHIA, 2*(1), 49–66.

Rodriguez, N. M., Martino, W. J., Ingrey, J. C., & Brockenbrough, E. (Eds.). (2016). *Critical concepts in queer studies and education: An international guide for the twenty-first century.* Palgrave Macmillan. https://doi.org/10.1057/978-1-137-55425-3

Roth, A. (2015). Einer der am Bau schafft ist nicht schwul: Zum Umgang mit Homosexualität an Berufsschulen. In M. Breckenfelder (Ed.), *Homosexualität und Schule* (pp. 249–296). Barbara Budrich.

Shure, S. (2021). *De_Thematisierung migrationsgesellschaftlicher Ordnungen. Lehramtsstudium als Ort der Bedeutungsproduktion.* Beltz.

Spivak, G. C. (1993). *Outside in the teaching machine.* Routledge.

Spivak, G. C. (1996). Bonding in difference: Interview with Alfred Arteaga. In D. Landry & G. Maclean (Eds.), *The Spivak reader* (pp. 5–28). Routledge.

Stockton, K. B. (2009). *The queer child, or growing sideways in the twentieth century.* Duke University Press.

Thomas, W. I., & Znaniecki, F. (1996). *The Polish peasant in Europe and America.* University of Illinois Press. (Original work published 1920)

# CHAPTER 5
# Queered Failure and Management Education

NICK RUMENS

Notions of queering higher education have gathered pace and luminosity (Allen, 2015; Falconer & Taylor, 2017; Msibi, 2013; Rodriguez et al., 2016), but they have yet to extend into the realm of management education. At first pass, this might seem strange because management education is not an obscure dark corner within higher education institutions. It is a highly visible and profitable pedagogical field that continues to attract large numbers of students (Steyaert et al., 2016). While management education is seen as pivotal in generating the managers and leaders of the future (Starkey & Tempest, 2005), it also has a vital role to play in furnishing management students with the skills needed to cultivate and manage workplace diversity and inclusion in regard to lesbian, gay, bisexual, trans, and other nonnormative sexualities and genders (LGBT+). LGBT+ people are an important segment of the labor force, even if they are not always visible and their voices are unheard due to the regulatory effects of heteronormativity (Beauregard et al., 2018; Colgan & Rumens, 2014). On closer inspection, the paucity of queer theorizing about management education is not altogether surprising as the most likely undertakers of this are management scholars. The problem here is that queer theory is not a go-to resource in the grab bag of management theory. Management education tends to place emphasis on a specialist, practice-oriented education that is technical in nature (Steyaert et al., 2016), in which queer theory is likely to be perceived by management scholars as having no obviously productive role.

Nick Rumens, *Queered Failure and Management Education* In: *Queer Studies and Education*. Edited by: Nelson M. Rodriguez, Robert C. Mizzi, Louisa Allen, and Rob Cover, Oxford University Press. © Oxford University Press 2023. DOI: 10.1093/oso/9780197687000.003.0006

Yet, it is recognized that management education has long been informed and shaped by philosophical and theoretical approaches and perspectives derived from the humanities and social sciences (Gagliardi & Czarniawska-Joerges, 2006). Striving for a more humanistic management education can encourage students to foster a critical disposition that challenges what we take for granted about the world of management, raising penetrating questions about, for example, the ontological status of "organizations" and how to reclaim the "human" in human resource management practices. In light of the above, I address the question: how might we approach the idea of queering management education?

In what follows, I argue for a notion of queering management education that concentrates on the fruitfulness of failure. I draw from Halberstam's (2011) writing on queer failure to elaborate my ideas on how heteronormativity can be exposed and challenged in management education. Heteronormativity is regarded in this chapter as a toxic normative regime that relies on and sustains sexual (heterosexual/homosexual) and gender (male/female; masculine/feminine) binaries (Ahmed, 2006; Warner, 1993). These binaries do not hold or validate nonnormative sexualities and genders, limiting opportunities for human flourishing. That management education can reproduce the regulatory effects of heteronormativity has been framed as a grave concern (Gedro & Chapman, 2009; McQuarrie, 1998; Rumens, 2017). As such, rupturing heteronormativity in management education through the idea of queered failure is something that has excited me, not least because LGBT+ people can be understood as exemplars of failing heteronormativity (Halberstam, 2011). Exploring this in the context of management education may occasion opportunities for (re)thinking how LGBT+ issues appear and are approached in management curricula. Crucially, the discussion that follows is not to be read as a definitive account of how management education can be queered. Queering is neither a static nor an essentialist critical practice but fluid and contextually contingent. Queering management education may be confected in different ways, many of which are currently unforeseen, and this chapter offers an assemblage of ideas and speculations as to how we might commence this endeavor. I begin by outlining briefly why and how management education can be understood and experienced as heteronormative.

## HETERONORMATIVITY AND MANAGEMENT EDUCATION

Management education has been a feature of the higher education landscape in Europe and North America for nearly 200 years. ESCP Europe in

Paris, France (French: École Supérieure de Commerce de Paris), was established in 1819, followed much later in the United Kingdom in 1902 at the University of Birmingham, the first English university to offer a business degree. From these humble beginnings in the United Kingdom, something like a revolution took place in the following decades in how management education gained popularity and prominence, to the extent that it now forms a highly lucrative educational offering in many universities. Steyaert et al. (2016) have pointed out that the "field of management and business studies is now the single largest area of research and education in the UK higher education system" (p. 3). Accordingly, debates about the purpose and scope of management education have increased in temperature. For example, searing criticism has been leveled at management education for failing to provide ethically minded leaders (apposite in the aftermath of the financial crash and Great Recession in 2008), entrenching the managed corporation as the most desirable mode of organization, and becoming detached from the humanities (Colby et al., 2011; Grey, 2004; Reedy & Learmonth, 2009; Steyaert et al., 2016; Toubiana, 2014). The main thrust of this critique has been directed also at the business and management schools in which management education programs are nested, being derided by some scholars as little more than finishing schools for managers (Grey, 2002). In the thick of these debates other criticisms circulate, less conspicuous but no less significant, which are germane to the purpose of this chapter.

These center on how management education and business and management schools reproduce gender and sexual inequalities (Fotaki, 2011; Kelan & Jones, 2010; Rumens, 2016). Fotaki (2011) is one of a number of scholars who have exposed and critiqued a dominant masculine rationality, encoded in terms of competitiveness, control, and objectivity, which is pervasive in management education and business schools. Women's relative absence from senior roles in business and management schools is one marker of how masculinity and men's practices have stymied many women (and some men) from participating fully within these institutions. Kelan and Jones (2010) argued that postfeminist sensibilities operate within the master's in business administration (MBA), often regarded as the jewel in the management education crown. They found that female MBA students made sense of gender by accepting extant gender inequalities and/or insisting gender does not matter, partly to avoid being positioned as inferior to their male work colleagues. Kelan and Jones (2010) expressed concern at how management education can endorse such sensibilities in the wider social, cultural, and economic context of major gender inequality. While the role of management education in reproducing gender inequalities has received some but not enough scholarly attention, we are a long way from understanding fully how heteronormativity also operates within management education.

McQuarrie (1998) was one of the first to argue that sexual orientation is often missing in management curricula, even in the subject of diversity management, where sexual orientation is most likely to feature as a topic. Drawing on her experiences of teaching in the management classroom, McQuarrie exposed the prevalence of homophobia, one effect of which is the othering of gay and lesbian sexualities that renders discussion of gay and lesbian topics difficult but, crucially, as McQuarrie argued, integral to management education. Similarly, Chapman and Gedro (2009) hold that, while human resource development (HRD) programs place emphasis on valuing workplace diversity and engendering social change, HRD curricula seldom addresses LGBT+ issues. Clearly, there are problems with management education as a site of heteronormativity that can marginalize and exclude LGBT+ issues. There are a number of reasons why this is the case. Management educators may be uneducated and unconfident educating students on LGBT+ issues. LGBT+ sexualities and genders are complex and often freighted within controversy, such as when they intersect with religious beliefs that continue to link them to sin, vice, and perversion (Falconer & Taylor, 2017). Classroom discussion about LGBT+ workplace issues can be uncomfortable as sexuality continues to be a site of cultural control and regulation, even though sexuality has long been associated with the private realm (Allen, 2015). Another reason concerns the operation of heteronormativity within business and management schools, the effects of which are brought to light in research on the experiences of LGBT+ educators. Studies of business school LBGT+ educators are scarce, and the exceptions make for sober reading (Giddings & Pringle, 2011; Ozturk & Rumens, 2014). Giddings and Pringle's (2011) firsthand account of their experiences as lesbian academics in a university business school in New Zealand is one such example. In light of one female lesbian student claiming she had only heard the term *lesbian* uttered twice throughout her business degree course, Giddings and Pringle (2011) discussed their ongoing commitment to disclose their identities as lesbians to reassure LGBT+ students that claiming a lesbian identity can be something to be proud of. However, identity disclosure can be challenging for LGBT+ educators in business and management schools, as Ozturk and Rumens's (2014) study illustrated. Visible gay male identities within business school contexts tended to be those that adhered to heterosexual norms that endorsed White, middle-class respectability and gender conformity, while identifying as queer was seen to be "dangerous" given its perceived affiliations with sexual promiscuity, radical politics, and disruptiveness. In this scenario, heteronormativity can reproduce a cultural logic of exclusion that positions queer as the other, as something that could bring universities into disrepute (Morrish & O'Mara, 2011). The implications of the heteronormative contours of management curricula and the institutions within which management course content is delivered are stark. Future managers and leaders may not acquire the skills needed to advocate and support more sophisticated, perhaps queered, forms of LGBT+ diversity and inclusion in the workplace (Rumens, 2017). Relatedly, LGBT+ management education students may feel their sexual and gender identities are not recognized, out of place in the world of work, or abnormal. Management research on LGBT+ workplace issues may also be discouraged and/or marginalized, thereby hampering research-led teaching practice in this area.

Acting in a corrective fashion, some management and business scholars have advanced feminist, queer, and critical pedagogies to open up spaces for sexuality and gender within the management curricula (Chapman & Gedro, 2009; Rumens, 2017; Sinclair, 2000). It is in this body of work that hope is kept alive for the educating future managers and leaders that LGBT+ issues are to be taken seriously, and not just confined to discrete subject areas such as equality and diversity management. Additionally, this scholarship has only just started to provide insights into how management education dialogues with LGBT+ students lived realities in the management education curricula. Notions of queering management education in this literature are emergent and empirically open.

## QUEERED FAILURE

Given what we currently know about management education and its checkered record of accomplishment on LGBT+ issues, it is little wonder that queer theory occupies a marginal position within business and management schools (Rumens, 2018). Explaining this, Parker (2016) observed that the "majority of business school academics are not charmed by queer . . . and they never have been" (p. 72). It is precisely because queer theory is seen to be an unpalatable, radically critical theoretical resource that makes it unattractive to management educators. After all, queer theory has no appetite for improving organizational efficiency and performance. As such, management school educators may rationally discard queer theory because it offers little help in teaching students how to manage the diversity of organizations in ways that produce economic diversity dividends, such as increased profitability and job performance. From my experience, when queer theory comes up in conversation in business and management schools, puzzled expressions soon follow, as do phrases such as "far too abstract," "unpractical," and "a theory for the gays." There was a time when these responses would make me frustrated, dejected even, but now they remind me that queer theory has not yet been normalized within these institutions, as it appears to be within other parts of the academy, or so some scholars suggest (Halperin, 2003). In other words, it still has the potential to disrupt, startle, and disturb. Viewed as such, queer theory holds enormous potential for interrupting and problematizing heteronormativity in management education. I regard this as an imperative of queering management education, although not the only one as queering is a flexible and capacious practice, just as queer theory is an expansive field of concepts and theories. At this juncture, then, it is helpful to outline what queer concepts I mobilize in the remainder of this chapter.

The notion of queer failure, or queered failure as I prefer to word it in order to avoid essentializing the dynamic between queer and failure, has been valuable for helping me to think through notions of queering management education. In particular, I draw on Halberstam's (2011) writing on "queer failure," which we might think about as an example of a discourse of queer negativity. This "negativity" concerns how LGBT+ subjects (and others) can revel, embody, and live out such things as shame, refusal, failure, forgetting, and unknowing. Halberstam (2011) acknowledged the work of others who have written on failure queerly. Muñoz (2009) asserted that failure is often understood as failure because it "rejects normative ideas of value" (p. 173). The failure to achieve heteronormative constructions of value, as in how some bodies, identities, and selves are ascribed value while others are not (see also Butler, 1993), does not necessarily mean the end of hope or that we are stuck in the here and now. Specifically, Muñoz regarded queer failure as a mode of politics, one that is about "doing something else" (2009, p. 154), typically antinormative, to propel us beyond current normative protocols and constraints. Sympathetic to Muñoz's (2009) reading of failure, Halberstam (2011) has projected a different vision of the epistemological and ethical potential of negativity. Halberstam's vision of failure is grounded in "low theory" and popular culture (e.g., children's animated films, queer artists, punk and avant-garde performance), all of which run the risk of not being taken seriously, yet harbor potential for thinking about "ways of knowing and being that stand outside of conventional understandings of success" (2011, p. 2). One of Halberstam's main contentions is that a queer perspective on failure can "dismantle the logics of success and failure with which we currently live" (2011, p. 2). Success, as Halberstam pointed out, is tightly bound to "specific forms of reproductive maturity combined with wealth accumulation" (2011, p. 2). Expressed differently, Halberstam (2011) used a particular permutation of queer negativity to problematize a heteronormative notion of failure as a negative consequence of a bad attitude on the part of the individual (e.g., the inability to accumulate wealth) and instead focus on the benefits of failure.

In contrast, failure in management education tends to be defined narrowly in pedagogical terms, such as the failure to meet learning objectives, in the case of students, and in failure to teach and assess student learning, in the case of educators. While there are negative connotations associated with this type of failure, students and educators can be reassured they can learn and recover from such failures, but, in the context of management education, largely for the purposes of reconstituting themselves as recognizable managerial subjects, such as aspiring managers or as "good" management educators. Failure in this instance barely resembles what Halberstam (2011) called queer failure, representing a missed opportunity in management curricula to expose its own heteronormativity and how heteronormativity configures intelligible subjects in the workplace. So, how can we imagine failure as a mode of interrupting the heteronormativity of management education?

## ACKNOWLEDGING QUEERED FAILURE

In one sense, we are all failures. We fail a lot and failure is a ubiquitous feature of everyday life. Crucially, failure is manifestly diverse, and there is one incarnation of failure that can be mobilized as a resource for management educators. By this, I mean the failure we experience trying to cite or approximate the norms of heteronormativity. LGBT+ people are not alone in failing to meet the normative standards of heteronormativity; there are plenty of heterosexuals who fail also in that regard, but Halberstam (2011) singled out LGBT+ people as exemplary failures: "Failing is something queers do and have always done exceptionally well" (p. 3). Countless LGBT+ people wrestle with heteronormativity every day, failing to cite the sexual and gender norms that would constitute them as culturally recognized subjects. We might see examples of these failures in the workplace, such as when gay men are othered for being too feminine in professions associated with heteronormative masculinity (Rumens & Broomfield, 2012) and when lesbians who identify as masculine and "butch" struggle to cite organizational norms of femininity (Woodruffe-Burton & Bairstow, 2013). LGBT+ people who seek to normalize their sexuality and gender within heteronormative places of work to gain recognition as "good gay" employees also encounter failure (Williams et al., 2009) because meeting the standards of heteronormativity every day, all the time is a fantasy. As Judith Butler (1990, 2004) pointed out, there are slippages in how sexual and gender norms are cited, especially when (un)planned digressions occur. In that regard, our failures may (not) go (un)noticed, and for many of us, perhaps, these kinds of failures are to be avoided, covered up, and remedied in fear that we should be disavowed as recognizable sexual and gendered subjects. However, Halberstam's (2011) idea of queered failure compels us to explore how these failures can be embraced and celebrated, whether that be as a mode of identity, lifestyle, or way of life.

One queer proposal is that management educators show students how heteronormativity makes failures of us all. Of course, asking management educators to interrogate failure and heteronormativity in a relationship of failure is likely to raise derision as well as eyebrows. Heteronormative failure seems wildly out of place in management curricula that is so entrenched in producing intelligible managerial subjects. However, queer ideas and politics rarely ask us to adopt the line of least resistance. A politics of queered failure may involve risk, putting ourselves at risk of failing in conventional pedagogical terms, of not teaching management students the "correct" topics and skills. Here, we may learn from students who identify as queer, such as one student in Renn's (2007) research who said she was willing to put her life at risk to campaign for a queerer world in which to live. That being said, proposing that management educators embrace failure does not need to entail putting lives at risk, articulating a roll call of failures, or unraveling the failed self to a point of disintegration. Instead, I suggest we can treat the management curricula and management classroom as an incubator for propagating queered failure. In other words, management educators can galvanize queered failure as a mode of critique and politics in the management classroom to challenge heteronormativity. Such an approach is likely to involve developing a new vocabulary of failure and addressing LGBT+ issues in ways that exceed pedagogical interventions that add LGBT+ issues into management curricula in order to tick a box that says we have created "inclusive" course content or an "inclusive" management classroom. The challenge of queering failure will be formidable in some management education contexts, but in an effort to show how such a project can commence, we can at least begin by reflecting on our own failures as management educators.

[106]   *Nick Rumens*

## FAILING TO FAIL QUEERLY IN A U.K. MANAGEMENT CLASSROOM

At this juncture, I want to connect with wider conversations about queer pedagogy because they can support classroom activities focused on queered failure (Allen, 2015; Britzman, 1995; Kumashiro, 2002; Luhmann, 1998; Talburt & Rasmussen, 2010). Queer pedagogy, like queer theory, resists attempts to fix it as a discrete and stable entity (Schlasko, 2005). In practice, we might speak of queer pedagogies, although this does not mean to say that queer pedagogy means anything anyone wants it to. Queer pedagogy has attachments to queer theory and critical pedagogy, so it has acquired a bibliographic shape. Luhmann (1998) elucidated this, arguing that critical or progressive pedagogy is already queer because, in part, it engages students in the project of showing how bodies are assembled and in whose interests are particular bodies of knowledge constructed. Critical pedagogies seek to question hegemonies and inspire students to critique the limits imposed by hegemonies on alternative forms of human becoming. What Luhmann (1998) named as "queer pedagogy" is a result of what happens when critical pedagogies are queered. In other words, queer pedagogy represents a set of theoretical possibilities for questioning normative processes of "learning and teaching, reading and writing" (1998, p. 151). Or, as defined in Britzman's (1995) seminal work on this topic, queer pedagogy is "one that refuses normal practices and practices of normalcy" (p. 165). Crucially, a queer pedagogy has potential to nurture queered notions of failure in management education.

Contrary to convention, I am not illustrating my ideas with a "good practice" example of queered failure. Rather, I want to dwell on a "failure" or form of heteronormative success that, when read through Halberstam's (2011) notion of "queer failure," can be understood as failing to fail queerly. This idea may include those instances of failure that (in)advertently reinforce heteronormativity in such a way that snuffs out any light for illuminating nonnormative modes of human becoming and flourishing. Pursuing this, I reread my experience as an early career academic teaching a Level 3 (final year) undergraduate module on HRD. I do this to expose my complicity in reproducing the heteronormativity that averts the possibilities for understanding how LGBT+ sexualities may be lived queerly.

It is important to acknowledge the U.K. context of my failing to fail queerly, as other higher education settings vary considerably in the expectations placed on early career academics and how the management curriculum should be delivered (Steyaert et al., 2016). Early careers in U.K. academia can be understood in terms of identity construction, whereby academic identities are formed that later act as markers of subject expertise and knowledge (Crozier & Woolnough, 2020). It is a time also characterized by vulnerability and insecurity (Bristow et al., 2017; Ratle et al., 2020). While U.K. academics do not have to deal with job tenure in the same way that their U.S. counterparts do, insecurity can be experienced in struggling to meet institutional targets and standards of academic excellence in order to advance along a trajectory expected of those wishing to transition to fully fledged academics (Clarke et al., 2012). As such, the importance of attaining high student satisfaction scores, receiving positive student feedback and demonstrating teaching "excellence" cannot be underestimated as factors that can shape, both positively and negatively, the careers of early academics in management and business schools (Adcroft & Taylor, 2013). In an institutional context characterized as such and at an early point in my academic career, I taught an undergraduate module on HRD. Enthusiastic in my ambition to inject criticality into the module, which was previously taught from a managerialist perspective, I was eager to introduce the subject of sexuality and gender into the module. Teaching sexuality and gender to management students can be a fraught business, involving resistance and even hostility from some management students (Ozturk & Rumens, 2014; Sinclair, 2000). One reason is that classroom discussions about sexuality and gender can be inhibited by competing discourses in which gender and sexuality are constructed as private, embarrassing, and taboo (Allen, 2015). Acknowledging this and my fears about how students would react to these topics, I decided to draw on a discourse of diversity management, an approach I envisioned would make LGBT+ issues more "palatable" as diversity management is framed as a management intervention that seeks to integrate and harness human diversity in the workplace. Discussing my intentions with colleagues provoked a variety of responses: Some tried to dissuade me, citing it as a "sensitive" topic that might elicit negative student feedback that would adversely affect my student satisfaction scores; some applauded my "ambition"; while others read my inclusion of LGBT+ issues on an HRD module as "progressive." With this in mind, I felt a trailblazer within the business school, someone who might be queering the management curriculum.

To begin, I used organizational case studies to encourage students to think through LGBT+ sexualities and genders in terms of workplace diversity and inclusivity. Specifically, the point of these case studies was to show how and why LGBT+ sexualities and genders deserve inclusion within the work environment and how HRD professionals can help LGBT+ people fit into diverse work cultures in order to advance careers as productive employees. Rather than dwell on the exact detail of the methods I deployed, I want to reflect on the comments I received from one student, written in an anonymous module evaluation questionnaire:

> Dr Rumens, I love your approach to the module. This is the first time we have been taught gay issues and I'm grateful for it, as I'm straight. But I don't fit into the type of workplace we've been discussing. I'm queer, not gay, so the push for inclusion feels to me like a prison. I can't see queers in your teaching, just cardboard cut outs of gay people. I thought you might like to know just in case you have any more queer students.

I was deflated after reading the feedback. While I had not failed as far as the program director was concerned, satisfied as he was by my overall student satisfaction rate, I had failed to fail queerly. Indeed, Halberstam's (2011) notion of queered failure unearths the heteronormative traps I had fallen into.

One aspect of this failing relates to how I handled classroom discussions of workplace homophobia. Seminar discussions tended to treat homophobia as a problem of ignorance without considering its relationship with heteronormativity. What I did not anticipate here was that new knowledge was required about how homophobia is linked to heteronormativity; instead, we approached the problem of homophobia as an organizational and individual matter, one that required the development of appropriate policies and individuals to correct homophobic behaviors. It did occur to me at the time that we ought to delve more deeply into homophobia's relationship with heteronormativity, but since the discussion was flowing well, I opted to go with the flow. This was a missed opportunity. Apprehensive that I might be negatively construed as pushing a queer agenda by encouraging students to grasp the nettle of heteronormativity, a regime no doubt benefitting some of my HRD students, I avoided the subject and minimized the risk of incurring student dissatisfaction. On reflection, teaching queered failure would seem to me to require a queer pedagogy that enables management educators to confront the prospect that risk and uncertainty among students are necessary emotional responses, particularly if we mean to bring the heterosexual/homosexual binary to a point of collapse. It might require students to reflect on their own investments in heteronormativity and the consequences of surrendering that privilege if such regimes are dismantled.

Similarly, I was naïve to think that simply including LGBT+ sexualities and genders into the HRD curriculum was enough to queer the management curriculum. Although helpful, as noted by the student's comment above, an add-and-stir approach falls short of interrogating how the field of HRD can operate as a technology of power to normalize LGBT+ people as knowable subjects, which in a pedagogical setting Luhmann read as "merely another form of subjection to normalization" (1998, p. 146). Queered failure can teach us that we need to question the core norms that govern what "counts" as legitimate bodies of management knowledge worth knowing in the classroom. On reflection, my efforts had stalled that endeavor. I had encouraged students to engage with my teaching materials in a way that endorsed the benefits of what has been dubbed as a "gay-friendly closet," a closet that permits the visibility of those LGBT+ employees who conform to the heteronormative configuration of "normal" LGBT+ organizational subjects (Williams et al., 2009). In so doing, I unwittingly reinforced the type of LGBT+ inclusivity in which LGBT+ people become overincluded as they are assimilated into heteronormativity.

Furthermore, I recognize how my teaching might have been directed too heavily toward heterosexual students, motivated by a desire to say that it is OK to be LGBT+. While none of the students on the module openly contested this contention, it is underwritten by a logic that keeps heterosexuality intact by making no demands on heterosexual students to question their own or others' failure to cite sexual and gender norms. How heterosexuality is a site of failure is an important topic that has yet to feature prominently in management course content, but it represents another means by which heteronormativity can be interrupted. As my failure shows, if we relax into reciting repetitions of what is already known and what is knowable about LGBT+ people within heteronormative culture, then we cut short any ambition we might harbor in the management classroom to understand new ways of becoming through failing to do heteronormativity.

As I have suggested above, embracing queered failure to problematize heteronormativity is likely to cause discomfort and dissatisfaction among students who have investments in acquiring the types of knowledge these norms codify. This poses a dilemma for management educators seeking to engage with students queerly because discomfort and dissatisfaction create discordance within the paradigms of "good teaching" that many universities favor. Traditionally, feelings of dissatisfaction and discomfort among students are construed as "negative" outcomes (Allen, 2015). Academics who incite those responses among students are likely to be viewed as having "failed" to do their jobs (Alexander, 2014), and in the worst cases business and management schools can adjudicate on whether these academics have no future in academia. As I have learned, queered

[110]   *Nick Rumens*

failure as a pedagogical practice requires from educators a conscious effort, courage, and determination to fail their students well.

## CONCLUSION

In this chapter, I have sought to explore how management education can be queered through Halberstam's (2011) notion of queer failure. Management education is an epistemological site that can reproduce heteronormativity in management curricula content. This should be more of a concern for management educators than it currently is. LGBT+ people are an important segment of the management student body, so the heteronormativity of the management curriculum may be felt acutely by many members of this cohort. Additionally, management students need to acquire the knowledge and skills about how heteronormativity operates in the workplace and what to do about it. As one of many queer concepts available to management educators (see Rumens, 2018), queered failure is distinct in transforming harmful heteronormative tropes of failure into a mode of critique and politics that can embrace and celebrate the dysfunctionality of failing heteronormativity. By interrogating my own failure to fail queerly, I hope to have shown how queered failure is motored by an antinormative impulse as well as demonstrating what is at stake for those of us (not) involved in its practice. I am certain that some management education scholars will dismiss my incursion into queered failure as whimsical, impractical, or utopian. Yet, queer failure is hardly any of those things as many folks, LGBT+ people especially, are failing queerly in everyday life. Importantly, it may be the only way for some of us to live liveable lives, to coin Butler's (1990, 2004) terminology. In other words, failing queerly is a necessity for some of us to flourish as sexual and gendered subjects. As management educators interested in pursuing queered failure, we risk offending students and incurring student dissatisfaction and negative student feedback. Failure, whether queered or not, is not something all of us can afford, and its "feels like shit" dimension should not be underestimated (Johnson, 2015, p. 255). Still, this chapter not only provides some signposts to the obstacles and consequences to failing queerly, but also takes some modest steps to engage with it pedagogically. As someone who is engaged in failing queerly, queered failure holds potential for generating new forms of knowing that alter how managerial subjects of the future are educated and recognized as such.

## REFERENCES

Adcroft, A., & Taylor, D. (2013). Support for new career academics: An integrated model for research intensive university business and management schools. *Studies in Higher Education, 38*(6), 827–840. https://doi.org/10.1080/03075 079.2011.599378

Ahmed, S. (2006). *Queer phenomenology: Orientations, objects, others.* Duke University Press.

Alexander, K. B. C. (2014). Teaching discomfort? Uncomfortable attachments, ambivalent identifications. *TransFormations: Journal of Inclusive Scholarship and Pedagogy, 22*(2), 57–71. http://www.jstor.org/stable/10.5325/trajincsch ped.22.2.0057

Allen, L. (2015). Queer pedagogy and the limits of thought: Teaching sexualities at university. *Higher Education Research & Development, 34*(4), 763–775. https://doi.org/10.1080/07294360.2015.1051004

Beauregard, A. T., Arevshatian, L., Booth, J. E., & Whittle, S. (2018). Listen carefully: Transgender voices in the workplace. *International Journal of Human Resource Management, 29*(5), 857–884. https://doi.org/10.1080/09585 192.2016.1234503

Bristow, A., Robinson, S., & Ratle, O. (2017). Being an early-career CMS academic in the context of insecurity and "excellence": The dialectics of resistance and compliance. *Organization Studies, 38*(9), 1185–1207. https://doi.org/10.1177/ 0170840616685361

Britzman, D. P. (1995). Is there a queer pedagogy? Or, stop reading straight. *Educational Theory, 45*(2), 151–165. https://doi.org/10.1111/ j.1741-5446.1995.00151.x

Butler, J. (1990). *Gender trouble: Feminism and the subversion of identity.* Routledge.

Butler, J. (1993). *Bodies that matter: On the discursive limits of "sex."* Routledge.

Butler, J. (2004). *Undoing gender.* Routledge.

Chapman, D. D., & Gedro, J. (2009). Queering the HRD curriculum: Preparing students for success in the diverse workforce. *Advances in Developing Human Resources, 11*(1), 95–108. https://doi.org/10.1177/1523422308329091

Clarke, C., Knights, D., & Jarvis, C. (2012). A labour of love? Academics in business schools. *Scandinavian Journal of Management, 28*(1), 5–15. https://doi.org/ 10.1016/j.scaman.2011.12.003

Colby, A., Ehrlich, T., Sullivan, B., & Dolle, J. (2011). *Rethinking undergraduate business education: Liberal learning for the profession.* Jossey-Bass.

Colgan, F., & Rumens, N. (2014). Understanding sexual orientation at work. In F. Colgan & N. Rumens (Eds.), *Sexual orientation at work: Contemporary issues and perspectives* (pp. 1–20). Routledge.

Crozier, S. E., & Woolnough, H. (2020). Is age just a number? Credibility and identity of younger academics in U.K. business schools. *Management Learning, 51*(2), 149–167. https://doi.org/10.1177/1350507619878807

Falconer, E., & Taylor, Y. (2017). Negotiating queer and religious identities in higher education: Queering "progression" in the "university experience." *British Journal of Sociology of Education, 38*(6), 782–797. https://doi.org/10.1080/ 01425692.2016.1182008

Fotaki, M. (2011). The sublime object of desire (for knowledge): Sexuality at work in business and management schools in England. *British Journal of Management*, 22(1), 42–53. https://doi.org/10.1111/j.1467-8551.2010.00716.x

Gagliardi, P., & Czarniawska-Joerges, B. (Eds.). (2006). *Management education and humanities*. Edward Elgar Publishing.

Chapman, D. D., & Gedro, J. (2009). Queering the HRD curriculum: Preparing students for success in the diverse workforce. *Advances in Developing Human Resources*, 11(1), 95–108. https://doi.org/10.1177/1523422308329091

Giddings, L., & Pringle, J. (2011). Heteronormativity at work: Stories from two lesbian academics. *Women's Studies Journal*, 25(2), 91–100. http://www.wsanz.org.nz/journal/back-issues/25-2.htm

Grey, C. (2002). What are business schools for? On silence and voice in management education. *Journal of Management Education*, 26(5), 496–511. https://doi.org/10.1177/105256202236723

Grey, C. (2004). Reinventing business schools: The contribution of critical management education. *Academy of Management Learning & Education*, 3(2), 178–186. http://www.jstor.org/stable/40214248

Halberstam, J. (2011). *The queer art of failure*. Duke University Press.

Halperin, D. M. (2003). The normalization of queer theory. *Journal of Homosexuality*, 45(2–4), 339–343. https://doi.org/10.1300/J082v45n02_17

Johnson, M. L. (2015). Bad romance: A crip feminist critique of queer failure. *Hypatia*, 30(1), 251–267. https://doi.org/10.1111/hypa.12134

Kelan, E. K., & Jones, R. D. (2010). Gender and the MBA. *Academy of Management Learning & Education*, 9(1), 26–43. http://www.jstor.org/stable/25682431

Kumashiro, K. K. (2002). *Troubling education: Queer activism and anti-oppressive pedagogy*. Routledge.

Luhmann, S. (1998). Queering/querying pedagogy? Or, pedagogy is a pretty queer thing. In W. F. Pinar (Ed.), *Queer theory in education* (pp. 120–132). Lawrence Earlbaum Associates.

McQuarrie, F. A. E. (1998). Expanding the concept of diversity: Discussing sexual orientation in the management classroom. *Journal of Management Education*, 22(2), 162–172. https://doi.org/10.1177/105256299802200204

Morrish, L., & O'Mara, K. (2011). Queering the discourse of diversity. *Journal of Homosexuality*, 58(6–7), 974–991. https://doi.org/10.1080/00918369.2011.581966

Msibi, T. (2013). Queering transformation in higher education. *Perspectives in Education*, 31(2), 65–73. https://www.ajol.info/index.php/pie/article/view/97077

Muñoz, J. E. (2009). *Cruising utopia: The then and there of queer futurity*. NYU Press.

Ozturk, M. B., & Rumens, N. (2014). Gay male academics in U.K. business and management schools: Negotiating heteronormativities in everyday work life. *British Journal of Management*, 25(3), 503–517. https://doi.org/10.1111/1467-8551.12061

Parker, M. (2016). Queering queer. *Gender, Work & Organization*, 23(1), 71–73. https://doi.org/10.1111/gwao.12106

Ratle, O., Robinson, S., Bristow, A., & Kerr, R. (2020). Mechanisms of micro-terror? Early career CMS academics' experiences of "targets and terror" in contemporary business schools. *Management Learning*, 51(4), 452–471. https://doi.org/10.1177/1350507620913050

Reedy, P., & Learmonth, M. (2009). Other possibilities? The contribution to management education of alternative organizations. *Management Learning, 40*(3), 241–258. https://doi.org/10.1177/1350507609104338

Renn, K. A. (2007). LGBT student leaders and queer activists: Identities of lesbian, gay, bisexual, transgender, and queer identified college student leaders and activists. *Journal of College Student Development, 48*(3), 311–330. https://muse.jhu.edu/article/215257

Rodriguez, N. M., Martino, W. J., Ingrey, J. C., & Brockenbrough, E. (Eds.). (2016). *Critical concepts in queer studies and education: An international guide for the twenty-first century.* Palgrave Macmillan. https://doi.org/10.1057/978-1-137-55425-3

Rumens, N. (2016). Towards queering the business school: A research agenda for advancing lesbian, gay, bisexual and trans perspectives and issues. *Gender, Work & Organization, 23*(1), 36–51. https://doi.org/10.1111/gwao.12077

Rumens, N. (2017). Queering lesbian, gay, bisexual and transgender identities in human resource development and management education contexts. *Management Learning, 48*(2), 227–242. https://doi.org/10.1177/1350507616672737

Rumens, N. (2018). *Queer business: Queering organization sexualities.* Routledge.

Rumens, N., & Broomfield, J. (2012). Gay men in the police: Identity disclosure and management issues. *Human Resource Management Journal, 22*(3), 283–298. https://doi.org/10.1111/j.1748-8583.2011.00179.x

Shlasko, G. D. (2005). Queer (v.) pedagogy. *Equity & Excellence in Education, 38*(2), 123–134. https://doi.org/10.1080/10665680590935098

Sinclair, A. (2000). Teaching managers about masculinity: Are you kidding? *Management Learning, 31*(1), 83–101. https://doi.org/10.1177/1350507600311007

Starkey, K., & Tempest, S. (2005). The future of the business school: Knowledge challenges and opportunities. *Human Relations, 58*(1), 61–82. https://doi.org/10.1177/0018726705050935

Steyaert, C., Beyes, T., & Parker, M. (Eds.). (2016). *The Routledge companion to reinventing management education.* Routledge.

Talburt, S., & Rasmussen, M. L. (2010). "After-queer" tendencies in queer research. *International Journal of Qualitative Studies in Education, 23*(1), 1–14. https://doi.org/10.1080/09518390903447184

Toubiana, M. (2014). Business pedagogy for social justice? An exploratory investigation of business faculty perspectives of social justice in business education. *Management Learning, 45*(1), 81–102. https://doi.org/10.1177/1350507612454097

Warner, M. (Ed.). (1993). *Fear of a queer planet: Queer politics and social theory.* University of Minnesota Press.

Williams, C. L., Giuffre, P. A., & Dellinger, K. (2009). The gay-friendly closet. *Sexuality Research and Social Policy, 6*(1), 29–45. https://doi.org/10.1525/srsp.2009.6.1.29

Woodruffe-Burton, H., & Bairstow, S. (2013). Countering heteronormativity: Exploring the negotiation of butch lesbian identity in the organisational setting. *Gender in Management: An International Journal, 28*(6), 359–374. https://doi.org/10.1108/GM-01-2013-0015

CHAPTER 6

# Navigating Personal and Professional Identities in the Higher Education Workplace

## A Facilitated Autoethnography

CRAIG M. MCGILL, TONETTE S. ROCCO,
JOSHUA C. COLLINS, LORENZO BOWMAN,
ROD P. GITHENS, HOLLY M. HUTCHINS,
NATHAN VICTORIA, SAUL CARLINER, GISELA P. VEGA,
JULIE GEDRO, AND THOMAS NECHODOMU

Higher education is a workplace in a complex industry that employs four million people in the United States (Steinberg, 2017) and "a major economic player in markets around the world" (Koprowski, 2016, para. 1). To maintain production, institutions of higher education must create and maintain a complex ecosystem of people working in a variety of roles, such as faculty, attorneys, health professionals, administrative and support staff, custodians and groundskeepers, and student affairs personnel. Each of these workers has a sense of self and their purpose at the institution. For some of these workers, this sense of self and purpose becomes part of a professional identity, which is based on prior education and academic preparation, life experiences, socialization, professional role, and personal dispositions (Slay & Smith, 2011). Professional identity involves the

Craig M. McGill, Tonette S. Rocco, Joshua C. Collins, Lorenzo Bowman, Rod P. Githens, Holly M. Hutchins, Nathan Victoria, Saul Carliner, Gisela P. Vega, Julie Gedro, and Thomas Nechodomu, *Navigating Personal and Professional Identities in the Higher Education Workplace* In: *Queer Studies and Education*. Edited by: Nelson M. Rodriguez, Robert C. Mizzi, Louisa Allen, and Rob Cover, Oxford University Press. © Oxford University Press 2023. DOI: 10.1093/oso/9780197687000.003.0007

> continual interplay between structural and attitudinal changes that result in a self-conceptualization as a type of professional. This self-conceptualization . . . serves as a frame of reference from which one carries out a professional role, makes significant professional decisions, and develops as a professional. (Brott & Myers, 1999, p. 339)

The social construction of professional identity is shaped by discourse and interactions within and beyond professional contexts (Bierema, 2010). Professional identity is a self-image enhanced by belief in one's expertise: the ability to perform tasks and problem-solve at a high level.

Professional identity is the amalgamation of life histories and experiences, education and training, personal dispositions, mental and physical well-being, and attitude toward work and profession (Tickle, 2000). Professional identity is influenced by the perception and meanings people associate with themselves in terms of other identity vectors (e.g., race, gender, class, sexuality), the views of institutions where they work, and contextual forces (Abu-Alruz & Khasawneh, 2013). One's development as a professional has a bearing on clients in both explicit and implicit ways. For instance, the development of an educator's professional identity impacts the learning of their students (Beckett & Gough, 2004; Krejsler, 2005; Robinson & McMillan, 2006). Professional identity is never achieved or actualized; it is always becoming.

Our sense of ourselves shapes the work that we do, and the work we do shapes our sense of ourselves. Yet, societal scripts dictate that nondominant workers must compartmentalize their identities and leave matters of personal identity at home and separate from professional identities. If we are to be whole, our identities are always with us, including within our professional work. Professional identity theories isolate one aspect of a person's identity: their work role. They do not examine intersectionality of identity characteristics such as physical identities (e.g., gender, race, sexuality, disability, appearance, age); social identities (e.g., class, work roles, professional status, ethnicity, veteran experiences, religion); and political identities (e.g., queer, feminist, immigrant). Intersectionality is a "lens through which you can see where power comes and collides, where it interlocks and intersects" (Crenshaw, 2017, para. 5). Identity characteristics can intersect to create power or marginalization depending on the context.

Professional identity development enhances an individual's self-worth as one gains knowledge, technical skill, interpersonal skill, judgment, reasoning, self-reflection, and self-direction (Paterson et al., 2002). The image of a professional is someone educated, knowledgeable, wise, and skilled, which creates social capital and symbolic capital (Noordegraaf

& Schinkel, 2011). The presentation of professional identity intersects with, complicates, and at times eclipses personal identity in both helpful and harmful ways, as might be the case for professionals who are sexual minorities (Rocco & Gallagher, 2006).

Despite constituting a significant portion of the workforce, the workplace experiences of sexual minorities have been underexamined (Federman & Rishel Elias, 2017; McFadden, 2015; Ozeren, 2014; Schmidt et al., 2012) or examined from a deficit perspective (Reinert & Yakaboski, 2017). When research focuses on sexual minorities in nonacademic work settings, the purpose is to examine their experience as a victim, for example, coping with workplace minority stress (Randall et al., 2017), workplace protections (Rhodes & Stewart, 2016), employee networks (McFadden & Crowley-Henry, 2018), and hostile workplace climates (Kwon & Hugelshofer, 2010). Research on sexual minorities in academic workplaces examined coming out (Braun & Clarke, 2009); homophobia (Wickens & Sandlin, 2010); and campus climate (Vaccaro, 2012). Few studies examined the intersection of personal and professional identities of sexual minority workers.

Pfohl (2004) examined the intersection of personal and professional identities of sexual minorities who were supervised by heterosexual supervisors. Pfohl focused on the power of straight supervisors to mentor, teach, and coach sexual minority subordinates. Craig et al. (2017) found social workers with gender and/or sexual marginalized identities from the United States and Canada desired more personal and professional identity integration in their work. Regarding their academic preparation for social work, many participants believed their coursework was devoid of queer or LGBTQ content. A consequence of this missing content was the placement of the responsibility of educating their straight and/or cisgender peers on the social workers with gender and/or sexual marginalized identities. Baumle (2018) studied activist attorneys and how the changing legal landscape impacted the facilitation of their personal and professional identities. Participants expressed the difficulty of navigating their identities in an uncertain and ever-changing society. A study of LGBT physicians (Eliason et al., 2011) revealed they were denied referrals, harassed, socially ostracized, and witnessed discriminatory care and disrespect of LGBT patients and colleagues. Each of these studies, although in different professional contexts, suggested sexual minority professionals have often been closeted, hypercognizant of their behavior, and concerned with the perceptions of others.

Identifying as LGBTQ and working at an institution of higher education presents a distinctive experience of performance (Butler, 1993) and commodification (Hennessy, 2002). Employees are aware their behavior can influence the perceptions of others. Behavior or image that confirms sexual minority status can have implications for employment (Rocco & Gallagher, 2006). Sexual minorities are vigilant at work, managing their personal identity to prevent or lessen backlash to their professional identity. An examination of the intersection of sexual minority and professional identity and the management of this intersection is needed. Therefore, the purpose of this facilitated autoethnography (FAE; Grenier & Collins, 2016) is to examine the experiences of lesbian and gay professionals in a higher education workplace managing their intersecting personal and professional identities. We are considering the experiences of lesbian and gay professionals in higher education institutions, the nature of professional identity, and how professional and personal (sexual) identities intersect and are co-constructed.

## DISENTANGLING QUEER EXPERIENCES OF PROFESSIONALISM

Queer theory is one lens to examine the experiences of LGBTQ employee experiences in higher education settings. Although initially a pejorative term, queer has come into the academic lexicon to represent ideologies and identities falling outside of the status quo. Queer "focuses on mismatches between sex, gender and desire" (Jagose, 1996b, p. 3). Thus, queer serves "as an umbrella term for a coalition of culturally marginal sexual self-identifications" and as "a category in the process of formation. It is not simply that queer has yet to solidify and take on a more consistent profile, but rather that its definitional indeterminacy, its elasticity, is one of its constituent characteristics" (p. 1). Queer identities position a person as a member of a minority group in terms of their sexual orientation, gender identity, and/or gender expression. However, all sexual minorities do not consider themselves queer or embrace the concepts of queer theory that question norms, performativity, and heteronormativity. Yet,

> the unknown potential of queer suggests that its most enabling characteristic may well be its potential for looking forward without anticipating the future. Instead of theorising queer in terms of its opposition to identity politics, it is more accurate to represent it as ceaselessly interrogating both the preconditions of identity and its effects. (Jagose, 1996a, p. 47)

Queer theory posits that our sexuality is connected to our social existence. Societal attitudes about sex, emotion, and erotic activities reveal a lot about who we are as a society. Heterosexism is the dominant social discourse and is embedded in institutions of higher education as it is in other workplaces, such that

> heterosexism or heterosexual privilege is a system of oppression that reduces the experience of sexual minorities to medical or criminal causes while victimizing through violence or diminished opportunity people that are seen as sexual minorities. Heterosexism sustains a legal system that denies equal protection and property rights (such as marriage) and holds in contempt the personal relationships of sexual minorities. (Rocco & Gallagher, 2006, p. 30)

Certain sexualities/practices are privileged. Rubin's (1984) charmed circle illustrates the ways some types of sex are privileged over others. The charmed circle is at the peak of the hierarchy and encompasses "good, normal, natural, blessed sexuality" (Rubin, 1984, p. 109), in other words, private sex between heterosexual adults of childbearing age in a monogamous relationship. However, those who engage in sex outside of the charmed circle experience "extreme and punitive stigma" (Rubin, 1984, p. 107). The charmed circle exemplifies heterosexism's control over what is deemed normal sexual practice, while highlighting abnormal sexual practices and desires. Negative social attitudes about sexual practice and desire impact individual psychosocial development, sustain myths and immorality tales, and create distinctions between individuals' public and private lives (Rocco et al., 2019). Heterosexism also normalizes ways of knowing and being (Sullivan, 2003), which "placed queers in a constant existential state of questioning ourselves, our identity, and how we should act" (Tierney, 1997, p. 39). This questioning has led to fugitive knowledge based in the cultural work of queer history and studies encompassing ways of knowing not controlled by the heteronormative discourse (Grace & Hill, 2001; Hill, 1996). Queer studies and queer theory help to explain and disentangle some of the complexities that emerge at the intersection of professional and queer identity for queer professionals in higher education. When we tie queer theory specifically and only to LGBT experiences, it loses its potentially radical opportunity for reimagining a different future.

## METHOD

Our research aims to center queer voices in the (re)telling of what it means to be a queer professional in higher education. We situate our work both philosophically and methodologically in queer theory:

> Like critical qualitative research in general, research grounded in critical queer theory "moves beyond" experience (as given) and understands the "materiality" of culture as the historical conditions and the social and economic—the material—structures which in fact produce that "experience." (Wickens & Sandlin, 2010, p. 656)

To this end, we leveraged a FAE methodology to achieve this purpose (Grenier & Collins, 2016). A FAE has a facilitator who encourages others, referred to as "leads," to tell their stories, which might otherwise go untold. The facilitator gathers these stories and acts as collaborator and guide through a four-phase CORE process: create, obtain, reflect, and establish. FAE is particularly well suited for queer research approaches because it provides opportunities for queer people to participate in research while also maintaining power over the narrative as collaborators. The facilitator for this project is a straight White woman, full professor, whose scholarship is focused on social justice specifically in terms of LGBTQ/sexual minorities/queer theory. The leads are cisgender lesbian women and gay men who are scholars and practitioners in a variety of higher education contexts in the United States and Canada. We use the word queer here and throughout this chapter to refer to the collective group of leads and to better encompass the range of complex and intersectional and fluid identities present among them, which necessarily influence, complicate, and explain their experiences as professionals in higher education. In the sections that follow, we further describe our positionalities and the CORE process utilized in our study.

### Create

During the first phase of the CORE process, the facilitator and leads agree on an approach "for eliciting and capturing the Lead's experiences and learning" (Grenier & Collins, 2016, p. 367). In our case, the facilitator (Tonette) approached three of the potential leads and sought guidance regarding the best way to elicit stories about our experience as queer professionals working in higher education. This encompassed process, time commitment, and timeline. The facilitator and the first three potential leads then collectively honed their focus and decided that initial data collection would take place via the leads' responses to a series of questions formulated by the group. The facilitator and the first three potential leads then determined which additional leads should be asked to join based on their knowledge, experiences, backgrounds, and interest.

Ultimately, our FAE team included 1 facilitator and 10 leads. The facilitator invited all but one lead, who was told about the project by another lead and asked to join the project. No one was invited who was bisexual, trans, or questioning. This is simply because no one in the facilitator's professional circle who works in higher education identifies as bisexual, trans, or questioning or has disclosed this to her. The facilitator has served as faculty advisor to three (Joshua, Craig, Gisela) and coauthored with six (Julie, Joshua, Craig, Gisela, Rod, Lorenzo). Seven have produced chapters for a book or journal the facilitator has edited (Holly, Julie, Rod, Lorenzo, Joshua, Saul, Craig). One lead is a recent acquaintance (Nathan), and another is a lead the facilitator has never met (Thomas). Many of the leads know other leads, but only one lead (Joshua) and the facilitator know 9 of the 10 leads. The leads included seven gay men and three lesbian women. Nine leads work in institutions of higher education in different regions of the United States and Canada, and one works in a higher education professional association. At the time of data collection, the leads' professional positions included academic advising, instructional designer, LGBTQ specialist, faculty at different ranks, and deans at different ranks. See Table 6.1 for a listing of relevant information on the leads at the time of data collection.

Once all 10 of the leads had agreed to the project, the research entered the second phase.

*Table 6.1* LEAD CHARACTERISTICS

| Lead | Professional Title | Identity Characteristics |
| --- | --- | --- |
| Lorenzo Bowman | Senior Professor | Black male, single |
| Saul Carliner | Professor and Interim Chair | White male, married |
| Joshua Collins | Assistant Professor | White male, married |
| Julie Gedro | Associate Dean/Professor | White female, single |
| Rod Githens | Assistant Dean/Associate Professor | White male, married |
| Holly Hutchins | Associate Professor | White female, married |
| Craig M. McGill | Senior Academic Advisor | White male, single |
| Thomas Nechodomu | Instructional Designer | White male, married |
| Gisela Vega | Associate Director for Multicultural Programs and Services' LGBTQ Initiatives | Latinx female, committed relationship |
| Nathan Victoria | Senior Director | Filipino American male, married |

### Obtain

The second phase of the CORE process is to "obtain and document the stories in accordance with the established process" (Grenier & Collins, 2016, p. 367). In this phase, the facilitator sent out the series of questions to each of the leads, "[providing] prompts, encouragement, and/or support" (p. 367). The questions asked leads to describe their professional identity, job, responsibilities, work environment, coming out, and management of professional and personal identities:

1. Describe your professional identity.
2. What is your title?
3. What does your job encompass? What are you responsible for?
4. Describe coming out at work.
5. What are the issues that you perceive with being LG/q/Q in terms of your job category/job title/position?
6. What is your experience with professional and personal identities intersecting?
7. How and why would you try to separate your professional and personal identities?
8. What are your experiences with professional colleagues who are peers?
9. What are your experiences with professional colleagues who are subordinates?
10. What are your experiences with professional colleagues who are supervisors or of a higher rank?
11. What are your experiences with students?
12. What issues related to your sexuality do you experience personally?
13. What are the issues you experience in terms of personal identity and professional identity?
14. Describe a time when you had to negotiate your sexual identity in a work context.
15. Describe your work environment.
16. How does your identity as a gay man or lesbian woman affect your work? The way you see your job?
17. How does your identity as a gay man or lesbian woman affect your professional status?

The leads were asked to (a) reflect on the relevant experience(s) and to (b) "recall and capture the stories and anecdotes" (p. 367). After answering the questions, each Lead emailed their responses to the Facilitator.

[122]   *McGill et al.*

## Reflect

The third phase of the CORE process is to "reflect on the stories to reveal underlying assumptions, beliefs, or realizations" (Grenier & Collins, 2016, p. 367). The facilitator gathered all responses and then "format[ted] and organize[d] the stories" and "probe[d] for further detail and clarification" (p. 367). After reading the responses, which varied from 4 to 14 pages of text, the facilitator reread the responses and recorded observations about each lead's experience on separate documents and general, overarching observations on another document. The facilitator's notes and the leads' responses were reviewed again, searching for themes, which were recorded and set aside. The facilitator then organized the responses by question to get a sense of the similarities and differences in the leads' responses to each question.

Next, one of the leads (Craig) reviewed the work of the facilitator. He was selected for this task because his primary research interest is on professions and professional identity within higher education. He reviewed the preliminary themes, responses by question, and the facilitator's observations. After a move across the United States for a new position caused a 9-month delay in analysis, Craig reapproached the data with fresh eyes. He took time to consider a narrower focus on professional identity, personal identity, and their intersection and "chunked out" the relevant data. Saldaña (2015) referred to this process as "splitting," in which the researcher can "generate a more nuanced analysis" (p. 24) by taking a closer look. Through a reexamination of the data, Craig identified five broad areas:

1. Descriptors of the nature of professional identities
2. The intersection of personal and professional identities
3. Issues with experiences with the intersection of personal and professional identities
4. Reasons for separating professional and personal identities (the why)
5. Strategies for separating professional and personal identities (the how).

## Establish

The final phase of the CORE process is to "establish the findings of analysis within a meaningful cultural framework" (p. 367). Craig and Tonette (facilitator) conferred via phone and email. Her suggestions included describing the "range of nuance involved with describing professional identity as a concept," how personal identity (with a primary focus on sexual identity) intersected with professional identity, and reasons for separating personal and professional identity. Having worked out three important areas that seemed prominent in the data, Craig began organizing the "range of nuance" found in each of these areas. The leads then responded to remaining facilitator questions and interpretation, providing feedback to enhance the extent to which the interpretation represented their stories. We describe each of these below.

## FINDINGS AND DISCUSSION

Our analysis revealed three areas of concern: the lack of consensus around professional identity, the intersection of personal and professional identity, and reasons and strategies for separating personal and professional identities.

### Experiences of Professional Identity

First, there was a lack of consensus regarding the nature of professional identity. Conceptions of professional identity ranged from simplistic lists of roles (e.g., scholar, researcher, administrator, etc.) to several pages of factors influencing a current description of one's identity. Some described identities as fluid and shifting over time; others connected their professional identity to a field or role. For instance, Rod identified more as a professor than as a practitioner, even though he began as a practitioner in the field of human resources and organizational development. Craig discussed growing out of one role and into another and how his evolution felt very fluid. Although this was, at times, uncomfortable, Craig saw parallels in this professional fluidity to the queer identity processes he had experienced earlier in life. Thus, queer theory became a means of theorizing professional identity development, building on his meandering experiences coming to terms with his gay identity in previous years.

We found it interesting to consider the range of nuance involved with describing professional identity as a concept. Compare Nathan's understanding that "professional identity varies as it is to enact, enable, and encourage these spaces, but it varies dependent upon my power within the space" to Thomas, who did the equivalent of thumbs up/thumbs down: "My professional identity is pretty informal although I pull out the formal side

[124]   *McGill et al.*

whenever it's needed and even then, it's a pretty casual version of 'formal.'" In its emphasis on destabilizing the status quo, Nathan's response engages with the political power of queer theory to scrutinize the role of power within work contexts.

Some of us (the leads) described specific roles within our self-concept of professional identities: scholar, faculty, practitioner and teacher (Holly); scholar/researcher/practitioner (Craig); administrator, scholar, researcher and educator, human resources professional/scholar/higher education administrator (Julie); academic (Lorenzo); student affairs practitioner, a diversity advocate, and a gender/queer and social justice educator (Gisela); writer (Saul). Others (Joshua, Lorenzo, Thomas) described behaviors. Joshua's identity comes from his active decision to be a "rebel":

> I'm a rebel in my critical and social justice-oriented research in a discipline that is still highly performative and traditional. I'm a rebel in my teaching because I refuse to lecture for hours on end as if my voice is the most important in the room. I'm a rebel in my service because I'm not shy about taking on roles and responsibilities that some may assume should be, and generally are, reserved for more senior academics. Being a rebel doesn't mean that I don't still meet or exceed all the necessary benchmarks and standards other tenure-track faculty are held to; it just means I'm only willing to do those things if I can do them on my own terms, and so far I have been able to.

Here, Joshua expressed his identity as a focus on the quality and timing of work, controlling when and how work is done. His focus on disrupting traditional classroom norms embodies the goals of queer theory and constitutes queering the curriculum (Chapman & Gedro, 2009). "Queer theory is related to forms of critical pedagogy . . . in the way that it promotes more participatory and inclusive discourse" (Spurlin, 2002, p. 97). Joshua's resistance to normative and asymmetrical power boundaries between professor and students, demonstrated by his "refusal to lecture for hours on end" and the concomitant dislocation of privilege, presents a queer classroom dynamic. His lack of shyness regarding taking on roles "reserved for more senior academics" destabilizes tacitly held assumptions about generational privileges that result in fixed boundaries and narrow access to power and influence in academic workplaces. For Lorenzo: "The essence of who I am is embodied in the work that I do." Nathan, "as a gay, practicing Catholic, Filipino American male," described his professional identity as a "conflicted disruptor." In seeming contradictory roles, Nathan "struggled choosing between these polarizing options—either challenge the system or accept it as reality." Although expressed in a different way, Craig experienced bifurcation in navigating different professional spaces and a constant feeling that he was living in "two different worlds":

> I have felt divided in my own job. I had a dual report structure that required me to report to two bosses in two different directions. . . . Although I report to the college, my physical location and the people with whom I most connect professionally, are within the department. Thus, I feel like sort of an outsider in both worlds: I'm not an advisor in the college's advising center; but I'm not a faculty member in this department. I have a unique role. I suspect many of the faculty in this department respect me and what I do, but I still am not *one* of *them*.

Although far more satisfied in his role, Saul also expressed a dual identity:

> I have academic and professional identities in training and development and in professional communication. I have held academic and professional posts in both and continue to maintain academic and professional profiles in both. In a way, it's like being bilingual because when I'm with the training and development community, I know the correct language to use and ideas to cite. . . . Similarly, I know the correct language to use when I'm with the communicators. I take pride in being culturally appropriate in terms of occupational cultural norms with the different groups with whom I identify. But there's actually a singular identity at the core of all this: the identity of a writer, which is my primary professional identity.

The leads' stories indicated an overall tacit acceptance and lack of deconstruction of the heterosexism foundational to any occupational norm or acknowledgment that what is culturally appropriate in most professions is controlled by heteronormative discourse (Grace & Hill, 2001). This absence of interrogation on the part of leads about what it means to be a professional is not uncommon. Identifying as gay or lesbian does not mean a person deconstructs events and concepts using queer theory. Nor were leads invited to join this project because of their views on or use of queer theory. Unfortunately, the image of a professional is of a straight cisgender (often White) male, an image that must be challenged. Professional identity should be challenged as a heteronormative concept so that the experience of gay physicians being ostracized as not part of the professional medical community (Eliason et al., 2011) becomes less a reality. Professional identity built on a foundation of heteronormativity relegates LGBT clients as "other" and their needs as special concerns and not part of day-to-day life (Rocco & Gallagher, 2006).

## Intersection of Personal and Professional Identity

Our second area of concern was the intersection of personal and professional identities. Some of the leads (Rod, Craig, Lorenzo, Julie, and Gisela) experienced our personal and professional identities as one. Lorenzo noted his inability to "separate my professional and personal identities at this point in my career." Julie, "an extroverted person . . . [with] a long journey through developing self-confidence and comfort with herself not only as a lesbian but also as a person who has the good fortune to be a person in long-term sobriety," noted "the lines between my identities are porous." Julie's self-characterization serves as a representation of queer theory; the natural and progressive manner in which heretofore stigmatized aspects of her identity are now composite, problematized, fixed boundaries. There are two mutually informing aspects of queer identity embedded in Julie's observations. First, the very dynamic of fluidity is a queer phenomenon because it breaks down impermeable categories and acknowledges a dislocation of those categories. Second, the *content* of what is being disrupted—sexual minority status and status as a sober person—are also a queer phenomenon because her acceptance and confidence decenters the stigma that could otherwise be cloaked in silence and other forms of closeting regarding these aspects of her identity.

Part of living with marginalized identities is learning to be authentic and open about who we are. For Holly and Nathan, authenticity is a value one must put into practice. Holly noted the importance of "faculty self-disclosures and modeling as one of the more potent ways to depower a classroom (i.e., move power to the students). I often disclose about my family and how this intersects with my growing appreciation and work in critical HRD [human resource development]." Nathan reflected:

> I'm from a world where there is no personal and professional. Where work/life balance is better phrased as work/life integration . . . where I am able to initiate change on a systemic-level by making more inclusive policies and practices. Where all of my values align completely and where I help colleges and universities distill the potential and ignite the passion of the future of all of our worlds. That despite all the constructs and contradictions, I can push the envelope and use my voice and help others find theirs. I am from a place that not only asks why, but questions why we ask why in the first place.

Nathan also discussed his daily efforts to "force" his personal and professional identities to intersect. Both he and his husband work for the same organization, so everyone is in our business. We recently adopted a baby girl, and they all know about her and the process. I don't feel like I could have privacy within the organization, but I also believe that is partly due to our choices in how we live our lives.

Similarly, Gisela and Joshua noted the work of communicating to others the boundless terrain between personal identities and professional work: The personal *is* professional. This stance provides insight into the fluidity of queer identities, individual resilience, and the ability to interrogate heterosexist norms, which would separate queer identities from professional ones (Jagose, 1996a; Tierney, 1997). Gisela described the constant negotiation of these intersecting identities when faced with other identity factors, such as culture and religion:

> As a queer Latina Lesbian of color working at a Hispanic Serving Institution, my professional and personal identities intersect constantly. Challenging and trying to change stigma and discrimination among the Latino community has been difficult to do due to religious and cultural beliefs. This is a daily part of my life.

Still others described the constant need to gauge the safety and wisdom of coming out in certain professional situations or circumstances (Tierney, 1997). Although "coming out" is sometimes discussed as a one-time life event in which one ceremoniously comes out to the world, the reality is that queer people must maneuver disclosure on a daily basis prior to almost every exchange in terms of when and why, to whom, and how much. In considering issues experienced when personal and professional identities intersect, Holly reflected:

> Still having to consider, even in a split second, is this a good and safe situation to come out. Is it worth it? Sometimes the answer is still "no" when I just don't want to exert the extra effort and tolerate the uncertainty of how it will land on people.

Some of us considered how our identity impacts or changes our work. For instance, Holly discussed the self-imposed pressure to work harder to establish herself with certain male audiences in their executive business graduate program. As faculty, Joshua and Lorenzo feared being treated differently because of their gay identity. For Joshua, it had less to do with his safety and more to do with being relatable to a larger audience: "I worry that maybe my colleagues don't take my work seriously because I'm focused on what is seen as a relatively small population's experiences rather

[128]   *McGill et al.*

than larger trends that may impact more people." These examples provide a glimpse of the complexities faced by queer scholars (e.g., managing an audience for safety), yet challenging that same audience by producing knowledge the audiences cannot control (Hill, 1996).

Thomas and Nathan discussed the benefits of working in higher education as gay men. In particular, Nathan reflected on being in student affairs, a field that has long been social justice oriented. At its core, student affairs is concerned with "the whole student," and therefore, a value of the field is authenticity, where one can be open about who they are. In his description, Thomas went further and described the experience of being gay within a network of queer people and thus having opportunities one might not otherwise have. Within his professional context, he described being a gay man as a privileged identity:

> I frequently joke that our university is run by "the gays." There is a family, of sorts, among the gays of academia (even if they're not all as open as each other) and I often perceive that if you're gay you're more likely to be liked by some people and are even more likely to be offered more interesting opportunities over others.

In his reflection, Craig described the experience of becoming an ally. There is a perception that if one identifies as LGBTQ they must automatically be an ally to an LGBTQ person. Craig discovered when one is raised in a heteronormative society, one must fight internalized homophobia/biphobia/transphobia just as one fights racism and other forms of bigotry. Fighting heterosexism means fighting the heteronormative ways of knowing and being (Sullivan, 2003) that cause LGBT people to otherwise *other* LGBT people or not be as supportive as we might be for fear of the ramifications of being "so" out (Rocco & Gallagher, 2006). Queer theory demands we resist our heterosexist indoctrination by using our voices and doing the critical work necessary to make change (Gedro & Mizzi, 2014).

## Reasons and Strategies for Separating Personal and Professional Identities

Third, in investigating the intersection of our personal and professional identities, we considered reasons why we might separate them and strategies for how we could. The primary reason we engaged in separating our personal and professional identities is if we did not feel safe to be authentic at work or for job protection. For instance, as a faculty member,

Joshua noted that although he is "out" in the classroom, he did not discuss his activism work before earning tenure. Being out and being an activist are steps necessary to challenge heterosexism in the higher education workplace (Grace & Hill, 2001; Rocco & Gallagher, 2006).

Being out serves as a reminder that heterosexism as the norm is being challenged. Although Rod has always felt safe in academia, he might be more likely to separate out his personal and professional identities if he worked in a different industry. Holly sometimes has to do a cost/benefit analysis when negotiating disclosure:

> I would separate the two when I feel like I need to assimilate to the norm of my audience. However, I have disclosed my personal identity as a lesbian just to test the reaction of this type of audience. I think it goes to vulnerability. How safe do I feel? Do I want to/feel like experiencing the additional emotional labor of the awkward pause or looks? My disclosure almost always has some disruptive effect, even among supportive people, so I have to be willing to do it. There is usually always a risk.

Thus, even in environments that appear safe and with supportive people, marginalized individuals must always weigh possible ramifications or costs of coming out at work. Saul described instances when he had to assess how open the other person was:

> On a few occasions, I downplayed my personal identity when I get the impression someone may not be comfortable with me talking openly about my spouse. I acknowledge that I'm making assumptions about people based on possibly superficial observations, but as a gay man, I've had to learn a certain level of defensive maneuvering when it comes to human relationships as a means of protecting myself emotionally and physically. I've never had to separate myself to the point of feeling like I was completely denying my personal identity though, I don't think I'll ever do that again in my life.

Joshua also expressed his desire to separate his personal and professional identities as a "form of protection." He described the power he has over disclosing when and how his identities intersect:

> I want to be able to go to LGBTQ spaces and interact with my community without people knowing where I work or what I do, unless I choose to reveal that information, and I don't want my institutional colleagues knowing too much about how I choose to spend my time off campus.

[130]   *McGill et al.*

While queer theory supports disrupting the status quo (Teman, 2019), being out to any degree is often disruptive to those that hold heterosexuality as sacred. This creates a dilemma faced by all in the Queer community: how much weight should be given to safety and comfort and how much to representing the Queer community as a role model (Rumens, 2016). This dilemma is not an easy one to resolve. Yet, the leads in this chapter work in higher education in regular contact with students who desperately need such role models.

Some of us (Craig, Julie, Lorenzo, Gisela, Thomas, Nathan) felt there was no reason to separate identities. For Craig, "It feels very natural for them to intersect." Julie noted:

> I do not separate my identities. In all aspects of my life—friends, family, church, nonprofit leadership and other dimensions—anyone who knows me beyond a very superficial level, knows much about me. I am not advocating that my way of being in the world is better than compartmentalizing, but I would say that it works very well for me and that I flourish this way.

Julie noted the importance of being open and out regarding her sobriety; the synthesis of her sexual orientation, gender expression, and status as a sober person serves an important role in her overall health and well-being. While some of us discussed this intersection as natural or a passive act, Gisela and Nathan described it as intentional and a daily act. They described these identities as "inseparable," and that it was important to model to others "normal" and how healthy it is to be authentic and open. They discussed this display of intersecting identities as a commitment they enacted daily. Gisela noted:

> It is important to me that other queer people of color see positive LGBTQA professionals in higher education. This is something that I have dedicated my life to. I have seen too many other professional LGBTQA colleagues struggle with their professional and personal identities. The fear of being fired, harassed, and even personal safety has kept professionals silent about their queer identity.

Joshua and Nathan were the only two who went into detail about how they do (Joshua) or how they might (Nathan) use strategies for separating professional and personal identities. Joshua described the following ways he worked to compartmentalize his identities:

- He refrains from bringing activism into the classroom;
- Expresses very little about his work in his social life when he is out with his husband; and
- Has little interaction with colleagues outside of work and does not generally connect with them on social media.

Although he discussed intentionally integrating personal and professional identities (even mentioning that he does have work colleagues, family, and friends all on social media), Nathan suggested how he might separate these identities by subverting societal expectations of disclosure:

> It depends on how cheeky I'm feeling in the day and my relationship with the individual/organization but I could just answer the question from the vendor or the random member "what's your wife do" with "marketing and communications" rather than adding a "he" or "my husband does. . . ." So I would just not challenge when there is an assumption made that I'm straight, in particular, now that I have a wedding ring. Additionally, I also think sometimes people norm gay as white, so when they see I'm brown (many people don't know whether I'm Asian or Latinx), they assume I am straight.

Gisela, too, described the experience of passing as straight: "Many people have assumed that I am straight, but I have no problems or concerns correcting their assumption." Because being gay is not a visible identity marker (in the way that race, for instance, might be in some cases), some people are able to pass as straight. In a heteronormative society and from a gay and lesbian studies perspective (Rollins & Hirsch, 2003), straight is the default: straight until proven otherwise. What is our responsibility in outing ourselves in order to push the status quo? What is at stake for the people to assume that we are straight? Do we cheat cisgender or heterosexual people of enlightenment by not openly identifying? Do we harm students by not openly identifying and becoming a role model of what is possible? Do we cheat ourselves when we are not out visibly demonstrating that queer is flamboyant Pride celebrations *and* professional, educated, and living the American Dream? From a queer theory perspective, we should out ourselves, take a radical approach, and speak up (Rollins & Hirsch, 2003). As professionals in higher education, we regularly engage in conversations regarding the need for role models for our racially and ethnically diverse students. Yet rarely do we hear or stand up and state queer students need role models, too.

## IMPLICATIONS FOR HIGHER EDUCATION

Higher education is responsible for the education of vast numbers of adults who develop a sense of community, identity, and morality while pursuing that education. Higher education is a major industry employing millions of people (Steinberg, 2017). The higher education workplace might seem to some to be a place where all people are accepted, professionals who work as staff or faculty are able to be their authentic selves, and micro and macro aggressions do not occur. However, our findings suggest that marginalized individuals still must routinely negotiate their identities even in these spaces.

Many campuses have student services designed to support students from a variety of minority and affinity groups, which would lead some to think this is a sign that professionals, members of these minority groups, working on these campuses would enjoy support and not be subject to macro or micro aggressions. Yet each lead described considering when and how to disclose their personal identities at work. Taking time to consider an action could be an indicator that the psychosocial safety climate—"organizational policies, practices, and procedures for the protection of worker psychological health and safety" (Dollard & Bakker, 2010, p. 580)—does not exist for all faculty and staff. While organizations have a responsibility to develop policies and practices that provide a safe workplace for all workers, how do organizations control behavior of individual workers?

Negotiated identity also relates to allies supporting marginalized individuals in higher education. For example, the facilitator (Tonette) works at an institution with several gay or lesbian professionals working in the upper level of administration as high as provost. This would lead many to think the institution is supportive and open. Yet that is not the reality. When an LGBTQ support group was formed at the university, not one of the more than a dozen LGBTQ faculty in her college joined with her. Nor did any of them want her to connect them to the group, even though they would speak to her about their concerns. One person being fearful might be an individual choice, but so many faculty not wanting to be so visibly out speaks to the university climate not being safe or inclusive for the professional staff and faculty. So, although an institution can have policies and procedures on paper, this is not enough to change culture. This is the difference between diverse and inclusive: A policy aimed at promoting diversity of people and ideas may be implemented, but individuals still may not feel safe or encouraged to be included.

Inherent in professional status is an implied authority, knowledge, and economic stability. This enhances the privilege of the professional who may also have privilege from other identity characteristics, yet sexual minority status is not a privileged identity. So, should sexual minority faculty and staff professionals use that privilege to disclose and become more visible? Could the climate of higher education institutions be changed by sexual minorities being more visible? Certainly, many organizations believe diversity is important and have policies in place to encourage diversity and inclusion. But how can a LGBTQ voice be added to the other diverse voices if people who identify as LGBTQ are hesitant to disclose and be visible? These questions, albeit rhetorical, raise issues that should be further researched and considered by organizational policymakers.

We intended to use queer theory to challenge essential identities and resist categorization, and yet, to examine the work lives of sexual minorities, we have reduced ourselves to a category, professional, and to an essential identity, lesbian or gay. We cannot raise awareness without naming the identity, troubling identity, and seriously considering what it means for others in an organization when professional status does not seem enough in all contexts for complete openness risk free.

## REFERENCES

Abu-Alruz, J., & Khasawneh, S. (2013). Professional identity of faculty members at higher education institutions: A criterion for workplace success. *Research in Post-Compulsory Education, 18*(4), 431–442. https://doi.org/10.1080/13596 748.2013.847235

Baumle, A. K. (2018). LGBT family lawyers and same-sex marriage recognition: How legal change shapes professional identity and practice. *Journal of Homosexuality, 65*(14), 2053–2075. https://doi.org/10.1080/00918 369.2017.1423215

Beckett, D., & Gough, J. (2004). Perceptions of professional identity: A story from pediatrics. *Studies in Continuing Education, 26*(2), 195–208. https://doi.org/ 10.1080/158037042000225218

Bierema, L. L. (2010). Professional identity. In C. E. Kasworm, A. D. Rose, & J. M. Ross-Gordon (Eds.), *Handbook of adult and continuing education* (pp. 135–146). Sage.

Braun, V., & Clarke, V. (2009). Coming out and negotiating heteronormativity in higher education. *Lesbian & Gay Psychology Review, 10*(1), 3–7.

Brott, P. E., & Myers, J. E. (1999). Development of professional school counselor identity. *Professional School Counseling, 2*(5), 339–348.

Butler, J. (1993). Critically queer. *GLQ: A Journal of Lesbian and Gay Studies, 1*(1), 17–32. https://doi.org/10.1215/10642684-1-1-17

Chapman, D. D., & Gedro, J. (2009). Queering the HRD curriculum: Preparing students for success in the diverse workforce. *Advances in Developing Human Resources, 11*(1), 95–108. https://doi.org/10.1177/1523422308329091

Craig, S. L., Iacono, G., Paceley, M. S., Dentato, M. P., & Boyle, K. E. (2017). Intersecting sexual, gender, and professional identities among social work students: The importance of identity integration. *Journal of Social Work Education, 53*(3), 466–479. https://doi.org/10.1080/10437797.2016.1272516

Crenshaw, K. (2017, June 8). Intersectionality, more than two decades later. Faculty Scholarship and Ideas. https://www.law.columbia.edu/news/archive/kimberle-crenshaw-intersectionality-more-two-decades-later

Dollard, M. F., & Bakker, A. B. (2010). Psychosocial safety climate as a precursor to conducive work environments, psychological health problems, and employee engagement. *Journal of Occupational and Organizational Psychology, 83*(3), 579–599. https://doi.org/10.1348/096317909X470690

Eliason, M. J., Dibble, S. L., & Robertson, P. A. (2011). Lesbian, gay, bisexual, and transgender (LGBT) physicians' experiences in the workplace. *Journal of Homosexuality, 58*(10), 1355–1371. https://doi.org/10.1080/00918 369.2011.614902

Federman, P. S., & Rishel Elias, N. M. (2017). Beyond the lavender scare: LGBT and heterosexual employees in the federal workplace. *Public Integrity, 19*(1), 22–40. https://doi.org/10.1080/10999922.2016.1200410

Gedro, J., & Mizzi, R. C. (2014). Feminist theory and queer theory: Implications for HRD research and practice. *Advances in Developing Human Resources, 16*(4), 445–456. https://doi.org/10.1177/1523422314543820

Grace, A. P., & Hill, R. J. (2001). *Using queer knowledges to build inclusionary pedagogy in adult education* (ED481587). Proceedings of the 42nd Annual Meeting of the Adult Education Research Conference, Lansing, MI. ERIC. https://newprairiepr ess.org/cgi/viewcontent.cgi?article=2301&context=aerc

Grenier, R. S., & Collins, J. C. (2016). "Man, have I got a story for you": Facilitated autoethnography as a potential research methodology in human resource development. *Human Resource Development Review, 15*(3), 359–376. https:// doi.org/10.1177/1534484316656658

Hennessy, R. (2002). *Profit and pleasure*. Routledge.

Hill, R. J. (1996). Learning to transgress: A social-historical conspectus of the American gay lifeworld as a site of struggle and resistance. *Studies in the Education of Adults, 28*(2), 253–279.

Jagose, A. (1996a). *Queer theory*. Melbourne University Press.

Jagose, A. (1996b). *Queer theory: An introduction*. New York University Press.

Koprowski, E. (2016). The growth of the higher education sector as an industry: What we can learn from Australia. Keystone Academic Solution. https://www.keyst oneacademic.com/news/the-growth-of-the-higher-education-sector-as-an-industry-what-we-can-learn-from-australia-1261

Krejsler, J. (2005). Professions and their identities: How to explore professional development among (semi-) professions. *Scandinavian Journal of Educational Research, 49*(4), 335–357. https://doi.org/10.1080/00313830500202850

Kwon, P., & Hugelshofer, D. S. (2010). The protective role of hope for lesbian, gay, and bisexual individuals facing a hostile workplace climate. *Journal of Gay & Lesbian Mental Health, 14*(1), 3–18. https://doi.org/10.1080/19359700903408914

McFadden, C. (2015). Lesbian, gay, bisexual, and transgender careers and human resource development: A systematic literature review. *Human Resource Development Review, 14*(2), 125–162. https://doi.org/10.1177/153448431 4549456

McFadden, C., & Crowley-Henry, M. (2018). "My People": The potential of LGBT employee networks in reducing stigmatization and providing voice. *International Journal of Human Resource Management, 29*(5), 1056–1081. https://doi.org/10.1080/09585192.2017.1335339

Noordegraaf, M., & Schinkel, W. (2011). Professionalism as symbolic capital: Materials for a Bourdieusian theory of professionalism. *Comparative Sociology, 10*(1), 67–96. https://doi.org/10.1163/156913310X514083

Ozeren, E. (2014). Sexual orientation discrimination in the workplace: A systematic review of literature. *Procedia-Social and Behavioral Sciences, 109*(8), 1203–1215. https://doi.org/10.1016/j.sbspro.2013.12.613

Paterson, M., Higgs, J., Wilcox, S., & Villenuve, M. (2002). Clinical reasoning and self-directed learning: Key dimensions in professional education and professional socialisation. *Focus on Health Professional Education, 4*(2), 5–21.

Pfohl, A. H. (2004). The intersection of personal and professional identity: The heterosexual supervisor's role in fostering the development of sexual minority supervisees. *Clinical Supervisor, 23*(1), 139–164. https://doi.org/10.1300/J001v23n01_09

Randall, A. K., Totenhagen, C. J., Walsh, K. J., Adams, C., & Tao, C. (2017). Coping with workplace minority stress: Associations between dyadic coping and anxiety among women in same-sex relationships. *Journal of Lesbian Studies, 21*(1), 70–87. https://doi.org/10.1080/10894160.2016.1142353

Reinert, L. J., & Yakaboski, T. (2017). Being out matters for lesbian faculty: Personal identities influence professional experiences. *NASPA Journal About Women in Higher Education, 10*(3), 319–336. https://doi.org/10.1080/19407882.2017.1285793

Rhodes, C. D., & Stewart, C. O. (2016). Debating LGBT workplace protections in the Bible belt: Social identities in legislative and media discourse. *Journal of Homosexuality, 63*(7), 904–924. https://doi.org/10.1080/00918369.2015.1116341

Robinson, M., & McMillan, W. (2006). Who teaches the teachers? Identity, discourse and policy in teacher education. *Teaching and Teacher Education, 22*(3), 327–336. https://doi.org/10.1016/j.tate.2005.11.003

Rocco, T. S., & Gallagher, S. J. (2006). Straight privilege and moral/izing: Issues in career development. *New Directions for Adult and Continuing Education, 2006*(112), 29–39. https://doi.org/10.1002/ace.234

Rocco, T. S., Landorf, H., & Gallagher, S. J. (2019). Dismantling straight privilege: Alternative conceptions of identity and education. In P. M. Jenlink (Ed.), *Sexual orientation and teacher identity: Professionalism and LGBT politics in teacher preparation and practice* (pp. 117–132). Rowman & Littlefield.

Rollins, J., & Hirsch, H.N. (2003). Sexual identities and political engagements: A queer survey. *Social Politics: International Studies in Gender, State and Society, 10*, 290–313.

Rubin, G. S. (1984). Thinking sex: Notes for a radical theory of the politics of sexuality. In C. S. Vance (Ed.), *Pleasure and danger: Exploring female sexuality* (pp. 267–319). Routledge.

Rumens, N. (2016). Sexualities and accounting: A queer theory perspective. *Critical Perspectives on Accounting, 35*, 111–120. https://doi.org/10.1016/j.cpa.2015.05.003

Saldaña, J. (2015). *The coding manual for qualitative researchers*. Sage.

Schmidt, S. W., Githens, R. P., Rocco, T. S., & Kormanik, M. B. (2012). Lesbians, gays, bisexuals, and transgendered people and human resource development: An examination of the literature in adult education and human resource development. *Human Resource Development Review, 11*(3), 326–348. https://doi.org/10.1177/1534484312447193

Slay, H. S., & Smith, D. A. (2011). Professional identity construction: Using narrative to understand the negotiation of professional and stigmatized cultural identities. *Human Relations, 64*(1), 85–107. https://doi.org/10.1177/001872671 0384290

Spurlin, W. J. (2002). Theorizing queer pedagogy in English studies after the 1990s. *College English, 65*(1), 9–16. https://doi.org/10.2307/3250727

Sullivan, N. (2003). *A critical introduction to queer theory*. NYU Press.

Steinberg, B. (2017). Higher education employment report (Fourth quarter & annual 2016). HigherEdJobs. https://www.higheredjobs.com/documents/HEJ_Em ployment_Report_2016_Q4.pdf

Teman, E. D. (2019). Queer theory: Queercrit. In K. T. Han & J. Laughter (Eds.), *Critical race theory in teacher education: Informing classroom culture and practice* (pp. 92–102). Teachers College Press.

Tickle, L. (2000). *Teacher induction: The way ahead*. Open University Press.

Tierney, W. G. (1997). *Academic outlaws: Queer theory and cultural studies in the academy*. Sage.

Vaccaro, A. (2012). Campus microclimates for LGBT faculty, staff, and students: An exploration of the intersections of social identity and campus roles. *Journal of Student Affairs Research and Practice, 49*(4), 429–446. https://doi.org/10.1515/jsarp-2012-6473

Wickens, C. M., & Sandlin, J. A. (2010). Homophobia and heterosexism in a college of education: A culture of fear, a culture of silence. *International Journal of Qualitative Studies in Education, 23*(6), 651–670. https://doi.org/10.1080/09518390903551035

CHAPTER 7

# Shifting the Gaze

## A Decolonial Queer Analysis of Photographs of the Canadian Indian Residential Schools

SPY DÉNOMMÉ-WELCH AND ROBERT C. MIZZI

In this chapter we draw on decolonial queer theory to inform our work with historical photographs of the Canadian Indian residential school system. We met as graduate students at York University in 2006 and over the years have been collaborating together to explore topics on gender and sexuality, education, and Indigenous/non-Indigenous representation in the public sphere (e.g., Dénommé-Welch & Mizzi, 2019). Spy is an Indigenous scholar (Algonquin-Anishnaabe) originally from northeastern Ontario. Robert is a White, queer, first-generation settler in Canada with mixed heritage from Malta and England. We are both concerned with Indigenous representations in educational discourses. We chose to work with archival photographs as they offer an opportunity to investigate what can be considered and expressed as queer within a colonizer-educational context, without it being named as such, while moving toward decolonial thinking. The term *queer* in a decolonial sense is defined as a noun, verb, and adjective; it considers and expands beyond heteronormativity to uncover and share sexual and gender minority histories and narratives (Perez, 2006). Heteronormativity explores how colonialism has imposed a sex-gender system situated within European colonies that renders White, heterosexual, Eurocentricity as universal (Pereira, 2019).

Spy Dénommé-Welch and Robert C. Mizzi, *Shifting the Gaze* In: *Queer Studies and Education*. Edited by: Nelson M. Rodriguez, Robert C. Mizzi, Louisa Allen, and Rob Cover, Oxford University Press. © Oxford University Press 2023. DOI: 10.1093/oso/9780197687000.003.0008

In response to the ongoing denial of Two-Spirit[1] and queer Indigenous identities, this project returned to the roots of the matter by investigating archival photographs and historical images that were taken of Indian residential schools as a means to examine the structural methods that embedded and imposed heteronormativity and gender binary systems within the architecture and design of these spaces. As Perez (2006) wrote: "Decolonial queer theorists must deconstruct coloniality before excavating the lives of queer subaltern citizens" (p. 25). Furthermore, this work examined how these sites are staged in such ways that tended to curate heteronormative expressions of gender by regulating the bodies of Indigenous students and their White teachers in the photographs. The chapter continues with an exploration of decolonial queer theory, explanation of the Indian residential schools, and our research project. A conclusion summarizes key points made in the chapter.

## DECOLONIAL QUEER THEORY

When traveling to a Global South context, queer theory often encounters challenges of being relevant and being understood in a different political structure and therefore viewed as a form of colonialism due to its Global North origins (Alqaisiya, 2018). Yet, certain interpretations of queer theory can inspire decolonial thinking when it comes to recognizing that queer does not have a fixed value. We draw on Jagose's (1996) work as an example of where there can be some congruency in the deployment of queer theory in a non-Western context. Jagose suggested that identities are fictitious, produced by material effects that are motivated by arbitrary and ideological concerns. Queer may connect with other identities, but it is not a category or a state of being. Jagose wrote: "Queer describes those gestures or analytical models which dramatise incoherencies in the allegedly stable relations between chromosomal sex, gender and sexual desire" (p. 3). Jagose recognized that sexuality has been individualized in and influenced by 20th century Western thought and in a way that renders sexuality private and primitive. Jagose argued that queer has the potential to be stronger than promoting nonidentity or anti-identity positionalities. There can be a relationship of sexual identities, behaviors, discourses, and spatial sites that may be regarded as queer. Jagose's views may help address some of the documented exclusion tendencies within queer theory, especially when it comes to matters that relate to race, colonialism, or globalization, similar to how Hames-García (2011) questioned how queer undermines or hides other identities. That said, our goal is not to add race and colonialism to queer theory or to dismiss how queer theory has been rooted in Eurocentric values and colonial power.

Decolonial thinking can include Indigenous queer critiques of historical and contemporary forms of colonialism (Dénommé-Welch, 2018; Pereira, 2019; Pyle, 2018). Decolonial thinking involves analyzing practices of resistance to sexualized violence (Hames-García, 2011) and an acknowledgment that resistance to colonialism is often rendered invisible within non-Indigenous queer spaces (Hunt & Holmes, 2015). As Hunt and Holmes (2015) wrote: "Part of this involves asking critical questions about non-Indigenous queer and trans claims for safe space, rights, and belonging in the context of ongoing colonial dispossession" (p. 155).

Decolonial queer theory draws attention to how Indigenous people are bound to strict heteronormative logics and histories around race, gender, and sexuality, which has harmful effects on cultural expression. Decolonial queer theory, as an embodied theory, does not separate bodies, genders, and sexualities from geography, language, culture, and history (Pereira, 2019). There is an effort to break away from colonial apparatuses and logics and an attempt to revisit and redesign concepts underpinned by White heteronormativity into new and respectful points of connection (Hunt & Holmes, 2015; Seely, 2020). There are three intersecting principles underpinning decolonial queer theory and praxis (Hunt & Holmes, 2015; Pereira, 2019).

First, decolonial queer theory "is an encounter, a project, and a search" (Pereira, 2019, p. 63) that functions to critique and transgress spatial and social boundaries, identities, and subjectivities from non-White and noncolonial positions and to deconstruct queer voices as a "white thing" (Perez, 1999, p. 124). Rather than reifying sexuality and desire as peripheral and private markers, decolonial queer theory centralizes sexuality and desire within political structures and challenges the dominance of Whiteness and Eurocentrism that underpins queer (Hames-García, 2011; Hunt & Holmes, 2015). Sexuality and desire look very different from a non-Eurocentric narrative in light of painful experiences with the slave trade, sexual persecution, colonialism, and war (Hames-García, 2011; Pereira, 2019). Spatial dimensions become more paramount, for example, when struggling to understand the effects of colonialism (De Leeuw, 2007). De Leeuw wrote that Indian residential schools in British Columbia, Canada, "may be understood as multi-directional and permeable sites nested within, yet crucial to, larger spatial colonial projects" (p. 343), and that these projects were designed to spatially disorient, dislocate, and expunge Indigeneity. The theoretical gaze shifts toward the oppressor and away from the oppressed, who have normative language, race, culture, sexuality, gender, and class constructions (Perez, 2003).

Decolonial queer theory confronts and deconstructs oppressor–oppressed relationships; how they are based on White, binary gender systems; and heteronormativity (Muñoz, 1999). Decolonial queer theory centers the experiences of the queer subject and uncovers voices from the past to reveal experiences that have fallen prey to a "white colonial heteronormative gaze" (Perez, 2006).

Second, decolonial queer theory sheds light on and reconstitutes a world preconceived and determined by the White colonial heteronormative mind and the rigid gender and sexual categories situated within (Hunt & Holmes, 2015). A decolonial queer critique cannot reduce, collapse, or conflate political identities and engagements to one issue (e.g., sexual regulation), but rather foreground a historical reality that reshapes multiple identities, realities, and fantasies (Perez, 2006). Euro-Western concepts of "civilization" disrupted and changed the sociocultural traditions and values of Indigenous peoples across Turtle Island (North America). Decolonial queer theory reimagines the production of White colonial heteronormativity and challenges notions of "civilization" through a different racialized, gendered, and sexualized account of human experience, and, furthermore, questions what "liberation" looks like through these experiences (Alqaisiya, 2018; Pereira, 2019; Perez, 2006).

Third, decolonial queer theory integrates analyses of power and desire, and that these analyses are paramount to understanding how subjectivity is bound to relationships, history, and experience (Hames-García, 2011; Pereira, 2019). Pereira (2019) explained:

> By seeking out a counter position to the various logics of coloniality, and by presenting other cultural, political, and economic experiences and productions of knowledge, decolonial thinking alerts us to a certain direction in the voyages of theories, and to a geopolitics that transforms certain people into suppliers of experiences, and others into exporters of theories to be applied and reaffirmed. (p. 47)

Decolonial queer theorizing, therefore, centralizes race, class, and other social locations as part of its analysis of sexuality and desire. It rejects sexuality as a site of oppression that stands in isolation from settler colonialism and, instead, seeks to dismantle colonial and normative structures (Alqaisiya, 2018).

Recently there has been engagement with Two-Spirit and queer Indigenous topics in the literature from various perspectives (e.g., Hunt & Holmes, 2015; Pyle, 2018; Ristock et al., 2019). We also argue that a colonial system forms the core of an assimilationist agenda in

Canada that methodically excluded expressions of queer, nonbinary, and nonconforming backgrounds and sexual diversity everywhere, which in turn silenced Two-Spirit or queer-identified Indigenous people. Exploring the history allows some insight into various contemporary struggles facing Two-Spirit and queer Indigenous people and helps us realize the negative impacts of this denial and systemic erasure on Indigenous understanding of these identities. Ristock et al. (2019) wrote: "Another substantial negative impact of the residential school system noted by the Urban Native Youth Association (2004) is that homophobia is now rampant in most Aboriginal communities in Canada" (p. 770).

While colonial influence may have affected perceptions and cultural understandings of gender and sexual diversity, efforts are being made to counter these biases through education, community activism, cultural recuperation, and public discourse (e.g., annual Two-Spirit gatherings, more Two-Spirit groups connecting through social media platforms, increased visibility of Two-Spirit authors). Though there is increased efforts to counter impacts of colonial heteronormativity, Two-Spirit and Indigenous queer people have been profoundly affected by the strict imposition of Western constructs of gender (gender expression, gender role expectations) and sexuality (heteronormativity) that have historically denied them their freedom to openly express and live as any of these identities (Wilson & Laing, 2018). Recognizing the ongoing work that needs to be done to redress these historical injustices, this chapter continues with exploring the history of Indian residential schools in Canada and its heteronormative and gender regulation roots.

## HISTORY OF INDIAN RESIDENTIAL SCHOOLS

The turbulent history that Indigenous people in Canada have faced, beginning from the point of European contact to the expansion of settler society, continues to be deeply felt into the current post–Truth and Reconciliation era. The historical impacts of this turbulent colonial history are experienced in a variety of ways, with, for example, the imposition of the reserve/reservation systems across North America (Canada and United States), which sought to forcibly displace and segregate Indigenous peoples from the larger society and, specifically in Canada, through the implementation of the Indian Act in 1876 that has served as a political apparatus to suppress Indigenous agency and sovereignty. Furthermore, the implementation of the Indian residential school system in Canada functioned as an aggressive policy under the Department of Indian Affairs, forcing Indigenous peoples

[142]   *Spy Dénommé-Welch and Robert C. Mizzi*

to abandon their cultural backgrounds, languages, and heritages, as well as assimilate into the new "Canadian" mosaic. As the broader North American society begins to recognize some of the historical and contemporary tactics used to undermine Indigenous identity, sovereignty, and self-governance by engaging in forms of land and resource extraction, Indigenous people (writers, community leaders, scholars, etc.) are increasingly redressing these inequities through various means, including, but not limited to, the publishing of memoirs about their experiences at Indian residential schools (Merasty, 2015) or creating film/video and documentaries on these very topics (e.g., Nadia McLaren's 2007 film *Muffins for Granny*), and participating in the development of resources aimed at educating about this history.

From the mid-1800s to mid-1990s, First Nation, Inuit, and Métis children were stolen from their families and communities and sent to government-funded, church-run Indian residential schools located across Canada as part of an imperialist and militarized agenda. The purpose was to systemically isolate Indigenous children from their familial and cultural influences and to assimilate them into Western culture so that they began to disassociate with their Indigenous roots, languages, and customs and, instead, speak English or French and study subject matter perceived more relevant to the project of nation-building (Fournier & Crey, 1997; Truth and Reconciliation Commission of Canada, 2015). The historical impacts of Indian residential schools on Indigenous people in Canada are significant and deeply felt. Though the doors to the last of the Indian residential schools in Canada closed in 1996, there remain the ongoing effects of emotional, spiritual, intellectual, and physical trauma, along with the enduring impacts of systematic oppression and the denial of Indigenous ways of being that still persist. These effects are witnessed through contemporary forms of intergenerational traumas (Smith et al., 2005) and ongoing struggles (e.g., plight of Missing and Murdered Indigenous Women and Girls, underfunding of on-reserve schools). Indian residential schools created the means to "destroy" Indigenous identities, languages, and cultures (Salem-Wiseman, 1996), which has fragmented and displaced many Indigenous peoples, their families, and communities, with Indigenous ways of living suppressed or outright erased. Furthermore, the residue of Indian residential school fallout lingers throughout various aspects of Canada's social, political, cultural, and economic systems, which continue to impose biased structures that disadvantage and discriminate against Indigenous peoples to the degree that First Nations, Métis, and Inuit peoples are significantly overrepresented in the child care system (Blackstock, 2016), Canadian justice system, and the prison complex, and disproportionate numbers of

Indigenous people continue to live below the poverty line. These disproportionate numbers and their relationship with colonialism need further exploration, as does the suppression of Indigenous cultural practices.

## Heteronormativity and Gender Regulation in the Indian Residential Schools

There have been a variety of Indigenous cultural practices and ceremonies (e.g., powwow gatherings, singing, dancing) that were outlawed by the Canadian government until the 1950s. Indigenous expressions of sexuality and gender, especially those that resisted heteronormativity, were also stifled. This exclusion was due, on one hand, to the criminalization of male homosexuality that was introduced during British rule of Canada and the categorization of homosexuality and transsexuality as being a mental illness (Drescher, 2010; Korinek, 2018), and, on the other hand, a gender regulation that reified a male/female binary and rigid gender roles in the Indian residential schools (De Leeuw, 2007). In the effort to regulate and assimilate Indigenous peoples and Western ways of being, Indian residential schools became a blueprint for ways to systematically conceive, organize, and impose systems, structures, and spaces that indoctrinated and strengthened Western Christianized understandings of gender (i.e., cisgender men and women as the only two genders); sexuality (i.e., heterosexuality as the only acceptable sexuality); and race (i.e., Whiteness as a social construct and White supremacy). Indian residential schools that screened out queerness are inescapable and fall under the wider project of heteronormative nation-building and citizenship. What was planned by school administrators was to develop "model" citizens based on notions of uniformity and restraint. A model citizenry considered, among many things, heterosexuality and binary gender systems as compulsory and normalized. Ristock et al. (2019), citing Taylor and Ristok, wrote: "The Christian religious dogma of residential schools erased a proud history of Two-Spirit people in most Indigenous nations where there had been room for alternative genders and sexual identities beyond that of male/female gender binaries and heterosexual orientations" (p. 770).

Erasing and policing of Indigenous expressions of gender took place in the Indian residential schools, aimed at controlling and suppressing nonconforming identities, queer expressions of sexuality, and a spectrum of gender identities through various social, political, and economic means (Robinson, 2020; Wilson, 2015). Margaret Robinson (2020) explained:

The forcible conversion of Indigenous people to Christianity—especially through residential and boarding Schools, most of which were run by Christian institutions—instilled binary gender and heteronormativity for generations. . . . By forcing Indigenous students to speak only in English or French, and severely punishing those who spoke their Indigenous language, residential and boarding schools played a key role in eliminating Indigenous gender systems. The intentional eradication of Indigenous languages erased traditional Indigenous ways of understanding the world, including perspectives on gender. (pp. 1676–1677)

Keeping Robinson's view in mind, we recognize that understanding the impact of colonialism is paramount before a queer analysis. This may mean investigating regulated aspects of gender and sexuality, and other social locations, when possible. Recognizing the history of assimilation in the Indian residential school system, the federal government of Canada issued a formal apology to First Nations, Métis, and Inuit people in 2008 and launched the Truth and Reconciliation Commission (TRC) from 2008 to 2015 to provide a national platform for survivors and their descendants to share their experiences at various Indian residential schools across Canada. According to the Final Report of the Truth and Reconciliation Commission of Canada, 139 Indian residential schools were identified for settlement; however, the commission noted the difficulty in determining the exact figure of all the schools where Indigenous people were sent (see Truth and Reconciliation Commission of Canada, 2015), and therefore the figure may be higher. The goal of the TRC was to facilitate reconciliation among survivors of residential schools, families, communities, schools, and all Canadians (Government of Canada, 2019). The efforts of the TRC culminated in a final report and a "94 Calls to Action" document that outlines what needs to occur in Canada for reconciliation to take hold (Truth and Reconciliation of Canada, 2015). While the TRC did difficult and meaningful work to gather testimonies about experiences from survivors of Indian residential schools across Canada, there was virtually little to no examination of the ways Indian residential schools affected and impacted Two-Spirit or queer-identified Indigenous peoples. Arguably, Pereira's (2019) version of heteronormativity appeared in the calls to action, which came as no surprise to Two-Spirit people due to their long history of exclusion in the Indian residential schools and elsewhere. Yet, at a time when Canada currently enjoys its recognition as an unwavering global leader for Two-Spirit, lesbian, gay, bisexual, trans, and queer (2SLGBTQ[2]) rights, there is a noticeable gap regarding the limited attention and consideration that is given to Two-Spirit perspectives in the public discourse.

For example, in 2017, Prime Minister Justin Trudeau included Two-Spirit people in his apology to civil servants and military personnel who were dishonorably discharged due to their homosexuality and transgender identity. This was one of the few times that the House of Commons heard about or acknowledged the existence of Two-Spirit people in Canada. An exploration into the conditions that shape gender and sexuality diversity, including gender fluidity and Two-Spirit representations, or broader social and gender difference, would address inaccuracies, assumptions, Eurocentrism, and incompletions in current theoretical understandings of sexuality and gender.

## A QUEER READING OF A DIFFERENT PATH: OUR RESEARCH JOURNEY

A decolonial queer critique includes reading how bodies are also racialized and gendered through the colonial machinery (Dénommé-Welch, 2018; Pereira, 2019). There has been research published on the topic of Indigenous Two Spirit and queerness, gender fluidity and expression in different areas such as cultural theory, Indigenous studies, anthropology, and also in the areas of literature and literary studies (e.g., Belcourt, 2020; Dénommé-Welch & Mizzi, 2019; Pyle, 2018; Robinson, 2020; Whitehead, 2018). That said, there is still very little research exploring the implications and impacts of Indian residential schools on Two-Spirit or queer Indigenous representation and identity expression or an understanding of how Indian residential schools suppressed any type of nonconformity (Two-Spirit or queer-identified bodies and identities).

During the course of this research, which initially began as a pilot project in 2013, we engaged with visual methodologies/ethnography and decolonizing methodologies to undertake the critical work of analyzing over 5,000 pieces of archival photographs and materials through the public institutions of the Library and Archives of Canada (Ottawa, Ontario), the National Centre for Truth and Reconciliation Commission (Winnipeg, Manitoba), and the not-for-profit Centre de Patrimoine (Winnipeg, Manitoba). With this approach, we could investigate how colonial structures and spaces were documented through photographic documentation, thus providing some new insights into how Indigenous people were institutionalized through Western educational systems. We observed incidences of White dominance, binary gender systems, and heteronormativity through characteristics of the Indian residential school structures and spaces and therefore theorized potential impacts on emerging Two-Spirit and queer Indigenous identities. We examined and unpacked new strategies and possibilities for redressing this impact by delving into historical documents, including archival images and photographs taken of the schools during their operation, and studied the ways that colonialism and heteronormativity underpinned Indian residential schools by the oppressor (i.e., the Canadian state). Despite the ongoing issues with harassment, abuse, and cultural erasure in the Indian residential school system, school administrators arranged to have annual photographs by photographers unknown to us of their schools in order to document and convey a "successful" model of assimilation happening in each school.

Our research journey sparked intrigue from others. It became no surprise when one archivist commented to us that there was little interest in these photographs and seemed surprised, if not became guarded, to learn we were interested in these very photographs and archival materials accumulated through Indian residential schools. This approach not only helped to facilitate our own experiences of these interactions, but also understand how these histories, as captured through photographic media, intersect with contemporary readings and ways of processing difficult and traumatic histories. Further, the process of engaging this research also opened up a series of questions about what it means to actually engage visual ethnographic research from both Indigenous and non-Indigenous perspectives and through the lens of decolonial queer theory. As explored previously, decolonial queer theory questions the institutionalization of sexuality and gender and brings to light how the photographs are rooted in a White, Eurocentric, heteronormative ethos. Through this lens, we can begin to envision how there is interference with queer or Two-Spirit development through such a highly structured context. From the outset of this research we had to be sensitive to a variety of complex questions around this work, which included asking what it means to take up a decolonial queer theoretical and analytical approach when looking at (re)storying a gendered understanding of Indian residential schools.

Our decolonial queer approach involved decolonizing the eye in which we methodologically examined aspects of gender segregation, racism, White dominance, and cultural erasure. We also analyzed a number of components, such as considering the physical spaces and constructs of the Indian residential school system through space (buildings, classrooms, land surrounding the school) and school culture (uniforms and curricula, e.g., boys made to do manual labor and girls assigned domestic tasks like sewing and crafts). As the work unfolded, we gradually came to understand what it means to examine and understand the underrepresentation, or

SHIFTING THE GAZE  [147]

otherwise outright erasure, of queer or Two-Spirit Indigenous identities in the Indian residential schools.

Although images taken from Indian residential schools are now made available through the public domain, including different archival institutions, as well as reproduced via various online sources, we purposefully decided not to reprint the photographs in this chapter as these are images that bring great pain to Indigenous people and exposes students who likely would not have given consent for these photographs to be taken. Further, while the study of images helped us to better understand some of the implications of heteronormativity and colonial erasure of Indigenous people through representations of gendered space, we recognized that these also come with some limitations in terms of interpretation, reading, and the speculation of queerness. When engaging and processing information through visual methodology and ethnography, Sarah Pink (2013) wrote that it is "a process of creating and representing knowledge or ways of knowing that are based on ethnographers' own experiences and the ways these intersect with the persons, places and things encountered during that process" (p. 35). Undoubtedly, we recognize that this work does not claim "to produce an objective or truthful account of reality" (Pink, 2013, p. 35), but instead it points to other ways to examine such phenomena. Therefore, as we examined the photographs through a decolonial queer lens as a starting point, a number of issues became apparent (or rather were revealed to us) that circulate around the themes of (1) structure and land as cultural hegemony, (2) gender binary dominance, and (3) refusal and resistance. We explain each below.

### Structure and Land as Cultural Hegemony

Decolonial thinking involves an analysis of spatial dimensions of oppression and marginalization (De Leeuw, 2007). Through this analysis, we began to notice that different Indian residential schools in southern parts of Canada (i.e., provinces from the western to eastern coasts) tended to focus more so on tall and wide buildings and architecture/structure, with students and teachers remaining in separate spaces in the photographs. There would be rows of students standing in uniform, and the images of them were reifying stereotypical ideas of sex segregation, with priests and/ or nuns, teachers, and principals standing on the outside. This was different from northern parts of Canada (i.e., the territories), where images were taken more so on the land or out on the schoolyards and blended students and teachers. For example, a nun would be mixed in with the students in

[148]  *Spy Dénommé-Welch and Robert C. Mizzi*

the Northwest Territories, on the land, and away from the school. There was more visible interaction among Indigenous and non-Indigenous people and genders, and there was greater physical freedom than in other regions. There were no displays of Indigenous culture anywhere in the spaces and/or structures.

A decolonial queer analysis of this difference between northern and southern Canada in the context of the photographs suggests a relational fluidity perhaps more prevalent in the north, and that rules surrounding the annual photographs became less regimented in the north. Students are smiling and more involved with their White teachers in the photographs of the north, suggesting a desire within a certain political structure that differently engages the dominance of Whiteness and Eurocentrism than in the south. If fluidity, both in policies and relationships, became a significant marker in Indian residential schools in the territories, then we question where else fluidity exists, and where did it end on reaching the south? Further, we are concerned with the highly regulated ways in which the photographs were taken in the south. It is clear that Pereira's (2019) view of heteronormativity can also be tied to the land and access to it and other public spaces; for instance, students must be "arranged" according to their male/female status, wear school uniforms, demonstrate no cultural expressions, and be serious in their presentation. These expectations were normative and resonated with the school architecture (most often angular and constrained)in schools across the country. Students were meant to show "presence" in the photographs, and yet, a decolonial queer analysis of these photographs could problematize what it means to be present in deeply oppressive societies, what the structures are that shape presence, and where there can be acts of resistance to the normative underpinnings of presence. We explore this point further in this chapter.

## Gender Binary Dominance

We observed in our reading of the images that a rigid expression of a masculine/feminine (male/female binary) divide was dominant across the majority of images. The photographs were largely staged and tightly framed within the square setting so that there is little questioning of what is going on outside the square (i.e., what is not being captured through the colonial lens). The images were prescriptive and hierarchical, with younger students in the front and older youth toward the back of the image. Indigenous students were assigned tasks according to assumptions made about their gender, with girls mainly in sewing rooms or kitchen settings and boys working in agriculture, machine, or carpentry class. Never was there mixing or opportunities for students to explore curriculum that countered gender role expectations. In another example, in whole-school photos, boys are placed at the top of the stairs or on the right side of the stairs, always separated from the girls. There are various written accounts from survivors describing the gender/sex identification division and separation, which took place in Indian residential schools regardless of actual sexuality or gender difference. For example, in a published collection of stories from various survivors, *Speaking My Truth: Reflections on Reconciliation & Residential School*, Garnet Angeconeb (2012) described how during his time at Pelican Indian Residential School he could see his brothers but not his sister, stating: "Although I saw my brothers, I had no contact with my little sister because boys and girls were kept separate" (p. 15).

There were images of empty and tidy classrooms and residences to demonstrate "compliance" and "order" in the Indian residential schools.[3] In one photograph, there was an image of a devil overlooking the space where students would work, assumingly to function as a way to keep students in line and afraid. We shift the gaze here in that while the presence of a devil figure may be used to teach obedience and keep students fearful, it is also an instrument of control. Since Christianization played a dominant role in the Indian Residential Schools, and that homosexuality is viewed as perverse in the Christian Bible, then there will be undoubtedly negative effects on queer Indigenous or Two-Spirit identities.

Overall, these photographs appear to serve as a form of demonstrative purpose, which a colonial agenda is used to control and organize and ultimately to circumvent Indigenous bodies, by means of containing non-White presence within the parameters of Eurocentric schools. Such attempts to rearrange Indigenous bodies and minds, whether it is physical, psychological, emotional, or spiritual, demonstrates how Western structures and institutions were organized and weaponized, while aimed at "correcting" and reconstructing Indigenous expression through a gender binary lens. A negative impact here would be on trans or Two-Spirit people, who would feel their gender expression confined to their assigned sex at birth.

**Resistance and Refusal**

We observed encounters of resistance and refusal by students in the photographs through countering of the expectation by White school leaders and teachers to maintain the status quo. We see Jagose's (1996) work as helpful, where gestures disrupt the stable relations between sex and structure. Further, decolonial queer theory according to Pereira (2019) seeks to dismantle colonial and normative structures that bind gender and sexuality. Yet, we also envision the disruptive potential of decolonial queer theory and suggest through these photographs that human agency can still continue, perhaps cloaked as rebellion or disorder, resulting in encounters with resistance and refusal to comply with the oppressor. These disruptive moments are queer because they are antinormalizing, antiracist, and anticolonial. We observed how these moments in the photographs not only signified resistance to Western expectations, but also functioned as a moment of disruption and refusal that challenged the normative depictions of school productivity and modernity, and consequently the colonial gaze. Resistance to systemic regulation takes multiple shapes. Resistance acts in the photographs can be a turned head, a smile or frown, or a subtle gesture and unplanned movement. Due to technology of that time, photographs could not be viewed instantly, and therefore educational leaders needed to see the photographs after they were produced. Arranging new photographs that involved all the students again in that era was timely and expensive. Since taking school photographs would not be entirely new to students as the photos are taken annually, it therefore presents an opportunity to resist the status quo and know that this resistance would be fixed in history. A decolonial queer analysis suggests that resistance can be useful clues toward understanding a historical reality that reshapes multiple identities and realities (Perez, 2006). Rather than Indigenous students being cast as victims, without agency, and compliant, depictions of resistance toward colonial oppression in the photographs generate a counternarrative worthy of exploration. In deeply regimented environments, resistance can also be nonconformity, such as a certain "look" or a bodily "turn" that begins a narrative nuanced by human agency, counternormativity, and activism. Or, in our case, conducting this research by viewing photographs creates a new line of thinking that institutions may be weary of and perhaps wish to suppress. While sexuality emerged in the photographs by way of symbols that remind students that "good" Christians abstain from sex or do not engage in homosexuality or through using storybooks or fairy tales that promote heteronormative relations, a decolonial queer critique also connects this oppression to explorations of dismantling colonial and normative structures of nation-building. Resistance to the colonial gaze demonstrated different strategies by which Indigenous refusal was enacted through visual discourse. Being forced to interface with the camera (subjected to colonial documentation) was clear in the photographs, but so was, paradoxically, a form of recording/documenting that signals resistance to control and a failure to completely control and erase human agency.

## CONCLUDING THOUGHTS

By and large, we observed through this research project that Indian residential schools maintained a heteronormative gender binary felt elsewhere in Canadian schools, and that this arguably has an impact on ways that Two-Spirit and queer identities are viewed in the contemporary, post–truth and reconciliation context. Increasingly, this research began to tackle broader questions about how the Indian residential school system was used as a means to impose Western norms and policy and moreover how the physical structures of education were used to push heteronormative ideologies on First Nations, Métis, and Inuit people, which ideologies ultimately undermine diversity of expression and gender difference among Indigenous peoples. To respond to this glaring gap in research, along with the desire to deconstruct Western heteronormative understandings of colonization and its systematic impacts on Indigenous Two-Spirit and queer identities, we looked to examine the role and function of space and how the physical spaces of and placement of bodies within Indian residential schools were structured and subsequently gendered in such ways as to enact and uphold cisgender heteronormative ideologies. As a research team we collaborated on this project, bringing together our research skills and interests to examine the implications of gender and sexuality expression in the history of Indian residential schools, which deepened our observations about the impacts of these schools and their current and future implications on Indigenous ways of living. If Canada is intent on seeing changes that effectively and adequately restore Indigenous agency and sovereignty, then it should take coordinated action and considerable determination to dismantle and untangle the colonial regime and structures that have been used to undermine Indigenous independence by breaking its treaty commitments and obligations for more than half a millennia. Part of this untangling process is to disrupt the heteronormativity that underpins the reconciliation effort. Furthermore, as the research uncovered new questions about the problematics of gender regulation within colonial logic systems, it also invited different ways to engage historical implications of Indian residential schools. Muñoz (1999) emphasized "to perform queerness is to constantly disidentify" (p. 78). This point reminds us that through the reading and engaging with archival photographic documentation of Indian residential schools that we encountered a different way to investigate the implications of colonial systems, structures, and spaces that have been historically used to undermine and erase gender diversity and nonbinary expression and the potential of positive Two-Spirit and queer development. What is helpful in this research were the frequent displays of resistance in the photographs, demonstrating that human agency cannot be entirely erased by staunch oppressive educational systems.

## NOTES

1. Two spirit is a term that was coined in the early 1990s as a means of providing Indigenous people with same-sex sexualities, gender fluidity, or identification with the lesbian, gay, bisexual, transgender/transsexual, and queer (LGBTQ) identity categorizations with a unique distinction in Indigenous culture. Two-Spirit people are viewed as "'bridge-makers' between male and female, the spiritual and the material, between Indigenous American and non-Indigenous American" (Wilson, 1996, p. 305). Not all Indigenous diverse sexual and gender identities employ Two Spirit; some may prefer queer, lesbian, gay, or bisexual labels. While we recognize the limitations of language and labels to express identity, we employ both Two Spirit and queer as means to respect both views.
2. In Canada, there is a building momentum to recognize Two-Spirit identities first in the acronym due to Two-Spirit people being among the first peoples of Canada.
3. Library and Archives of Canada have a digital collection of images from Indian residential schools at https://recherche-collection-search.bac-lac.gc.ca/eng/Home/Search?DataSource=Images&q=residential+schools&start=0&num=50

## REFERENCES

Alqaisiya, W. (2018). Decolonial queering: The politics of being queer in Palestine. *Journal of Palestine Studies*, *47*(3), 29–44. https://doi.org/10.1525/jps.2018.47.3.29

Angeconeb, G. (2012). Speaking my truth: The journey to reconciliation. In S. Rogers, M. DeGagné, & J. Dewar (Eds.), *Speaking my truth: Reflections on reconciliation & residential school* (pp. 11–36). Aboriginal Healing Foundation.

Belcourt, B.-R. (2020). *A history of my brief body*. Hamish Hamilton.

Blackstock, C. (2016). The long history of discrimination against First Nations children. Policy Options. https://policyoptions.irpp.org/magazines/october-2016/the-long-history-of-discrimination-against-first-nations-children/

De Leeuw, S. (2007). Intimate colonialisms: The material and experienced places of British Columbia's residential schools. *Canadian Geographer*, *51*(3), 339–359. https://doi.org/10.1111/j.1541-0064.2007.00183.x

Dénommé-Welch, S. (2018). Productive contrary: Counterperformative resistance of the queered-queer, the othered-other. In P. Dickinson, C. E. Gatchalian, K. Oliver, & D. Singh (Eds.), *Q2Q: Queer Canadian theatre and performance* (pp. 255–269). Playwrights Canada Press.

Dénommé-Welch, S., & Mizzi, R. C. (2019). Decolonizing influence: An exploration of queer sexuality in the film *Stryker*. *Postcolonial Directions in Education*, *8*(1), 95–119.

Drescher, J. (2010). Queer diagnoses: Parallels and contrasts in the history of homosexuality, gender variance, and the diagnostic and statistical manual. *Archives of Sexual Behavior, 39*(2), 427–460. https://doi.org/10.1007/s10 508-009-9531-5

Fournier, S., & Crey, E. (1997). *Stolen from our embrace: The abduction of First Nations children and the restoration of Aboriginal communities.* Douglas & McIntyre.

Government of Canada. (2019). About the Truth and Reconciliation Commission. https://www.rcaanc-cirnac.gc.ca/eng/1450124405592/1529106060525

Hames-García, M. (2011). Queer theory revisited. In M. Hames-García & E. J. Martínez (Eds.), *Gay Latino studies: A critical reader* (pp. 19–45). Duke University Press.

Hunt, S., & Holmes, C. (2015). Everyday decolonization: Living a decolonizing queer politics. *Lesbian Studies in Canada, 19*(2), 154–172. https://doi.org/10.1080/ 10894160.2015.970975

Jagose, A. (1996). *Queer theory: An introduction.* Melbourne University Press.

Korinek, V. J. (2018). *Prairie fairies: A history of queer communities and people in western Canada, 1930–1985.* University of Toronto Press.

McLaren, N. (2007). *Muffins for granny.* Mongrel Films.

Merasty, J. A. (2015). *The Education of Augie Merasty: A residential school memoir.* University of Regina Press.

Muñoz, J. E. (1999). *Disidentifications: Queers of color and the performance of politics.* University of Minnesota Press.

Pereira, P. (2019). *Queer in the tropics: Gender and sexuality in the global south.* Springer.

Perez, E. (1999). *The decolonial imaginary: Writing Chicanas into history.* Indiana University Press.

Perez, E. (2003). Queering the borderlands: The challenges of excavating the invisible and unheard. *Frontiers: A Journal of Women Studies, 24*(2&3), 122–132. https:// doi.org/10.1353/fro.2004.0021

Perez, E. (2006, October). Queer subaltern citizens: Agency through decolonial queer theory [Paper presentation]. Subalterns Citizens and Their Histories Conference, Emory University, Atlanta, United States. http://sarr.emory.edu/ subalterndocs/Perez.pdf

Pink, S. (2013). *Doing visual ethnography.* Sage Publications.

Pyle, K. (2018). Naming and claiming: Recovering Ojibwe and Plains Cree Two-Spirit language. *Transgender Studies Quarterly, 5*(4), 574–588. https://doi.org/ 10.1215/23289252-7090045

Ristock, J., Zoccole, A., Passante, L., & Potskin, J. (2019). Impacts of colonization on Indigenous Two-Spirit/LGBTQ Canadians' experiences of migration, mobility and relationship violence. *Sexualities, 22*(5–6), 767–784. https://doi.org/ 10.1177/1363460716681474

Robinson, M. (2020). Two-spirit identity in a time of gender fluidity. *Journal of Homosexuality, 67*(12), 1675–1690. https://doi.org/10.1080/00918 369.2019.1613853

Salem-Wiseman, L. (1996). "Verily, the white man's ways were the best": Duncan Campbell Scott, Native culture, and assimilation. *Studies in Canadian Literature, 21*(2), 120–142.

Seely, S. D. (2020). Queer theory from the South: A contribution to the critique of sexual democracy. *Sexualities, 23*(7), 1228–1247. https://doi.org/10.1177/13634 60719893618

Smith, D., Varcoe, C., & Edwards, N. (2005). Turning around the intergenerational impact of residential schools on Aboriginal people: Implications for health policy and practice. *Canadian Journal of Nursing Research*, 7(4), 38–60.

Trudeau, J. (2017). Remarks by Prime Minister Justin Trudeau to apologize to LGBTQ2 Canadians. https://pm.gc.ca/en/news/speeches/2017/11/28/rema rks-prime-minister-justin-trudeau-apologize-lgbtq2-canadians

Truth and Reconciliation Commission of Canada. (2015). *Canada's residential schools: The history, part 1. Origins to 1939. The final report of the Truth and Reconciliation Commission of Canada. Volume 1.* http://publications.gc.ca/collecti ons/collection_2015/trc/IR4-9-1-1-2015-eng.pdf

Whitehead, J. (2018). *Johnny Appleseed*. Arsenal Pulp Press.

Wilson, A. (1996). How we find ourselves: Identity development and two-spirit people. *Harvard Educational Review*, 66(2), 303–317. https://doi.org/10.17763/ haer.66.2.n551658577h927h4

Wilson, A. (2015). Our coming in stories: Cree identity, body sovereignty and gender self-determination. *Journal of Global Indigeneity*, 1(1), 1–7. http://ro.uow.edu. au/jgi/vol1/iss1/4

Wilson, A., & Laing, M. (2018). Queering Indigenous education. In L. Tuhiwai Smith, E. Tuck, & K. W. Yang (Eds.), *Indigenous and decolonizing studies in education* (pp. 131–145). Routledge.

CHAPTER 8

# "No Queers, No Marching Bands"

## Schools, Social Recognition, and Gender Visibility on the Brazil–Bolivia Border

TIAGO DUQUE AND GUSTAVO MOURA

This chapter analyzes the gendered experiences of young queer members of school marching bands in the Brazilian city of Corumbá. Corumbá is in the state of Mato Grosso do Sul and is considered the capital of Pantanal. Pantanal is one biome (Brazilian Institute of Geography and Statistics [IBGE], 2002) that encompasses the world's largest tropical wetland area and flooded grasslands. Over 110,000 inhabitants are living in Corumbá, and its greater area includes three other cities: Ladário in Brazil and the Bolivian cities of Puerto Quijaro and Puerto Soárez.

In Corumbá, like in several other Brazilian cities, the population that lives in the peripheral region of the city is poor. The people in these areas in Corumbá are originally of African–South American ethnicities. They are mostly of Paraguayan and Bolivian descent, which also grants them certain Indigenous phenotypes and therefore results in marginalization due to their race. Surely, there are families who come from European and Southwest Asian backgrounds, and they inhabit other areas of the city, especially the commercial downtown area. The living conditions of people in Corumbá do not necessarily keep different groups from interacting with each other. However, their interactions result in complex processes that

---

Tiago Duque and Gustavo Moura, *"No Queers, No Marching Bands"* In: *Queer Studies and Education*. Edited by: Nelson M. Rodriguez, Robert C. Mizzi, Louisa Allen, and Rob Cover, Oxford University Press.
© Oxford University Press 2023. DOI: 10.1093/oso/9780197687000.003.0009

intertwine hierarchies of national identity, racial phenotypes, and gender and sexuality issues (Costa, 2013; Duque, 2017).

Due to Corumbá's unique geographical position, the first author (as principal investigator) conceptualized and implemented a study that explored gender, queerness, and expression. All participants in this study were Brazilian, and although they lived in a Brazil–Bolivia port of entry city, they were not considered immigrants. These participants did not need or were accustomed to crossing the international border to work or study in Brazil or Bolivia, but they exchanged goods and were frequent tourists in both countries. Yet, space and locality are two concepts to be attentive to in this chapter, as people exercise and standardize norms within different communities (White & Downey, 2021).

Following migration sexualities and queering spaces lenses to unpack the role of space and locality in this chapter, gender and sexual identities were "constructed within multiple intersecting relations of power including race, ethnicity, gender, class, citizenship status and geopolitical location" (Murray, 2016, p. 3). When there is queer migration movement, the nature of the spaces changes, and such transformations enable the transgression of what is seen as static categories (Fikes, 2021; Vitry, 2021). In this study, straddling two different communities could be significant because there are multiple sociopolitical boundaries that influence movements and affiliations, allowing for greater plurality of identity and expression. For queer people, it may mean an ability to occupy a political space that allows greater "freedom" to express their authentic selves.

The participants in this current study were young queer people (from 18 to 25 years old) who identified themselves as effeminate gay men or transvestites and who were immersed in a border-crossing region where social influences, values, and standards flow frequently. These participants crossed gender and sexuality boundaries daily as they resisted conforming to hegemonic masculine gender and social rules (Butler, 2006). In Brazil, the experiences of effeminate gay men and transvestites vary enormously depending on regional and historical cultures (Fry & MaCrae, 1986), some being more in danger than others based on how they present themselves. In addition to challenging hegemonic practices of assigning gender identity categories (Butler, 2006), these study participants did not correspond to the prescribed script of "compulsory heterosexuality" either, as they were affectively and/or sexually attracted to other men and therefore felt free to express this desire (Butler, 2006; Rich, 2010).

Another key characteristic of study participants was that they were members of marching bands. Marching bands are musical groups formed at schools that consist of percussion instruments and some woodwind instruments. School students, both former and current ones, rehearse throughout the year to get ready for public presentations in the city. Not all participants in a marching band are queer, and you can find a mix of straight and queer people creating music together. Music becomes their connecting point, allowing for relationships to take shape. Their main performances happened in Corumbá during the city's anniversary parade and during the contest for the best regional marching bands, bringing schools from different cities and states as well.

The anniversary parade and the contest were organized by the city government of Corumbá. They were not organized by schools themselves, but educational institutions are always part of the events. The approximate number of participants, per school band, is 50 people. These members include those who play musical instruments and those who make up the color guard. The color guard members are responsible for carrying banners with the name and coat of arms of their schools and flags of the city or state they come from. Part of the color guard group consisted of young people who danced, entertained, and played with different props to engage the audience with the performance (Fernandes, 2018).

This chapter describes a study that aimed to understand how young queers acquire social recognition (Assmann, 2007; Knudsen, 2010) and comprised the effeminate gay men or transvestites who were part of different marching bands in Corumbá. Social recognition here was treated as recognition from people in schools and city spaces, acknowledging their participation and identities as queer members in school marching bands. In this sense, social recognition is something that necessarily takes place through a common path between singular histories. Such a path is cyclic (Assmann, 2007), and this is because "recognition is an intersubjective relationship, and for an individual to recognize the other, they have to resort to existing fields of intelligibility" (Knudsen, 2010, p. 168).

As discussed in this chapter, the social recognition of young queers who are part of marching bands happened mostly because these individuals did not challenge the existing fields of intelligibility that pertains to straight women. Hence, young queers and straight girls were acknowledged for their female gender, which is what is comprehensible for that particular society. Moreover, the fields of intelligibility of gender, as Knudsen (2010) argued, follows a binary systemic organization that urges queer scholars to problematize how queerness is being performed in spaces given as diverse and inclusive.

Data were collected through ethnographic observations and interviews during the marching bands' rehearsals and performances in Corumbá.

Ethnography is a methodological practice that involves observing and participating in the activities with the study participant groups (Magnani, 2009). Through ethnography, a transactional relationship is established, in which researchers intertwine their own theories with those of the groups they study "and thus try to leave with a new model of understanding or, at least, with a new clue that was not previously foreseen" (Magnani, 2009, p. 135). Interviews were conducted with five young queer marching band members and three school staff members (nonqueer teachers and instructors). The participants' identities have been protected, with no personal information or pseudonyms used in this chapter. As not many people who are openly "out" as queers in Corumbá, characteristics such as job position, grades, and schools that participants attended are omitted from our analysis to protect their identities as well.

Our analysis drew from queer theory (Butler, 2006) and demonstrated the importance of school spaces in developing antioppressive and safer spaces. That is, young queers can express their dissident gender and sexual identities without having to be discriminated against or become victims of any sort of harassment. The analysis also explored the extent schools emphasize binary gender expectations, impacting the integration of young queers into a process of social recognition, and considering social markers (e.g., nationality, religion) other than sex and gender determinants that influence identity and expression. In the next section, we unpack queer theory as a theoretical framework, following Butler's (2006) notion of representation of more fluid concepts of gender and sexualities. We then present the context of the study in more detail, exploring the ways young queers from school marching bands "perform" within a border context. Though the study participants did not cross international borders, the social context (e.g., people in the border community) and space (e.g., port of entry city) contained rich possibilities to enact meaningful and impactful experiences for queer people (White & Downey, 2021). Next, we discuss the role that young queers play in school marching bands in terms of gender and sexual identities. Finally, we analyze the process of social recognition that queer participants obtained through school marching bands. Overall, this chapter critiques the type of knowledge schools still promote in relation to emphasizing male and female expectations and not allowing young queers to perform masculine roles, for example, which limits the social recognition of young queers who can disrupt such binary gender systems. This criticism can be useful for the development of more antioppressive educational practices (Kumashiro, 2000) that disrupt boundaries and explore the significance of space.

## THE QUEER IN QUEERS: REIMAGINING IDENTITIES IN CORUMBÁ

Corumbá, as a diverse, energetic, and dynamic city on the border of Brazil and Bolivia, attracts different individuals for its carnival events, parades, and school marching band competitions. Within these festivities, the image of effeminate queer people can be a result of a cultural elaboration (Kulick, 1997). As an example, historically, feminine queer gays and transvestites "were most exuberantly visible during Brazil's Carnival, and any depiction or analysis of the festival would inevitably include at least a passing reference to them, because their gender inversions were often invoked as embodiments of the Carnival spirit" (Kulick, 1997, p. 575).

The term *queer* has been used in various research contexts as a nonconventional political inquiry (Jagose, 1996). Queer theorists in the 1990s started questioning gender expectation, gender bias, and heterosexism, which prompted a movement that challenged binary identity stereotypes (Butler, 2006; Jagose, 1996; Talburt & Rasmussen, 2010). Since then, in education for instance, queer studies have

> much to say about the production of the social and the social production of institutions; relations between citizenship, nation, pedagogy, and identity; and how young people are positioned by and position themselves in relation to institutions, social imaginaries, everyday public pedagogies, and popular culture. (Talburt & Rasmussen, 2010, p. 2)

This view of queer theories in education and its relation to the social aspect of people is important in the context of Corumbá because, we argue, queer people in that region are regulated and subsumed into traditional feminine and masculine roles. Within the queer community for instance, gay men could be either too masculine or too feminine, and their expectations evolve around masculinity being a synonym of dominance and femininity being a more passive role (Kulick, 2008). In Corumbá, young queers' experiences are overlooked by their gender expectations once they still reiterate gender standards.

That is, the effeminate gay men and transvestites in Corumbá commonly assume functions (e.g., jobs) that are more feminine, such as hairdressers, choreographers, and dancers. As mentioned in this chapter, the participation of these young queers in school marching bands also reiterates that flamboyant gay men and transvestites are accepted as long as they perform the feminine gender roles expected from individuals who identify themselves as following women's standards. Building on the notion of gender expectation, Seffner (2011) provoked notions of adequate behavior by saying that we need the strength of *bichas* ("effeminate gay men") to change the world. Disrupting binary concepts, even among queer people, requires transgressing gender and sexual norms as "one serious problem with this way of distinguishing between gender and sexuality is that, while denaturalizing sexual object-choice, it radically renaturalizes gender" (Sedgwick, 1993, p. 155).

Queer theory offers a deeper analysis about what diversity really looks like among nonqueer and queer experiences, particularly of those who occupy an "in-between" space. We challenge Corumbá's cultural outcomes of how society sees effeminate gay men and transvestites as we argue that a more critical lens is needed to problematize how the participation of young queers in school marching bands can corroborate to the dismantling of gender norms. We value the historical battles of queer theories against binary social functions and systems but propose that researchers better understand that male–female role expectations can still be rooted in queer research (Talburt & Rasmussen, 2010).

This study acknowledged that spaces in Corumbá "are seen as queer or having a queer effect" (Vitry, 2021, p. 942). However, our findings and discussions are paramount to broad queer research and queering spaces theories in the sense of questioning how much transgression of dominant binarism is essentially happening (Fikes, 2021) in such spaces. Furthermore, this chapter contrasts the different queer spaces defined by Fikes (2021) as personal and intimate spaces; city and public spaces; and larger geographies and the global spaces. For instance, from the young queers' personal and intimate stance, they are being seen and recognized as effeminate gay men and transvestites who perform the female gender expectations. From the city and public space perspective, there is a social response toward young queers' participation in such spaces, but that is because young queers' bodies are not disrupting gender binaries. Then, geographically and/or globally, the participation of young queers in marching bands does not challenge regimes of power and knowledge that oppress, exclude, and even kill queer people in the country (De Souza & Pádua Carrieri, 2015).

## YOUNG QUEERS ON THE BRAZIL–BOLIVIA BORDER: WHEN ONE SIDE IS DIVERSE BUT NOT THE OTHER

While in Corumbá, several participants reflected on the diversity of the city as different groups of people gathered in municipal and school events. For the young queers from marching bands, coexisting in a city like Corumbá, where people from different cultures come together, is part of the narratives of many who live in the region. On the national level, however, Brazil has one of the highest numbers of cases of violence against queer people in the world, and that number is greater in intersections of BIPOC (Black, indigenous, and people of color) and queer communities. The National Association of Transvestites and Transexuals (Benevites, 2022) indicated the average number of murders of transvestites and transsexuals from 2008 to 2021 was 123.8 murders/year. Another survey developed by the Gay Group of Bahia (Michels & Motti, 2018) concluded that Mato Grosso do Sul, the state where Corumbá is located, is the eighth most violent and dangerous place for queers in the country. The Brazilian Lesbian, Gay, Bisexual, and Transgender Organization also revealed that more than 60% of young Brazilians felt unsafe in their schools when expressing their sexual identities, and more than 40% are concerned about their safety when it comes to conveying their gender identities. These high percentages may be explained when educational institutions remain oblivious to how they perpetrate homophobic and transphobic behaviors and violence (Junqueira, 2009) in the country.

Despite the terrorizing scenario for queer people in Brazil, Corumbá does not fit into the national standards of violence and harassment against queers according to participants of the study. The participants felt that their queerness is celebrated when people "applaud the queers" (Participant) on the streets during school marching bands presentations, for example. Social applause becomes a form of social recognition for young queers, who understand that they can be accepted for who they are. Because school marching bands are embedded in a broader set of cultural activities within the city that include a varied range of people of different nationalities, races, class, sexual and gender identities, and religions, diversity is central to the participants' view that "Corumbá is a city free of homophobia" (Participant).

Indeed, one participant in the study shared that she was able to wear makeup and have her hair neatly done to engage the audience. She realized that regardless of her queer identity expressions (mostly through clothes, accessories, and mannerisms), people from different ages were watching her perform and enjoying it. Safety was not a concern for this participant. For two flamboyant boys, who played the cymbal among the girls, wearing the same uniform, props, and glitter makeup as the girls did not lessen their roles in the marching bands. While other boys were executing more masculine roles in the band (e.g., playing heavier and specific musical instruments), queers and nonqueers had flexibility to develop whichever role they felt most comfortable.

Drawing from Butler's (2006) work involving gender expectations, student groups were expected to act according to their gender functions, following the social matrix of intelligibility that determines what males and females ought to do (e.g., females play the cymbal in marching bands, males play heavier instruments, and young queers act according to female expectations as they are seen as feminine individuals). According to the participants of the study, queers and nonqueers are able to share the same space "without the fear of homophobic slurs" (Participant), and the participant attributed this to the geographical location of the city. The border location made it easy for diverse people to be integrated in different events that attract local, national, and international audiences. When plurality is a foundation of a constructed space, perhaps there is opportunity for greater queer expression.

The city is also a space for inclusive events for queer people, including gay-themed contests and matches (e.g., Miss Gay, Gay Muse of Carnival, and a queer soccer match). Assuredly, such events are important spaces for effeminate gay men's and transvestites' socialization and learning, mostly because the city does not have any gay bars or pubs, queer shops, or queer institutions (e.g., resource centers). Because of that, a more critical lens is needed to identify whether Corumbá is, in fact, a homophobia-free zone. For example, at the same time the city is advertising a soccer match by saying it is "the party of joy against prejudice," local newspaper headlines are showing "a 29-year-old transvestite being stabbed to death" (Diário Online, 2013) and "a man being assaulted in downtown Corumbá for dating a transvestite" (Silva, 2015).

The contrast between participants' views of queer acceptance and safety, and the news about homophobic and transphobic assaults in the area highlights a controversial issue created by the geographical location of Corumbá. Brazilians associate that people from the Bolivian side of the border are the ones full of prejudice and judgment. Historically, any Brazilian city that is a port of entry to any other country in South America has been associated with prejudice, misogyny, drug dealing, robbery, and danger to Brazilian citizens (Oliveira & Campos, 2012). The negative and dangerous aspects of the border regions become a cultural problem as they are deposited onto the figure of the other (Duque, 2017).

The belief that Corumbá is not homophobic was strengthened by the experiences of effeminate gay men and transvestites from the marching bands, who felt celebrated because it is the Bolivians who are seen as the strict and narrow-minded ones. One participant shared that in Bolivia: "There are no gay people at the border, I have never seen it." The derogatory use of the term "the border" (Costa, 2013) is used to describe the Bolivian town in the border region, and when deploying it, the Brazilian participants dissociate themselves from that location. The border, in all its negative effects, belongs to the Bolivians only and is part of a broader stigmatization effort (Banducci Júnior et al., 2019). Unfortunately, this study did not approach how Bolivians feel or act toward such prejudice against them, which implicates future studies need to further analyze the different individuals' experiences in a border context.

Brazilian citizens from Corumbá seek to erase the stigma of being associated with the border region and differentiate themselves from the Bolivians (others), who are the supposedly homophobic/transphobic ones in this scenario. These calculated actions of Brazilian people shape the power dynamics and constructions of subjectivities in the local contexts once they are valuing a "nonprejudiced" national identity of the Brazilian city of Corumbá. Local marching bands may be one space where these power dynamics play out as Brazilian people accuse Bolivians of having prejudice but not recognize that they are also part of the audience that applauds young queers and their marching bands. Avoiding acknowledging the latter highlights the power relations of Brazilians when they consider themselves morally more superior than the Bolivians. The power dynamics in this context impede Brazilians to realize the self versus other binary interlocution they portray, which consequently reflects that they also carry prejudices that affect young queers.

## SCHOOL MARCHING BANDS AND YOUNG QUEERS: ARE THEY REALLY DISRUPTING GENDER ROLES?

During rehearsals, family members, relatives, and friends of the members of the marching bands gather around the court, creating opportunities for interaction with one another. In one rehearsal observation, gendered expectations were emphasized in groups that had more masculine-looking boys playing heavier or other specific instruments and never being part of the choreographies of the color guard or of playing the cymbal, which is typically given to girls to play. However, it is also noticeable that the young queers cross such gender and sexuality boundaries as there are those who express their femininity in dance choreographies and engage performances normally reserved for girls (e.g., playing the cymbal and performing in the color guard).

When analyzing the role of schools in practices of cultural regulation, it is important to note that the experiences of sexual and gender visibility are seen in the ways they are performed in public spaces (Miskolci, 2014). In presentations of the school marching bands, for example, such visibility "translates into a sophisticated power relationship, as it is not based on direct prohibitions, but on indirect and highly efficient ways of managing what can be visible and acceptable in everyday life" (Miskolci, 2014, p. 62). That means young effeminate gay men and transvestites are not forbidden to participate in school bands and not discriminated against within those environments. However, their participation is limited to only female roles, and in the case of the more effeminate boys, we do not observe them playing or being a part of the band traditionally reserved for men.

This can be a sign of implicit discrimination (Fernandes, 2018) once the gender expectations in the marching bands are neither explicitly stated nor presented as a rule by the band instructors. There is not a specific rule that determines the role of each participant in the marching bands. The cultural elaboration of a regime of gender visibility, for instance, guarantees young queers' recognition in nonofficial terms. That means effeminate gay men and transvestites are able to be seen as queering the marching bands and the different spaces where they perform, but do not have the effect of reconceiving fixed notions of masculinity and femininity in those contexts (Fikes, 2021; Vitry, 2021).

Visibility, in the context of the study participants, had to do with the acceptance of these groups of people in roles originally given to girls. But at the same time, the limitation of such visibility and acceptance has historical roots in restrictions imposed by gender roles (Butler, 2006). Effeminate men, for example, are limited to female roles only due to their gender expression, but this is not bidirectional whereby women can play instruments traditionally reserved for men. These study participants were taught a series of codes and values that function as a type of grammar on how to act and be visible as queers (Passamani, 2018). Effeminacy seems to be guiding this pedagogy.

Through a queer lens (Butler, 2006; Louro, 2004; Miskolci, 2016), the effeminate gay men and transvestites are visible as young queers, but do not disrupt sexual and gender identities paradigms. These participants are gathering with nonqueer people as well, but their socialization is performed according to the expectations around being more feminine queer people. Moreover, the participants manage to be seen as trailblazers in terms of personal gender intelligibility, but in the broader social aspect of it, they do not press the boundaries of the binary male and female roles (Duque, 2019).

According to the gender intelligibility matrix by Butler (2006), the effeminacy of gay men and transvestites breaks the model male sex = male gender = desire for the opposite sex. In this context, these participants diverged from gender expectations as there was a failure to comply with the model previously mentioned. Though assigned as males at birth, these gay men and transvestites were effeminate, which dissociates from the dominant male gender stereotype. On a desire level, another disconnection to the gender matrix is that these participants are affectively and/or sexually attracted to other men rather than being attracted to the "opposite sex." Such intelligibilities do not marginalize these young queers; the same holds for their roles in the marching bands, but their performances can result in gender comparisons between what men assigned at birth, who are effeminate gay and transvestites, and straight men can do, and instances of homophobia as young queers do not perform masculine roles.

In Brazil, the construction of gender and sexuality knowledges is still binary, and this binary system implies that individuals' genders are revealed according to the gender matrix of intelligibility (Butler, 2006). For instance, effeminate gay men and transvestites cannot be seen playing a more masculine role because that would disrupt the gender binary framework (Kulick, 2008). Such a system is a threat to society as it normalizes social attitudes and behaviors and produces a unique mode of identification that can become a source of oppression, even for queer people.

For example, young queers are accepted in school marching bands as long as they "fit" into the traditional female gender roles. If, on the contrary, a nonqueer, straight male young person wanted to play the cymbal, that member would not have the same recognition since that is assigned to female or effeminate male members only. Therefore, queers in this study were still constrained to band functions that are assigned to straight female girls in light of their effeminate features. When thinking of the different band functions and who is assigned to them, the binary concepts of gender roles are not part of a discussion that schools and teachers approach in their rehearsals or day-to-day practices, which does not promote and reinforce a disruptive knowledge of gender systems and how they should work (Kumashiro, 2002; Miskolci, 2016). There is a missed opportunity for schools and band leaders to dismantle traditional gender roles, explore conceptualizations with masculinity and femininity, and deepen plurality.

This study demonstrated that young queers in marching bands do not disrupt assigned gender roles. The study participants' effeminacy was perceived as a weak femininity (i.e., they were assigned flamboyant and less strenuous roles in the marching band) and were not considered masculine in their own way. In terms of sexuality, they were still consistent with the expectations of desire within a binary system. For instance, this occurred even though knowing that the "desire to be penetrated" is much more in the binary cultural imaginary of Brazilians when it comes to the sexuality of effeminate gays or transvestites than in the practice itself of sexuality of these queer people. Despite this imaginary scenario, transvestite and effeminate gays do not always prefer to be penetrated in their affective/sexual relationships.

The importance of the school band for young queers is acknowledged for various reasons in this research. One participant shared that she did not need to tell the family she was gay because her family found it out when she decided to play the cymbals in her school band. She herself decided to play the cymbal to "come out" as gay. The choice was related to the way that the city appreciated those who play and perform in the bands, after all, according to her, coming out through being part of the band was a way of being valued. Moreover, it was a strategy to be recognized due to the status that the school marching bands have in the city. This way of coming out is more than vocalizing queerness. It also involves an accepted gendered performance of playing the cymbals in the school band, which can be culturally valued through applause and celebration.

Conversely, another participant in this study, who was not part of the school band, pejoratively stated that young queers are "society's clowns." This participant said that many people attend the parades and seem to find such events laughable. In other occasions, it is also common to see the audience laughing at young queers. The effeminacy of these young queers haunts some men who are not as effeminate. In this type of performance, the femininity of effeminate gay men and transvestites unveils a powerful sexist standpoint, even within the queer experience. Here, several gay men are reminded of the stigma of nonheterosexual sexuality (Sedgwick, 1991), in which being linked to a more flamboyant feature diminishes a sense of personhood. Social recognition and the different ways people feel visible, celebrated, judged, and/or discriminated are necessary explorations.

## ON DIFFERENCES AND SOCIAL RECOGNITION FROM SCHOOL MARCHING BANDS

The visibility of young queers in school band presentations is mediated by the institutional interests of schools. According to one of the city band instructors, a school he worked for did not allow him to put young queers at the front of the marching bands to carry one of the school flags. He was not allowed to use a young queer as a leader either because the school administration thought it would not bring a positive image for the school. Borrowing from Britzman's (1995) concept of inclusion, the criteria for participation of young queers in marching bands is used to mask broader exclusion experiences of these participants. In this context, the school administration has minimal impact on expanding the social recognition of ephemeral gays and transvestites in the region.

In Corumbá, the binary gender expectation is socially developed and carries a large set of regulations on how young men, for example, should act. The expectations of schools to perform well and win contests, the focus on improving skills rather than teaching new skills, and the male/female binary functions of members of the marching bands are some of the examples that society demands when dealing with these individuals. For instance, as shared by a band instructor, an effeminate gay or transvestite would not only be poorly accepted into playing instruments reserved for traditional masculine boys, but also "spoil the image and synchrony of the choreography" that nonqueer men do. Therefore, choreographies of school marching bands are also predetermined following gender rules, and those in the band still need to conform to the binary male–female roles, even when they are queer.

The difference in treatment between effeminate gay men and transvestites and nonqueer members in marching bands implicates processes of identity and social differentiation ultimately because each participant is socially authorized to meet their own universalized role in the marching bands (e.g., men will play percussion instruments and that is it). According to Hall (2000), the differentiation occurs due to discourses of the "other" and the solidification of symbolic boundaries. For these processes to happen, we need to categorize what is left out or, in other words, the outsider that constitutes marginalization and oppression (Hall, 2000). Thus, not surprisingly, the cymbals, as the most feminine instrument in the marching bands, cannot be played by a socially determined masculine boy.

After all, according to one of the band's players and choreographer, no matter how good a boy is at playing the cymbal: "He ought to do it gracefully, just like the girls do when they play it." In the process of being differentiated, in this case categorizing effeminate gay men and transvestites as effeminate, this choreographer explained that queers need to be even more delicate than girls. As explained to the lead researcher, if

[168] *Tiago Duque and Gustavo Moura*

queers are breaking gender paradigms, they at least must prove that they can perform a function that is considered difficult to other men. We noted little self-reflexivity in this dialogue with the choreographer, such as seeing the value of having gender-neutral marching bands.

Notwithstanding the success of these marching bands and the fact that young queers supposedly put on makeup and sew costumes better than anyone else, they still do not dismantle male and female gender norms. That is, the stereotypical views of queer men's fashion and makeup skills led different city schools to reproduce a jargon that says: "Without the queers, you cannot win a marching band contest." Among queer people themselves, the allusion to their important role in marching bands becomes a reason to be proud and included, when in fact it is a problematic affirmation of gender binarism.

The stereotypes are also emphasized when non-queer men decide to join the marching bands. When a "straight-acting" boy reaches out to participate in rehearsals, it is expected that they know how to play percussion instruments, for example. Besides gender, religious experiences are also used to distinguish who plays a percussion instrument in marching bands. For instance, the Brazil–Bolivia border is well known for its Afro-Brazilian religious rituals that culturally divide men and women by gender. Men, in those rituals, are expected to play percussion drums; therefore, when a boy, who is assumed to come from that background and participates in the marching band, is expected to play a percussion instrument.

Roles and expectations, often established by binary gender norms, of queer and nonqueer people in Corumbá allow the coexistence of different groups of people in the city. School marching bands across the region are certainly proud of the "respect" they enforce among their groups as "all bands have queer members," as said by one teacher. Yet, it is still limiting for those queer people who have not disclosed their sexuality or gender, for example, and those still need to conform to gender roles that they might not relate to. The visibility that effeminate gay men and transvestites are getting is transgressive (Duque, 2017, 2019), but not enough to normalize nonbinary perspectives or disrupt gendered experiences of marching bands more broadly.

That said, the social recognition that school marching bands afford is that of an intersubjective relationship (Knudsen, 2010). Such relationship allows an individual to recognize the other, but in the case of effeminate gay men and transvestites in this study, the other is still conveyed through a binary regime. The image of young queers, in Corumbá, can be respected, celebrated, and able to blend in with others (nonqueers). However, their queerness is limited and only associated with male and female standards (Kulick, 2008).

## TOWARD ANTIOPPRESSIVE PRACTICES

In this Brazil–Bolivia border context, the young queers of school marching bands do not entirely escape the matrix of intelligibility of gender and sexuality (Butler, 2006). This is because the visibility of young queers in school marching bands corresponds to a certain gender performance expected by effeminate gay men, transvestites, and girls who do not identify as queer. Since young queers cannot escape the matrix of intelligibility of gender and sexuality (Butler, 2006), they are still presumed to exercise roles that are predetermined by a binary system, such as playing instruments that the girls play or performing in the color guard.

The lack of options young queers have when participating in school bands is particularly oppressive. First, it normalizes the participation of young queers in school marching bands only if they correspond to the codes and values of femininity when playing the cymbal or presenting as color guard performers. Then, the local culture and locality, through the schools and city, use this kind of gender visibility of young queers in school marching bands to problematically define themselves as inclusive and antihomophobic and oppressively classify Bolivians as homophobic/transphobic. Therefore, it becomes urgent to think that an "anti-oppressive education" (Kumashiro, 2000) is needed to "work against the privileging of certain groups, and the normalizing of certain identities" (Kumashiro, 2000, p. 34).

One way to address queer oppression might be for schools to establish a practice that adopts the construction of the normality of queers and nonqueers participating in marching bands, but not having to fit into gender roles and expectations. The idea is not to completely abolish gender roles, but rather dismantle power hierarchies that will consequently allow diverse gender expressions to be performed in contexts that are not oppressive. Currently, the gender visibility of queers in school bands allows the city to be not only recognized as inclusive and antihomophobic, but also contributes to Bolivians being the cultural counterpoint for being seen as homophobic. When schools include young queers in their marching bands, the acceptance of difference is not entire, mostly because queers still need to conform to their norms (of gender, sexuality, religiosity, nationality, etc.).

In conclusion, the kind of knowledge that schools need to promote is one that ensures social recognition of queer youth in its breadth. That is, an antioppressive knowledge that, according to Britzman (1995), is a kind of pedagogical stake that "thinks ethically about what discourses of difference, choices, and visibility mean in classrooms, in pedagogy, and in how education can be thought about" (p. 152). Schools are responsible for promoting the disruption of binary knowledge in order to discuss when the idea of a "nonhomophobic" city hides its own prejudice against the "others." Disruptive knowledge, through a queer lens, would also allow an understanding of how much nonqueer boys are also produced in terms of hegemonic gender and sexuality paradigms and how much the compulsory heterosexuality is still a cultural experience.

In schools, disruptive knowledge means more than thinking of gender expectations through a relational lens. The idea is to go beyond that different gender identities and expressions relate and complement each other. Moreover, disrupting knowledge through learning involves a set of ongoing lessons that show how an individual's positionality establishes the image of the other. For example, in this study, the role of young queers and the space they occupy automatically creates and contrasts with the identities of other straight women and men and the spaces they engage with. In this process of disruptive teaching and learning, unveiling power dynamics is key to critically analyze universalized inclusive practices as well.

For instance, the acceptance of young queers in marching bands needs to be carefully considered because what is apparently diverse and all encompassing can in fact have marginalizing effects on individuals. The general matrix of intelligibility (Butler, 2006) is a determinant of how gender expectations are fixed, generalized, and universal, and considering the different intersectional layers such as race, class, and nationality of individuals in this study poses different questions about what queerness is like in border regions and how education systems perpetuate oppressive sociocultural attitudes and behavior.

That said, future queer research in education ought to delve deeper into an analysis of what inclusion of young queers looks like in different schools. Researchers are urged to explore different perspectives, especially in border regions where individuals go back and forth and their sociocultural backgrounds constantly transgress and reshape teaching and learning. Along with problematizing and redesigning the gender matrix of intelligibility, studies need to include aspects of other identities (e.g., religion, nationality, race, class, etc.) to continue discussions about the complexities of creating disruptive knowledge in different educational contexts.

## REFERENCES

Assmann, S. J. (2007). Human condition versus "nature." Dialogue between Adriana Cavarero and Judith Butler. *Revista Estudos Feministas, 15*(3), 650–662. https://doi.org/10.1590/S0104-026X2007000300008

Banducci Júnior, Á., Passamani, G. R., & Duque, T. (2019). Fora chollos: Gender, sexuality, otherness and differences on the Brazil-Bolivia border. *Revista De Antropologia Da UFSCar, 11*(1), 577–598. https://doi.org/10.52426/rau.v11i1.302

Benevites, B. G. (Orgs.). (2022). *Dossier murders and violence against Brazilian transvestites and transsexuals in 2021.* Distrito Drag, ANTRA.

Brazilian Institute of Geography and Statistics (IBGE). (2002). *Map of Biomes of Brazil.* https://www.ibge.gov.br/geociencias/cartas-e-mapas/informacoes-ambientais/15842-biomas.html

Britzman, D. P. (1995). Is there a queer pedagogy? Or, stop reading straight. *Educational Theory, 45*(2), 151–165. https://doi.org/10.1111/j.1741-5446.1995.00151.x

Butler, J. (2006). *Gender trouble: Feminism and the subversion of identity.* Routledge. https://doi.org/10.4324/9780203824979

Costa, G. V. L. da. (2013). The invisible wall: Nationality as a reified discourse on the Brazil-Bolivia border. *Social Time: Sociology Review at USP, 25*(2), 141–156. https://doi.org/10.1590/S0103-20702013000200008

De Souza, E. M., & de Pádua Carrieri, A. (2015). When invisibility is impossible: Body, subjectivity, and labor among *travestis* and transsexuals. *SAGE Open, 5*(2), 1–11. https://doi.org/10.1177/2158244015585406

Diário Online. (2013, September 15). Travesti de 29 anos é assasinado com facada no pescoço. Correio do Estado. Cidades. https://www.correiodoestado.com.br//noticias/travesti-de-29-anos-e-assassinado-com-facada-no-pescoco/193917

Duque, T. (2017). "There is no gay there": Border and neighborly relations involving dissident genders and disparate sexualities in Corumbá (MS). *MNEME, 18*(40), 111–124. https://periodicos.ufrn.br/mneme/article/view/12275/9335

Duque, T. (2019). The transvestite, the jaguar and the sucuri: Reflections on the regime of visibility in the Pantanal, MS. *Século XXI: Revista De Ciências Sociais, 9*(1), 93–122. https://doi.org/10.5902/2236672536923

Fernandes, S. F. (2018). The trajectories of "trans youth" on the Brazil/Bolivia border: (In) visibility in public schools in Corumbá (MS) [Unpublished master's thesis]. Federal University of Mato Grosso do Sul.

Fikes, E. (2021, April 23). Chusid, Segade, Warke discuss queer/queering spaces. *Cornell Chronicle.* Cornell University. https://news.cornell.edu/stories/2021/04/chusid-segade-warke-discuss-queer-queering-spaces

Fry, P., & MaCrae, E. (1986). *What is homosexuality.* Editora Brasiliense.

Hall, S. (2000). Who needs identity? In P. du Gay, J. Evans, & P. Redman (Eds.), *Identity: A reader* (pp. 15–30). Sage.

Jagose, A. (1996). *Queer theory: An introduction.* New York University Press.

Junqueira, R. D. (2009). "Here we don't have gays or lesbians": Discursive strategies of public agents regarding measures to promote the recognition of sexual diversity in schools. *Bagoas, 3*(4), 171–189. https://periodicos.ufrn.br/bagoas/article/view/2302

Knudsen, P. P. P. da S. (2010). Talking about psychoanalysis: Interview with Judith Butler. *Revista Estudos Feministas, 18*(1), 161–170. https://doi.org/10.1590/S0104-026X2010000100009

Kulick, D. (1997). The gender of Brazilian transgendered prostitutes. *American Anthropologist, 99*(3), 574–585. https://doi.org/10.1525/aa.1997.99.3.574

Kulick, D. (2008). *Transvestite: Prostitution, sex, gender, and culture in Brazil.* Fiocruz.

Kumashiro, K. K. (2000). Toward a theory of anti-oppressive education. *Review of Educational Research, 70*(1), 25–53. https://doi.org/10.3102/00346543070001025

Kumashiro, K. (2002). *Troubling education: Queer activism and anti-oppressive pedagogy.* Routledge. https://doi.org/10.4324/9780203819753

Louro, G. L. (2004). *A foreign body: Essays on sexuality and queer theory.* Autêntica.

Magnani, J. G. C. (2009). Ethnography as practice and experience. *Horizontes Antropológicas, 15*(32), 129–156. https://doi.org/10.1590/S0104-71832009000200006

Michels, E., & Motti, L. (2018). *Violent death of LGBT+ in Brazil report 2018.* Gay Group From Bahia.

Miskolci, R. (2014). Negotiating visibilities: Secret and desire in male homoerotic relationships created by digital media. *Bagoas, 8*(11), 51–78. https://periodicos.ufrn.br/bagoas/article/view/6543

Miskolci, R. (2016). *Queer theory: Learning through differences.* Autêntica Editora: UFOP—Federal University of Ouro Preto.

Murray, D. A. B. (2016). *Queering borders: Language, sexuality, and migration.* John Benjamins Publishing Company.

Oliveira, M. A. M. de, & Campos, D. L. (2012). Migrants and the border: Subversive logic, referred lives. In J. H. do V. Pereira & M. A. M de Oliveira (Eds.), *Migration and integration: Results of research in Mato Grosso do Sul* (pp. 17–37). UFGD.

Passamani, G. R. (2018). *Confetti battle: Aging, homosexual behavior and visibility regime in Pantanal-MS.* Wild Papers.

Rich, A. (2010). Compulsory heterosexuality and lesbian existence. *Bagoas, 4*(5), 17–44. https://periodicos.ufrn.br/bagoas/article/view/2309

Sedgwick, E. K. (1991). How to bring your kids up gay. *Social Text, 29*, 18–27. https://doi.org/10.2307/466296

Sedgwick, E. K. (1993). How to bring your kids up gay: The war on effeminate boys. In E. K. Sedgwick (Ed.), *Tendencies* (pp. 163–176). Routledge. https://doi.org/10.4324/9780203202210-11

Seffner, F. (August 2011). *Compositions (with) and resistance (to the) norms: Thinking LGBT of body, health, politics, and rights.* [Paper Presentation], Stonewall 40+ in Brazil? Salvador, UFBA. https://www.researchgate.net/publication/343386200_Stonewall_40_o_que_no_Brasil

Silva, E. (2015, April 23). Após assumir namoro com travesti, homem ê agredido no centro de Corumbá. *Capital News*, Polícia. https://www.capitalnews.com.br/policia/apos-assumir-namoro-com-travesti-homem-e-agredido-no-centro-de-corumba/277439

Talburt, S., & Rasmussen, M. L. (2010). "After-queer" tendencies in queer research. *International Journal of Qualitative Studies in Education, 23*(1), 1–14. https://doi.org/10.1080/09518390903447184

Vitry, C. (2021). Queering space and organizing with Sara Ahmed's queer phenomenology. *Gender, Work & Organization, 28*(3), 935–949. https://doi.org/10.1111/gwao.12560

White, S., & Downey, J. (Eds.). (2021). *Rural education across the world: Models of innovative practice and impact.* Springer.

# CHAPTER 9

# Timely Interventions

## Queer Activist Early Childhood Teaching in Aotearoa New Zealand

ALEXANDRA C. GUNN

In 2017, just over 30 years since homosexual law reform in Aotearoa, the New Zealand government finally began a political and legal process to enable the expunction of historical convictions for New Zealand men convicted of offenses under the crimes act for consensual homosexual acts. The scheme came into place in April the following year (Criminal Records [Expungement of Convictions for Historical Homosexual Offences] Act, 2018). My sense of this moment was that it was about time. During the homosexual law reform activism of the late 1980s, the depth of public opposition and debate was significant and hostile. At that time I was a senior secondary school student. Media images of New Zealanders wrangling over placards and shouting each other down at public meetings as hatred and fear spilled freely remain clear in my mind. Though I had not yet identified queerly, my allegiances I recall were clearly on the side of those calling for reform.

In my adult life, my tools of choice for continued activism with respect to queer scholarship and social advocacy have become research and education, and I am not alone. Over the past 15 years, within my professional and academic fields of early childhood education, I have increasingly seen queer thinking influencing Aotearoa New Zealand studies. A growing

Alexandra C. Gunn, *Timely Interventions* In: *Queer Studies and Education*. Edited by: Nelson M. Rodriguez,
Robert C. Mizzi, Louisa Allen, and Rob Cover, Oxford University Press. © Oxford University Press 2023.
DOI: 10.1093/oso/9780197687000.003.0010

number of researchers and practitioners have set about examining persistent issues of gender and sexuality inequality and the social inclusion of diverse families and educators in the field (Cooper, 2015; Jarvis & Sandretto, 2010; Lee, 2010; Morgan, 2020; Morgan & Kelly-Ware, 2016; Surtees, 2006; Zou, 2015). As a period of the life span replete with normative discourses about gender, sexuality, and the family form, the early childhood years, especially those parts of them lived collectively within formal institutions of early childhood education, provide a multitude of entry points for comprehending and raising awareness about the repetitive impositions of heterosexual hegemony and associated heteronormative thinking and practice.[1] But also, young children sometimes say and do the queerest things, acting freely outside of normative structures not yet internalized, to assert different possibilities for who and how individuals might claim or know themselves to be. I have long argued that the astute educator in early childhood education can use such ordinary moments to critically queer | query early childhood curriculum and in doing so expand the learning of all.

In this chapter, I write from my early childhood educator and queer feminist activist perspectives to describe how thinking and practicing queerly can improve the quality of early childhood education provision in Aotearoa New Zealand. By situating my account among contingent turns of historical events, specifically changes in Aotearoa New Zealand family and child law, education curriculum development, and a tendency toward critique of modernist thinking and practice more broadly, I illustrate how in these short 30 years it has become possible to not only ask queer questions of ourselves, our children, and the early childhood institutions we create, but also be queer in this place as we make visible a multitude of possibilities of existence for actual and possible selves.

## DECLARING QUEER AND ITS DEPLOYMENT IN MY RESEARCH ABOUT EARLY CHILDHOOD EDUCATION

For me queer theory is one among a number of contemporary critical poststructural theories that bring to attention the ways people use and are imbued with discourses of modernity that

- infuse the body with power;
- shape subjectivities and, with particular reference to genders and sexualities,

[176]   *Alexandra C. Gunn*

- establish the grounds for who and what is to be considered normal (Butler, as cited in Ahmed, 2016; Davies, 1994; Sedgwick, 1990).

My turn to queer theory emerged in the context of study into heteronormativity and early childhood education (Gunn, 2008). I was conducting research with tools of discourse analysis and genealogy (Foucault, 1977, 1978) to explore the workings of power and heteronormativity in everyday language and practices of early childhood education. I intended working queerly on data from the study, which informed by Sedgwick (1990, 1994) meant I would maintain a focus on sexuality as a discrete element of personhood and explore normative thinking and practice in relation to this as a priority. I intended the study to work in the interests of queer identities, social justice, and inclusion as I sought to explore reasons for the exclusion from early childhood education of knowledges, experiences, and subjectivities of nonheterosexual folk (queers) and nonheterosexual sexualities. My aim in this was to advance thinking and practice in early childhood education beyond the (hetero)norm.

My investments in working queerly had begun close to home, within experiences of my own family's positioning as abnormal due to an oversupply of mothers in our lesbian-led household. One school year, one of our children's primary school teachers refused to recognize our child's parents "as parents." Subsequently the teacher refused to work in partnership with us as a family at the school. He would, for instance, only talk about our child to their biological mother; the "other mother" in his view, had no legal right to be in the conversation. Throughout that long year, our child's teacher repeatedly drew on heteronormative discourses to produce us, our child's parents, and our family as abnormal and illegitimate. I committed then to speak back to heteronormative discourses in education settings, to use the considerable power and advantage I had in my position as academic, researcher, and writer, and to draw strength from queer studies (education-related research that questioned forms of normative thinking and practice as well as studies whose content addressed matters of nonheterosexual sexualities) and queer theorists (scholars whose identities were nonheterosexual as well as scholars whose work was informed by queer studies or queer theory) to support that work.

When I began my research, the disruption of heteronormativity was identified as a key project of queer scholars and queer research (Sumara & Davis, 1999; Warner, 1991). As I was both queer (nonheterosexual, cisgendered, lesbian) and conducting a study about queer concerns (heteronormativity), I sought to learn from studies in education concerning the experiences of nonheterosexual folk like me that addressed heteronormativity in teaching and learning or that took up analysis of gender and sexualities matters in education (e.g., Britzman, 1995; Morris, 1998; Sumara & Davis, 1999; Taylor & Richardson, 2005). These studies led me to orient strategies for analyzing accounts of early childhood education practice that illustrated how relations of sexuality, gender, family, and power intersected with notions of normal and deviant to privilege and silence certain subjects, knowledges, and practices. I was exploring heteronormative discourse to better understand heterosexual hegemony in my field.

Lived experiences of a teacher's refusal to recognize my partner's and my own parenting subjectivities as legitimate, particularly in relation to those children in the family who we'd not birthed, meant that my interest in concepts of "the subject" and "subjectivities" was also piqued. So, when I began to deploy Foucault's discourse analysis (1977, 1978) in my study and to think queerly in my exploration of how subjectivities were produced within heteronormative discourses, I turned to Bronwyn Davies (1994) and Judith Butler's (1990) feminist poststructuralist explanations of genders, of categories of personhood, and of subjectivities to augment Foucault's ideas of the same. Butler (1990) and Sedgwick's (1990) ideas firmed up my queer thinking, especially around notions of norms, normal, and normativity in relation to genders, sexualities, and the family form; and following Britzman's (1995) advice to "stop reading straight," the questioning of normativity by thinking "at odds" with the data I had produced became a significant queer theory–inspired strategy of my research. Davies's (1994) analysis of binary thinking was also instructive, particularly for understanding how power relations within binary structures worked (e.g., heterosexual/homosexual establishes heterosexual as the normative standard against which homosexual and other nonheterosexual forms of sexuality could be produced). Many possibilities for analysis arose: How was one subjectivized through and subjected to norms of sexuality, gender, and the family? How was this happening in everyday early childhood practice? How does "normal" get figured in early childhood education anyway? Could teachers in my field begin to think at odds with the norm (in whichever context it was being asserted)? When I then returned to Foucault to explore the workings of heteronormativity more queerly through discourse analysis and his form of genealogy, I became intent on exploring how power was moving through, making, and maintaining so-called normal gendered, sexual, and family-oriented subjectivities in early childhood education (Gunn, 2008, 2011). I was also interested in working on how such understandings and practices were not only malleable but also resistant to change. Thus, the impulse to work at odds (which I think of as working queerly) with the heteronormative practices I had experienced as a parent

[178]   *Alexandra C. Gunn*

and in early childhood education more broadly connected me firmly with queer theory as I sought to understand more about how heteronormative discourses produce, maintain, and support the workings of power and heterosexual hegemony in early childhood education.

Following Foucault (1978), I understand power to be entwined with knowledge and exercised within as well as on bodies. Power may be thought of as an active relation such that behavior may be directed in particular ways (by the self or another) in order to produce bodies as "docile" (Foucault, 1977, p. 138). Through such processes, society's so-called normal and abnormal bodies and persons may be demarcated, reified, and subjected to law and prescription aimed at achieving the body or person as recognizably so-called normal. Queer theory provided me avenues for understanding such processes in relation to notions of im/proper sexualities and, by association, genders, patterns of family formation, and close interpersonal relationships. My work has drawn on queer scholarship to advance thinking and practices that disrupt heteronormativity (Gunn, 2015). Contemporary debates about the directions in which queer theory may have turned: too academic, too elitist, too White (Butler, as cited in Ahmed, 2016; Talburt & Rasmussen, 2010); or the *proper* subject/s of queer theory (Halley & Parker, 2007; McKee, 2007); and definitional precision about what "queer" might possibly mean and when (Freccero, 2007; Green, 2007) have brought challenges and expansive thinking to the field since I began to think and do things more queerly in my work. However, I have stuck close with those initial ideas I formed from the field when I first engaged: researching to emphasize the production of normative forms of sexualities (and relatedly, genders and in early childhood education the family form); considering what and who is constituted as normal in early childhood education (in terms of related phenomena of sexualities, gender, and the family form, and more generally); and from this thinking at odds with those norms by resisting and challenging them and interrogating any associated binary thinking (after Britzman, 1995; Davies, 1994; Sedgwick, 1990). I am intensely interested in figuring out how institutions maintain, entrench, and challenge normative thinking, practice, and power (after Foucault, 1977, 1978) and how institutions work to reproduce certain sexualities and related subjectivities and subject positions as legitimate, or normal, or not (after Butler, 1990; Sedgwick, 1990, 1994).

My localized activism also seeks recognitive social justice (Fraser, 1997) through a normalized and affirming representation and recognition of diverse sexualities, genders, and families within early childhood education. I encourage any practitioner or scholar within the field to engage with thinking or practicing queerly in order to advance a more inclusive and welcoming practice for themselves and others. This approach is both cognizant of and an attempt to suspend "identitarian politics" (so called by Fraser, 2000, p. 120), which have been argued as insufficient for addressing deeply rooted institutional bases of inequity and injustice. In this way, I think any person can teach at odds with (hetero)normativity and work toward disrupting heterosexual hegemony and, in doing so, draw from queer theory to pursue equity and inclusion.

Having ended up working in the academic and professional context of early childhood education, which like the concept of queer itself has been largely produced through modernist technologies of health disciplines, psychology, and the law, I engage with queer theory as a means of identifying, contesting, and exceeding patterns of (hetero)normative thinking and practice, especially in relation to the imposition of fixed notions of genders, sexualities, and the family form (Gunn, 2011). Moreover, I consider that working queerly provides a means for recognizing subjectivities that exceed the hetero(norm), for resisting a strict adherence to fixed and historically dominant identity forms, and for addressing institutional formations that lead to experiences of misrecognition and marginalization. As Butler (as cited in Ahmed, 2016) recognized, anybody can act and think queerly because heteronormativity imposes particular social patterns and ways of being on us all; within the heterosexual/homosexual binary, we are all subject to the workings of inequitable power relations.

## ABOUT EARLY CHILDHOOD EDUCATION

Formal contemporary practices of early childhood education and care have been built on modernist humanist norms associated with health disciplines, psychology, and the law to form concepts of the child, the family, gender, sexuality, and so on that have particular meanings for pedagogical practice (Beatty et al., 2006; Burman, 2008). Influences from educational philosophy, the learning sciences, and developmental psychology have intersected with governments' imperatives for social and economic development to produce a sense of early childhood education in Aotearoa New Zealand as absolutely necessary for individuals' and nations' prosperity and development. The rise of early childhood education as a formal institution of education in the minority world[2] has come with a vision of early childhood education as a panacea for addressing myriad social, educational, and economic development issues (see, e.g., the 2011 government's Early Childhood Education Taskforce report: *An Agenda for Amazing Children*). The market has also profited greatly—over the past two decades

[180]  *Alexandra C. Gunn*

in Aotearoa New Zealand investment in early childhood education by corporate and for-profit organizations has grown astronomically (Mitchell, 2019). The time has arrived for almost all children in Aotearoa New Zealand to attend some form of early childhood education despite it not being compulsory to do so. National Ministry of Education data also show that participation in early childhood education has been increasing for children in all age groups, and that children are attending for longer hours (Ministry of Education, 2019). For families raising young children then, the chances they'll engage with some form of early childhood education are significant. As institutions, early childhood education services can play a significant role in supporting families, shaping parental identities, and fostering the social inclusion of a diversity of people and groups (Gunn, 2015). Thus, paying attention to the ways early childhood education works to construe concepts of child, parent, gender, sexuality, teacher, family, and so forth is an important goal for queer activist-minded scholars and practitioners who are invested in positive educational systems change.

I argue that we, members of the early childhood profession, can help reify the expectation that everyone can and should belong within an education system that recognizes individuals' languages, cultures, and identities in terms acceptable to these individuals (Gunn et al., 2020). Armed with such expectations, the optimistic view suggests that families, children, and parents may demand the same consideration by others as they transition from early childhood education into the compulsory education sector: to be known on their terms in ways that affirm their experiences and identities. Thus, I argue that by drawing attention to how early childhood teachers think about, practice, and understand the potential impacts of a more queer teaching practice, transformation in the education system more broadly may be supported. Educators from different education sectors may learn from their early childhood education colleagues' experiences and also seek to resist heteronormativity. Thus, it seems even more achievable that queer thinking and practice within early childhood education can support the education system in Aotearoa New Zealand to be actively dismantling the (hetero)norm.

## RE-FORMING QUEER IN AOTEAROA NEW ZEALAND

Local queer activism of the 1970s and 1980s was not at all the origin of queer awareness in Aotearoa New Zealand, but it was my introduction to it. Since then I have come to appreciate how British colonial settlers brought with them norms and social expectations that contributed systematically to the dismantling and marginalization of myriad Māori understandings, culture, and practices, including in relation to sexuality. Evident in traditional narratives, chants, whakatauki (proverbs), and sculptural/visual arts (carving) depicting Te Ao Māori | Māori worldviews and Māori lives, Ngahuia Te Awekotuku (2005) explained an etymology of the word *takatāpui*, a term still used contemporarily, in reference to an "intimate companion of the same sex" (p. 8). The term is located historically in accounts from the 1800s by Ngāti Rangiwewehi leader and scholar Wiremu Maihi Te Rangikāheke.[3] Te Rangikāheke produced many manuscripts concerning Te Ao Māori | Māori worldviews during his tenure as advisor to Governor George Grey, then governor of New Zealand (1845–1853); he, Te Rangikāheke, was a recognized authority and public servant. Te Awekotuku (2005) wrote of Te Rangikāheke's accounts of an important historical figure from the Rotorua region in the North Island, Tutānekai. Tutānekai, arguably known even more for a heterosexual love affair with the highborn Hinemoa, describes to his father his grief, as he pines for his beloved Tiki, another man. Elaborated in a PhD thesis by Kerekere (2017), contemporary takatāpui identity and behavior are thus predicated on "Māori identity with a spiritual connection to the takatāpui tupuna (ancestors)" (p. 5). Yet as Te Awekotuku (2005) illustrated, understandings of same-sex sexualities in Te Ao Māori have been lost to many as indigenous knowledge and life were systematically reshaped through colonization, and artifacts depicting same-sex relations were "destroyed or secreted away in private collections" (p. 8).

Heteronormativity in relation to the family rests on the nuclear family form and on participants in families occupying recognizably gendered, sexualized, and age-related positions. The nuclear family form differed from established whānau and whanaungatanga practices within Māori society (Metge, 1995); however, much of Aotearoa New Zealand's social policy in the first three-quarters of the 20th century came to revolve around a notion of family as nuclear and patriarchal. The patriarchal nuclear family relies on a structure comprising two opposite-gender adults whose heterosexual union results in the birth of children. Given this structure, we expect children's parents to comprise one each of the mother and father description, who will be biologically and/or legally related to the children. Furthermore, the parents are assumed to be heterosexual because of the expectation for procreation within their union. So, within this single notion of traditional (nuclear) family, heteronormative constructions of sexuality, gender, and close-interpersonal relations are entwined and underscored. If, in educational institutions, teachers, administrators, and policymakers go on to privilege such normative thinking when imagining the families they

[182] *Alexandra C. Gunn*

will work with, the resulting practices for anybody whose family, parents, and life experiences don't fit this pattern are potentially marginalizing and exclusionary (Gunn, 2009; Surtees & Gunn, 2010; Terreni et al., 2010).

However, as argued previously, thinking queerly about phenomena of family, gender, sexuality, and close interpersonal relationships can help progress change, equity, and inclusion. Thinking queerly involves first recognizing when heterosexual hegemony and associated fixed (and often binary) thinking about phenomena such as family, gender, sexuality, and close interpersonal relationships is shaping one's thoughts, attitudes, and practices. Then, it means we attempt to understand how consequences of such patterns of thought may privilege and marginalize folk with whom we work. The third aspect is to then think at odds with this by imagining what it would look and feel like to disrupt the imposition of those historical constructions on people and perhaps to even imagine inverting any to help understand how they sustain relations of power in social and political life. The process requires one to recognize how some folk's lived experiences exceed the (hetero)norm and with what consequences. The impulse is not to ignore, dismiss, or necessarily even devalue heterosexuality, traditional nuclear family structures, or historical binary gender configurations; rather, it is to set these in the context of the range of possible sexualities, genders, and family formations and to open up those categories to expressions beyond the fixed and heteronormative configurations alone. Thinking and practicing queerly is an invitation to do more, know more, and recognize more with respect to such phenomena.

## BUILDING A CONTEXT FOR THINKING AND DOING QUEER IN EARLY CHILDHOOD EDUCATION

It has become easier to call for queer-minded educational reform in Aotearoa New Zealand's education system since broader legislative and social reforms took hold in the late 20th and early 21st century. Various provisions in the Care of Children Act (2004) came into force after July 1, 2005, and provided scope for formal arrangements between adults who were or wished to be recognized as parenting a child or being a guardian. Soon thereafter the Civil Union Act (2004) passed into law recognizing same-gender and opposite-gender civil partnerships. Marriage equality for same-gender couples was achieved in 2013. Since then, it has become possible for same-gender couples to have their parenting status as "mother," "father," or "parent" recorded accurately on children's birth certificates (previously only one spot for "mother" and/or "father"/"other parent" was recorded). That only two named parents can still be recorded thus is testament to the strength of heteronormativity in the legal and social spheres. Nonetheless, it has become more ordinary for some people in Aotearoa to live openly nonheterosexual lives. If anything, homonormativity associated with an assumption that queer families are just like normal families but with same-gender parents in them may be becoming an area of new resistance (Brown, 2009). I argue that in this broader context of progressive social and legal reform it is more doable than ever to think and practice queerly in early childhood education.

## WHAT MIGHT QUEER THEORY–INFORMED PRACTICE AND THINKING LOOK LIKE IN EARLY CHILDHOOD EDUCATION AND BEYOND?

As previously noted, the locus of heteronormativity in early childhood education forms around central concepts of the family and, by association, genders and sexualities. I next explore how the curriculum context for early childhood education in Aotearoa opens the possibility that queer-minded teachers might challenge (hetero)normative discourses in their work. To advance that argument, I draw from the concept of working theories as a means of recognizing how it may be possible to engage with queer ideas in children's play. Working theory is a concept embedded in the Aotearoa New Zealand early childhood curriculum framework and is one of three high-level valued learning outcomes of that framework (Hedges & Jones, 2012; Ministry of Education, 2017; Reedy, 2019). Hedges's (2014) description of the concept suggests that working theories are "thinking and learning processes that may connect . . . [children's] interests and efforts to make sense of their worlds" (p. 35). Through the curriculum framework, teachers are encouraged to prioritize the "development of children's learning dispositions and working theories because these enable learning across the whole curriculum" (Ministry of Education, 2017, p. 23). The idea of working theory is helpful for showing how queer-minded teachers may intervene in and explore children's working theories about sexuality, gender, and family with them. The chapter then draws to its conclusion by underscoring why it is ever more possible now for queer theory to inspire critical and relevant educational practice in Aotearoa New Zealand.

The early childhood curriculum framework (hereafter *Te Whāriki*, Ministry of Education, 2017) describes a broad aspiration for children's empowerment and urges teachers to recognize and support children's active participation in worlds of which they are part. *Te Whāriki* expects

[184]   *Alexandra C. Gunn*

educators to build children's senses of themselves as strong learners whose mana[4] is imperative, and whose agency is recognized and valued. Furthermore, the framework expects that children's learning dispositions and capabilities will transfer into schooling and beyond. The learning and teaching theory of the curriculum framework rests on sociocultural underpinnings, and the policy understands that child well-being and educational success is tightly tied to whānau | family well-being and also that of the wider community. The working theories aspect of the curriculum provides avenues for the exploration of children's diverse ideas, including about those queer-related concerns, of sexualities, genders, close interpersonal relations, and the family form. Closely related with learning dispositions, over time children's working theories become more intricate, connected, and refined. Teacher-designed learning environments that engender dispositions of courage, curiosity, trust, playfulness, perseverance, confidence to express ideas and feelings, and to take responsibility in a social setting provide a context within which children make sense of the natural, social, physical, and material worlds through working theories. In this light, recognizing and responding to children's diverse ideas about how people form and perform family, do and experience gender, and understand sexuality and close interpersonal relationships are entirely reasonable expectations. Teachers' capacities to support such thinking by children may be hindered by senses of risk and safety (Gunn, 2008; Kelly-Ware, 2018), as well as discourses of childhood innocence and of sexuality that posit it as irrelevant to young children (Surtees & Gunn, 2010). Yet, it is well understood that children's everyday play sees them engaging in family-centered sociodramatic play scripts; births, deaths, marriages, and the like feature regularly in these. That such play so often goes unremarked as evidence of children constructing working theories about matters of gender, sexuality, and the family is testament to the pervasive nature of (hetero)normative discourses in early childhood education.

Kelly-Ware's (2018) thesis stressed that diversity can be a rich resource for learning when teachers recognize how normalizing discourses may influence children's sense of themselves and others. Focusing on children's theories about what is fair, who is a friend, genders, sexualities, and ethnicities, Kelly-Ware's study illustrates how children's working theories are influenced by people and things beyond children's immediate family, including peers and popular culture. Hence, why children may hold ideas different from those their teachers may anticipate. Of interest here is that children's understandings may routinely exceed those of their teachers and family members. It is imperative therefore for teachers to listen closely to children's points of view, even if fleeting, and to be able to identify instances from the everyday happenings where children's working theories open up possibilities for knowing and being differently. An example from a study[5] I worked on that explored children's storytelling and teachers' support of children's narratives is illustrative (Bateman et al., 2017). The data extract that follows is a transcript of video footage involving several children in free play at kindergarten.

## MUMS AND DADS AND KIDS AND CARS

Jacob and Mitch, two children identified as and who identify themselves as boys, have been playing with toy cars in the sandpit. Two other cisgender boys, Rory and Kurt, approach to join them. After first being told they cannot play, Rory joins in the car game. Mitch and Rory, with two of the cars, are driving around tracks they've made in the sand. Jacob is doing his own driving of a tractor nearby. Kurt sits on the edge of the sandpit watching them. Jacob drives the tractor toward the group:

JACOB: "Here comes the robber!" [Jacob drives the tractor toward Mitch and Rory; Rory moves his hand to avoid being hit with the tractor.]
JACOB [TO RORY]: "I know, you can be the kid."
MITCH: "Me?"
JACOB: "No, Rory."
MITCH: "Yeah."
JACOB: "Rory do you want to be the kid?"
RORY: "Yep."
JACOB: "And I'm the dad."
RORY: "Who's gonna be the mum?" [Rory pats Mitch on the head in reference to a different storyline he'd observed Jacob and Mitch playing earlier; Mitch had been and still was, in part, Jacob's dog.]
MITCH: "R- . . . ah, Kurt can."
JACOB: "What?"
MITCH: "Kurt can."
RORY [TO KURT]: "You're the mum."
KURT: "No! I'm not playing. . . . No, there's not . . . mum in this game."
MITCH: "Yes, there is."
JACOB: "Mums and dads. See? We'll play mums and dads and kids."
RORY: "And cars."
KURT: "How about we have two dads?" [Mitch's attention is drawn back to the previous story, and in character as "dog" Mitch is ordered to bed by Jacob. The Mums, Dads, Kids and Cars story ends.]

There are many possible interpretations to make here about working theories regarding family, gender, and sexualities being verbalized by the boys as they work to negotiate the rules of how they'll play their game. Initially among the children there is an accepted understanding that for there to be a family it has to comprise children and parents, one each of the Mum and Dad type. Furthermore, it seems tolerable, as far as Mitch and Rory are concerned, to have a mother figure played by a boy. Their principle objective seems to be launching the family play rather than quibbling over the gender of someone who might play Mum. I interpret Jacob's "what?" after Mitch suggests Kurt can be "Mum" as a request for clarification after Jacob misheard Mitch's suggestion, although it could equally have been "What? You can't be serious" as well. For Kurt, the suggestion that he could play Mum was never going to fly, even if it was a strategy that allowed him access to the game. It seemed inconceivable to him that he might be cast in a female role; his priority at that moment seemed to be more concerned with maintaining a coherent gender performance and identity for himself. Kurt's suggestion of there being two dads in the game would have achieved this for himself; relatedly, it also opened up the possibility of developing a play script that would involve a family configuration involving same-gender parents. However, it may have also been in Kurt's mind that the dads weren't necessarily coparents to "kid," so the same-gender parented family may equally as not have emerged. Although, my interpretation of them being "kid's parents" comes from the fact Kurt was working to solve a problem over who was able to play "Mum" in the family that was being arranged and by changing Mum and Dad to "two Dads," parents could be achieved. In any case, none of Mitch, Jacob or Rory agreed, negotiations came to an end as did the play.

The queer activist teacher in me noticed this fleeting exchange between the boys and recognized its potential for expanding thinking, knowledge, and practice beyond (hetero)normative discourses. Had I been part of the play, it may have been possible to have acted in support of Rory and Mitch's suggestion of Kurt playing Mum or supported Kurt's response that there just be two dads instead—suggestions that in my experience would have likely led to further discussion among the group about just who might constitute the family in their play script at the time. Instead, I was doing "researcher" at the time so remained as an observer while my mind raced with questions and thoughts: What made it possible for Mitch and Jacob to suggest Kurt could be Mum? Was it because they understood that it was only a game, so Kurt's gender integrity as boy could be maintained in spite of him taking up a differently gendered role? Why was Kurt reluctant to play Mum? Was Kurt's investment in being boy a barrier to the play? Why didn't Kurt's two-dad suggestion get taken up? Could this group have been encouraged to play family in a way that made same-gender parenting or gender fluidity more possible? Why/why not? And so forth. There are many avenues for thinking about these boys' exchanges and for revisiting these ideas with the children later or with the teaching team. The queer-minded teacher, who is open to the possibility of children's experiences exceeding so thought normal conventions, has plenty to work with here.

My argument that it is now even easier for queer theory–inspired thinking and practice to feature in early childhood education and beyond relies on Foucault's concept of genealogy (1977) for its coherence. Genealogies, for Foucault, make visible the mutual constitution of knowledge-power and reveal how truths and senses of what's normal become established, entrenched, sustained, and imposed in social life (Gunn, 2019). By tracing turns of contingent historical events and change over time, it is possible to see how in a moment something that has been inconceivable before might now be able to be. The example of constituting same-gender headed families as legitimate after civil union and marriage equality laws passed is a relevant example here. Those changes occurred after decades of activism and technological and social change such that it was almost impossible to think that the law, early in the 21st century, might not eventually catch up. Likewise, the confluence of factors that make engagements with queer thinking and practice possible in early childhood education today are theoretical and cultural, related to broader social reform and legal change and supported by increased capacity for queer lives to be lived out and ordinary in Aotearoa New Zealand society. Recent research, awareness, and trans*[6] activism (Kroeger, Recker, & Gunn, 2019; Kroeger & Regula, 2017; Ministry of Education, n.d.), for example, have been bringing to light the ways educational institutions might usefully change to reflect an increasing awareness of gender nonbinary experiences and identities. That such work is being recognized and used to support policy development means that educational practice and thinking may expand again. Ministry of Education guidelines (Ministry of Education, n.d.) for schools working with gender and sexually diverse students suggest four strategies that I think are equally as legitimate to advance in early childhood education. They involve the building of knowledge among teachers and institution-wide interventions such as sound inclusive policy. I have long advocated for inclusive education policy in early childhood education to stipulate that homophobia, heterosexism, and sexism will not be tolerated, and that awareness and support for gender, sexuality, and family diversity is a priority for practice. By articulating with the existing national guidelines for schools, early childhood education also may well change. The ministry guidelines suggest that environmental, physical, and social needs for gender and sexuality diverse students be addressed, and that an inclusive curriculum be practiced. All such strategies will move thinking toward awareness of the normative practices and regimes of truth supported through outdated institutional structures and formations. With such advice being promulgated in the schools sector in Aotearoa New Zealand, it seems immanently more possible that similar advice could support thinking and practice in early childhood education beyond the (hetero)norm.

## CONCLUDING THOUGHTS

I began this chapter with a nod to time, recognizing that it was about time (in 2017) that men in Aotearoa New Zealand who carried historical convictions for homosexual acts had those convictions expunged—finally, 30 years after homosexual law reform in this country. The theme of time has been interwoven with my arguments as I have described my first encounters with queer activism, queer theory, and research practice in early childhood education that has sought to query and queer elements of early childhood education thinking and practice. I have argued that it is now timely and in our interests to progress early childhood education in ways that engage with queer theory because to do so is to advance a more equitable, inclusive, and socially just education practice with young children and their families—a practice that others may learn from and use to shape teaching and learning in other education spaces. I have suggested it is time to rethink some of the normative ways we have constructed notions of sexualities, genders, family structures, and close interpersonal relationships in our early childhood education work because by doing so we can expand our thinking and practice beyond the (hetero)norm. Timely interventions in children's play, to connect with their working theories about doing family, gender, sexuality, and the like can provide scope within curriculum to query and challenge heteronormativity; capitalizing on professional advice provided to schools, where it seems more possible to acknowledge and respond positively to queer concerns, may support queer activist teachers in early childhood education to achieve the same.

If we are to intervene in heterosexual hegemony and disrupt heteronormativity in our thinking and practice in education, I believe we must work at multiple levels and across the spectrum of the early childhood community to effect change. We, early childhood teachers, must think queerly, at odds with those norms that settle into and around our work, especially those norms concerned with matters of sexuality, gender, family, and close interpersonal relationships. We must listen closely to children and their working theories to capitalize on those moments when children's capacities to position themselves and others outside of the impositions of heterosexuality open up different ways to know and to be. We must harness the contexts of broader change in education and in society more generally and work to make visible our own divergent thinking and knowledge, as well as that of the children and families with whom we work. For me the promise of queer theory's relevance in early childhood education is broad and full of potential and, now more than ever, seems a good time to act.

## NOTES

1. I use heterosexual hegemony to refer to the ways heterosexuality as a social construct has been inserted into social and political life and upheld as a standard for all to meet and heteronormativity to refer more specifically to the governing of language and practices that shape social and political life toward that normative standard.
2. Minority world nomenclature rejects the categorizing of world countries according to the established binary of developed/developing (or first/third world). When employing a practice inspired by queer theory, the disruption of binary thinking typically concerns the inversion of the heterosexual/homosexual binary. However, as I have explained, working queerly for me also means to resist, disrupt, or draw attention to all forms of normative thinking (working "at odds" to the norm). So, by using the term *minority world* in reference to those countries typically categorized as "developed" or "First World" countries, and not using the established binary, the power relation usually invoked through such binarisms is troubled and less intelligible (due to the absence of the binary configuration). Minority world language recognizes that the majority of the world's population lives in so-called Third World or developing nations, while a minority of the world's population holds economic wealth that drives much global policy, which is a thought "at odds" with normal associations of the terms.
3. A short bibliography of Te Rangikāheke (Wiremu Maihi) is included on *Te Ara: The Encyclopedia of New Zealand* and can be retrieved at online: https://teara. govt.nz/en/biographies/1t66/te-rangikaheke-wiremu-maihi
4. Mana is a concept Te Ao Māori | a Māori worldview referring to one's power, authority, and influence. Tilly Te Koingo, Lady Reedy (2019), explains in relation to the image of the child in *Te Whāriki* that having mana "is the enabling and empowering tool to controlling their own destiny" (2019, p. 37).
5. The project from which data in this chapter is drawn was funded by the *Teaching and Learning Research Initiative* under Grant 9146.
6. After Burford, MacDonald, Orchard & Wills (2015), the signifier 'trans' with an asterisk reminds us that a number of words, representing diverse and connected divergent gender identities may follow (gender, sexual, feminine, masculine).

[190]   *Alexandra C. Gunn*

## REFERENCES

Ahmed, S. (2016). Interview with Judith Butler. *Sexualities, 19*(4), 482–492. https://doi.org/10.1177/1363460716629607

Bateman, A., Carr, M., Gunn, A. C., & Reese, E. (2017). *Literacy and narrative in the early years: Zooming in and zooming out.* Teaching and Learning Research Initiative.

Beatty, B., Cahan, E. D., & Grant, J. (Eds.). (2006). *When science encounters the child: Education, parenting and child welfare in 20th Century America.* Teachers College Press.

Britzman, D. (1995). Is there a queer pedagogy? Or, stop reading straight. *Educational Theory, 45*(2), 151–165. https://doi.org/10.1111/j.1741-5446.1995.00151.x

Brown, G. (2009). Thinking beyond homonormativity: Performative explorations of diverse gay economies. *Environment and Planning A, 41*(6), 1469–1510. https://doi.org/10.1068/a4162

Burford, J., MacDonald, J., Orchard, S., & Wills, P. (2015). (Trans)gender diversity, cisnormativity and New Zealand education cultures. In A. C. Gunn & L. A. Smith (Eds.), *Sexual cultures in Aotearoa/New Zealand Education* (pp.147–169). Otago University Press.

Burman, E. (2008). *Deconstructing developmental psychology* (Rev. ed.). Routledge.

Butler, J. (1990). *Gender trouble: Feminism and the subversion of identity.* Routledge.

Care of Children Act (NZ). (2004). https://www.legislation.govt.nz

Civil Union Act (NZ). (2004). https://www.legislation.govt.nz/act/public/2004/0102/latest/DLM323385.html

Cooper, K. (2015). *"I just want to be who I am." Exploring the barriers faced by lesbian early childhood teachers as they disrupt heteronormative practices in Aotearoa/New Zealand* [Unpublished master's thesis]. University of Canterbury.

Criminal Records (Expungement of Convictions for Historical Homosexual Offences) Act (NZ). (2018). https://www.legislation.govt.nz/act/public/2018/0007/latest/DLM7293253.html

Davies, B. (1994). *Poststructuralist theory and classroom practice.* Deakin University Press.

Early Childhood Education Taskforce. (2011). *An agenda for amazing children: Final report of the ECE Taskforce.* NZ Government Print.

Foucault, M. (1977). *Discipline and punish* (A. Sheridan, Trans.). Penguin Books.

Foucault, M. (1978). *The history of sexuality, volume 1: An introduction* (R. Hurley, Trans.). Random House.

Fraser, N. (1997). *Justice interruptus: Critical reflections on the "postsocialist" condition.* Routledge.

Fraser, N. (2000). Rethinking recognition. *New Left Review, 3*, 107–120. https://newleftreview.org/issues/ii3/articles/nancy-fraser-rethinking-recognition

Freccero, C. (2007). Queer times. *South Atlantic Quarterly, 106*(3), 485–494. https://doi.org/10.1215/00382876-2007-007

Green, A. I. (2007) Queer theory and sociology: Locating the subject and the self in sexuality studies. *Sociological Theory, 25*(1), 26–45. https://doi.org/10.1111/j.1467-9558.2007.00296.x

Gunn, A. C. (2008). *Heteronormativity and early childhood education: Social justice and some puzzling queries* [Unpublished doctoral dissertation]. University of Waikato.

Gunn, A. C. (2009) "But who are the parents?" Examining heteronormative discourses in New Zealand government early childhood reports and policy. *Early Childhood Folio: A Collection of Recent Research, 13*, 27–30. https://doi.org/10.18296/ecf.0175

Gunn, A. C. (2011). Even if you say it three ways, it still doesn't mean it's true: The pervasiveness of heteronormativity in early childhood education. *Journal of Early Childhood Research, 9*(3), 280–290. https://doi.org/10.1177/1476718X11398567

Gunn, A. C. (2015). The potential of queer theorising in early childhood education. In A. C. Gunn & L. Smith (Eds.), *Sexual cultures in Aotearoa New Zealand education* (pp. 21–34). Otago University Press.

Gunn, A. C. (2019). Foucauldian discourse analysis in early childhood education. In G. Noblit (Ed.), *Oxford research encyclopedias* (Online). Oxford University Press. https://doi.org/10.1093/acrefore/9780190264093.013.333

Gunn, A. C., Surtees, N., Gordon-Burns, D., & Purdue, K. (Eds.). (2020). *Te Aotūroa Tātaki inclusive early childhood education: Perspectives on inclusion, social justice and equity from Aotearoa New Zealand* (2nd ed.). NZCER Press.

Halley, J., & Parker, A. (2007). Introduction: After sex? On writing since queer theory. *South Atlantic Quarterly, 106*(3), 421–432. https://doi.org/10.1215/00382876-2007-001

Hedges, H. (2014). Young children's "working theories": Building and connecting understandings. *Journal of Early Childhood Research, 12*(1), 35–49. https://doi.org/10.1177/1476718X13515417

Hedges, H., & Jones, S. (2012). Children's working theories. The neglected sibling of Te Whāriki's learning outcomes. *Early Childhood Folio, 16*(1), 34–39. https://doi.org/10.18296/ecf.0140

Jarvis, K., & Sandretto, S. (2010). The power of discursive practices: Queering or heteronormalising? *New Zealand Research in Early Childhood Education, 13*, 43–56.

Kelly-Ware, J. (2018). *Negotiating fairness and diversity: Stories from an Aotearoa New Zealand kindergarten* [Unpublished doctoral dissertation]. University of Waikato.

Kerekere, E. (2017). *Part of the whānau: The emergence of takatāpui identity. He Whāriki takatāpui* [Unpublished doctoral dissertation]. University of Victoria Wellington.

Kroeger, J., Recker, A., & Gunn, A. C. (2019). Tate and the pink coat: Exploring gender and enacting anti-bias principles in practice. *Young Children, 74*(1), 83–92. https://www.naeyc.org/resources/pubs/yc/mar2019/exploring-gender-enacting-anti-bias

Kroeger, J., & Regula, L. (2017). Queer decisions in early childhood teacher education: Teachers as advocates for gender non-conforming and sexual minority young children and families. *International Critical Childhood Policy Studies, 6*(1), 106–121. https://journals.sfu.ca/iccps/index.php/childhoods/article/view/59

Lee, D. (2010). Gay mothers and early childhood education: Standing tall. *Australasian Journal of Early Childhood, 35*(1), 16–23. https://doi.org/10.1177/183693911003500104

McKee, A. (2007). (Anti)queer. Introduction. *Social Semiotics, 9*(2), 165–169. https://doi.org/10.1080/10350339909360430

Metge, J. (1995). *New growth from old: The whānau in the modern world*. Victoria University Press.

Ministry of Education. (n.d.). Guide to LGBTIQA+ students. https://www.inclusive.tki.org.nz/guides/supporting-lgbtiqa-students/

Ministry of Education. (2017). *Te Whāriki, He Whāriki mātauranga mō ngā mokopuna o Aotearoa, Early Childhood Curriculum*.

Ministry of Education. (2019). *He taonga te tamaiti—Every child a taonga: Early learning action plan, 2019–2029*.

Mitchell, L. (2019). Turning the tide on private profit-focused provision in early childhood education. *New Zealand Annual Review of Education, 24*, 75–89. https://doi.org/10.26686/nzaroe.v24i0.6330

Morgan, K. (2020). *Early childhood teachers' use of picture books to counter heteronormativity: Children's working theories about gender diversity and LGBTIQ-parented families* [Unpublished master's thesis]. University of Canterbury.

Morgan, K., & Kelly-Ware, J. (2016). "You have to start with something": Picture books to promote understandings of queer cultures, gender and family diversity. *Early Childhood Folio, 20*(1), 3–8. http://dx.doi.org/10.18296/ecf.0016

Morris, M. (1998). Unresting the curriculum: Queer projects, queer imaginings. In W. F. Pinar (Ed.), *Queer theory in education* (pp. 275–286). Lawrence Erlbaum Associates.

Reedy, T. (2019). Tōku rangatira nā te mana mātauranga: Knowledge and power set me free. In A. C. Gunn & J. Nuttall (Eds.), *Weaving Te Whāriki: Aotearoa New Zealand's early childhood curriculum document in theory and practice* (3rd ed., pp. 25–44). NZCER Press.

Sedgwick, E. (1990). *Epistemology of the closet*. University of California Press.

Sedgwick, E. (1994). *Tendencies*. Routledge.

Sumara, D., & Davis, B. (1999). Interrupting heteronormativity: Toward a queer curriculum theory. *Curriculum Inquiry, 29*(2), 191–208. https://doi.org/10.1111/0362-6784.00121

Surtees, N. (2006). *Sexualities matters in early childhood education: The management of children/bodies and their unsettling desires* [Unpublished master's thesis]. University of Canterbury.

Surtees, N., & Gunn, A. C. (2010). (Re)marking heteronormativity: Resisting practices in early childhood education contexts. *Australasian Journal of Early Childhood, 35*(1), 42–47. https://doi.org/10.1177/183693911003500107

Talburt, S., & Rasmussen, M. L. (2010). "After-queer" tendencies in queer research. *International Journal of Qualitative Studies in Education, 23*(1), 1–14. https://doi.org/10.1080/09518390903447184

Taylor, A., & Richardson, C. (2005). Queering home corner. *Contemporary Issues in Early Childhood, 6*(2), 163–173. https://doi.org/10.2304/ciec.2005.6.2.6

Terreni, L., Gunn, A., Kelly, J., & Surtees, N. (2010). In and out of the closet: Successes and challenges experienced by gay- and lesbian-headed families in their interactions with the education system in New Zealand. In V. Green & S. Cherrington (Eds.), *Delving into diversity: An international exploration of issues of diversity in education* (pp. 151–161). Nova Science Publishers.

Te Awekotuku, N. (2005). He reka anō—Same sex lust and loving in the ancient Māori world. In A. J. Laurie & L. Evans (Eds.), *Outlines: Lesbian and gay histories of Aotearoa* (pp. 6–9). Lesbian and Gay Archives of New Zealand.

Warner, M. (1991). Introduction: Fear of a queer planet. *Social Text, 29*, 3–17. http://www.jstor.org/stable/466295

Zou, P. (2015). Diverse sexualities in the early childhood setting in New Zealand: Theories, research and beyond. *He Kupu the Word, 4*(1), 5–11. https://www.hekupu.ac.nz/article/diverse-sexualities-early-childhood-setting-new-zealand-theories-research-and-beyond

CHAPTER 10

# Beyond "Abstinence Only"

*The U.S. Christian Right's "Pro-Family"*
*Countermovement against Comprehensive Sexuality*
*Education and Sexual and Reproductive Rights in Eastern*
*and Southern Africa*

FINN REYGAN AND HALEY MCEWEN[*]

Over the course of the past 15 years, a transnational countermovement has been steadily developing advocacy against sexual and reproductive health and rights (SRHR), the rights of individuals who identify as lesbian, gay, bisexual, transgender, intersex, and queer (LGBTIQ+), comprehensive sexuality education (CSE), Gender Studies, and the rights of young people in relation to their ability to access sexual health information and services.

---

[*] Professor Finn Reygan passed away prior to the publication of this chapter. At the time of writing, Finn was a Research Director at the Human Sciences Research Council and also had an affiliation with the University of the Western Cape as an Extraordinary Professor in the Department of Educational Psychology. He will forever be remembered as a committed scholar and activist who was dedicated to the struggle against exclusion, injustice, and oppression, particularly for sexual and gender minority youth. His wholeheartedly generous, energetic, and joyful approach to the work will continue to reverberate through our research and advocacy for decades to come. Haley McEwen is a Postdoctoral Researcher in the Department of Political Science at Gothenburg University. She is also an affiliated Research Associate of the Wits Centre for Diversity Studies at the University of the Witwatersrand, Johannesburg.

Finn Reygan and Haley McEwen, *Beyond "Abstinence Only"* In: *Queer Studies and Education*. Edited by: Nelson M. Rodriguez, Robert C. Mizzi, Louisa Allen, and Rob Cover, Oxford University Press. © Oxford University Press 2023.
DOI: 10.1093/oso/9780197687000.003.0011

This movement, and the "anti-gender" political agendas, campaigns, and discourses it promotes, has been increasingly documented by scholars and activists who have been alarmed by increasing attacks on sex, sexuality, and gender-related rights, and LGBTIQ+ people, in various global contexts (Biroli & Caminotti, 2020; Kováts & Pető, 2017; Kuhar & Paternotte, 2017).

The efforts of pro-family, or "anti-gender," organizations to influence sexual politics in Africa have been increasingly documented. Kapya Kaoma (2009, 2012) has made significant contributions to knowledge about the U.S. Christian Right and its deployment of American-style culture wars against LGBTIQ+ rights and sexual and reproductive rights (SHRH) in Africa, while progressive civil society and philanthropic organizations have also been working to uncover the financial sources that are enabling U.S. Christian Right organizations to expand their agendas beyond North America (Global Philanthropy Project, 2018; Provost & Archer, 2020). As these reports have indicated, pro-family activists have been propagating anti-LGBTIQ+ and antiabortion discourses in Africa for at least a decade. While sexuality education has been on their agenda for a number of years, the movement's anti-CSE campaigning has intensified over the course of the past 5 years.

LGBTIQ+ and SRHR civil society and advocacy organizations in Eastern and Southern Africa (ESA) are increasingly encountering opposition to CSE within government, traditional leadership, and school communities. In a project led by Reygan to facilitate the implementation of CSE and SRHR across 21 countries in ESA, partners increasingly reported "backlash" against their efforts within communities and policy debates. Across ESA, it has become clear that a coordinated countermovement against CSE is working to convince governments and communities that CSE is inappropriate for children and should therefore be rejected by government officials, teachers, and parents. As this chapter discusses, while opposition against CSE has in many ways appeared to be the product of local grassroots concern about CSE, there is ample evidence suggesting that anti-CSE campaigning has been mobilized by well-resourced conservative "pro-family" organizations in the United States. We discuss the U.S.-driven pro-family movement behind anti-CSE campaigning, revealing the otherwise obscure transnational and geopolitical dimensions of this countermovement against sex, sexuality, and gender-related rights. In doing so, we aim to provide a deeper understanding of the implications of efforts to close down CSE in the region and those of the pro-family discourse and activism more broadly.

We argue that opposition against CSE in the region of ESA cannot be entirely understood without an understanding and grasp of the pro-family

[196]   *Finn Reygan and Haley McEwen*

movement and its global efforts to reverse many of the gains made in advancing SRHR and sexual orientation, gender identity and expression, and sex characteristics (SOGIESC) rights over the course of the past 50 years. The key research questions guiding this chapter are: What are the transnational connections and ideologies of the countermovement to CSE in schools across ESA? What are the implications of this in terms of normative understandings of gender and sexuality in schools in the region? And finally, how do these dynamics reveal the ways in which heteronormativity is far from "natural," but is actively produced, in this case, through geopoliticized messaging and narratives about CSE and SRHR. This chapter begins with a broad overview of adolescent SRHR as manifest in the ESA commitment to CSE. It continues with an exploration for the global pro-family movement and the implications of its activities for the ESA region. The chapter then engages with the methodological framework for this study, followed by case studies of two countries in the region: South Africa and Zambia. The chapter then concludes and offers recommendations for strategic sectoral responses to the attempted rollback of youth rights across ESA.

## THEORETICAL FRAMEWORK

Our approach to the analysis of U.S.-based pro-family advocacy in ESA is grounded and informed by a decolonial queer critique of heterosexuality and the nuclear family model as forms of cultural imperialism that accompanied colonization (Lugones, 2007; McClintock, 1995; Ndjio, 2012; Oyěwùmí, 1997; Smith, 2006; Stoler, 1995; Tamale, 2011). As these decolonial and anti-imperialist queer and feminist scholars have shown, the gender binary and compulsory heterosexuality were mechanisms of colonial conquest, functioning to destroy indigenous ways of knowing and doing what the English language refers to as "gender," "sexuality," and "family." As these scholars have shown, the process of imposing and enforcing heteropatriarchal Eurocentric norms and values of what it means to be male/man/father/husband and female/woman/mother/wife interlocked with other colonial processes underway, such as Christianization and colonial missionary schooling, the implementation of a wage labor system, and the development of a civil society and capitalist economy. In addition to the implementation of colonial biopolitics, legislation was created that criminalized deviation from heteronormativity. Colonial antisodomy laws, some of which have been retained within postindependence legislation, were therefore only one dimension of how European nations were concerned with the regulation of sexuality in the colonies. From this perspective, we understand current pro-family advocacy in the region as an effort to retain the sex and gender norms entrenched through the process of colonial rule (McEwen, 2017). In this regard, we pursue the opportunity that queer theory presents to interrogate the ideological work of the pro-family movement as a site in which hegemonic forms of power intersect and interlock to retain heteropatriarchal and geopolitics power.

The method and design of the research informing this chapter has therefore been shaped by the paradigm of social justice research and the imperative of interrogating problems of social inequality, injustice, prejudice and discrimination. On the one hand, social justice research draws purposefully on methods that are available and required to understand the intersectional ways in which forms of power and oppression limit the life opportunities of individuals on the basis of race, gender, sexual orientation, class status, ability, religion, and other markers of difference. On the other hand, and less acknowledged, social justice research compels the study of how racist, heterosexist, classist, and ableist forms of power, hegemony and dominance intersect, interlock, and co-construct one another (Steyn, 2015). As problem-oriented research, this approach to knowledge production requires an intersectional understanding of not only marginality, but also hegemony. As something that works to actively erase itself and the trail of evidence it leaves behind (Pascale, 2010), power and hegemony must be interrogated using techniques of data collection and analysis that can uncover the forms of injustice that are often disguised as "common sense."

This methodological approach has epistemic and ontological connections with the theoretical frameworks provided by a queer critique of heteronormativity, heteropatriarchy, and the power of the gender binary in structuring our societies, economies, and imaginaries. Both of us are also queer identified, which also brings our own lived experiences on the margins of heteronormativity to bear on the topic under discussion. Our positionalities also inform our sense of urgency in naming and challenging pro-family efforts to erode gains made by sexual minorities and women globally and in Southern Africa especially. Moreover, while both of us have resided in South Africa for a number of years, we come from two different countries in the Global North where gender and sexuality diversity and reproductive rights have been deeply contentious and polarizing issues. Reygan is from Ireland, and McEwen is from the United States of America. Having been born and raised in these contexts, where issues of gay rights and abortion have become lightning rods for ultraconservative political mobilization and deeply divisive political rhetoric, we both have long-standing personal and professional interest in making sense of the politics of sex and gender. Our concerns about the countermovements against CSE curricula are also informed by existing research in the region showing the forms of prejudice, exclusion, and violence that LGBTIQ+ learners face in schools (see for instance Msibi, 2012; Bhana, 2014; McArthur, 2015; Francis & Brown, 2017; Daniels et al., 2019; Francis et al., 2019), and the forms of heteronormativity that are embedded within school curricula and policy (see for instance Potgieter & Reygan, 2012; Francis, 2016; Ngabaza & Shefer, 2019; Reygan, 2021; Ubisi, 2021; Francis & McEwen, 2023).

## METHODOLOGY

The idea for this chapter was catalyzed by the currently unfolding debates about CSE in ESA, and conversations between the two of us about the emergence of coordinated and well-resourced anti-CSE opposition in the region. Finn Reygan has been engaging with government, civil society organizations, and community-based activists about the need for CSE and SRHR to be accessible to young people in the region. He has extensive experience leading multicountry projects in the region focused on diversity, inclusion, violence, and SRHR in school systems. His publications initially focused on queer experiences of othering in schooling systems and have since begun to focus on troubling the broader, regional schooling space in terms of power, privilege, and authority. The second author of this chapter, Haley McEwen, has conducted extensive research about the pro-family movement and the efforts of conservative U.S.-based activists and organizations to expand their networks and agendas in African contexts. In writing this chapter together, we bring in and apply our relevant areas of expertise and knowledge in order to unpack the current rise in anti-CSE campaigning in the region. In doing so, we hope to first provide insights that can be beneficial to efforts to make CSE and SRHR accessible to young people in ESA. This objective also has a wider imperative to raise awareness about the pro-family movement more broadly and to provide SRHR, SOGIESC, and CSE advocacy groups working around the world with critical insights into the workings and implications of this movement, which have such dangerous consequences for queer communities and young people in the region.

This chapter draws on data that show how the pro-family movement is operating to mobilize opposition against CSE in ESA in the immediate sense. The methods used to collect data about anti-CSE advocacy in the region involved desktop study and document analysis, including online materials, that sought to understand the countermovement against CSE across the ESA region. Desktop studies and document analyses are methods utilized

BEYOND "ABSTINENCE ONLY" [199]

in qualitative research to critically review and analyze secondary data sources (Denzin & Lincoln, 2017). This includes a broad literature review of the relevant knowledge base on the topic, including but not limited to the academic literature. In the present study the authors critically engage with different kinds of texts, such as academic literature and research, policies, online articles, government statements, and statements that reveal the contestations over CSE in ESA. As further discussed below, critical review and analysis builds on our previous published research about both the pro-family movement and SRHR in the education sector and are combined with the newsprint and other online data presented in this study. By means of critical, comparative analyses that focused on discourse and the construction of the other (Denzin & Lincoln, 2017), we attempt to capture some of the varied standpoints and worldviews of both the pro-family movement and CSE supporters. These competing and contrasting perspectives are presented below with supporting evidence from the desktop review and document analysis along with the three case studies.

In addition to collecting data demonstrating and providing insight into the discursive and networking strategies used by U.S.-based pro-family activists and organizations in the region, the chapter draws on the larger body of research developed by McEwen that has investigated pro-family advocacy in a range of contexts and in relation to various other issues that the movement is working to counter, such as children's rights, LGBTIQ+ rights, and the academic freedom of feminist and queer scholars. In addition to the already mentioned techniques of data collection, this research involved a broader literature review as well as participant observation at an international pro-family gathering that took place in Salt Lake City, Utah, in 2015, as well as online participant observation of pro-family webinars and presentations and the collection and analysis of a broad range of pro-family texts (i.e., newsletters, reports, website content). Data informing this project have also been informed by Reygan's ongoing research and writing about sexuality and gender diversity in the region, with a particular focus on schools and youth. This research has also involved a broader literature review as well as ongoing reflections on the need for SRHR access in schools.

Analysis of anti-CSE campaigning in the ESA region is therefore informed by, and draws on, extensive prior research and investigation. For both of us, techniques of thematic and critical discourse analysis have been central methods used to uncover the coloniality of anti-CSE campaigning in the region. In the data we present here, critical discourse analysis made it possible to uncover the forms of injustice that are embedded within, and advanced by, pro-family narratives. Significantly, pro-family activists

[200]   *Finn Reygan and Haley McEwen*

are not explicitly hateful or violent in their rhetoric and actively deny that they advocate for LGBTIQ+ or women's oppression. Rather, they have developed sophisticated discursive techniques that conceal violence and oppression within the terms of "tradition," "culture," "family values," and "morality" communicating their ideas through politically acceptable rhetoric of "rights," "family," and child "protection" that works to disguise and conceal the underlying prejudiuce and exclusion structuring pro-family ideology. Therefore, in examining pro-family advocacy and discourse in the three countries examined here—Zambia, Namibia, and South Africa—we set out to interrogate the deeper geopolitical, ideological, and epistemic forms of power to which anti-CSE opposition is tethered.

## THE NEED FOR COMPREHENSIVE SEXUALITY EDUCATION AND SEXUAL AND REPRODUCTIVE HEALTH AND RIGHTS IN EASTERN AND SOUTHERN AFRICA

Adolescents and young people, particularly those in Africa and other developing countries, are faced with a multitude of sexual and reproductive health (SRH) challenges. These include, but are not limited to, high HIV and other sexually transmitted infections (STIs) and low contraceptive prevalence, resulting in high pregnancy rates and unsafe abortions (Fatusi, 2016). African governments are committed to various continental and international policy frameworks intended to amplify the health and wellbeing of adolescents and young people. International treaties such as the Convention on the Rights of the Child, the Committee on the Elimination of Discrimination Against Women, the International Conference on Population and Development in 1994, and the Beijing Platform for Action all uphold the right of all children and adolescents to receive SRH information, education, and services in accordance with their specific needs. In Africa, the Maputo Plan of Action and the African Youth Charter are examples of continental declarations that "further stress the need for education on HIV, reproductive health and gender" (United Nations Educational, Scientific, and Cultural Organization [UNESCO], 2013, p. 21).

For a long time, the agenda around adolescent and youth SRH in the region has largely been about abstinence. The abstinence approach has largely portrayed sex as a negative activity, associated with guilt, shame, danger, and disease (Glover & Macleod, 2016). However, the portrayal of sex by the media and among peers tends to be more positive, conflicting with many of the key messages within abstinence-only approaches to sexuality education. This means that adolescents and young people receive conflicting messages and norms around sex. Furthermore, as Santelli writes, abstinence-only approaches to youth SRH are "ethnically problematic" in that they fail to grasp the realities that young people face, relying on scare tactics about contraception and sex rather than providing accurate information that could be potentially life saving:

> Current federal abstinence-only legislation is ethically problematic, as it excludes accurate information about contraception, misinforms by overemphasizing or misstating the risks of contraception, and fails to require the use of scientifically accurate information while promoting approaches of questionable value. (Santelli et al., 2006, p. 86)

It is for this reason that "there is increasing evidence to show that abstinence-only programmes are ineffective" (International Planned Parenthood Federation, 2010, p. 4). In an effort to advance the health and well-being of adolescents and young people, in particular their SRHR, ministers from health and education in 20 African countries gathered in Cape Town on December 7, 2013. During the meeting, all 20 countries signed the ESA Commitment, agreeing to

> work collaboratively towards a vision of young Africans who are global citizens of the future, who are educated, healthy, resilient, socially responsible, informed decision-makers, and have the capacity to contribute to their community, country, and region. They affirmed a commitment to the right to the highest possible level of health, education, non-discrimination, and well-being of current and future generations. (UNESCO et al., 2016, p. 12)

The commitment by ESA governments has put a spotlight on sexuality education (UNESCO et al., 2016). An overview of the ESA Commitment 2015 targets regarding sexuality education are as follows: 15 out of 21 countries reported that they offer CSE/life skills in at least 40% of primary schools, while in 6 countries the implementation of these classes is in progress; second, there were 12 out of 21 countries who indicated that they provide CSE/life skills in at least 40% of secondary schools, while in 9 countries the implementation of these classes is in progress; and third, 16 out of 21 countries have policies or strategies relating to sexuality education for out-of-school youth (UNESCO et al., 2016). Also, a quick glance at the international, national declarations or commitments showed that there is an agreement that adolescents and young people need accurate and reliable SRHR information and services. There is no doubt that the introduction of comprehensive sexuality education programs in schools offers an opportunity to

[202]   *Finn Reygan and Haley McEwen*

provide adolescents and young people with accurate information regarding their SRH: "There is clear evidence that CSE has a positive impact on sexual and reproductive health (SRH), notably in contributing to reducing STIs, HIV and unintended pregnancy" (UNESCO, 2015, p. 14). Despite progressive gains made, there are still countless challenges that disrupt the implementation and delivery of CSE. These challenges also remain deeply shaped by legacies of the colonial enforcement of the sex and gender binaries and hierarchies and normative notions of the nuclear family. As the following section shows, contemporary pro-family campaigning against comprehensive sexuality education reinforces restrictive notions of gender, sexuality, and family, while also undermining the rights of young people to potentially life-saving knowledge and support services.

The geopolitical dimensions of pro-family campaigning also reveal the unequal North-South relations that are reproduced through pro-family campaigning. As we show in the following section, the drive to roll back the gains made by CSE in school systems across Africa is led by conservative pro-family advocacy groups from the United States who have invested millions of U.S. dollars promoting antifeminist and anti-LGBTIQ+ agendas internationally (Provost & Archer, 2020). Furthermore, U.S.- and Africa-based organizations campaigning against CSE are employing narratives that have been prevalent among U.S. antiabortion and antigay movements from the 1970s in response to the sexual revolution. As previously stated, this movement has developed transatlantic networks in Africa and has encouraged and mentored African political, religious, and thought leaders to implement campaigns against SRHR, SOGIESC, and CSE across the continent. Here, we share our findings about anti-CSE campaigning in South Africa while also drawing connections to the ESA region more broadly. After presenting these data, we conclude with a discussion of the implications of these findings for CSE, SRHR, and broader struggles for sex and gender justice in the region and globally.

## PRO-FAMILY ATTACKS ON COMPREHENSIVE SEXUALITY EDUCATION IN EASTERN AND SOUTHERN AFRICA

In November 2019, a series of images began circulating on community and parents' WhatsApp groups across South Africa. Said to be "leaked" content from the Department of Basic Education, a set of five images appeared to depict human reproduction, beginning with sexual intercourse in the form of missionary-style penetrative sex between a man and a woman and ending with the woman lying naked on a table, holding up a newborn baby as the now-clothed man and a doctor look on, with pleased looks on their faces. The images circulated with the following "warning":

> This is the rubbish that the department of education will teach our kids from next year on. To think your 8 year old daughter's private parts will be touched by a boy because it will be part of their practical. Now think about it, think about it again and again and again. Than decide what will you do about it (sic).

Many of those who circulated the message perhaps did so out of a sense of duty to protect the children of South Africa from what appeared to be explicit content developed by the Department of Basic Education. The notification that new content was being added to the Life Orientation curriculum about sex education came as a surprise to many, but most shocking of all was the assertion that the new content would include the images contained in the "warning" message. While a simple Google image search of the images revealed that their source was not the South African Department of Basic Education at all, but a 1975 Danish children's book called *How a Baby Is Made*, the disinformation had the effect of stirring moral panic about the introduction of new sexuality education curricula, feulling notions that the content was being imposed by White westerners. Despite semiotic indications that the images were not South African (mainly because all characters depicted are White), their graphic nature and claims that they were to be included in the curriculum catalyzed a significant amount of moral outrage among parents, teachers, and communities more broadly.

In the days and weeks that followed the circulation of these images through social media platforms, large blue banners began appearing around Johannesburg motorways with anti-CSE messages, such as "Teach kids Maths, not Masturbation," and its rough isiZulu translation "Fundisa a batwana Bethu ezi'balo haye uqhansi." Below these slogans in smaller text, the banners read "X Families say NO to CSE." The posters were the work of the Cape Town–based organization the FPI, whose name was also printed in white on the bottom left corner of the banners.

At the same time, a letter addressed to the South African Minister of Basic Education, Angie Motshekga, was being circulated via the conservative online petition forum CitizenGo and was making its way through virtual networks. The petition letter addressed the Department of Basic Education, claiming that CSE was "not approved by South African parents and is being taught in schools behind their back" (Family Policy Institute, 2016). The petition further stated that the CSE curriculum is "destructive to children," encourages promiscuity and disregards "parental values and parental involvement in education . . . demeaning "'traditional' moral, religious, and cultural values shared by families and the community." According to the letter, comprehensive sex education wages an all-out war on the society, threatening children and the traditional values of parents and families. This messaging reproduces colonial and Christian morality politics that informed Eurocentric notions of "civilization." As decolonial feminists have shown, the gender binary and nuclear family model were used by colonial regimes to construct indigenous people who did not practice gender and kinship as Christian Europeans did as "uncivilized," "savage," and in need of saving by colonial administrations (Kitch, 2009, p. 56). It was through this history that notions of the gender binary and hierarchy became an integral component of the system of racial classification and ranking that positioned male dominance as a signal of cultural advancement (Kitch, 2009, p. 56). As Oyěwùmí has discussed, the enforcement and institutionalization of the European concept of the family formed the ideological basis of gender and race "as two fundamental axes along which people became oppressed" in colonized African societies (Oyěwùmí, 2002, p. 3).

When recontextualizing the argument that reproductive and LGBTIQ+ rights will destroy civilization for audiences in ESA, and audiences in the Global South more broadly, these heterosexist and patriarchal instigations of moral panic are combined with a geopolitical narrative constructing CSE and SRHR as part of a "global sexual rights agenda" driven by U.N. agencies and international donors. In placing emphasis on U.N. agencies and international SRHR organizations, U.S. Christian Right groups mobilizing against CSE demonized human rights while also obscuring the ways in which their discourse and ideology reinforced social arrangements and imaginaries that have been complicit in the exploitation and oppression of African and other colonized societies.

After setting out the alleged "dangers" of CSE, the petition letter continued, compelling readers to agree that CSE "is a dangerous proposal that must be stopped," in part because it was directed by foreign powers who are working in secret cahoots with the government:

> We are deeply concerned that multiple UN agencies, federal and local governments, and school administrations are implementing, promoting and/ or funding controversial comprehensive sexuality education programs that sexualize children and take away their innocence. (Family Policy Institute, 2016)

According to the petition letter, local forces, backed by international donor funding, are working to smuggle comprehensive sex education into the school curriculum. The letter concludes with the final attempt to ignite public fears about the consequences of comprehensive sex education, proclaiming that these programs "are designed to change all of the sexual and gender norms of society."

The claim that CSE, SRHR, and LGBTIQ+ rights are being imposed by foreign powers has become a cornerstone of U.S. Christian Right efforts and strategies to gain allies and exploit existing anxieties about coloniality and Western hegemony. As shown in the following section, the threat that CSE and SRHR seek to eradicate old norms and introduce new, "perverse," and foreign ideas about gender and sexuality has been an influential means of growing opposition to CSE. Furthermore, it has been through this rhetorical strategy that predominantly White and middle-class pro-family actors from the United States position themselves as allies who want to protect African people from dangerous Western progressives, obscuring the unequal relations of power that structure their relationships with the African communities they address.

## THE STOP CSE CAMPAIGN

While the letter discussed above had the appearance of being produced by local organizations, a search of its content revealed that identical letters had also been circulated in Nigeria, Zambia, Kenya, and Ghana. The original version of the letter is hosted on a website created by a U.S.-based organization, Family Watch International (FWI). This organization, which is based in Gilbert, Arizona, has launched a global campaign called Stop CSE, although its current emphasis is clearly in ESA. Materials produced by the Stop CSE campaign, such as policy briefs, policy tools, documentaries, and pamphlets, have been circulated widely across the region.

### South Africa

In South Africa, FWI partnered with local groups, Family Policy Institute (FPI), the African Christian Democratic Party (ACDP), Freedom of Religion South Africa, and others to mobilize the Stop CSE campaign. The FPI was founded by conservative Christian activist Errol Naidoo in 2007, in Cape Town, South Africa. Naidoo established the organization after returning from Washington, D.C., in 2006, where he received mentorship at the Family Research Council (which was established in 1983 and has since operated as a leading conservative "think tank" that has led political lobbying against LGBTQIA+ rights, SRHR, and CSE in the United States).

[206]   *Finn Reygan and Haley McEwen*

According to the organization's website, FPI was founded "with the single-minded objective of making the restoration of marriage and the family the cornerstone of South African social policy." Since 2007, Naidoo has participated in international pro-family gatherings convened by the World Congress of Families, positioning himself at the forefront of pro-family activism in Southern Africa. Naidoo's links with U.S.-based pro-family organizations are clear in his presence at these events and also through the partnership between FPI and FWI, which is frequently mentioned in FPW newsletters.

Naidoo was previously a member of the ACDP, which has also taken up the cause of opposing CSE, echoing the pro-family rhetoric espoused by the FWI and other U.S. Christian Right organizations. In 2020, the Rev. Kenneth Meshoe, president of the ACDP, indicated his commitment to fight the plan to treat

> masturbation, gender nonconformity and single parent families as a mainstream. . . . What the Department of Basic Education plans to do is wicked and must be stopped. (Independent Online, 2020)

The Christianview Network and the ACDP continue to argue that CSE will sexualize children:

> The planned sexuality education to be introduced in schools attempts to normalise lesbianism, sodomy and sex outside marriage. In addition to that, it is an assault on the sexual health and innocence of children. . . . The "hero role models" promoted lean disproportionately in favour of LGBT including Zachie Achmat (in both grade 11 and 12). In the book "Defiant Desire" (Gevisser & Cameron, 1995) Achmat boasts about his sex with older men while a child. (Former Constitutional judge) Justice Edwin Cameron who wrote the book "Defiant Desire" full of stories of a diverse forms of sex outside of marriage is also listed as a "hero." (IOL, 2020)

Akin to FWI's claims about CSE, the ACDP's Rev. Meshoe argued that CSE promoted a liberal agenda in schools, including sexual experimentation and gender fluidity, and that while the ACDP didn't have a problem with traditional sex education, CSE was a version of UNESCO's curriculum:

> CSE that is developed and promoted by UNESCO does not promote abstinence but rather encourages dangerous and reckless sexual activities, habits and promiscuity. . . . By introducing UNESCO-developed CSE, it seems apparent that one of the main objectives of the department with CSE is to change the sexual and

gender norms of society—especially one like South Africa, that has strong traditional and religious beliefs. (IOL, 2020)

Meshoe argued that the government must prioritize the interests of South African children and push back against a White, anti-African agenda

above those of foreign agencies who seem intent on destroying the future of our children. We also call for CSE developed by UNESCO to be scrapped and for government to revert back to traditional sexuality education which was previously taught in the Life Orientation curriculum. We must start applying African solutions to African problems.

## Zambia

Debates are currently underway about the national curriculum in Zambia, and CSE is a key topic within these discussions. Inclusion of CSE has been a constitutional mandate in the country, and until recently, there had been widespread support for CSE. Grassroots SRHR, gender-based violence and HIV and AIDS advocacy groups have noted that while there has been awareness of existing opposition to CSE in the sector, there has been an increasingly organized and vocal countermovement against CSE.

Those involved in CSE advocacy have indicated that the recent call for the banning of CSE has been organized and well resourced, and that FWI has played a key role in mobilizing existing opposition. Organized, in that those leading the opposition have been lobbied through the use of FWI's anti-CSE campaign materials, including their "War on Children" documentary, which was being circulated among governmental and traditional leadership. It is also apparent that this emerging opposition to CSE is highly financed. Activists have commented that the upcoming renewal of the ESA commitment to implement CSE and SRHR in the region has been a key factor that explains the timing of the emergence of new, highly organized, well-resourced efforts to counter CSE.

In early 2020, a petition, "Protect Zambia Children," was circulating, warning readers about the alleged dangers of CSE. The petition is hosted on the FWI online campaign against comprehensive sexuality education. Similar to the South African version, this petition asserts that "ineffective and highly controversial CSE programs pushed by foreign entities are harming Zambia's children and must be stopped immediately!" After significant influencing by anti-CSE campaigners in Zambia, the minister of religious affairs and other key government officials began questioning the role of CSE after a public announcement by two key religious leaders in September 2020 on the dangers of CSE. This ultimately led to a debate in the Zambian parliament on the removal of CSE, a proposal that was ultimately rejected.

Clearly, FWI's Stop CSE campaign has been mobilized in a number of countries in ESA in their efforts to block further efforts to make CSE and SRH services available to young people. In its use of metaphors associated with geopolitical conflict and colonization to characterize efforts by UNFPA, UNESCO, IPPF, and other international nongovernmental organizations to implement CSE and SRHR, pro-family leaders actively work to geopoliticize the issues of gender and sexuality. In doing so, they activate the narrative that homosexuality is "un-African," and connect issues of gender and sexuality to neocolonial imperatives. According to FWI's Stop CSE campaign video, *War on Children*, CSE content is a form of "mental molestation" that manipulates, indoctrinates, and confuses children through its "pornographic" and "obscene" content. According to the Stop CSE petition, which is also hosted on the campaign website:

> We are deeply troubled that these dangerous programs that are sexualizing children around the world, threatening their health and compromising their innocence are being aggressively promoted and/or funded by organizations, such as Planned Parenthood (See InvestigatePlannedParenthood.org), as well as various UN agencies, including UNICEF [originally U.N. International Childen's Emergency Fund], the World Health Organization, UNFPA, UNESCO, and the [Office of the High Commissioner on Human Rights], largely funded by Western governments and donors.

Characterizing CSE as a form of cultural imperialism, the Stop CSE campaign works to create alarm, in the Global South especially, about the impetus behind and the effects of CSE. The Stop CSE campaign has been circulating this petition, along with their "defenders toolkit," to government representatives, religious leaders, and school communities in South Africa, Zambia, Namibia, Uganda, Tanzania, and Ethiopia. While Stop CSE campaigning in each of these countries typically has the appearance of originating in grassroots-level outrage, the U.S.-based organization catalyzing this movement, FWI, remains largely obscured from view. While FWI has tapped into some conservative local sentiments about sexuality and gender, they work to ignite moral panic about the need to protect children from global progressive actors. As the following section discusses, the countermovement against sex and gender-based rights is not only led by U.S. based conservative advocacy groups, but works to uphold Eurocentric and colonial notions of the gender binary, compulsory heterosexuality, and the nuclear family model in their global promotion of pro-family agendas.

## THE GEOPOLITICIZATION OF GENDER AND SEXUALITY

The current Stop CSE campaign in ESA is only one example and site of the antirights campaigning that the pro-family movement has catalyzed in many parts of the world in recent years. While the origins of the pro-family movement can be traced to the North American Christian Right family values movement of the 1970s that sought to counter the sexual revolution, this movement has expanded its geopolitical horizons since the 1990s. Over the course of the past three decades, U.S.-based family values or pro-family groups have made a concerted effort to globalize the countermovement against feminist and queer advocacy and knowledge production (Buss & Herman, 2003). Growing countermovements against LGBTIQ+ rights and sexual and reproductive rights, pro-family groups have capitalized on the enduring effects of colonialism and the social arrangements it destroyed and created in African societies. As decolonial feminist scholar María Lugones (2007) wrote, colonialism introduced gender as not only a system of constructing and regulating "men" and "women," but also a mode of organizing and institutionalizing relations of production, property relations, cosmologies, and ways of knowing (p. 210). Speaking to the broader material and epistemic interests at stake within the colonial enforcement of the gender binary and hierarchy, Lugones pointed to other systems of power and control that are at stake within contemporary pro-family activism.

Awakened to advances being made in relation to women's rights and LGBTIQ+ rights at the 1994 UN International Conference on Population and Development in Cairo and the 1995 World Conference on Women in Beijing, the U.S. Christian Right began to develop its own transnational networks and agendas to extend its advocacy beyond U.S. borders and politics (Cupać & Ebetürk, 2020, p. 704). According to pro-family activists, the SHRHs, women's rights, and gay rights being tabled in these U.N. gatherings threatened the so-called traditional or natural family, putting societies and nations in peril. Within pro-family discourse and advocacy, the UNFPA, UNESCO, and UNICEF have been key agencies that pro-family activists have accused of driving a nefarious global sexual right agenda that undermines the traditions, values, and sovereignty of formerly colonized nations.

[210]   *Finn Reygan and Haley McEwen*

Over the course of the past 25 years, American pro-family organizations have used a variety of strategies to build networks and gain allies in Africa, South America, Europe, and Southeast Asia. Online and offline campaigns, political lobbying in domestic and international governance, events, and demonstrations are some of the key methods used by pro-family organizations to grow their networks and support. While they typically present themselves as sympathetic to the concerns of local communities and as allies of historically oppressed groups (McEwen, 2018), their pro-family ideology aims to reinforce and deepen the exclusion of LGBTIQ+ people within policy language and all spheres of society.

As a countermovement to the sexual and gender revolutions, the pro-family movement and the discourses it propagates work to protect sexed, gendered, and geopolitical forms of power and dominance that have historically served the interests of White, heterosexual, middle-class, and Christian men from wealthy, industrialized nations. The movement's efforts to construct U.S.-based conservative organizations with predominantly White and middle-class leadership as allies of the historically oppressed have strategically negated the power relations between these organizations and the communities they address in the Global South. As Buss and Herman (2003, p. 77) wrote, U.S.-based conservatives have been successful at constructing themselves as more in touch and sympathetic to the needs of local communities than their progressive Western counterparts, who they claim are trying to import nefarious foreign agendas on African and other societies in the Global South.

The movement has dedicated a great deal of attention to African countries and has gained a number of African allies in recent years. Currently, the movement's campaign against CSE and SRHR is gaining traction, threatening programming in these areas in ESA. Organizations tasked with advancing CSE and SRHR in the region are encountering pro-family opposition among political and religious leadership. The renewal of the ESA commitment at the end of 2020 has no doubt catalyzed pro-family activism in the region, and the effects of the movement's intervention within local policy debate are increasingly noted by SRHR and CSE advocacy groups. While the focus of anti-CSE campaigning has been directed at specific countries in ESA, pro-family campaigning has implications for other countries in the region and within regional intergovernmental bodies, such as the African Union and the Southern African Development Community. Recent efforts to prevent the renewal of the 2013 ESA Ministerial Commitment on CSE and SRH services reflect the regional strategy that anti-CSE campaigning has adopted over the course of the past few years.

## CONCLUSION

Overall, significant gains have been made globally since the post-WWII period in advancing LGBTIQ+ rights, women's rights, and SRHR. These gains, however, have not come without resistance. Over the course of the past two decades, a global movement has emerged in opposition to advances made by queer and feminist advocacy and scholarship. While opposition to changing norms about sex, sexuality, and gender has always existed, it is clear that there is a concerted effort being made to consolidate and constellate conservative sentiment and advocacy. As investigative journalists and forensic financial investigators have shown, these efforts have been funded by U.S. Christian Right organizations and other conservative global powers from Eastern and Western Europe who have become aligned with the pro-family agenda in often contradictory and surprising ways.

The strategic conservative efforts to challenge CSE in African countries should also be seen in relation to attacks on gender studies in other parts of the world, such as Latin America (Jaschik, 2017; Pele & Assy, 2019) and Europe (Geva, 2019; Korolczuk & Graff, 2018; Mayer & Birgit, 2017). As a field of knowledge intertwined with advocacy for LGBTIQ+ rights and gender justice, gender studies has also become a target of antigender activism for having developed what the movement refers to as "gender theory." Although gender studies and CSE are different in terms of their immediate objectives and audiences, both have played significant roles within advocacy for sex, sexuality, and gender-related rights. In the effort to discredit these fields of knowledge, the pro-family movement is working to dislodge and delegitimize the epistemic foundations of increasingly visible and vocal queer and feminist advocacy in Global South and North countries. Challenges to the hegemonic status of heteropatriarchy challenges not only cisgender and heterosexual normativity, but also the White supremacist colonial foundations of the notions of the gender binary and hierarchy.

Epistemic attacks on CSE and gender studies thus constitute efforts to discredit and erase knowledge that challenges not only heteronormativity and male dominance, but also Eurocentric and colonial ways of knowing and doing gender, sexuality, and family. The hegemony of heteropatriarchal and colonial ways of knowing and defining sex, sexuality, and gender have been central to the ability of these forms of social dominance to be perpetuated and reproduced amid increasing calls for equal recognition of gender and sexuality diversity in societies around the world.

While the efforts of the pro-family movement to discredit CSE and gender studies are certainly cause for alarm within queer and feminist

[212]   *Finn Reygan and Haley McEwen*

social movements, it is also confirmation of the power and potential of these fields of knowledge to dismantle the forms of power that are so vehemently working against them. It is also a powerful reminder that rights once gained cannot be taken for granted as having been permanently won. Moreover, as the current countermovement against CSE in ESA shows, attacks on forms of knowledge that support SRHR and LGBTIQ+ rights are as significant as, and entangled with, attacks on the rights themselves.

## REFERENCES

Bhana, D. (2014). *Under pressure: The regulation of sexualities in South African secondary schools*. Braamfontein: Ma'Thoko's Books.

Biroli, F., & Caminotti, M. (2020). The conservative backlash against gender in Latin America. *Politics & Gender, 16*(1), E1. https://doi.org/10.1017/S1743923X20000045

Buss, D., & Herman, D. (2003). *Globalizing family values: The Christian Right in international politics*. University of Minnesota Press.

Cupać, J., & Ebetürk, I. (2020). The personal is global political: The antifeminist backlash in the United Nations. *The British Journal of Politics and International Relations, 22*(4), 702–714.

Daniels, J., Struthers, H., Maleke, K., Catabay, C., Lane, T., McIntyre, J., & Coates, T. (2019). Rural school experiences of South African gay and transgender youth. *Journal of LGBT Youth, 16*(4), 355–379.

Denzin, N., & Lincoln, Y. (2017). *The SAGE handbook of qualitative research*. SAGE.

Family Policy Institute. (2016). Stop CSE in South African Schools. https://citizengo.org/en/fm/35997-stop-cse-south-african-schools

Fatusi, A. O. (2016). Young people's sexual and reproductive health interventions in developing countries: Making the investments count. *Journal of Adolescent Health, 59*(3), 1–3. https://www.jahonline.org/article/S1054-139X(16)30162-8/fulltext

Francis, D. A. (2016). *Troubling the teaching and learning of gender and sexuality diversity in South African education*. Springer.

Francis, D. A., & Brown, A. (2017). "To correct, punish and praise" LRC leaders experiences and expressions of non-heterosexuality in Namibian schools. *International Journal of Inclusive Education, 21*(12), 1276–1293.

Francis, D. A., Brown, A., McAllister, J., Mosime, S. T., Thani, G. T., Reygan, F., Dlamini, B., Nogela, L., & Muller, M. (2019). A five country study of gender and sexuality diversity and schooling in Southern Africa. *Africa Education Review, 16*(1), 19–39.

Francis, D., & McEwen, H. (2023). Normalising intolerance: The efforts of Christian Right groups to block LGBTIQ+ inclusion in South African schools. *Culture, Health & Sexuality*, 1–12.

Geva, D. (2019). Non Au Gender: Moral epistemics and French conservative strategies of distinction. *European Journal of Cultural and Political Sociology, 6*(4), 393–420. https://doi.org/10.1080/23254823.2019.1660196

Gevisser, M., & Cameron, E. (Eds.). (1995). *Defiant desire*. Routledge.

Global Philanthropy Project. (2018). *Religious Conservatism on the Global Stage: Threats and Challenges for LGBTI Rights.* https://globalphilanthropyproject.org/2018/11/04/religious-conservatism-on-the-global-stage-threats-and-challenges-for-lgbti-rights/

Glover, J., & Macleod, C. (2016). Rolling out comprehensive sexuality education in South Africa: An overview of research conducted on Life Orientation sexuality education [Unpublished policy brief document, Critical Studies in Sexualities and Reproduction, Rhodes University]. http://srjc.org.za/wp-content/uploads/2017/06/Life-Orientation-Policy-Brief_Final.pdf

International Planned Parenthood Federation. (IPPF). (2010). *IPPF framework for comprehensive sexuality education (CSE).* IPPF.

Independent Online. (2020). Sex education will normalize lesbianism, sodomy and promiscuity. https://www.iol.co.za/the-star/news/sex-education-will-normalise-lesbianism-sodomy-promiscuity-christian-groups-37186239 (Accessed February 15, 2022).

Jaschik, S. (2017, November 13). Judith Butler discusses being burned in effigy and protested in Brazil. Inside Higher Ed. https://www.insidehighered.com/news/2017/11/13/judith-butler-discusses-being-burned-effigy-and-protested-brazil

Kaoma, K. (2009). Globalizing the culture wars: US conservatives, African churches, and homophobia. Political Research Associates. https://www.politicalresearch.org/2009/12/01/globalizing-culture-wars

Kaoma, K. (2012). Colonizing African values: How the U.S. Christian Right is transforming sexual politics in Africa. Political Research Associates. https://politicalresearch.org/2012/07/24/colonizing-african-values#toc-pdf-file

Kitch, S. (2009). *The specter of sex: Gendered foundations of racial formation in the United States.* SUNY Press.

Korolczuk, E., & Graff, A. (2018). Gender as "Ebola from Brussels": The anticolonial frame and the rise of illiberal populism. *Signs: Journal of Women in Culture and Society, 43*(4), 797–821. https://doi.org/10.1086/696691

Kováts, E., & Pető, A. (2017). Anti-gender movements in Hungary: A discourse without a movement? In R. Kuhar & D. Paternotte (Eds.), *Anti-gender campaigns in Europe: Mobilizing against equality* (pp. 117–131). Rowman & Littlefield International.

Kuhar, R., & Paternotte, D. (Eds.). (2017). *Anti-gender campaigns in Europe: Mobilizing against equality.* Rowman & Littlefield.

Lugones, M. (2007). Heterosexualism and the colonial/modern gender system. *Hypatia, 22*(1), 186–219. https://doi.org/10.1111/j.1527-2001.2007.tb01156.x

Mayer, S., & Birgit, S. (2017). "Gender ideology" in Austria: Coalitions around an empty signifier. In R. Kuhar & D. Paternotte (Eds.), *Anti-gender campaigns in Europe: Mobilizing against equality* (pp. 23–40). Rowman & Littlefield.

McArthur, T. (2015). Homophobic violence in a Northern Cape school: Learners confront the issue. *Agenda, 29*(3), 53–59.

McClintock, A. (1995). *Imperial leather.* Routledge.

McEwen, H. (2018). Nuclear power: The family in decolonial perspective and "pro-family" politics in Africa. *Development Southern Africa, 34*(6), 738–751. https://doi.org/10.1080/0376835X.2017.1318700

Msibi, T. (2012). "I'm used to it now": Experiences of homophobia among queer youth in South African township schools. *Gender and Education, 24*(5), 515–533.

Ndjio, B. (2012). Post-colonial histories of sexuality: The political invention of a libidinal African straight. *Africa: Journal of the International African Institute, 82*(4), 609–631. https://doi.org/10.1017/S0001972012000526

Oyěwùmí, O. (1997). *The invention of women: Making African sense of western gender discourses*. University of Minnesota Press.

Oyěwùmí, O. (2002). Conceptualizing gender: The Eurocentric foundations of feminist concepts and the challenge of African epistemologies. *JENdA: A Journal of Culture and African Women Studies, 2*(1), 1–9.

Pascale, C. M. (2010). Epistemology and the politics of knowledge. *The Sociological Review, 58*(2), 154–165.

Pele, A., & Assy, B. (2019, November 5). Academic freedom(s) in the drift towards authoritarianism (3/4). *Droit & Société: Theorie et sciences sociales du droit*, p. 1–7. https://ds.hypotheses.org/6354

Potgieter, C., & Reygan, F. C. (2012). Lesbian, gay and bisexual citizenship: A case study as represented in a sample of South African Life Orientation textbooks. *Perspectives in Education, 30*(4), 39–51.

Provost, C., & Archer, N. (2020, October 27). Revealed: $280m "dark money" spent by US Christian Right groups globally. openDemocracy. https://www.opendemocracy.net/en/5050/trump-us-christian-spending-global-revealed/

Reygan, F. (2021). "I just want to have a better life and be who I want to be": Competing perspectives on LGBTI inclusion in South African schools. In W. Pearson, Jr. & V. Reddy (Eds.), *Social justice and education in the 21st century: Research from South Africa and the United States* (pp. 113–128). Springer. https://doi.org/10.1007/978-3-030-65417-7_7

Santelli, J., Ott, M. A., Lyon, M., Rogers, J., & Summers, D. (2006). Abstinence-only education policies and programs: A position paper of the Society for Adolescent Medicine. *Journal of Adolescent Health, 38*, 83–87.

Smith, A. (2006). Heteropatriarchy and the three pillars of white supremacy. In A. Smith, B. Richie, J. Sudbury, J. White, & the INCITE! (Eds.), *Color of violence: The INCITE! anthology* (pp. 66–73). South End Press.

Steyn, M. (2015). Critical diversity literacy: Essentials for the twenty-first century. In S. Vertovec (Ed.), *Routledge international handbook of diversity studies* (pp. 379–389). Routledge.

Stoler, A. L. (1995). *Race and the education of desire: Foucault's history of sexuality and the colonial order of things*. Duke University Press.

Tamale, S. (2011). Researching and theorizing sexualities in Africa. In S. Tamale (Ed.), *African sexualities: A reader* (pp. 11–36). Pambazuka Press.

Ubisi, L. (2021). Queering South Africa's protective school policy for LGBT+ youth: The Nare Mphale case. *Journal of Educational Studies, 2021*(si1), 106–138.

United Nations Educational, Scientific, and Cultural Organization (UNESCO). (2013). Experts in Southern and Eastern Africa call for renewed commitment on sexuality education and health services. https://en.unesco.org/news/experts-southern-and-eastern-africa-call-renewed-commitment-sexuality-education-and-health

United Nations Educational, Scientific, and Cultural Organization (UNESCO). (2015). Emerging evidence, lessons and practice in comprehensive sexuality education: A global review. https://unesdoc.unesco.org/ark:/48223/pf0000243106

United Nations Educational, Scientific, and Cultural Organization, United Nations
        Population Fund, & United Nations Joint Program on HIV/AIDS (UNESCO,
        UNFPA, & UNAIDS). (2016). Fulfilling our promise to young people today
        2013–2015: Progress review: The Eastern and Southern African Ministerial
        Commitment on comprehensive sexuality education and sexual and
        reproductive health services for adolescents and young people. https://healt
        heducationresources.unesco.org/sites/default/files/resources/fulfilling_our_
        promise_to_young_people_today_esa_2013-2015_progress_review_en.pdf

CHAPTER 11

# Queering School Sport and Physical Education

RICHARD PRINGLE AND DILLON LANDI

Critical researchers have predominantly viewed school sport and physical education (PE) spaces as heteronormative and homophobic (e.g., McGlashan, 2013; Sykes, 2011). The research that has prompted these views has typically focused on LGBT student and teacher identities and their associated experiences of disaffect and abuse within sport and PE settings. Although we recognize the good intentions of these scholars, we are also concerned that much of the research repeatedly seeks to reveal problems but offers little direction in how to think differently about diverse genders and sexualities moving forward. In this chapter, we aim to examine queer thinking about sport and PE contexts and promote alternative, more optimistic ways for viewing these spaces.

The argument we develop begins with the recognition that school sport and PE spaces are never purely heteronormative or homophobic (lisahunter, 2019). In contrast, we contend these spaces are much messier than that, and in recognizing this complexity we hope that cracks of resistance can be opened up to forge greater acceptance of queer ways of being within PE. Relatedly, we adopt a more fluid view of sexualities and question, drawing from Foucault (2014), why one would want to "lock in" their broader identity to one particular form of sexual performance? In this manner, we question how identities, as linked to sexualities, have been conceptualized within existing research concerning PE. We accordingly argue that it is the seemingly normative gender/sexuality framework that has underpinned

Richard Pringle and Dillon Landi, *Queering School Sport and Physical Education* In: *Queer Studies and Education*. Edited by: Nelson M. Rodriguez, Robert C. Mizzi, Louisa Allen, and Rob Cover, Oxford University Press.
© Oxford University Press 2023. DOI: 10.1093/oso/9780197687000.003.0012

much of the LGBT research in sport and PE spaces that ultimately needs to be challenged if we are to "free" ourselves of identity dilemmas. We conclude by presenting a narrative of a queer student's experiences related to sexuality in school sport and PE to illustrate how desires can disrupt and transform allegedly heteronormative spaces. We develop our argument in three sections. First, we begin by providing a brief historical sketch of the linkages between sport, bodies, genders, sex, and sexualities to illustrate how various gender and sexuality troubles have developed within this sporting assemblage. We then critically review research that has examined gender and sexuality issues within school sport and PE. We draw specifically from the international research of Eric Anderson (England), Michael Gard (Australia), Dillon Landi (USA/New Zealand), and Håkan Larsson and colleagues (Sweden). Drawing from this research, we highlight three promising research approaches that offer hope for thinking and performing differently within PE spaces. We conclude by presenting a PE narrative of queer transformation based on the experience of a sexuality diverse young person from Aotearoa New Zealand.

## SPORT/GENDER/SEX/SEXUALITY/EDUCATION ASSEMBLAGES

Sport/gender/sex/sexuality assemblages have historically been understood, via queer theorists, as interconnected in a fluid but somewhat troubling manner. In this section we provide a *brief historic sketch* to illustrate how sporting assemblages allegedly link to gender/sexuality troubles and how these troubles can be found in school sport and PE. We do so in relation to the contemporary dilemma of sex testing in sport. Sport is one of the last remaining social institutions to divide individuals based on biological conceptions of sex. This sexual division is still viewed as extremely important as sporting associations, such as the International Olympic Committee (IOC), go to great cost to devise and implement techniques for determining whether certain bodies can be scientifically classified as female or male. In this essentialist context, certain female bodies, such as Caster Semenya's,[1] gain dubious media and medical attention due to speculation that they are not 100% female and, relatedly, *might* have an unfair "male" (i.e., testosterone) sporting advantage (Karkazis et al., 2012; Schultz, 2011). Yet, this concern about unfair advantage is unfounded on three fronts. First, there is little scientific evidence to support the notion that elevated testosterone levels in females improve sport performance (Karkazis et al., 2012). Second, the issue of sport fairness at the elite open level has never been an issue in relation to an athlete's height, weight,

[218]   *Richard Pringle and Dillon Landi*

strength, limb length, or any other bodily attribute or ability—attributes that undoubtedly give some competitors unfair(?) advantage over others. Third, there has never been a case in which a "male" athlete has been caught in a deliberate attempt to compete as a female in order to gain sporting glory. Despite the lack of a clear and consistent rationale for sex testing, many elite female athletes—and only female athletes—have been subject to visual, invasive, and biochemical testing for decades (Schultz, 2011).

Underpinning this interest in the maintenance of scientifically derived sexual divisions in sport, we contend, is an apparent attempt to use sport to maintain a traditional "gender/sexuality order" (see Connell, 1995). Sport has been widely recognized as a prime gendering institution, particularly in the production of masculinities (Connell, 2008; Messner, 2006). Indeed, sport was historically developed by men for the benefit of men (Messner, 2002). And until the 1970s, sport was principally viewed as a male domain or preserve (Theberge, 1985). Female athletes have accordingly been barred from competing in numerous sporting competitions. In the inaugural 1896 Olympics, for example, only males were allowed to compete. The founder of the modern Olympics, Pierre de Coubertin, clarified his position about women by stating: "At the Olympic Games their role should be above all to crown the victors, as was the case in the ancient tournaments" (as cited in Houry, 2011, pp. 59–60). Females were also denied entry into many other sporting spaces throughout much of the 20th century unless they were servicing men's sport, such as by serving beer in the clubrooms, laundering uniforms, or cheering on the sidelines (Thompson, 1999).

Sport has also been widely valued for its alleged masculinizing abilities. Young boys were/are often encouraged to participate in sports, including those with high injury rates, as parents and teachers believe that sport will help these boys develop good masculine characters: As the sexist cliché asserts, "sport turns boys into men." The characteristics most valued in sport align closely with masculine notions, such as competitiveness, aggression, strength, perseverance, leadership, and pain tolerance. The sporting assemblage accordingly connects sport with dominant forms of masculinities and, by default, heterosexuality. The sporting domain has correspondingly been assembled as a predominantly masculine and heterosexual space. Within this space, it is still rare for an elite sportsman to "come out" as gay or bisexual.

When females were finally "allowed" to participate in various sporting codes they were widely regarded as *athletic intruders* (Bolin & Granskog, 2003). This access was only typically granted, however, after sustained protest and political action. The history of women's sport, as such, has been one of struggle for acceptance and equity (Cox & Pringle, 2012). Moreover, these victories in sport occurred late in comparison to other gender equity fights. The right for equal pay for female teachers was granted in 1972 in Australia, yet it was only in 2007 that the Wimbledon tennis tournament offered equal prize money and 2018 with respect to the World Surf League. In other sporting competitions, the status of equal pay has not yet been reached, thus indicating female sport participants are still not valued as highly as sportsmen. The pioneering sportswomen, particularly in sporting codes deemed masculine (e.g., soccer, rugby, American football), often faced derision and ridicule in their early attempts to enjoy the benefits of sport. Female soccer players from the early 1970s, as an example, reported they were often mocked as dykes or lesbians (Cox & Pringle, 2012).

The advent of strong athletic sportswomen has undoubtedly troubled the traditional gender/sexuality order. C. L. Cole (2000) correspondingly argued that the sex testing of female athletes had little to do with ensuring fairness in sport competition but was primarily concerned with policing gender and producing firm binaric boundaries: male/female, masculine/ feminine, straight/gay. Cole argued this boundary production was interconnected with the promotion of sport as a wholesome and moral activity. She referred to the disqualified athletes as *boundary creatures* as they illustrated the divide between the normal and the abnormal, while indirectly promoting the sporting context as a level or "moral" playing field. Andy Miah (2010) similarly contended that the IOC members are portrayed in the media as moral vigilantes in their attempts to rid the sporting world of "sexual misfits" and drug cheats to ensure the integrity of the sporting world.

We concur with Cole (2000) and Miah's (2010) arguments and understand that the IOC desires to prevent some sportswomen from participating— those who appear too manly or too good to be real women—via the dubious task of sex testing (see also Kelly, 2018). Yet, given the difficulty encountered in trying to ascertain what constitutes "a woman" (e.g., visual inspection is not proof enough and internal examination and the genetic/ hormonal testing has been subject to stern critique), the sport sex-testing debacle has indirectly supplied scientific evidence that sex boundaries are indeed blurred and fluid social constructions. Ironically, therefore, the IOC sex-testing approach supports a queer and disruptive stance through revealing that biological sex cannot be easily determined. When we also consider that most PE curricula are dominated by sport, it is not surprising that gender and sexuality scholars have found these spaces to also be homophobic and heteronormative. In the following section, however, we aim to engage in the queer process of troubling the idea that spaces can be labeled in such a straightforward manner.

## GENDERS AND SEXUALITIES IN PHYSICAL EDUCATION:
## A QUEER EXAMINATION

The dominant research approach for examining gender/sexuality issues in PE draws on the identity-bound notions of LGBT. Findings from this research tend to highlight how LGBT persons suffer various negative experiences within school sport and PE. The explanatory "cause" for these troubling experiences rests with the acceptance that these spaces are heteronormative and homophobic and therefore spaces of discrimination and exclusion. Although we do not doubt the existence of dimensions of heteronormativity and homophobia within PE spaces, we worry that such a straightforward labeling of these spaces can unintentionally prop up normative assumptions about sex and gender in a manner that reproduces the idea that there are clear divisions between differing "types" of subjectivities (e.g., female/male, gay/straight, femininities/masculinities). Further, we contend that it is this normative framework of thinking that reproduces notions of normality and abnormality that are tied into sex, gender, and sexuality assemblages. In doing so, the reproduction of this normative framework in LGBT research actually works to reinforce the various forms of discrimination felt by some students in PE. To develop this argument, we critically review key literature that has examined LGBT experiences in PE and school sport.

The following quotations attest to the issue that researchers who have examined genders and sexualities in school sport and PE spaces often instigate their research with the understanding that "homophobia and heteronormativity are central to the culture of sport" (Drury, 2014, p. 309). Sykes (2010), for example, began her chapter on student experiences of queerness in Canadian PE by stating:

> Many students have alienating or embarrassing experiences in physical education that deter them from developing confidence in their physical ability. Often these embarrassing or alienating moments in physical education arise from discrimination based on sexual orientation, gender expression and body shape/ size. (p. 123)

Similarly, Atkinson and Kehler (2012) assert that PE classes are sites "of ritual masculinizing practices through which boys learn, embrace and embody, or are damaged by, particular codes of dominant masculinity" (p. 166). And Joanne Hill (2013) began her review article by simply proclaiming: "It has been consistently identified that sport and physical education have a heterosexual and masculine bias which has implications for the development of young people's identities or subjectivities" (pp. 428–429).

The "knowledge" that school sport and PE are heteronormative and homophobic spaces has been of concern for critical scholars for three prime reasons. First, the discrimination of LGBT students deters these individuals from participating in sport, so they do not gain the alleged social, health, and affective benefits (Sykes, 2010). Second, LGBT students experience forms of marginalization, discrimination, and outright abuse that act to "damage" these individuals to the extent that this felt sense of abjection can encourage some LGBT students to "harm" themselves. The rates of self-harm and suicide by queer students is well known by scholars of sexualities, as Sedgwick (2013) pointed out: "I think everyone who does gay and lesbian studies is haunted by the suicides of adolescents" (p. 3).

Finally, there is concern that school sport and PE are formative spaces within which students learn, and become confined, by accepted ways of performing masculinities or femininities and associated sexualities. In other words, school sport and PE are viewed as sites that reproduce and reinforce dominant ways of performing genders and sexualities within which students learn what they can and cannot do with their bodies. Although these are legitimate concerns, we are also worried that research findings repeatedly reveal problems but offer little hope in how to think differently and promote greater acceptance, perhaps even celebration, of queer ways of being and performing. In the following section, we review three recent research approaches that seemingly allow hope for thinking differently about PE, sexuality, and gender.

## THREE PROGRESSIVE WAYS OF VIEWING SCHOOL SPORT AND PE SPACES

Over the last 15 years, alternative views of PE have developed that offer the promise of a more inclusive queer future. In this section, we examine three of these notable approaches. The first approach, drawing from what Eric Anderson (2012) called inclusive masculinity theory, suggests that there has been a dramatic decrease in levels of homophobia within sport settings and PE and associated evidence of increased inclusion of gay males within these settings. Anderson (2012), for example, concluded from an ethnographic examination of high school PE that there was "an absence of homophobia and homophobic discourse, the abatement of violence, the absence of jock-ocratic school culture, and the emotional support of male friends" (p. 151). Additional findings suggest that concerns about homosexuality have decreased to such an extent that straight sportsmen are no longer concerned to change with gay men in a locker room (Magrath et al., 2015), and that some sportsmen can even engage in cuddling, kissing, and spooning or sleeping with other men, without concerns that such behaviors might threaten their heterosexual status (Anderson & McCormack, 2015). The picture painted is one of a somewhat radical transformation with respect to the acceptance of (homo)sexualities within sport and PE settings.

Despite this apparently positive social change, inclusive masculinity theory is underpinned by an identity-based approach that does little to challenge normative notions of genders/sexualities. This theoretical lens does not, therefore, queer understandings of sexualities but works to classify and separate individuals based on reductive classifications of select sexual practices, which leads us back to Foucault's (2014) concern with the futility of attempting to find out the "truth" of one's sexuality. This mission, he believed, was a trap: How do you know when you have reached the ultimate truth? Is there another layer we could potentially pull back to get to our "real" selves? As an antiessentialist, he dismissed this approach and, more importantly, became concerned to understand how power operates in a manner to encourage our search for the alleged truth of our sexual selves. In drawing from Foucault, we suggest that power operates within inclusive masculinity theory to encourage classification of identities and, as such, it locks in the normative genders/sexualities framework. At this point, it is worth representing Foucault's (2014) long-term vision in relation to sexual identity politics:

> In my opinion, as important as it may be, tactically speaking, to say at a given moment, "I am a homosexual," over the long run, in a wider strategy, the question of knowing who we are sexually should no longer be posed. It is not then a question of affirming one's sexual identity, but of refusing to allow sexuality as well as the different forms of sexuality the right to identify you. The obligation to identify oneself through and by a given type of sexuality must be refused. (p. 261)

Foucault wanted to overturn the dominant and oppressive sexualities framework in order to offer greater "freedom" in the long-term from identity politics. Yet the inclusive masculinity theoretical perspective does not have this ambition and, by default, works to lock in the normative framework: a framework that some view as the source of sexuality troubles (Storr et al., 2022). For example, an associated danger of inclusive masculinity theory, as Sam de Boise (2015) argued, is that it "conflates the hard-fought legal rights won by gay rights activists with a mistaken belief that because homophobic speech and violence are less apparent in public contexts, that we are nearing some historical end-point for gender and sexuality discrimination" (p. 334). Indeed, although changes are occurring with respect to wider acceptance of gay marriage and diverse sexualities, there is overwhelming evidence that the endpoint is not fast approaching.

The second alternative approach for understanding gender/sexuality issues in PE rests on the assumption that as an educational space, PE can be used to challenge normative understandings of sexuality and gender. Research in this light offers strategies toward a queer PE pedagogy. Gard (2008) advocated, for example, the use of dance in PE as a tool for boys and girls to experiment with different ways of moving, understanding, and being. He argued "that the restrictions boys and men place on the ways they use their bodies are linked to the restrictions boys and men place on what it means to be male" (p. 186). Gard suggested that PE students should, accordingly, interrogate the norms of gender and their own emotional investments in these forms of gender via the lens of dance. Within this context, boys and girls can experiment with the pleasures and discomforts of alternative ways of moving and dancing. Gard added that student explorations of their emotional investments within differing ways of moving provide critical avenues to challenge "homophobia, stereotypes, difference, diversity and the way culture shapes who we are and what we do" (p. 192).

Larsson et al. (2014) have similarly used dance within PE to create a heterotopia or countersite that enables resistance to normalizing processes. With respect to gender/sexuality norms, they used dance so that the students could experience physical closeness with a variety of boys and girls (e.g., girl-girl, boy-boy, girl-boy). Through these experiences of dance, Larsson and colleagues advocated that PE teachers can encourage students to not only reflect on heteronormativity and develop an ability to identify when it is occurring but also become equipped "with the means to challenge cultural norms" (p. 147).

These queer pedagogies revolve around the potential of disruptive and discomforting experiences in order to challenge heteronormativities and produce opportunities for social change. Yet, these pedagogies require well-trained, knowledgeable, and value-invested teachers, as their implementation could potentially spur student resistance to such critical aims. As Gard (2003) noted: "We cannot be sure how students, particularly male students who are accustomed to getting their way in physical education, will react when asked to create and do dance" (p. 220).

The third research approach that offers new ways for thinking about gender/sexuality in PE starts from the outset that PE is already a queer

[224]    *Richard Pringle and Dillon Landi*

place. Lisahunter (2019) noted that despite PE's apparent disconnect from queer topics, it has been identified by some as a queer space for many years, given it is a subject with many lesbian teachers and queer-identified people. Lenskyj (1997) concurred by suggesting with respect to sporting contexts:

> On the one hand, women's sport provided a haven for women who preferred a homosocial environment, ostensibly free from pressure to behave and present oneself in a conventionally heterosexual manner, and as such it was well known by lesbians as a place where one might find other lesbians. (p. 11)

Drawing on the idea that PE is already a queer place, Dillon (Landi, 2019) explored the possibilities of queering the PE space drawing on ethnographic interview data with 11 queer-identified men. In it, Dillon argued the PE field can play an active role in producing homoerotic desire, and that this "desire can reciprocally affect the field and its practices" (p. 1). To do so, Dillon highlighted how his interviewees believed the prime purpose of PE was to work on the body to produce good health; his interviewees suggested the ideal masculine body assembled within PE would be viewed as fit, healthy, muscular, and athletic. Several of Dillon's interviewees further noted how the production, and active display, of particular "healthy" male bodies affected or induced their queer desire. These interviewees also noted the presence of their queer desire produced a transformative element within their PE classes as, at the least, it allowed queer students to use desire, in various ways, to challenge heteronormative practices.

In the following section, we continue this notion of using queer desire to disrupt heteronormativity. To do so, we draw from data from an earlier project that involved interviews with a purposeful sample of 11 men to examine their understandings and lived experiences of diverse sexualities within sporting/PE contexts (see Pringle & Landi, 2016). In this prior study, we deliberately sought out individuals who identified as queer or straight: Four identified as gay and seven as straight. Our empirical task was to document the array of bodies, technologies, affects, and events involved in the local assemblages of sporting sexualities. In this chapter, we focus our examination on the interview undertaken with Sione (a pseudonym). Sione, was 21 years old at the time of the interview and was studying at university. During the interview, Sione was asked to reflect on his experiences in school sport and PE. Sione revealed that he came out while in high school, and although he was subject to some forms of abuse, his narrative revealed how his desires disrupted and transformed the heteronormative PE space. Our narrative representation that follows is underpinned by the *ambition* that queer can become "productive for thinking and doing educational projects that reach beyond the subjects and objects of sex, gender, and sexuality" (Rasmussen & Allen, 2014, p. 442). In other words, the narrative is underpinned by a desire to challenge the normative in a broader sense than just sexualities. We also note that we have taken liberty with the interview transcript to retell and recraft aspects of Sione's story to provide a more coherent narrative but have remained true to the key elements of his story.

## A QUEERING NARRATIVE OF PE DESIRES

My name is Sione, which is a fairly common Samoan name for a boy but less common for a Tongan. And that is what I am: in fact, I consider myself a Tongan New Zealander. I've grown up all my life in Auckland. South Auckland to be more precise, it's a part of the city with lots of Pasifika people and with a real Pasifika feel. It's where you can buy pig heads at the butchers, kava at the corner shop and colourful "Island" shirts abound. It's also a place where some boys can be girls, or as Fa'afafine's as we say in Samoan, and that is pretty much accepted by most of us. So, I am a proud South Aucklander. I am a big boy also and have been all my 21 years of life. I stand over six feet tall and weigh over 16 stone. My size has been an advantage as, even if people didn't like me, they didn't want to push me around. But that doesn't mean that I haven't experienced my fair share of putdowns and abuse. And I have to admit that PE was one of the worst parts of school, at least when I first began high school. It's not that I wasn't good at sport or that I didn't enjoy playing a sport but that the other boys in PE were simply, I guess, dickheads for want of a better word or perhaps I should say immature.

Oh, and I should let you know that I was "out" early in life. I had always known that I liked boys and I thought others could also tell, so what was the point of hiding it? By the time I was 15, I was out, "loud and proud". And I had thick skin. I think. I needed it, as people would tell me things that they thought would affect me but it would bounce off my resplendent dark skin. Like in PE when we were playing touch rugby and someone would say to the teacher, "we don't want to play with Sione, as he might touch us inappropriately." I would just roll my eyes and sometimes even pretend to be trying to touch them by having my hands reaching out and fingers waggling. They, no doubt, thought they were being funny. And during PE, they would sometimes call me names like faggot and sissy. Literally. The teacher of course could hear them, but he did nothing. He probably thought it was good that I was being identified correctly—ha!

It was often worse in the changing rooms, that's where I would get called "fuck arse" and "poo jammer"—really crude things. When I was getting changed the captain of the school rugby team would sometimes stand behind me and mimic a sexual action. At times, I would go along with it to make it seem like I was part of the joke. Some would even grab my arse—I mean physically they would grab my arse—unbelievable really. So, they weren't the best of times. No one wants to be different and we all want to be accepted, so of course it did hurt. In the end, I refused to change in the locker rooms and I would get changed in this little dark room next to the gym that had old mats and gym equipment in, it smelt very musky, but was really private. Prior to that I had liked getting changed with all the boys, especially if they showered. I would always look but I had to do it carefully, so I would use mirrors to check out some guy's butt or at other times, I would walk past someone as they were changing and drop something so that I would have to pick it up right next to him. And I would have a good look! It was exciting for me. In fact, there were times that I would have to sit with cross legs not to reveal my excitement.

Then there was the moment that changed everything for me: an epiphany of sorts. One day the captain of the rugby team, Mike, followed me into my private "change room" as I was getting changed. I didn't know he was there at first, so was surprised when I looked up and realised he was standing and looking at me. I thought he was going to make fun of me. But he was just staring at me, and not saying a word. And then he moved a little closer, so I worked out what was happening and I tentatively flirted with him. That is, I let my undies "slip". And he still stood there quietly so I let him touch me briefly and he was real keen. But I told him "no, it's not safe here." Not long after that brief encounter we met several times after school for some intimate experimentations. I said it was an epiphany of sorts, as I slowly realised something else about the sexuality of others, that perhaps others are just as confined by the whole male sex system that tells us who we should be and what we should do, or not do, with our bodies. It allowed me to realise I was not the only one pushed around by what I call the sex system.

Looking back, I think that the fact that I was openly gay, encouraged Mike to think about his own sexuality or perhaps it encouraged him to explore some fantasies. Perhaps if I had never been out, he wouldn't have tried what he did and he wouldn't have found that he liked it? Who knows? Although Mike has never identified as gay—he even has a girlfriend now and I see him occasionally at university—I know he nevertheless enjoyed his sex with me. And it wasn't loving sex between us, it was just sort of physical and that's ok. Over time, another boy in my PE class approached me quietly and displayed an interest in me. I was happy to oblige. I began to wonder whether I had earlier been bullied in PE, as others couldn't come "out" and whether they were somehow envious of me. I don't know? Anyhow, by the time I was 16 I was feeling more confident—I was trying to live "loud and proud" and it was around this time that I started viewing PE differently and acting differently. I could now get away with being more flamboyant and with touching the other boys. PE actually encouraged the touch: in the scrums, on the basketball court, when wrestling or even doing gymnastics. PE also allowed me to see other boys naked, particularly when we did aquatics or when we were required to have showers after getting muddy and sweaty on the fields in winter. In time, I started doing things like jumping on other boy's backs in games of rugby and I guess I sort of taunted them or teased them with my physical closeness. At times it was hilarious and I loved it, it was fun, pushing boundaries and of course the physical closeness. Some knew it was like a joke, you know like "Oh no, Sione is hugging me again." At other times, such as when our team scored a goal, I would join the celebration and the hugging and even slip in a kiss on the cheek for some of the boys.

So, I would push boundaries and I found I could get away with it. If I had to summarise it, I slowly realised I could play an active role in making the boys more accepting of different ways of being. Over time, PE became a place that I enjoyed, a place where I felt less confined, a place where I could try different things with my body, and a place where I could express myself in different ways—sometimes tough and manly and other times, very "fem" and queer. So, unlike other academic subjects in school, it was a place of body experiment: a queer place.

## QUEERING PHYSICAL EDUCATION

In our narrative above, Sione's experiences in PE started out very typical, and like other LGBTQ+ young people he discussed his dislike of PE, how he was harassed by students and how teachers did little to intervene. Sione spoke of the homophobic and heteronormative nature of the subject— where he was also ostracized. As we dug deeper in questioning and learning more about Sione and his story, however, there was a more complex narrative to unfold. Sione was not a passive recipient of homophobic and heteronormative practices. Rather he played along with—and in many cases challenged—the behaviors of his classmates and teachers. For example, Sione often rolled his eyes and pretended to touch classmates in order to push back on homophobic culture.

Indeed, not all of Sione's experiences were positive. Some may argue that Sione's male classmates were "horsing around" or "playing along" with masculinities by performing "queer" behaviors and grabbing male arses. From Sione's perspective, however, he was being sexually assaulted, and straight men performing queer behaviors was more of a knock—an offensive grab for attention—rather than a shift in the types of masculinities acceptable in schools. Therefore, Sione chose to resist these spaces and the ostensibly inclusive performances by changing clothes in a private room. This is not to say that Sione did not enjoy some aspects of changing with classmates, such as the opportunities it provided to view male bodies. But at the end of the day, he did fear for his own safety and felt uncomfortable.

A watershed moment within the narrative, however, was when Sione realized that his body was *desired* by some of his classmates. Rather than him being the target of oppression, he was a target of sexual pleasure. As such, Sione felt being "loud and proud" helped other young men awaken their own curiosities around queer sexualities. Furthermore, as Sione started to feel more confident in PE settings, he started performing more flamboyant behaviors—and folding queer bodily movements into the gym (Landi, 2018). Thus, Sione's view of PE changed: He no longer viewed it as a restrictive and normalizing space but as a space of sensual and desirous opportunity. In drawing from Sione's narrative, we *optimistically* suggest that when young queer men have confidence, feel comfortable, and are encouraged to enjoy movement and touch, this allows possibilities to transform heteronormative and homophobic PE environments into queer expressive spaces.

## CONCLUDING THOUGHTS

Although gender and sexuality researchers have primarily represented school sport and PE spaces as problematic for queer students and as sites that entrench the gender status quo, these spaces are not only heteronormative and homophobic but also complex and messy. Indeed, school sport and PE can be thought of as queer school spaces as they are uniquely different from the ordered confines of the classroom and the serious focus on education, learning, and postschool vocations. Learning and education are valued within sport and PE, yet the prime focus is on body pleasure. Students primarily play sport for fun, and if it is no longer pleasurable, they stop. And PE teachers primarily aim to help students find a movement form they enjoy with the quixotic belief that this will translate to physically active adult lifestyles. In other words, the prime pedagogical goal in PE is to encourage students to have fun with their bodies (Gerdin & Pringle, 2017; Pringle, 2010)—a goal that is not always achieved or explicitly proclaimed.

Although these body pleasures are usually overtly nonsexual, covert links to sexuality are never far away. Females and males are, at times, still divided in these movement contexts so that, somewhat strangely, they become homosocial environments: contexts that demand same-sex seminudity and, at other times, close contact. Although looking is covert in male changing rooms, all sportsmen who shower together, irrespective of their sexual inclinations, know who has the biggest penis (Smith, 2014). The locker room, although a place of abuse, can also be a place of desire. The rugby field, although a place of aggressive competitiveness, can also be a space of cherished contact and close friendships. And, the swimming pool, not only a place of disciplined exercise but also a place where torsos and midriffs are visible, can be a space where bodies gain wanted or unwanted sexual attention. Unlike other school subjects, PE is a place where bodies and physical abilities are on display: a place of potential embarrassment and/or source of pleasure.

School sport and PE can also be considered queer places as females are encouraged to cherish so-called masculine qualities: to be competitive, aggressive, pain tolerant, dominant, and physical, whereas all students can be encouraged to be somebody else if a queer pedagogy is adopted in dance lessons. In this manner, PE can challenge normative thinking about gender and sexuality. So, what do we hope to gain politically through conceiving school sport and PE as queer spaces? Our hopes are threefold: (1) a contribution to a nonnormative way of viewing sport and PE, (2) an awareness that these spaces are messy and opportunities for resistance and transgressions potentially abound, and (3), a promotion of the idea that identities do not have to be bound to normative frameworks of thinking about sexualities and genders. It is perhaps easy to critique our "If you build it, they will come" stance (a notion popularized in the baseball movie *Field of Dreams*), yet we adhere to Foucault's underpinning aim "to make the strange familiar and the familiar strange."

## NOTE

1. Caster Semenya is a South African middle-distance runner, openly gay, and although raised a girl and with external female genitalia has faced bans from the International Amateur Athletic Association for having naturally high levels of testosterone.

## REFERENCES

Anderson, E. (2012). Inclusive masculinity in a physical education setting. *Boyhood Studies*, 6(2), 151–165. https://doi.org/10.3149/thy.0601.151

Anderson, E., & McCormack, M. (2015). Cuddling and spooning: Heteromasculinity and homosocial tactility among student-athletes. *Men and Masculinities*, 18(2), 214–230. https://doi.org/10.1177/1097184X14523433

Atkinson, M., & Kehler, M. (2012). Boys, bullying and biopedagogies in physical education. *Boyhood Studies*, 6(2), 166–185. https://doi.org/10.3149/thy.0601.166

Bolin, A., & Granskog, J. (Eds.). (2003). *Athletic intruders: Ethnographic research on women, culture, and exercise.* SUNY Press.

Cole, C. L. (2000). Testing for sex or drugs. *Journal of Sport and Social Issues*, 24(4), 331–333. https://doi.org/10.1177/0193723500244001

Connell, R. W. (1995). *Masculinities.* Allen & Unwin.

Connell, R. (2008). Masculinity construction and sports in boys' education: A framework for thinking about the issue. *Sport, Education and Society*, 13(2), 131–145. https://doi.org/10.1080/13573320801957053

Cox, B., & Pringle, R. (2012). Gaining a foothold in football: A genealogical analysis of the emergence of the female footballer in New Zealand. *International Review for the Sociology of Sport*, 47(2), 217–234. https://doi.org/10.1177/1012690211403203

De Boise, S. (2015). I'm not homophobic, "I've got gay friends": Evaluating the validity of inclusive masculinity. *Men and Masculinities*, 18(3), 318–339. https://doi.org/10.1177/1097184X14554951

Drury, S. (2014). Gay sports spaces: Transgressing hetero(/homo) normativity and transforming sport? In J. Hargreaves & E. Anderson (Eds.), *Routledge handbook of sport, gender and sexuality* (pp. 309–317). Routledge.

Foucault, M. (2014). *Wrong-doing, truth-telling: The function of avowal in justice.* University of Chicago Press.

Gard, M. (2003). Being someone else: Using dance in anti-oppressive teaching. *Educational Review*, 55(2), 211–223. https://doi.org/10.1080/0013191032000072236

Gard, M. (2008). When a boy's gotta dance: New masculinities, old pleasures. *Sport, Education and Society*, 13(2), 181–193. https://doi.org/10.1080/13573320801957087

Gerdin, G., & Pringle, R. (2017). The politics of pleasure: An ethnographic examination exploring the dominance of the multi-activity sport-based physical education model. *Sport, Education and Society*, 22(2), 194–213. https://doi.org/10.1080/13573322.2015.1019448

Hill, J. (2013). Queer bodies: Sexualities, genders and fatness in physical education. *Sport, Education and Society*, 18(3), 428–432. https://doi.org/10.1080/13573322.2013.737167

Houry, C. (2011). *American women and the modern summer Olympic Games: A story of obstacles and struggles for participation and equality* [Dissertation]. University of Miami. University of Miami Scholarly Repository: Open Access Dissertations, 571.

Karkazis, K., Jordan-Young, R., Davis, G., & Camporesi, S. (2012). Out of bounds? A critique of the new policies on hyperandrogenism in elite female athletes. *American Journal of Bioethics*, 12(7), 3–16. https://doi.org/10.1080/15265161.2012.680533

Kelly, M. (2018). Sports science, femininity, and athletic gatekeepers of gender. In D. Hutchinson & L. Underwood (Eds.), *Women, social change, and activism: Then and now* (pp. 33–41). Lexington Books.

Landi, D. (2018). Toward a queer inclusive physical education. *Physical Education and Sport Pedagogy*, 23(1), 1–15. https://doi.org/10.1080/17408989.2017.1341478

Landi, D. (2019). Queer men, affect, and physical education. *Qualitative Research in Sport, Exercise and Health, 11*(2), 168–187. https://doi.org/10.1080/21596 76X.2018.1504230

Larsson, H., Quennerstedt, M., & Öhman, M. (2014). Heterotopias in physical education: Towards a queer pedagogy? *Gender and Education, 26*(2), 135–150. https://doi.org/10.1080/09540253.2014.888403

Lenskyj, H. J. (1997). No fear? Lesbians in sport and physical education. *Women in Sport and Physical Activity Journal, 6*(2), 7–22. https://doi.org/10.1123/wspaj.6.2.7

Lisahunter. (2019). What a queer space is HPE, or is it yet? Queer theory, sexualities and pedagogy. *Sport, Education and Society, 24*(1), 1–12. https://doi.org/10.1080/13573322.2017.1302416

Magrath, R., Anderson, E., & Roberts, S. (2015). On the door-step of equality: Attitudes toward gay athletes among academy-level footballers. *International Review for the Sociology of Sport, 50*(7), 804–821. https://doi.org/10.1177/1012690213495747

McGlashan, H. (2013). *Dare to be deviant: Gay males reflective experiences of physical education* [Unpublished master's thesis]. University of Auckland.

Messner, M. A. (2002). *Taking the field: Women, men, and sports* (Vol. 4). University of Minnesota Press.

Messner, M. A. (2006). *Out of play: Critical essays on gender and sport.* SUNY Press.

Miah, A. (2010). Towards the transhuman athlete: Therapy, non-therapy and enhancement. *Sport in Society, 13*(2), 221–233. https://doi.org/10.1080/174304 30903522947

Pringle, R. (2010). Finding pleasure in physical education: A critical examination of the educative value of positive movement affects. *Quest, 62*(2), 119–134. https://doi.org/10.1080/00336297.2010.10483637

Pringle, R., & Landi, D. (2016, November 4). Are sporting masculinities really inclusive? A new-materialist study of (homo)sexualities and sport [Paper presentation]. North American Society for the Sociology of Sport Annual Conference, Tampa, FL, United States.

Rasmussen, M. L., & Allen, L. (2014). What can a concept do? Rethinking education's queer assemblages. *Discourse: Studies in the Cultural Politics of Education, 35*(3), 433–443. https://doi.org/10.1080/01596306.2014.888846

Schultz, J. (2011). Caster Semenya and the "question of too": Sex testing in elite women's sport and the issue of advantage. *Quest, 63*(2), 228–243. https://doi.org/10.1080/00336297.2011.10483678

Sedgwick, E. K. (1994). Queer and now. In D. Hall, A. Jagose, A. Bebell, & S. Potter (Eds.), *The Routledge queer studies reader* (pp. 3–17). Routledge.

Smith, R. (2014, March 18). Study: In the locker room size matters and straight guys act super gay. Queerty. https://www.queerty.com/study-in-the-locker-room-size-matters-and-straight-guys-act-super-gay-20140318

Storr, R., Jeanes, R., Rossi, T., & lisahunter. (2022). Are we there yet? (Illusions of) Inclusion in sport for LGBT+ communities in Australia. *International Review for the Sociology of Sport, 57*(1), 92–111. https://doi.org/10.1177/1012690221 1014037

Sykes, H. (2010). Looking back, looking sideways: Adult perspectives about student experiences of queerness in Canadian physical education. In M. O'Sullivan & A. MacPhail (Eds.), *Young people's voices in physical education and youth sport* (pp. 123–141). Routledge.

Sykes, H. (2011). *Queer bodies: Sexualities, genders, and fatness in physical education.* Peter Lang.

Theberge, N. (1985). Toward a feminist alternative to sport as a male preserve. *Quest,* *37*(2), 193–202. https://doi.org/10.1080/00336297.1985.10483834

Thompson, S. M. (1999). *Mother's taxi: Sport and women's labor.* SUNY Press.

CHAPTER 12

# Queer Screen Pedagogies

*Australian Queer Audiences and the Educational Value of LGBTQ Film and Television Stories*

ROB COVER

From a queer theory perspective, gender and sexual identities, selves, practices, and concepts are formed from an engagement with discourse. This is an engagement that operates across a very diverse range of pedagogies, whether formal education, media spectatorship, or creative meaning-making, to name a few. Within queer theory, all subjects form identities, behaviors, and ways of being in the world through that encounter, subsequently stabilizing a self-identity through taking up the norms, codes, and practices found in cultural discourses and performing those over time in a way that retroactively lends the illusion of agency and uniqueness. If we are to apprehend educational and pedagogic practices that foster identity, belonging, and social participation, we must take into account the *processes* through which that discursive encounter occurs, how it incorporates the utilization of a range of nonformal practices such as screen media spectatorship and how that subsequent broad range or "matrix" of pedagogies operates to condition ways of living, including ways of living a livable life. That is, in encountering discourse in its myriad and complex forms, we take on and cite the signifier, category, norm, or practice as codes of intelligible, coherent, and recognizable conduct that are prior to us and circulate as a "set of meanings already socially established"

Rob Cover, *Queer Screen Pedagogies* In: *Queer Studies and Education*. Edited by: Nelson M. Rodriguez, Robert C. Mizzi, Louisa Allen, and Rob Cover, Oxford University Press. © Oxford University Press 2023. DOI: 10.1093/oso/9780197687000.003.0013

(Butler, 1990, p. 140). All subjects perform variances on those discursively given codes in order to fulfill the cultural demand of intelligibility for belonging and social participation; all subjects perform across all aspects of life, whether in practices of speech, bodily composure, self-reflectivity, attitude, online articulation, desire, sexual and romantic expression, gender, and ways of practicing ethnicity, age, and other demarcations of distinctiveness and social difference.

With this in mind, an approach to queering our perceptions of education gains value if education is understood as one aspect or element of a wider "educational matrix" of pedagogies: resources, peer networks, private and public institutions, and—particularly in the context of this chapter—screen media as the range of interconnecting settings by which discourses of identity and subjectivity are formed. This chapter presents some findings from the project funded by the Australian Research Council, the *AusQueerScreen* study, in which key film and television production stakeholders and audiences from around Australia were interviewed and asked about their knowledge and views of the representation of gender- and sexually diverse minorities in Australian film and television. In many cases, both stakeholders and audience participants offered accounts of the pedagogical role of screen media in forming a sense of selfhood, recognition, and subjectivity through engagement with the narratives, themes, and characters depicted on screen; some focused on the intersection between local voices and global gender and sexual minorities and others.

This chapter begins with a summary of the AusQueerScreen study before presenting a queer-theoretical account of screen media cultural pedagogies. It then reports on three key findings from the study related to screen pedagogies: (1) Production stakeholders' perception of their role as "educators" in creating films with LGBTQ content; (2) an analysis of audience members' understandings of the encounter with gender- and sexually diverse content as an instance of education; and (3) the parasocial relationships with key characters that inform roles and decision-making. A significant finding from this study is that screen media texts continue to play an unexpectedly powerful pedagogical role. In the mid-1990s, it was acceptable to find that the relatively small number of queer characters, themes, and narratives in film and television were of value in a period in which queer content in formal education and other settings was substantially less available or in some jurisdictions legally suppressed (Cover, 2000). What is remarkable today, given some of the findings of the study, is the extent to which young audience members continue to find pedagogic value in ordinary, everyday queer entertainment texts, despite the "progress" in educational content, positivity, and situatedness within other pedagogical settings, including formal sex and relationships education (Rasmussen et al., 2016). Furthering our understanding of the intersection of screen media and pedagogy provides us with new approaches to thinking about how education is positioned alongside other cultural institutions and practices.

## THE AUSQUEERSCREEN STUDY

Despite an often-repeated journalistic cliché that gender- and sexually diverse characters are relatively absent from film and television, Australian screen creative production has indeed a very rich history of representing sexual and gender diversity on screen: greater than 19 mass-circulation films since 1993, including internationally recognized films such as *Priscilla, Queen of the Desert* (1994); *The Sum of Us* (1994); *Head On* (1998); and *The Monkey's Mask* (2000). Nine Australian films with LGBTQ, gender, and sexually diverse themes were released between 2013 and 2018, indicating an entrenchment of LGBTQ representation on Australian screens. Characters in major Australian television dramas and soap operas such as *Home and Away* and *Neighbours* have increased in presence, regularity, and complexity of storyline over the past two decades. Sexual stories, including narratives of minority sexual lives, have never, of course, been repressed or invisible but, according to Ken Plummer, have long been central to contemporary Western culture (Plummer, 1995, p. 4). Stories representing gender- and sexually diverse subjects, depicting identity struggles and articulating minority health outcomes are a major and ongoing part of Australian creative production. What is significant in cultural analysis is *not* questions of visibility or invisibility, but how the continuities and disruptions of depictions of gender and sexual minorities play a significant, pedagogical role in social participation, social harmony, acceptance, individual health and well-being, and community belonging. Indeed, rather than a focus on visibility, it is more important to acknowledge not only that range, extensiveness, and depth of queer characterizations are the key queries for the 2020s or how many queer characters are represented, but also *what audiences do with those representations* (Cover & Dau, 2021) that provides valuable knowledge on pedagogical potential.

The AusQueerScreen ("Representation of Gender and Sexual Diversity in Australian Film and Television, 1990–2010") study investigated gender- and sexually diverse LGBTIQ+ characters, themes, and narratives in Australian film and television (1990–present) and their impact on health, identity, and culture. Funded by the Australian Research Council,

[236]   *Rob Cover*

the study provided one of the first comprehensive accounts of Australian media production's contribution to gender/sexual minority representation in the context of its importance for fostering (1) healthy identities and (2) acceptance of minorities to mainstream audiences in a digital media era. Setting out to provide a framework for better understanding the role of screen media and entertainment in mental health, well-being, and social harmony among both minority youth audiences and their mainstream peers, the project undertook literature reviews and archival analysis and gathered new data from interviews with film and television stakeholders (producers, scriptwriters, actors) and audience members (aged 18–50) from across most regions of Australia, including both urban and rural/regional settings.

Among the study's key insights has been that while there are persistent public and discursive claims of a widespread "invisibility" of gender- and sexually diverse characters, themes, and stories, Australia has a very rich, long history of including gender- and sexually diverse content in its television and film production; that there is an overrepresentation in Australia, in contrast to English language screen media from the United Kingdom and the United States, of suicidality among queer young people (Cover, 2021); that there is widespread interest in gender diversity across several generations of Australian screen texts, including particularly intersections between trans subjectivity and drag performance which may or may not be productive (Cover et al., 2021); and that younger audience members tend to be more critical of the quality and depth of queer characters, while older audience members tend to celebrate any visibility, indicating a substantial shift toward a more critical form of spectatorship. For the purposes of this chapter, I am interested in cases in which creative production stakeholders and audience members interviewed articulated ideas that implied an educational practice in the production, circulation, and reception of Australian gender- and sexually diverse texts.

## CULTURAL PEDAGOGIES, QUEER THEORY, SCREEN MEDIA

A cultural pedagogy acknowledges that experiences and opportunities of "education" are dispersed across institutional and noninstitutional settings, through everyday engagement with the environment, via nonauthorized and noninformational sources, and—particularly in the contemporary era—through practices of engagement and spectatorship of media, including screen media in the forms of film and television entertainment and digital content. For theorist Henry Giroux (2004), "Pedagogy, at its best, implies that learning takes place across a spectrum of social practices and settings" (p. 61). The kind of pedagogy that Giroux envisaged is somewhat removed from the more formal framework of educational institutions, including particularly those that have been transformed negatively by transactional approaches to education in an era of neoliberalism (Duggan, 2003, p. 21; Giroux, 2010, p. 185). Recognizing, then, that pedagogical practices that operate alongside—and in interrelationships with—formal educational settings involve acknowledging the significance of entertainment media, which themselves are among the most powerful setting for the telling of stories through narrative that give meaning to otherwise disjunct and disconnected events and phenomena in everyday life (Plummer, 1995). What operates, then, is a broad media matrix that performs a pedagogical role. For Barbara Creed (2003), this matrix is a set of interlinked institutions, texts, practices of engagement, and forms of spectatorship through which stories are told and audiences read and engage with those stories in complex, diverse practices of interpretation and meaning-making. And these meaning-making practices are not only across media texts or "intertexts" but also ostensibly intersect with the meanings made and to be made in a wider range of institutional settings.

Making sense of the cultural pedagogy of screen media, its competitiveness and intersections with other formal educational settings, and what that implies for the constitution of gender- and sexually diverse identities among young people can take advantage of the long-standing benefits of queer theory, which, itself, could be aided by some further injection of media and cultural theory. Although queer theory approaches to identity are now over 30 years old, including particularly Judith Butler's poststructuralist theorization of gender performativity, they remain powerful conceptual frameworks for understanding the relationship between discourse, information, practice, and subjectivity and can be understood in the context of pedagogies generally and media pedagogies specifically. Queer theory developed in the late 1980s and early 1990s with theorists examining in critical detail the ways in which sexuality, gender, and subjectivity are socially constructed. Drawing on Michel Foucault's *History of Sexuality* (1990), Eve Kosofsky Sedgwick pointed to the ways in which the commonly known categories of sexuality—"heterosexual" and "homosexual"—are presented through a binary that is historical, mythical, and without "natural" or "essentialist" foundation (Sedgwick, 1990). Sedgwick's analysis of the binary has been a significant cornerstone of much queer theory work, which has often sought to deploy deconstructionist analyses to rethink sexuality along lines alternative to the dominant classification of sexual desire and identity in hetero and homo terms. By starting with the notion that sexual identities only emerged in the 19th century (there were always heterosexual and homosexual acts, but no identities or personages built on these acts) when particular Western medical and psychiatric discourses began to dominate and describe sexuality through these two identity categories (Foucault, 1990), queer theory opened a number of questions: (1) What other ways of categorizing or depicting sex, sexualities, and sexual behaviors were there historically, before the dominance of contemporary discourses of sexuality? (2) What alternative ways of thinking about sexuality can be developed in the future? (3) Who is excluded from the contemporary discourses of sexuality and the hetero- and homo- classifications? (4) In what ways do these categorizations constrain and/or regiment subjects in their sexual behavior, preference, or identity?

Butler articulated one of the most useful poststructuralist articulations of how identity is constructed and constituted in language, culture, and discourse and the means by which many of us have such a deep attachment to our identities despite their contingency and the fact that linguistically they tend to undo themselves. Her approach lends itself well to an understanding of discourse that incorporates media creative and reception practices, allowing us to go beyond the idea of media as simply some kind of benign conveyor or disseminator (Cover, 2006). Butler demonstrated that identities are constituted through performances that are "in accord" with preexisting culturally given categories of identity. For example, a queer male performs homosexuality through acts, desires, attractions, behaviors, and tastes that are recognizably homosexual as learned in discourse. In performing an identity—which is never a conscious or voluntary act—one cites and repeats the category and the information given culturally that makes that category intelligible and recognizable to oneself and to others. Such performances are repetitive and come to stabilize over time, retroactively producing the *illusion* that the performances manifest from a fixed, inner identity core (Butler, 1990, p. 143). That is, our actions and performances do not stem from an inner essence but constitute it.

Following Nietzsche, she pointed out that there is no "doer behind the deed," that is, no static sexual subject (being) is revealed through sexual behavior or desire (doing). Rather, we perform our sexual identities *over time* in accord with discursive expectations and cultural demands for coherence, intelligibility, and recognizability. Identity is the compulsion to reiterate "a norm or set of norms" that "conceals or dissimulates the conventions of which it is a repetition" (Butler, 1993, p. 12). The performative expression of same-sex desire, attractions, and behaviors that occur in line with recognizable and discursively given norms constitute the queer subject much as the articulation of opposite-sex desire forms the heterosexual subject.

That is, all identities are constituted within ambiguities, incoherences, and inconsistencies, but for the sake of coherence we are required to disavow, suppress, or reinscribe in order to perform as an intelligible and coherent self (Butler, 1990, pp. 31–32, 1997, p. 27). The cultural demand to articulate sexual identity as constant, fixed, coherent, and intelligible means such disavowals of any alternative are produced through cultural regimentation and regulation. For Butler, identity is thus manufactured in the languages, concepts, and ideas available to a culture at a specific point in time, meaning that the engagement with discourse includes the complicated, creative, diverse ways in which people engage with media that construct, circulate, reframe, and condition interpretations.

Most scholarship on the *representation* of gender- and sexually diverse (LGBTQ+) subjects has been grounded in literary and textual analysis, focused on understanding the meanings in film and television texts, with only a very small amount of scholarship intent on theorizing and testing how meanings are made by audiences, what audiences do with queer texts, and how those texts operate in pedagogic ways for audiences that are implicated in identity performativity (Cover & Dau, 2021). In that sense, this scholarship lacks an engagement with queer theories of identity and pedagogy. At the same time, however, media theories of reception lack the depth of queer theoretical perspectives on reception and audiencehood's pedagogical practices. That is, most media analysis that takes into account diverse audience identity has tended to operate from a standpoint perspective, in which the identity of the audience member is understood and framed as "fully formed." For example, the approaches to media reception that have dominated much of cultural and media studies, from screen theory in the 1970s (Moores, 1993), through Stuart Hall's encoding/decoding framework of audience interpretation and meaning-making (Hall, 1993), through Janice Radway's (1984) study of audience practices, do not provide a mechanism for accounting for the ways in which a relational engagement with texts, intertexts, and contexts can present the discursive resources providing the signifiers, codes, and practices that, in the encounter with the text, are taken up, cited, and *utilized* for the coherent and intelligible performativity of minority subjecthood.

In perceiving the spectatorship of queer screen texts not as chosen by a particular preexisting, fixed identity but as associated with the formation, stabilization, or reconfiguration of identity, the concept of encounter is key. It is in the moment of encounter with the text, narrative, or discourse that a process of subjectivity is configured and recognized (or, indeed, re-cognized or re-thought). A trajectory for a particular kind of subject is initiated in that engagement, and that is a trajectory that responds to the wider cultural demand for coherent, intelligible, and recognizable subjectivity—what Jacques Derrida described as "the subject answerable as subject" (Derrida, 1995, p. 241). While that trajectory might be moved from a subjective "I" to a "lesbian I," as Butler (1991) suggested, it might also be the transition of a lesbian I to another form of gender or sexual diversity as this changes further over time and new configurations of subjectivity, categorization, and identity articulation emerge (Cover, 2019). What is needed, then, is a further understanding about what the encounter does—the practices of encountering, using, revisiting, thinking about, sharing, and discussing texts—whether the encounter is perceived by audience members as specifically pedagogical or not and the memorialized practices by which audience members subsequently reflect on textual encounters as pedagogical.

From a perspective attuned to theories of cultural identity, a media discourse of minorities "not only names, but forms and frames the subject" (Butler, 1997, p. 93); once encountered and recognized as a social logic, it can have an interpellative effect that constitutes identities in particular ways (Butler, 1993, p. 107). Since gender- and sexually diverse subjects often come to recognize such identities not through early years in a family environment but through discursive frameworks encountered elsewhere, the "matrix" of media discourses available to that subject may be empowering for some young people and vulnerabilizing for others, depending in part on how the discourse is read, interpreted, has its meanings activated, and is incorporated into the everyday sense of selfhood of the subject (Cover, 2017; Gill, 2012). In this context, media accounts dealing with minority sexualities and genders may, indeed, be more significant than other more formal resources, such as formal sex education in schools (Rasmussen et al., 2016) or peer education in online settings (Clarke, 2013; Clarke et al., 2018). Catherine Ashcraft has pointed out that popular culture is a site of struggle in which adolescent sexual identities can either be reinscribed or transformed (Ashcraft, 2003, p. 38), and certainly the reinforcement of suicide as a logic for young people experiencing adversity is one possibility, while popular screen media also have the potential to subvert and critique embedded discourses and social logics. Given the capacity of entertainment media *both* to reinforce social stereotypes of minorities *and* to provide the resources for a critical engagement with those stereotypes (Giroux, 2003), for the broader population of their peers, there is substantial further work needed to understand the pedagogical practices of screen media, the ways in which creative producers perceive and position their role in educational contexts, and how audience members make sense of media as a form of pedagogical engagement.

## SCREEN PRODUCTION PEDAGOGIES

The AusQueerScreen study spoke to a range of film and television producers, scriptwriters, actors, and others involved in the production process. As many were speaking to the researchers about their experiences that included constraints on production of gender- and sexually diverse content and negative reactions from key industry stakeholders, their interviews were undertaken on condition of anonymity. All key stakeholders were asked to discuss their views on the importance of their work to audiences, whether soap operas, independent or wide-circulation film, or television dramas. The majority discussed these issues and their experiences not only in terms of providing entertainment to audiences but also as having an explicit educational or pedagogical role or responsibility.

One creative producer's comments are broadly representative of the views held by the screen media stakeholders interviewed, including those who were active in the 1980s, 1990s and 2000s and currently:

> So many young people tell me that seeing [text name redacted] changed their life because they found some kind of validation in it about their own lives. I'm regularly approached by people who saw it at the start and for whom it was quite life changing, as well as young people discovering [it] now. . . . I wanted to create characters on screen that felt relevant to me. As an artist, I had a burning desire to express something about sexual identity, class and culture that spoke to a moment in time and to a very specific place. . . . It was educational but that was not always in a positive sense, because I was criticised for not always showing lesbians and gay men in only a flattering light but as well-rounded, complex characters. That teaches all the audience something about humanity and the complex lives.

What this statement indicates is a recognition by creative producers and scriptwriters that audiences were active in articulating their appreciation of screen texts that were reflective of their own perceptions of everyday life, and that in recognizing this creative production stakeholders dealing with gender- and sexually diverse content understood themselves to have a broader responsibility to present characters that had depth and complexity, rather than to rely on stereotypes or gestural characterizations. It remains, of course, to test further the extent to which creative personnel need to rely on audience feedback and the conditions of making such feedback available—which vary across different genres and production arrangements—to produce characters and narratives that are both representative and palatable to audiences. Ultimately, to be a producer, director,

[242]   *Rob Cover*

actor, or screenwriter working with gender- and sexually diverse content was broadly regarded as having a special kind of responsibility different from those working with more normativized content.

In a large number of cases, this responsibility was read by the interviewees through the lens of a pedagogical discourse. Importantly, the perception that to be a creative producer, scriptwriter, actor, or director of Australian screen entertainment media with queer characters was to be situated in an educational role was expressed on three occasions by the key phrase, or similar: "making a difference in young people's lives." It is helpful here to unpack what that "difference" might constitute. For several of the key stakeholders, there was a perception that while their representational work in creating LGBTQ+ characters or stories was not alone and clearly built on the previous work of others, each new instance was an opportunity to break new ground by providing a distinctly different character or story. We can witness this in the texts themselves. For example, the Australian film *The Adventures of Priscilla, Queen of the Desert* (1994), depicted gay male and transgender characters, all working as drag performers traveling from urban Sydney to outback Alice Springs. Unlike other 1990s and 2000s queer films that represented LGBTQ+ characters and stories wholly outside communities, *Priscilla* "broke ground" by situating Australian gender and sexual diversity within extant communities built on shared experiences, gay subcultural language, practices, jokes, and everydayness, including drag theatrics (McKinnon, 2016; O'Regan, 1996). It made apparent the significance of geographically located urban communities by taking three central characters outside of those communities whereby those characters— for whom their gender and sexual subjectivity is core to a sense of self-identity—were called on to acknowledge the relational framework through which those identities are expressed and acknowledged. Most of the creative stakeholders interviewed in this study not only were familiar with the film but also invoked it as a milestone against which they recognized their own, later work.

One later film, *Downriver* (2015), however, demonstrates the shift in the relationship between identity, selfhood, and space as a good example of breaking new ground. Although also set in an Australian rural region, several characters are gender or sexually diverse, have ostensibly same-sex sexual encounters and/or relationships, form various complex networks rather than geographic communities within a 21st-century postghetto framework (Cover, 2017). While reflecting the increasing understanding that young gender- and sexually diverse people are not necessarily isolated and alone in rural and country settings or necessarily driven to escape to an urban setting (Cover et al., 2020; Gray, 2009), the text powerfully relegates sexual identity to the background of everydayness rather than being depicted as a core "issue," "problem," or "stumbling block" in a filmic narrative. As one interviewee recognized: "It just makes it seem ordinary to be a queer kid in a country town, so it's quite different to all that 'finding yourself in the city' stuff you get from older movies. That was something as a city kid I learned from it [the film]."

While the points raised here are apprehended in textual and audience readings of the films rather than from the perspective of creative producers' and screenwriters' interviews, what is apparent in the idea of "breaking ground" for the educational benefit of audiences is that producers and scriptwriters understood their texts not as individual pieces, but as contributing to a wider corpus of Australian screen media that—taken as a whole—is pedagogical. As one screenwriter of an Australian drama series with young lesbian-identified characters put it:

> I know for a fact that people who will see these characters will probably have seen Australian lesbians before, whether it's *The Getting of Wisdom* or *Monkey's Mask* or something else. I *want* them to compare the characters, I *want* them to not see [redacted character names] as being the first ever Australian lesbians but as just one other kind of representation, different to those who went before and different to those who came later. I *want* people to learn something about sexuality by thinking about the differences. Obviously we can't just have a voiceover explaining this, it's up to the young people [the audience] to figure it out hopefully by watching a lot of movies and TV and watching them carefully. I don't know how you encourage that, maybe in schools?

Significant here, then, is the way in which this interviewee positioned their own work as part of a wider set of texts or "intertexts"—like a curriculum that builds sophistication and nuance over time—thereby helping to give meaning to the characters created for this soap series. Further, the invocation of school, education, learning, and critical engagement is notable as the way in which this is perceived. What this interviewee implies is not that people learn about sexuality from an ever-growing set of representations, but that they learn the range of nuanced performativities of identity and selfhood from being better positioned to *critically engage with and assess* those characterizations beyond the individual text.

Finally, one element of pedagogy discussed among screen media stakeholders used the discourse of "train the trainer," with the view that film and television might perform a pedagogic role, but that role needs to be learned as well. As an Australia actor who played a nonheteronormative television character put it:

[244]    *Rob Cover*

Performing is difficult and you need to have a level of experience behind you, and what worries me is that people aren't getting enough apprenticeships, and moving straight into these roles now, and that's a shame for them because I learnt over a long fifteen-year period, because I was allowed to and was nurtured to, and so what I'd love to see more apprenticeships, so that we can have the next generation trained up across all cultures and sexual orientations and identities and then they take the leads fully prepared. You know what I'm saying? So the audience learns what we've learned—not just from learning the craft but learning about diversity in the first place.

To put this into the perspective of a queer-theoretical cultural pedagogy, then, is to understand it as part of the intertextual interstices across a range of discourses that are made available in uneven ways. By ensuring those involved in creative production have wide experience of diverse identities (as older, more experienced subjects), the texts they are involved in producing are thereby able to have greater nuance. This, arguably, leads to fewer stereotypes or one-dimensional queer characters and, instead, provides young people who encounter and engage with those texts with a more nuanced, richer set of characters, role models, stories, and narratives from which—wittingly or unwittingly—to cite in the formation and performativity of a queer subjecthood.

## AUDIENCE UTILIZATION—ENTERTAINMENT OVER INFORMATION RESOURCES

Audiences utilize creative texts in diverse ways, which can include taking up an entertainment text designed exclusively to tell a pleasurable story as education resources informing cultural knowledges (Giroux, 2003). To suggest that audiences utilize texts is to begin by acknowledging that audiences' members are not tabula rasa, blank slates, to be conditioned by the media they encounter as a result of now long-critiqued pedestrian ideas about "media effects." Such ideas make the erroneous assumption that screen media is more powerful than it is, and that audiences are on the whole are passive, disinterested, without agency, and without the capabilities of critique and reflexivity. Rather, from a uses and gratifications theory perspective, audiences are understood as active agents who select, make use of, preference, interpret, and engage with media to serve particular needs (Blumler & Katz, 1974). A users and gratifications approach allows us to make sense of the engagement with screen media texts as something that, potentially, can occur in ways not envisaged in the production, authorship, distribution, or marketing of those texts. For example, while much film and television based on fictional texts is marketed expressly as entertainment, for pleasurable consumption and for practices of leisure, the idea of uses and gratifications calls on asking if audiences make use of those texts for other reasons, including educational. More pertinently, a sophisticated utilization of a uses and gratifications approach obliges us to ask if there might be multiple uses (informational, entertainment, etc.) and if there might be ostensible and unwitting utilizations occurring at the same time (utilized as an entertainment without realizing until later that a film, e.g., provided substantial information and role modeling for the formation of a coherent identity).

Audience members interviewed were asked if there were any lessons they learned about life, gender, or sexuality from Australian film and television that depicted LGBTQ+ characters, stories, and themes. More than half stated that they did so, and regularly the interviewees made contrastive remarks about film and television serving an educational purpose due to an absence of nonheteronormative and noncisgender content in sex and relationships education in school:

> I did not have any real-world role models growing up at all. You know, I thought I was the only one in the world, which is what I'm so grateful to see now, the kids that, you know, it's out there [on screens] and spoken about and, you know, I know it's not in all relationship education/sex education in schools, unfortunately. It should be, but, no.

In some cases, however, participants did not make sense of this distinction as a dichotomy between suppressed education in school settings and greater representation in media. Rather, they understood the potential for the utilization of the latter in schools. For example, one participant discussed the absence of queer film and television in school curricula, suggesting its inclusion would provide greater opportunities for an expanded sex and relationships education program:

> We also need to have more conversations in educational environments, in primary schools and secondary schools, and have more of that content being used in those environments so it does become run of the mill; normal stuff.

While none explicitly unpacked Australian screen media's educational potential to the extent of identifying what aspects, texts, or ways of viewing would be educational as opposed to noneducational, most implied there was a pedagogical component to viewing queer texts if one was a queer young person.

Arguably, entertainment media may be more significant than information resources (handbooks, educational programs, online support advice, etc.) for its pedagogical role in naturalizing a set of ideas about gender- and sexually diverse subjectivity, relationships, behaviors, and ways of being. This is particularly the case for younger persons, given that such media are used as a resource by young people in the construction and performance of minority sexual and gender identities and in developing practices for coherent and intelligible social belonging (McKinnon, 2016). Screen media texts dealing with minority sexualities and genders may, indeed, be more significant than other more formal resources, such as formal sex education in schools (Rasmussen et al., 2016) or peer education in online settings (Clarke et al., 2018) because they present information in narrative form— that is, the emphasis is on story. As one participant put it:

> It was the fact it was stories that made it meaningful to me. I think in watching how a character changed over time, or how they combatted difficult people, or maybe how they worked out their problems in being gay that I was able to go, "oh, that's one thing I can do to keep my straight friends and gay friends getting along" or whatever.

Narratives present textuality in the context of spatial and temporal forms, both displacing the viewer from the text that is read and incorporating a primary similitude because spatial engagement and lives lived through temporal sequences are immediately familiar (Silverstone, 1981, p. 76). Where informational texts might describe a way of being or defining the self (as a noncisgender person, e.g., for example, depicted as *this is what* x *is*), a narrative text that tells a story by depicting the stages of change, development, self-perception, and transition invites a viewer to make sense of themselves in the context of that narrative of change, development, and stabilization.

To put this into a queer theoretical framework, then, if identities— and we might say, healthy, stable, and livable identities as one mode of subjectivity—are formed through the encounter with discourse that provides the codes, behaviors, and norms for coherent and intelligible self-hood, then a narrative text encourages a mapping out of selfhood across a temporality. In that sense, then, a film or television narrative does not always present the "finished product" of a character (*this is what a gay man is, looks like, acts like and does—a stereotype*) but as a subject always in the process of formation (*this is how a person who may or may not end up a gay man negotiates their subjectivity in relation to other characters*). Film and television have long been understood as a site with the potential to provide positive role models for minorities in circumstances where they might otherwise be absent—for example, empowered women characters (Helford, 2000), young minority men taking on leadership roles (Larbalestier, 2002), racial minorities as nonstereotypes (Edwards, 2002), and so on. Indeed, it has been argued that role models work best when they are represented and apprehended alongside other characters in other texts—an empowered young woman on television is recognized as a role model when differentiated from, say, virgin and vamp stereotypes of available positions for women in earlier television texts (Daugherty, 2001, p. 148). At the same time, however, it is in presenting that role model through narratives that tell a story in temporal contexts, and in articulating that narrative in the context of relationality with other characters, spaces, frameworks, and ways of being, that they invoke identification.

## REPRESENTATION, ROLE MODELS, AND PARASOCIAL RELATIONSHIPS

Finally, I would like to raise one element of the pedagogic function of fictional characters in screen media texts that emerged from the AusQueerScreen study: the parasocial relationship of identification that operates in fictional characters that bear a geographic, social, national, or otherwise "local" resemblance to the viewer. This is to take up one key question that emerged as a point of distinction among the audience interviewees: watching local rather than international (typically North American) content on screens. As one participant put it in discussing whether or not the fact content was "Australian" mattered:

> I don't know how much particularly local media has that capacity [to attract audiences] anymore. And for me, that's because I sense that people are perhaps consuming less local media than they once were, less Australian media than they once were.

On the other hand, most participants did acknowledge there was something very important and powerful about local voices, accents, and settings, even if they themselves preferred to engage with North American content, including North American queer film and television. For those who indicated the local element was particularly meaningful to encounter while growing up, it included the implication that it de-alienated gender- and sexually diverse identities because it reduced the inherent foreignness of LGBTQ+ subjectivity through reducing the explicit foreignness (North American-ness) of nonheteronormative and noncisgender subjectivity. Arguably, the dominant representation or media archetype of gay male subjectivity was, throughout the 1980s and 1990s, a North American one, what Dennis Altman (1982) referred to as the "Americanization" of the homosexual. Participants in the study pointed to what they saw as benefits of LGBTQ+ characters marked by character aspects that were more representably Australian.

In the following case, the interviewee was discussing the 1994 Australian film *The Sum of Us*, which was performed by stereotypically masculine Australian actors Russell Crowe and Jack Thompson:

> It was about relationships between men, as in father and son—and sporty men. And that, like all of that combination—like I grew up in a family of football players, and, you know, very devoted family. Nobody gay, apparently, in any part of this massive family. And, like, I just, you know, I just didn't know that you could be supported like that in a family. I didn't know it, until—yeah, until I started to see those representations. . . . I mean, that was an era where we were beginning to get much more positive pride based stories, I think, in the world, but not that really Australian kind of accent and sporty kind of culture, masculinity.

For this participant, in referring to the inherent "Australianness" and Australian brand of masculine bravado in the characterizations and choice of actors, the film stands out as something that teaches a lesson that was, in the 1990s, absent in other parts of cultural life: that a gay man can representably be a sporty, rugged, blue-collar tradesperson preferring a beer over champagne and a bawdy joke over sophisticated appreciation of opera (Cover, 2015). This is not, of course, to suggest that the "Australianization" of gay male relationality is necessarily in itself a positive framing of diversity since, as Jasbir Puar (2007) rightly pointed out, the reframing of homosexuality in nationalist terms, or "homonationalism," undoes the long-standing critical potential of gender and sexual diversity to present relational norms that reject racist and nationalist ways of being. Rather, it is to suggest that there is a point of *identification* that can be made by audience members who otherwise see too great a distinction between queers on screen and their own background, class, or personal circumstances.

Texts that are framed as having more recognizably local content are therefore opportunities that create the conditions for what one participant described as a more *intimate* form identification:

> But also, for some people, the closest they will actually get to an experience with somebody who is outwardly or openly trans or openly gay or lesbian, bisexual, is on the screen, and it is actually a very—it's intimate—when you're in your lounge room with the lights off, it's an intimate experience. You are actually in a position where you might absorb, that you might actually be positioned to come around to it, if that makes sense. And so I do feel like that's very important.

The recognizability of the characters on screen aids in establishing what has sometimes been understood in media theory as a "parasocial relationship." Parasocial relationality is a concept developed in the 1950s by David Horton and Richard Wohl (1956) and taken up again in the 1990s by Joshua Meyrowitz (1997). It describes the psychological perception by audience members that media characters are knowable, and in which one develops attachments of intimacy, perceived friendship, and identification. In discussing some of their favorite characters in Australian screen texts, several of the participants indicated a parasocial relationship that emerged out of a sense of similitude of background or circumstance that may not exist with texts from other parts of the world.

In its role as provider of narratives that operate as a resource for the construction and constitution of minority subjectivities and make available the codes for recognizable, coherent, and intelligible performativities, media texts that present localized gender- and sexually diverse minorities present the space for the development of parasocial relationships that have a meaningful pedagogical function because they encourage identification. Acts of identification, which Diana Fuss (1995, p. 2) argued has been the significant absence in queer theories of identity construction, are at the core of the study participants' attachments to texts not because those texts present queerness, but because they depict characters that share *other* aspects of background and experience that, in the case of this study, can include the experience of growing up in Australia. The ability of the character in a parasocial relationship is to stand in for the pedagogical friend or "peer"—someone who represents codes of behavior that guide everyday decisions. This part of the AusQueerScreen study did not interview "mainstream" (cisgender and straight-identifying) audience members about their experiences with such texts, but it might be speculated that a further aspect of their pedagogical potential, then, is to encourage everyday audiences to be more accepting of gender and sexual diversity because those texts place that diversity not among North American or European cities, but in the everydayness of Australia.

## CONCLUSION

This chapter argues that screen media have significant potential to operate as a form of unwitting education or what has been identified as cultural pedagogies that provide, in a queer theory sense, the resources for the constitution of intelligible performative identities. Creative producers, directors, screenwriters, and actors who were interviewed for the AusQueerScreen study made reflective comments that could be read as articulations of perceiving themselves in educator roles on the basis of the distinctiveness of the subject matter of their film and television works, and many openly saw themselves as providing an educational resource to their audiences.

The audience members interviewed in this study likewise understood Australian film and television with gender- and sexually diverse characters, themes, and stories as providing various kinds of pedagogies. I described some of these above as being the result of entertainment providing greater capacity for role modeling that can resource stable identity formation due to its narrative functions and the temporality of storytelling and character development. I have also suggested that where the local geographical setting, characters, actors, accents, and frameworks enable a stronger parasocial relationality between audience and character facilitates identification as the necessary element in making an encounter with a media text meaningful in producing a performative subject.

## REFERENCES

Altman, D. (1982). *The homosexualization of America, the Americanization of the homosexual*. St. Martin's Press.

Ashcraft, C. (2003). Adolescent ambiguities in *American Pie*: Popular culture as a resource for sex education. *Youth & Society, 35*(1), 37–70. https://doi.org/10.1177/0044118X03254558

Blumler, J. G., & Katz, E. (1974). *The uses of mass communications: Current perspectives on gratifications research*. Sage.

Butler, J. (1990). *Gender trouble: Feminism and the subversion of identity*. Routledge.

Butler, J. (1991). Imitation and gender insubordination. In D. Fuss (Ed.), *Inside/out: Lesbian theories, gay theories* (pp. 13–31). Routledge.

Butler, J. (1993). *Bodies that matter: On the discursive limits of "sex."* Routledge.

Butler, J. (1997). *The psychic life of power: Theories in subjection*. Stanford University Press.

Clarke, K. (2013). Pedagogical moments: Affective sexual literacies in film. *Sex Education, 13*(3), 263–275. https://doi.org/10.1080/14681811.2012.718992

Clarke, K., Cover, R., & Aggleton, P. (2018). Sex and ambivalence: LGBTQ youth negotiating sexual feelings, desires and attractions. *Journal of LGBT Youth, 15*(3), 227–242. https://doi.org/10.1080/19361653.2018.1469449

Cover, R. (2000). First contact: Queer theory, sexual identity, and "mainstream" film. *International Journal of Gender and Sexuality, 5*(1), 71–89. https://doi.org/10.1023/A:1010189618801

Cover, R. (2006). Audience inter/active: Interactive media, narrative control and reconceiving audience history. *New Media & Society, 8*(1), 213–232. https://doi.org/10.1177/1461444806059922

Cover, R. (2015). *Vulnerability and exposure: Footballer scandals, masculine identity and ethics*. Scholarly.

Cover, R. (2017). Learning about mobile sexual identities from *Queer as Folk*. In L. Allen & M. L. Rasmussen (Eds.), *The Palgrave handbook of sexuality education* (pp. 455–472). Palgrave Macmillan.

Cover, R. (2019). *Emergent identities: New sexualities, gender and relationships in a digital era*. Routledge.

Cover, R. (2021). Gender and sexual diversity and suicide on Australian screens: Popular culture, representation and health pedagogies. *Journal of Popular Culture, 54*(2), 365–387. https://doi.org/10.1111/jpcu.13012

Cover, R., & Dau, D. (2021). Placing the queer audience: Literature on gender and sexual diversity in film and television and reception. *MAI Feminism & Visual Culture, 7*. https://maifeminism.com/literature-on-gender-and-sexual-divers ity-in-film-and-television-reception/

Cover, R., Prosser, R., & Dau, D. (2021). The corporeality of sound: Drag performance, lip-synching and the popular critique of gendered theatrics in Australian film and television. *Media International Australia, 182*(1), 81–94. https://doi.org/10.1177/1329878X211031582

Cover, R., Aggleton, P., Rasmussen, M. L., & Marshall, D. (2020). The myth of LGBTQ mobilities: Framing the lives of gender and sexually-diverse Australians between regional and urban contexts. *Culture, Health & Sexuality, 22*(3), 321–335. https://doi.org/10.1080/13691058.2019.1600029

Creed, B. (2003). *Media matrix: Sexing the new reality*. Allen & Unwin.

Daugherty, A. M. (2001). Just a girl: Buffy as icon. In R. Kaveney (Ed.), *Reading the vampire slayer: An unofficial critical companion to Buffy and Angel* (pp. 138–165). Tauris Parke.

Derrida, J. (1995). The rhetoric of drugs (M. Israel, Trans.). In E. Weber (Ed.), *Points . . . interviews, 1974–1994* (pp. 228–254). Stanford University Press.

Duggan, L. (2003). *The twilight of equality? Neoliberalism, cultural politics and the attack on democracy*. Beacon Press.

Edwards, L. (2002). Slaying in black and white: Kendra as tragic Mulatta in *Buffy*. In R. V. Wilcox & D. Lavery (Eds.), *Fighting the forces: What's at stake in Buffy the Vampire Slayer* (pp. 85–97). Rowman & Littlefield.

Foucault, M. (1990). *The history of sexuality: An introduction* (R. Hurley, Trans.). Penguin.

Fuss, D. (1995). *Identification papers: Readings on psychoanalysis, sexuality, and culture*. Routledge.

Gill, R. (2012). Media, empowerment and the "sexualization of culture" debates. *Sex Roles: A Journal of Research*, 66(11–12), 736–745. https://doi.org/10.1007/s11199-011-0107-1

Giroux, H. A. (2003). Public pedagogy and the politics of resistance: Notes on a critical theory of educational struggle. *Educational Philosophy and Theory*, 35(1), 5–16. https://doi.org/10.1111/1469-5812.00002

Giroux, H. A. (2004). Cultural studies, public pedagogy, and the responsibility of intellectuals. *Communication and Critical/Cultural Studies*, 1(1), 59–79. https://doi.org/10.1080/1479142042000180926

Giroux, H. A. (2010). Bare pedagogy and the scourge of neoliberalism: Rethinking higher education as a democratic public sphere. *Educational Forum*, 74(3), 184–196. https://doi.org/10.1080/00131725.2010.483897

Gray, M. L. (2009). *Out in the country: Youth, media, and queer visibility in rural America.* New York University Press.

Hall, S. (1993). Encoding/decoding. In S. During (Ed.), *The cultural studies reader* (pp. 90–103). Routledge.

Helford, E. R. (Ed.). (2000). *Fantasy girls: Gender in the new universe of science fiction and fantasy television*. Rowman & Littlefield.

Horton, D., & Wohl, R. (1956). Mass communication and para-social interaction: Observation on intimacy at a distance. *Psychiatry*, 19(3), 215–229. https://doi.org/10.1080/00332747.1956.11023049

Larbalestier, J. (2002). *Buffy's* Mary Sue is Jonathan: Buffy acknowledges the fans. In R. V. Wilcox & D. Lavery (Eds.), *Fighting the forces: What's at stake in* Buffy the Vampire Slayer (pp. 227–238). Rowman & Littlefield.

McKinnon, S. (2016). *Gay men at the movies: Cinema, memory and the history of a gay male community*. Intellect Books.

Meyrowitz, J. (1997). The separation of social space from physical place. In T. O'Sullivan & Y. Jewkes (Eds.), *The media studies reader* (pp. 41–52). Edward Arnold.

Moores, S. (1993). *Interpreting audiences: The ethnography of media consumption*. Sage.

O'Regan, T. (1996). *Australian national cinema*. Routledge.

Plummer, K. (1995). *Telling sexual stories: Power, change and social worlds*. Routledge.

Puar, J. (2007). *Terrorist assemblages: Homonationalism in queer times*. Duke University Press.

Radway, J. (1984). *Reading the romance*. University of North Carolina Press.

Rasmussen, M. L., Cover, R., Marshall, D., & Aggleton, P. (2016). Sexuality, gender, citizenship and social justice: Education's queer relations. In A. Peterson (Ed.), *Handbook of education for citizenship and social justice* (pp. 73–96). Palgrave Macmillan.

Sedgwick, E. K. (1990). *Epistemology of the closet*. Penguin.

Silverstone, R. (1981). *The message of television: Myth and narrative in contemporary culture*. Heinemann.

CHAPTER 13

# The Possibilities and Futurities of LGBTQ Youth

## Thinking From a Queer of Color Critique in Educational Research

ANDREA VASQUEZ AND CINDY CRUZ

To speak of LGBTQ people in the United States is to enter an often-contradictory conversation around notions of identity, violence, and safety coupled with ideas of visibility, civil rights, and social justice movements. In recent years, the United States has moved forward, both politically and culturally, allowing for a seemingly more equitable lifestyle for LGBTQ people: Same-sex marriage was legalized, federal hate crime legislation such as the 2009 Matthew Shepard and James Byrd Jr. Hate Crimes Prevention Act was enacted, political positions in government are now filled by out LGBTQ folk, the 2020 U.S. Supreme Court affirmed that the Civil Rights Act of 1964 that outlaws employment discrimination on the basis of sex must also be interpreted to protect gay and transgender people, professional athletes and actors are coming out, and hit television shows like *Transparent*, *This Is Us*, and *One Day at a Time* not only have queer and trans characters but also include queer and trans *youth* characters. By such societal shifts, it would seem that the country is finally addressing homophobic and transphobic oppression. Yet, despite these social and cultural advances, the current political climate in the United States and a renewed emergence of anti-LGBTQ—more specifically antitrans

Andrea Vasquez and Cindy Cruz, *The Possibilities and Futurities of LGBTQ Youth* In: *Queer Studies and Education*. Edited by: Nelson M. Rodriguez, Robert C. Mizzi, Louisa Allen, and Rob Cover, Oxford University Press. © Oxford University Press 2023. DOI: 10.1093/oso/9780197687000.003.0014 youth legislation—renders visible, once again, the urgency to stay attuned to the multifaceted ways in which LGBTQ young people are made invisible, marginalized, and targeted, as well as how these oppressive forms are resisted and challenged.

For many young LGBTQ people, their lived experiences are entangled with and spread across educational settings and institutions of learning. Currently, for LGBTQ youth in the K–12 school system, this urgency has been exasperated not only by the continual and perpetual (re)production of hegemonic societal structures in their schools (Aronowitz & Giroux, 1994), but also by a series of school-related matters affecting all students in the United States. In recent years, K–12 education in the United States was affected by the appointment of conservative and neoliberal philanthropist Betsy Devos, whom as secretary of education enacted policy promoting the privatization of public education and lessened current antisexual harassment laws on university and public school campuses, along with legislation created by then California district attorney Kamala Harris's truancy laws that punished parents (some with jail time) for habitually truant students, and the sudden increase of school shootings that has sparked a nationwide youth-led movement for young people's lives. Unfortunately, for young queer students of color (QSoC), the stakes are much higher. Amid schooling experiences of academic underperformance (Diaz & Kosciw, 2009) and institutional exclusion (McCready, 2004b, 2005, 2010), lives of QSoC in the United States are also tainted by media representation of police brutality against the Black community, specifically police brutality against young Black boys, as well as anti-immigration rhetoric, and an unapologetic push for the construction of a wall at the southern border of the country. As such, QSoC find themselves fighting against not only homophobia and transphobia in and out of their schools, but also the many other forms of societal oppression that are inheritably tied to their *whole* being.

Much of the scholarly focus on lesbian, gay, bisexual, and transgender youth has examined the impact of oppressive social structures on the lives of these youth. This literature has provided numerous theoretical and pedagogical insights, such as theorization of the queer brown body, reflexive antioppressive curriculum and practices, trans-youth ontologies, and the experience of belonging by LGBTQ students on university campuses (Cruz, 2001; Duran et al., 2020; Kumashiro, 2001, 2003; Salas SantaCruz, 2020). However, though this scholarship has profoundly changed the way that LGBTQ students are perceived and advocated for in different discourses of equity and inclusivity within the field of education, "LGBTQ scholarship" has maintained the focus and analysis on the oppressive structures and experiences of LGBTQ students and has failed to take into consideration the ways in which sexuality, gender, class, and race are mutually constituted (Brockenbrough, 2013; Brockenbrough, 2015; Hames-García, 2011; La Fountain-Stokes, 2011; McCready, 2010). As such, this scholarship has failed to critically examine what it might mean—in theory and in practice—to encompass a nonvictimized, antideficit identity and has missed the opportunity to learn and highlight the agency and practices of structural and symbolic disruption of QSoC (Brockenbrough, 2013; Brockenbrough, 2015). Furthermore, "political" push to move away from the identitarian-based labels of lesbian, gay, bisexual, and transgender toward a reclamation of the word "queer" has epistemological and ontological consequences for the study of LGBTQ youth. Since this theoretical move, queer frameworks have been utilized to analyze the experiences of LGBTQ youth and in the process have made queer and LGBTQ youth experiences synonymous with "White, able-bodied, and middle-class" (Renn, 2010, p. 135).

The purpose of this chapter is to center queer of color critique within education research to analyze the potentiality and limitations of "queerness" (Brockenbrough, 2015; Hames-García, 2011) and expose the ways in which QSoC resist oppression in the K–12 education context. Starting with the premise that "queer theory would be able to make sexuality and desire central rather than peripheral to radical politics" (Hames-García, 2011, p. 20), we pay special attention to a shift from LGBTQ and queer studies in education to a move toward a queer of color framework, scholarship whose efforts to unveil liberatory possibilities are blocked by the given state of affairs, including a critical understanding of race, class, gender, and capitalism. In contextualization of the discussion between queer studies and queer of color critique, this chapter explores the disruptions and contributions of a queer of color analysis by situating its academic roots in race and ethnic studies and U.S. women of color (WOC) theory. Last, by exploring the lack of literature on queer youth of color resistance, this chapter asks education researchers to reflect on their scholarship with LGBTQ students and the ways in which they disrupt deficit notions of race and class with QSoC.

## A SHORT NOTE ON QUEER THEORY

Michael Hames-García attributed two dominant genealogies to the birth of queer theory: a separatist narrative and an integrationist narrative (Hames-García, 2011, p. 21). The two different genealogies of queer theory differ in what they argue to be the ontological oppression of sexuality and what knowledge can be afforded from sexuality studies. For these reasons, these two genealogies have two different epistemological and ontological orientations, especially in the way sexuality relates to other forms of socialities. This is important to note because both provide insight into the different ways that queer theory, and queer studies broadly, invisibilize and decenter notions of race and class.

Starting with Gayle Rubin's (1998) *Thinking Sex* and later influencing Eve Sedgwick's (1990) *Epistemology of the Closet*, proponents of the separatist account of queer theory focus on the politics of sexuality *separate* from gender, race, and class, opposed to contemporary feminist thought, which treats sexuality as a derivation of gender (Hames-García, 2011; Rubin, 1998). Queer theory's separatist scholars argue that the politics of sexuality should not be reduced to the politics of gender in order to avoid placing feminism (the epistemology of the politics of gender) as the privileged site for understanding the workings of sexuality (Hames-García, 2011, p. 22). Thus, in articulating sexuality as distinct from gender, race, and class through the onto-epistemological rejection of multiple feminisms, the intelligibility of these narratives has depended on the erasure of several decades of persistent calls within feminisms, antiracist movements, and lesbian and gay of color theory and activism that underscore the ways that different aspects of identity intersect and constitute each other.

Conversely, the integrationist account of queer theory attempts to respond to the challenges posed by the multiplicity of identities that the separatist account avoids. While the separatists attempt to distinguish sexuality from race and gender, integrationist approaches advocate for queer theory as a field of study that addresses the multiple relations among race, gender, class, and sexuality. However, integrationists address this complexity by deploying the category of *queer* to blur the lines among different social locations. Drawing from poststructuralism, integrationist models see identity as oppressive and thus opt to replace identity—and to some extent the corporal body—with "discourse," "practices," and "subjects" (Hames-García, 2011; Lugones, 2011). As Hames-García (2011) wrote:

> The key issues separating integrationist from separatist accounts is most sharply honed in the work of Judith Butler, for whom the very existence of identity is at least part of the problem. For Butler, the individual subject comes into existence as subjugated by identity. Since there is "no outside" to the constituted frame of domination, resistance lies in dismantling identity through parody and reiteration. (p. 25)

Queer theory of the integrationist approach counters the challenges put forward by interlocking identities by focusing on the movement *away* from identity-based theorizing and rather privileging power and desire as fundamental to the construction of subjectivity by using the term *queer* as all encompassing. However, by eliminating identity-based politics, integrationist queer scholars also ignore earlier calls for understanding interconnections among multiple forms of identity, the relationships between power, race, gender, ability, immigration status, and as such, recenter White logics. Without recognizing these intermeshments of power and histories of nondominant communities, queer theory alone is an insufficient framework to understand the multiple ways that QSoC subjectivities and politics are enacted in various worlds. It is a queer of color critique, grounded in feminist of color practices, that is theoretically inclusive to mark these relationships and resistance of QSoC as agential and creative.

## TOWARD A QUEER OF COLOR CRITIQUE

Beginning from Rodrick Ferguson's (2004) materialist analysis of the formation of Black queer subjectivities, queer of color critique names and arranges an interdisciplinary body of scholarship—mostly outside education studies—that seeks to understand the relationship between authoritative and normative ways of being and the practices of resistance to the hegemonic structures that have come to shape the lived experiences of queer people of color in the United States (Brockenbrough, 2013, 2015; Ferguson, 2004). Central to a queer of color critique is the need to make visible the social and historical forces that give rise to the continuous marginalization of queer people of color by exposing the structural forces— such as housing and school segregation, the histories of a community's migration to the United States and the economic and political foundations that are allotted to certain kinds of communities and to others none at all—that produce queer of color marginality. Paying special attention to the quotidian everyday realities of queer people of color and the political and economic ecologies around them, queer of color critique opens the landscape by which queer of color resistance can be explored (Allen, 2011). Like the legal scholarship of critical race studies, the body of literature that uses a queer of color critique is rooted in the lived experiences of queer people of color. By acknowledging queer of color modes of being, resistance, and agency, queer of color critique's strongest theoretical move is a recentering of queer people of color's liberatory knowledge production and practices of resistant socialities.

Two theoretical frames anchor queer of color critique. First, although queer of color critique emerges from the lived experiences of queer people of color, it does not dismiss queer theory's aim to disrupt heteronormative

[258]   *Andrea Vasquez and Cindy Cruz*

and patriarchal gender and sexual formations (Brockenbrough, 2015; Ferguson, 2004). As Brockenbrough (2015) noted, by rendering visible and challenging the logics that construct a "queer deviancy" and queer otherness, queer theory informs efforts within queer of color critique scholarship to explore meanings and expressions by those who have been historically marginalized and excluded due to their sexuality. Second, queer of color critique is informed by U.S. women of color (WOC) feminism. The work of scholars like Gloria Anzaldúa (Anzaldúa, 1987; Moraga & Anzaldúa, 1983), Barbara Smith (1983), Audre Lorde (1983), and the Combahee River Collective (1983) outline a *politics of difference* that acknowledges the multiple and intersecting subjectivities of WOC in the United States. By paying attention to the ways in which class, gender, and sexuality are jointly constructed, WOC theorizing provides a generative and political source of antihegemonic scholarship useful when theorizing from an intersectional standpoint. More than just highlighting power struggles, WOC theorizing provides the language to name and express the different strategies of resistance used by WOC to respond to the intersecting systems of oppression that have othered not only WOC, but also multiple communities of color in the United States. As such, WOC theorizing also casts light on queer theory's shortcomings. As Hames-García (2011) and others (La Fountain-Stokes, 2011; Lugones, 2011) have pointed out, queer theory's failure to engage an intersectional analysis beyond just heteronormativity and patriarchy make queer theory insufficient to understand a queer of color subjectivity. However, by bringing together queer theory's strengths and feminist of color theorizing, queer of color critique constructs an analytic lens that "names and contextualizes the marginalization of QOC [queer of color] difference; and it differentiates strategies of resistance to account for the shifting exigencies of the lives of queers of color" (Brockenbrough, 2015, p. 30). Because these affordances are understood by acknowledging the experiences of queer people of color as the primary sources of knowledge production, queer of color critique is a compelling approach to begin investigating queer of color existence in multiple contexts and settings, including public education.

## QUEER OF COLOR CRITIQUE AND EDUCATION

The scholarly body of queer of color critique has made critical contributions to a project that demystifies the lives and resistance of QSoC. However, perhaps because this interdisciplinary body of literature emanates from academic fields outside education scholarship, this body of work has yet to influence—and be influenced by—education research. Since the groundbreaking anthology *Troubling Intersections of Race and Sexuality: Queer Students of Color and Anti-oppressive Education* (Kumashiro, 2001) over two decades ago, scholars like Cindy Cruz (2008, 2011, 2013), Edward Brockenbrough (2013, 2015), and Lance McCready (2004a, 2004b, 2010) have paved the way for education researchers to think through the ways in which hegemonic structures are perpetuated in educational settings and resisted by QSoC. With the emergence of this scholarship, higher education research has increasingly examined the experiences of queer people of color as they navigate colleges and universities (Duran, 2019). Yet, despite the steady growth of studies centering the experiences of LGBTQ college students, there still is a concerning lack of research that explores the ways young queer people of color experience the K–12 system (5–18 years of age) and practice resistance to multiple oppressions.

## METHODOLOGY

As a result of situating queer of color critique as the main tool of excavation, there are several tenets of this framework that help address the experience of QSoC. First, queer of color critique centers an intersectional conceptual framework that accounts for not only for sexuality, but also gender, class, and race. Second, a queer of color critique moves past the unearthing of oppressive structures that alienate and victimize QSoC and instead center student practices of resistance or ways to foster such practices; and last, this framework concerns itself with the experiences of students in K–12 (or youth approximately 5 to 18 years of age). Though these criteria derived from queer of color critique frameworks, these requirements, per se, are both intentional and political. For example, queer of color critique has a deep respect for the lived experiences of queer people of color and defends the knowledge that emanates from such lived experiences as the primary source of agency and resistance. However, far from just being an integral part of queer of color critique, highlighting youth's resistance is also an attempt to move education scholars away from "damaged-centered" research (Tuck, 2009). Defined as "research that intends to document peoples' pain and brokenness to hold those in power accountable for their oppression" (Tuck, 2009, p. 409), damaged-centered research operates within a flawed theory of change. The flaw is in the dialectic between intention and impact. That is, while this type of research intends to use its findings as leverage for reparations and resources for marginalized communities, it does so at the expense of reinforcing and reinscribing notions of victimization, resulting in the perpetual conceptualization of communities as "depleted, ruined, and hopeless" (Tuck, 2009, p. 409). QSoC in these instances of damage-centered research become nothing but oppressed, utterly victimized, with few (or none at all) instances documenting young people talking back to oppression. Research that indexes oppression from LGBTQ youth experiences reinscribes the logics of oppression onto queer student bodies, invisibilizing youth agency and their talking back. For these reasons, agency and resistance are central in a queer of color critique with LGBTQ youth communities.

Additionally, this critique of the literature is restricted to young queer people in the K–12 U.S. school system or the like for several reasons. First, as noted by Duran's (2019) review of scholarship in higher education concerning queer and trans students of color, there is far greater work on LGBTQ college students than K–12 students. Fortunately, this corpus of literature is ever growing and its contributions to issues of diversity, access, retention, and health in higher education will be impactful. However, though queer students in higher education continue to face hostile campus climates and lack of resources and visibility (Duran, 2019), all of which are agitated by the complexity of an intersectional identity for QSoC, a university education also affords several privileges. For many LGBTQ college students, their journey to higher education can signify a certain amount of freedom to explore identity in all its complexities and allows students to exercise self-expression and pursue individual interests (Covarrubias et al., 2019). These allowances may not be readily available for queer students in K–12 educational spaces.

## QUEER STUDENTS OF COLOR'S PRACTICES OF RESISTANCE AND AGENCY

Queer youth of color have a history of social activism in and out of their schools (Blackburn, 2003, 2005; Blackburn & McCready, 2009; D. Johnson, 2007a, 2007b; McCready, 2010; Terriquez, 2015). In fact, D. Johnson (2007a) suggested that queer student organizations like gay–straight alliances (GSAs) attributed to more complex and intersectional QSoC identities. Established in 1979, the goal of the George Washington QSoC organization was to create a safer, more tolerant climate for all students in their school (D. Johnson, 2007a). In D. Johnson's (2007a) archival work on the history of the group, she pointed out that QSoC not only shared oppression of all high school students, but also were "organizing under a multi-issue coalition politics framework" (D. Johnson, 2007a, p. 384). Today,

QSoC organizing continues to incite social movements in the United States. For example, sociologist Veronica Terriquez (2015) writes of the ways in which queer undocumented youth, or undocuqueer youth, advocate for a queer inclusive immigration movement and share strategies for coming out twice—as undocumented and as queer. Her work reminds scholars that QSoC's intersectional identities are a source of resistance, and many become well versed in the strategic deployment of multiple ways of being (K. Johnson, 2016; Seif, 2014; McCready, 2001; Quinn, 2007; Terriquez, 2015). A good example of this negotiation is Theresa Quinn's (2007) work with queer girls of color who started a GSA in their public high school. In this work, Quinn documented how lesbian students claimed both cultural and sexual specificity by acting loud and often masculine. In their rejection of normative gender roles reserved for young WOC, new and innovative ideals of leadership that are valued in the school and society emerged. Similarly, K. Johnson's (2016) work demonstrated how queer youth combat bullying by enacting performances of "seduction" and pretending to flirt with their straight counterparts. It is also important to note, however, that QSoC also downplay their queer identity when necessary and opt to highlight their ethnic and racial identity when necessary. For example, McCready's (2001, 2004a, 2004b) ethnography of Black gay boys showed how and why Black gay boys intentionally downplayed their queerness to secure membership and safety in school-based racial communities.

Queer students of color are also versatile "space makers" and have gained skills to make places for their subjectivity and assert themselves through different media. For instance, Blackburn (2003) showed how a Black lesbian student contested curriculum by sharing lesbian love poetry. Similarly, McCready (2010) and Grady et al. (2012) demonstrated the ways in which queer youth embody resistance by making space for their own representations and performances of dance. By engaging in their own take on African dance and vogue culture (McCready, 2010), queer students challenged normative gendered and racial forms of conventional dance.

Central to this literature is the conceptualization of queer youth as active knowledge producers. Though all the scholarship presented thus far has in one way or another demonstrated the ways in which queer youth contest and challenge mainstreams ways of knowing, Cruz (2013) and Johnson (2017) directly took on this challenge. Through her work with QSoC in continuation schools, Cruz's research revealed how video making is a conducive tool for fostering "storying of the self," where "narratives of the body—the scars and lesions of violence, neglect, and poverty that are often literally inscribed onto our bodies" (p. 442)—can be made manifest. Through video making, youth uncover and make visible these "scars"

[262]   *Andrea Vasquez and Cindy Cruz*

and produce ways to think critically of their experiences. Similarly, L. P. Johnson's (2017) work with Black queer youth in an afterschool writing club demonstrated the way that queer youth write themselves into subjectivity after being silenced in their classrooms. Here, L. P. Johnson exhibited how QSoC are critical of power structures by writing about being silenced and heteronormative expectations of parents, teachers, and administrators and documented how QSoC define themselves through their lived experience. As such, scholarship that centers the ways that QSoC resist not only the victimization of youth but also humanizes them, moves them away from deficit portrayals with more nuanced documentation of youth agency and resistance.

## FOSTERING QUEER STUDENTS OF COLOR AGENCY

Current research on QSoC also highlights the ways that educators can foster and recognize queer youth of color agency and resistance. Though less nuanced than the scholarship that centers on QSoC's experiences, and often written as a response to systems of oppression cultivated in schools, this work offers ways in which educators and schools can make space for the development of QSoC. By outlining the multiple ways that schools as institutions marginalized queer youth of color, McCready (2004a, 2004b, 2010) highlighted ways in which schools and educators can move toward an inclusive educational setting for QSoC. In order to do so, however, McCready advocated for a denormalization of Whiteness in curriculum and extracurricular settings and the creation of learning opportunities that allow educators to develop an awareness of the relationship between students' everyday contexts (e.g., the economics and politics of neighborhoods) and student participation in the classroom. Doing so will allow educators to gain a better understanding of the localized historical processes that mediated students' day-to-day lives in and out of schools.

Scholars have also advocated for a "queerly responsive" pedagogy (Brockenbrough, 2016; McCready, 2004b). Drawing from Ladson-Billing's (1995) culturally relevant pedagogy, queerly responsive pedagogy takes into consideration the sociocultural forms in which queer youth express themselves. Such practices could potentially involve alternative definitions of family, inclusion of house ball culture, health education about HIV advocacy, and visibility of queer historical figures in curriculum and school bulletin boards. Along these lines, scholars in library studies have advocated for librarians to utilize critical theoretical approaches that combat institutionalized oppression (Austin, 2019). Such library-centered approaches include the construction of literary collections that reflect the lives and identities of QSoC *in and out of formal education settings*. This last point is of importance. As scholars of critical QSoC education studies remind us, the lives of QSoC spread across multiple settings and included in safe school rhetoric is insufficient. Educators must learn to utilize spaces out of formal education settings, such as nonprofit organizations and afterschool programs to enhance QSoC positive perceptions of themselves and thus their resistances. It is only through critical conceptual frameworks and pedagogical practices that challenge multiple forms of hegemonic oppression that educators can help QSoC develop positively.

## IMPLICATIONS FOR LGBTQ AND QUEER EDUCATIONAL RESEARCH

The practices of queer of color critique highlight important implications for education research with QSoC. Queer of color critique makes a compelling case for the use of intersectional and intermeshing frameworks that will account for the complexity of LGBTQ students of color lives. A queer of color critique asks education researchers to stay vigilant of the ways that gender, race, sexuality, and class are mutually constituted and interlocked to shape the experiences of QSoC (Brockenbrough, 2013, 2015; Grady et al., 2012; Marquez & Brockenbrough, 2013; McCready, 2010, 2012). By doing so, researchers can gain insights into dominant discourse of problems affecting historically marginalized students on account of the multiplicity of their identity and the ways in which students may be speaking back to dominant rhetorics of Whiteness and oppression (Wargo, 2016; Brockenbrough, 2013; Cruz, 2013; McCready, 2013; Vaught, 2004). In this way, education research can move toward acknowledging the lived experience of the intersectional, multifaceted politics of knowledge production and queer visibility of QSoC (Brockenbrough, 2015). Far from just advocating for intersectional frameworks, queer of color critique also advocates for a multiplicity of methods and epistemological orientations that can guide a critical lens when working with QSoC. For example, Mayo (2007) encouraged educational researchers to pay attention to the defining categories that bracket queer youth's subjectivity as well as to the way that space and place influence QSoC ways of being. Following a queer of color critique analysis of QSoC lives demands special attention to the everyday lived experiences and practices of QSoC. For these reasons, queer of color critique also asks education researchers to think of what it means to witness youth resistance and to ponder ways in which an education researcher

[264]  *Andrea Vasquez and Cindy Cruz*

can stand in solidarity with QSoC as a "resistance researcher" (Cruz, 2011, 2013). Maintaining an awareness of QSoC's resistance mandates that educational research also be aware of the ways in which resistance manifests in different ways and thus find *creative* ways that stem from youth's lives to analyze such resistance (Love, 2017). For example, in working with Black queer youth in New Orleans, Love outlined the way in which a "ratchet" imagination can help uncover a resistance through hip-hop. Finally, using qualitative methods like ethnography and interviews, a queer of color critique also advocates for a community-based and participatory research agenda where queer youth gain agency by conducting research themselves. Queer of color critique and its emphasis on resistance research offers new ways of decentralizing oppressive discourses around queer youth and acknowledges the way in which QSoC can push the methods and the episteme within a participatory research framework (Chmielewski et al., 2016; Owens & Jones, 2004). By giving QSoC the autonomy to design and conduct research of their lived experience, QSoC gain the ability to talk back to stakeholders and create transformative change (Brockenbrough, 2016; Chmielewski et al., 2016; Owens & Jones, 2004).

## CONCLUSION

This chapter explores the scholarship that draws from a queer of color critique in education studies as it pertains to the experiences of QSoC in the K–12 school system in the United States. Scholarship published between 2000 and 2019 highlighted several themes as it pertained to QSoC agency and resistance: (1) Queer of color critique derives from a history of activism and advocacy in working-class, nondominant communities. (2) It presents a strategic use of the multiplicity of LGBTQ youth of color identities. (3) It also highlights practices of space making and the production of knowledge from queer of color lived experiences that contest and challenge mainstream curricular and heteronormative ways of being. Additionally, this framework uncovers ways in which educators and institutions of learning can affirm QSoC's subjectivity and ways in which education research can move away from oppressive and deficit portrayals of QSoC.

Despite the critical contributions of new scholarship that focuses on the everyday resistances of QSoC in the United States, research on queer youth of color continues to be slim. Most importantly, though, is that in this work that concerns itself with the experiences of queer, lesbian, gay, and bisexual youth, there is an urgency to explore and center the specific practices of resistance of transgender students of color, whose existence in public schools is currently under attack in many U.S. state legislatures, with antitrans bills moving forward policies that exclude and discriminate against trans students in K–12 schools (Keenan & Nicolazzo, 2021).

It is a capricious time in the United States. While it is true that young queer people are becoming more unapologetic about their disruptions and ways of resisting the everyday practices of antiqueer and antitrans student policies and practices in schools, the same holds true for homophobic and antitrans policy and open hostility against LGBTQ student of color communities. It is now more important than ever for education researchers to hold themselves accountable to create research that highlights the attributes of marginalized communities rather than perpetuate structures that maintain queer youth of color in the periphery.

## REFERENCES

Allen, J. S. (2011). *Venceremos: The erotics of Black self-making in Cuba*. Duke University Press.

Anzaldúa, G. (1987). *Borderlands/la frontera: The new mestiza* (3rd ed.). Aunt Lute Press.

Aronowitz, S., & Giroux, H. (1994). Reproduction and resistance in radical theories of schooling. In A. R. Sadovnik, P. W. Cookson, Jr., & S. F. Semel (Eds.), *Exploring education: An introduction to the foundations of education* (pp. 229–237). Allyn and Bacon. (Original work published 1985)

Austin, J. (2019). Representative library collections as a response to the institutional oppression of LGBTQ youth of color. *International Journal of Information, Diversity, & Inclusion (IJIDI), 3*(1), 91–111. https://doi.org/10.33137/ijidi. v3i1.32269

Blackburn, M. V. (2003). Disrupting the (hetero)normative: Exploring literacy performances and identity work with queer youth. *Journal of Adolescent & Adult Literacy, 46*(4), 312–324. https://www.jstor.org/stable/40013589

Blackburn, M. V. (2005). Agency in borderland discourses: Examining language use in a community center with Black queer youth. *Teachers College Record, 107*(1), 89–113. https://www.tcrecord.org/content.asp?contentid=11690

Blackburn, M. V., & McCready, L. T. (2009). Voices of queer youth in urban schools: Possibilities and limitations. *Theory Into Practice, 48*(3), 222–230. https://doi.org/10.1080/00405840902997485

Brockenbrough, E. (2013). Introduction to the special issue: Queers of color and anti-oppressive knowledge production. *Curriculum Inquiry, 43*(4), 426–440. https://doi.org/10.1111/curi.12023

Brockenbrough, E. (2015). Queer of color agency in educational contexts: Analytic frameworks from a queer of color critique. *Educational Studies, 51*(1), 28–44. https://doi.org/10.1080/00131946.2014.979929

Brockenbrough, E. (2016). Becoming queerly responsive: Culturally responsive pedagogy for Black and Latino urban queer youth. *Urban Education, 51*(2), 170–196. https://doi.org/10.1177/0042085914549261

Chmielewski, J. F., Belmonte, K. M., Fine, M., & Stoudt, B. G. (2016). Intersectional inquiries with LGBTQ and gender nonconforming youth of color: Participatory research on discipline disparities at the race/sexuality/gender nexus. In R. J. Skiba, K. Mediatta, & M. K. Rausch (Eds.), *Inequality in school discipline: Research and practice to reduce disparities* (pp. 171–188). Palgrave Macmillan.

Combahee River Collective. (1983). The Combahee River Collective statement. In B. Smith (Ed.), *Home girls: A Black feminist anthology* (pp. 264–274). Rutgers University Press.

Covarrubias, R., Valle, I., Laiduc, G., & Azmitia, M. (2019). "You never become fully independent": Family roles and independence in first-generation college students. *Journal of Adolescent Research, 34*(4), 381–410. https://doi.org/10.1177/0743558418788402

Cruz, C. (2001). Toward an epistemology of a brown body. *International Journal of Qualitative Studies in Education, 14*(5), 657–669. https://doi.org/10.1080/09518390110059874

Cruz, C. (2008). Notes on immigration, youth, and ethnographic silence. *Theory Into Practice, 47*(1), 67–73. https://doi.org/10.1080/00405840701764797

Cruz, C. (2011). LGBTQ street youth talk back: A meditation on resistance and witnessing. *International Journal of Qualitative Studies in Education, 24*(5), 547–558. https://doi.org/10.1080/09518398.2011.600270

Cruz, C. (2013). LGBTQ youth of color video making as radical curriculum: A brother mourning his brother and a theory in the flesh. *Curriculum Inquiry, 43*(4), 441–460. https://doi.org/10.1111/curi.12022

Diaz, E. M., & Kosciw, J. G. (2009). *Shared differences: The experiences of lesbian, gay, bisexual, and transgender students of color in our nation's schools.* Gay, Lesbian and Straight Education Network (GLSEN).

Duran, A. (2019). Queer *and* of color: A systematic literature review on queer students of color in higher education scholarship. *Journal of Diversity in Higher Education, 12*(4), 390–400. https://doi.org/10.1037/dhe0000084

Duran, A., Dahl, L. S., Stipeck, C., & Mayhew, M. J. (2020). A critical quantitative analysis of students' sense of belonging: Perspectives on race, generation status, and collegiate environments. *Journal of College Student Development, 61*(2), 133–153. https://doi.org/10.1353/csd.2020.0014

Ferguson, R. A. (2004). *Aberrations in Black: Toward a queer of color critique.* University of Minnesota Press.

Grady, J., Marquez, R., & McLaren, P. (2012). A critique of neoliberalism with fierceness: Queer youth of color creating dialogues of resistance. *Journal of Homosexuality, 59*(7), 982–1004. https://doi.org/10.1080/00918369.2012.699839

Hames-García, M. (2011). Queer theory revisited. In M. Hames-García & E. J. Martínez (Eds.), *Gay Latino studies: A critical reader* (pp. 19–45). Duke University Press.

Johnson, D. (2007a). "This is political!" Negotiating the legacies of the first school-based gay youth group. *Children Youth and Environments, 17*(2), 380–387. https://www.jstor.org/stable/10.7721/chilyoutenvi.17.2.0380

Johnson, D. (2007b). Taking over the school: Student gangs as a strategy for dealing with homophobic bullying in an urban public school district. *Journal of Gay & Lesbian Social Services, 19*(3–4), 87–104. https://doi.org/10.1080/10538720802161581

Johnson, K. (2016, February). Beyond victimization towards the pursuit of happiness: A phenomenological study of the role of happiness in the schooling experience of queer Black boys. *Soka Education Conference Proceedings* (p. 109).

Johnson, L. P. (2017). Writing the self: Black queer youth challenge heteronormative ways of being in an after-school writing club. *Research in the Teaching of English, 52*(1), 13–23. https://www.jstor.org/stable/44821285

Keenan, H., & Nicolazzo, Z. (2021). Trans youth are under attack. Educators must step up. *EdWeek*. https://www.edweek.org/leadership/opinion-trans-youth-are-under-attack-educators-must-step-up/2021/04

Kumashiro, K. (2001). Queer students of color and antiracist, antiheterosexist education: Paradoxes of identity and activism. In K. Kumashiro (Ed.), *Troubling intersections of race and sexuality: Queer students of color and anti-oppressive education* (pp. 1–25). Rowan & Littlefield Publishers.

Kumashiro, K. (2003). Queer ideals in education. *Journal of Homosexuality, 45*(2–4), 365–367. https://doi.org/10.1300/J082v45n02_23

Ladson-Billings, G. (1995). Toward a theory of culturally relevant pedagogy. *American Educational Research Journal, 32*(3), 465–491. https://doi.org/10.3102%2F00028312032003465

La Fountain-Stokes, L. (2011). Gay shame, Latina and Latino-style: A critique of White queer performativity. In M. Hames-García & E. J. Martínez (Eds.), *Gay Latino studies: A critical reader* (pp. 55–80). Duke University Press.

Lorde, A. (1983). *Sister outsider: Essays and speeches.* Crossing Press.

Love, B. L. (2017). A ratchet lens: Black queer youth, agency, hip hop, and the Black ratchet imagination. *Educational Researcher, 46*(9), 539–547. http://doi.org/10.3102/0013189X17736520

Lugones, M. (2011). It's all in having a history: A response to Michael Hames-García's queer theory revisited. In M. Hames-García & E. J. Martínez (Eds.), *Gay Latino studies. A critical reader* (pp. 46–54). Duke University Press.

Marquez, R., & Brockenbrough, E. (2013). Queer youth v. the state of California: Interrogating legal discourses on the rights of queer students of color. *Curriculum Inquiry, 43*(4), 461–482. https://doi.org/10.1111/curi.12021

Mayo, C. (2007). Intersectionality and queer youth. *Journal of Curriculum and Pedagogy, 4*(2), 67–71. https://doi.org/10.1080/15505170.2007.10411647

Mayo, C. (2017). Queer and trans youth, relational subjectivity, and uncertain possibilities: Challenging research in complicated contexts. *Educational Researcher, 46*(9), 530–538. http://doi.org/10.3102/0013189X17738737

McCready, L. T. (2001). When fitting in isn't an option, or why Black queer males at a California high school stay away from Project 10. In K. Kumashiro (Ed.), *Troubling intersections of race and sexuality: Queer students of color and anti-oppressive education* (pp. 37–53). Rowman & Littlefield.

McCready, L. T. (2004a). Some challenges facing queer youth programs in urban high schools: Racial segregation and de-normalizing whiteness. *Journal of Gay & Lesbian Issues in Education, 1*(3), 37–51. https://doi.org/10.1300/J367v01n03_05

McCready, L. T. (2004b). Understanding the marginalization of gay and gender non-conforming Black male students. *Theory Into Practice, 43*(2), 136–143. https://doi.org/10.1207/s15430421tip4302_7

McCready, L. (2007). Queer urban education: Curriculum and pedagogy for LGBTQI youth in the city. *Journal of Curriculum and Pedagogy, 4*(2), 71–77. https://doi.org/10.1080/15505170.2007.10411648

McCready, L. T. (2010). *Making space for diverse masculinities: Difference, intersectionality, and engagement in an urban high school* (Vol. 50). Peter Lang.

McCready, L. T. (2012). Call and response: How narratives of Black queer youth inform popular discourses of the "boy crisis" in education. *International Journal of Inclusive Education, 16*(4), 391–406. https://doi.org/10.1080/13603 116.2011.555094

McCready, L. T. (2013). Conclusion to the special issue: Queer of color analysis: Interruptions and pedagogic possibilities. *Curriculum Inquiry, 43*(4), 512–522. https://doi.org/10.1111/curi.12024

Moraga, C., & Anzaldúa, G. (Eds.). (1983). *This bridge called my back: Writings by radical women of color.* Kitchen Table Press.

Owens, D., & Jones, K. (2004). Adapting the youth participatory action research model to serve LBGTQ youth of color. *Practicing Anthropology, 26*(2), 25–29. https://doi.org/10.17730/praa.26.2.0456r98m2pvg200g

Quinn, T. M. (2007). "You make me erect!": Queer girls of color negotiating heteronormative leadership at an urban all-girls' public school. *Journal of Gay & Lesbian Issues in Education, 4*(3), 31–47. https://doi.org/10.1300/J367v0 4n03_04

Renn, K. A. (2010). LGBTQ and queer research in higher education: The state and status of the field. *Educational Researcher, 39*(2), 132–141. https://doi.org/ 10.3102/0013189X10362579

Rubin, G. (1998). Thinking sex: Notes for a radical theory of the politics of sexuality. In P. M. Nardi & B. E. Schneider (Eds.), *Social perspectives in lesbian and gay studies: A reader* (pp. 100–133). Routledge.

Salas-SantaCruz, O. S. (2020). Terca, pero no pendeja: Terquedad as theory and praxis of transformative gestures in higher education. *Association of Mexican American Educators Journal, 14*(2), 23–43. https://doi.org/10.24974/amae.14.2.357

Sedgwick, E. K. (1990). *Epistemology of the closet.* University of California Press.

Seif, H. (2014). "Coming out of the shadows" and "undocuqueer": Undocumented immigrants transforming sexuality discourse and activism. *Journal of Language and Sexuality, 3*(1), 87–120. https://doi.org/10.1075/jls.3.1.05sei

Smith, B. (Ed.). (1983). *Home girls: A Black feminist anthology.* Kitchen Table–Women of Color Press.

Terriquez, V. (2015). Intersectional mobilization, social movement spillover, and queer youth leadership in the immigrant rights movement. *Social Problems, 62*(3), 343–362. https://doi.org/10.1093/socpro/spv010

Tuck, E. (2009). Suspending damage: A letter to communities. *Harvard Educational Review, 79*(3), 409–428. https://psycnet.apa.org/doi/10.17763/ haer.79.3.n0016675661t3n15

Vaught, S. (2004). The talented tenth: Gay Black boys and the racial politics of southern schooling. *Journal of Gay & Lesbian Issues in Education, 2*(2), 5–26. https://doi.org/10.1300/J367v02n02_02

Wargo, J. M. (2016). Queer, quare, and [q]ulturally sustaining. In N. M. Rodriguez, W. J. Martino, J. C. Ingrey, & E. Brockenbrough (Eds.), *Critical concepts in queer studies and education: An international guide for the twenty-first century* (pp. 299– 307). Palgrave Macmillan. https://doi.org/10.1057/978-1-137-55425-3_29

CHAPTER 14

# An Assimilation or Transgression of "Normativities"

## A Qualitative Sociological Exploration of the Experiences of Gay and Lesbian Students at a South African University

TSHANDUKO TSHILONGO AND JACQUES ROTHMANN

The South African Constitution is regarded as the most progressive in Africa on the rights of LGBTIQ+[1] individuals. Section 9(3) and (4) of the Equality Clause (1996) in the South African Bill of Rights prohibits any discrimination toward people because of their gender identity, sex, and sexual orientation (Eslen-Ziya et al., 2015). However, the annual publication of the International Lesbian, Gay, Bisexual, Transgender and Intersex's *State-Sponsored Homophobia report* (Mendos, 2019) commented on the continued persecution sexual minorities face due to the conservative views on gender and sexual identity of African religious and political leaders and members of civil society (R. Brown, 2012; Epprecht, 2012; Msibi, 2014), hence the reference to homosexuality as supposedly being "un-African" (Reddy, 2010; I. Smith et al., 2012, p. 36). Such ideologies comment on the existence of an incongruence between these legal provisions and the actual life worlds of LGBTIQ+ people in civil society, typified by hate crimes, stereotyping, and prejudice (De Wet et al., 2016). These actions may occur because of the perceived threat sexual equality poses to heteronormativity (Judge, 2017).

Tshanduko Tshilongo and Jacques Rothmann, *An Assimilation or Transgression of "Normativities"*
In: *Queer Studies and Education.* Edited by: Nelson M. Rodriguez, Robert C. Mizzi, Louisa Allen, and Rob Cover,
Oxford University Press. © Oxford University Press 2023. DOI: 10.1093/oso/9780197687000.003.0015

South African studies on the experiences of LGBTIQ+ persons in educational contexts have mainly focused on students' experiences in school settings (Rothmann, 2016). In a recent review of studies on the latter focus, Francis (2017a) provided an overview of research on the significance of studying homosexuality, particularly in educational contexts, outlining findings showing that, in certain South African schools, teachers deny the existence of gay and lesbian learners (DePalma & Francis, 2014; Francis, 2017b; Msibi, 2012), discriminate against gender-non-conforming learners (A. H. Butler et al., 2003; McArthur, 2015), and uncritically ascribe a heterosexual label to their entire learner constituency (A. Brown et al., 2018; Francis, 2017b). He further cited other studies that reflected the possibilities associated with attempts to teaching and learning themes on gender and sexual diversity (Francis, 2017b; E. Richardson, 2008) that could benefit both heterosexual and LGBTIQ+ individuals.

Francis's (2017a) demarcation extended such foci to higher education. Sexual identities in universities have, however, not been explored extensively in South African academia. Studies undertaken include focus on attitudes to LGBTIQ+ students (De Wet et al., 2016; B. Johnson, 2014; Rothmann & Simmonds, 2015); prejudicial assumptions about homosexuality on university campuses (Jagessar & Msibi, 2015; Matthyse, 2017); and the influence of subtle heterosexism (Rothmann, 2016, 2017, 2018). Studies also center on the violence, prejudice, and harassment faced by LGBTIQ+ students in educational contexts (Francis, 2017b; McArthur, 2015; Msibi, 2012; E. Richardson, 2008); exclusion of LGBTIQ+ voices in university policies and curricula (Msibi, 2016); perceptions about lesbian, gay, and bisexual students (Bhana, 2014; A. H. Butler et al., 2003; De Wet et al., 2016; Rothmann & Simmonds, 2015); and the lived experiences of such students on campuses nationwide (Jagessar & Msibi, 2015; Lesch et al., 2017; Msibi, 2015; Rothmann, 2014).

The primary focus of the chapter is twofold. First, we focus on how some students assimilate into the potentially heteronormative or homonormative campus cultures of their university to curtail possible homophobia. Second, we engage the narratives of students who noted their attempts to transgress such "normativities." For the purpose of the present chapter, *heteronormativity* is defined as the set of cultural, legal, and institutional practices that privileges heterosexuality to the exclusion of so-called sexual "others," including gay and lesbian persons (D. Richardson, 2012, p. 37). *Homonormativity* has two meanings. First, it refers to how some gay and lesbian persons may either conform to certain forms of gay or lesbian expression that resemble heterosexual behavior in order to either gain equal rights or avoid discrimination (e.g., assimilating into the mainstream campus culture). Second, it also denotes how other gay and lesbian persons may rather opt to distinguish themselves from their heterosexual counterparts as completely different and unique by creating visible separate spaces (e.g., LGBTIQ+ student organizations on campus) (Ghaziani, 2014).

## A QUEER THEORETICAL CRITIQUE OF HETERONORMATIVITY AND HOMONORMATIVITY

According to Warner (1991), one of the themes with which queer theorists seek to engage is a critique of the generalization of the above reference to sexual "normality." This theme informs the discussion below. Its proponents discard a minoritizing notion of tolerance of sexual minorities in a mainstream heterosexual context (A. Smith, 2010). As noted above, the standards that inform heteronormativity function to preserve the domination of heterosexuality, thus inhibiting homosexuality from being equated with heterosexuality (Corber & Valocchi, 2003). Consequently, the supposed supremacy of heterosexuality often operates unconsciously. Due to this, it often makes it difficult for individuals to acknowledge that they unknowingly perform their gender and sexual identities in normative ways (J. Butler, 1999). Rich (2004, p. 10), in contemplating her work on "compulsory heterosexuality," argued that gender and sexuality researchers should "critique . . . the presumption that heterosexuality is 'beyond question.'" Eaton and Matamala (2014) also argued that heteronormativity creates a set of oppositional relations between femininity and masculinity, supporting men's greater power and status in relation to women and gay and lesbian individuals, thus explaining how heteronormativity per se both affects and is affected by our view of gender and sexuality (Bhana, 2012). However, queer theoretical scholars critique beliefs that leave the supposed dominance of heteronormativity unquestioned.

Owing to the fears of facing homophobia, sexual minorities may opt to remain closeted and assimilate into mainstream heterosexual *or* homosexual contexts. Proponents of queer theory are, however, critical of such assimilationist tendencies (Seidman, 2002). An assimilationist view foregrounds the importance for LGBTIQ+ persons to gain equal access to the rights of their heterosexual counterparts (Van den Berg, 2016). Queer activists, however, do not wish to retain such a status quo; instead, they oppose these normative societal expectations. From a South African perspective, Van den Berg (2016) asserted that, due to their need for equality, gay assimilationists consider LGBTIQ+ individuals as not necessarily being so different from heterosexuals, and they therefore deserve the same rights and treatment by heteronormative society.

By conforming to the tenets of heteronormativity, gay and lesbian identities may concurrently become mirror images of their heterosexual counterpart: hence a reference to homonormativity. Two meanings of *homonormativity* are worth noting. First, *assimilationist homonormative principles* seek to mediate gay and lesbian identities, guiding homosexual individuals to gain access to mainstream societal privileges (Croce, 2015), thereby facilitating heteronormative principles in the process of "doing gender" for gay and lesbian persons to perform socially acceptable behavior by conforming to heterosexual processes and norms that reaffirm compulsory heterosexuality (Asencio, 2011). Examples of this include gay men and lesbian women's need to be afforded the same rights as heterosexual men and women, for example, the right to marry and adopt children (Calhoun, 2008). Since this conceptualization of homonormativity is likely informed by heteronormative assumptions and values, gay and lesbian individuals risk being marginalized and experience discrimination and stigma from both communities for being either "too straight" or "too gay" (Wailing & Roffee, 2017). Homonormativity thus manifests as "the queer skin under the otherwise straight masks" (Milani & Wolff, 2015, p. 165) since it upholds and sustains heterosexist assumptions and institutions.

The second strand of homonormativity is typified as a *queer liberationist perspective*. According to Robson (2002), this ideology interprets gender and sexuality in a nonconforming way through an emphasis on their *differences* rather than their similarities, that is, emphasizing the critique of heteronormative structures. They therefore advocate for a societal change in people's perspectives on sexuality rather than advocating legal reform and rights-based activism (Yep et al., 2003). Proponents of this approach support a more radical change, often arising from outside the political mainstream (Van den Berg, 2016). Queer liberationists do not conceal their sexuality and gender identity; they rather embrace it with pride, defining themselves by their own criteria, and oppose ideas fostering heteronormative standards of normality (Eide, 2010). In so doing, LGBTIQ+ persons, according to them, should disassimilate through the coming out process, proclaiming their differences and uniqueness (Robson, 2002).

Thus, regardless of the critique toward the influence of heteronormativity and the noted differentiation between the two strands of homonormativity, these "normativities" arguably continue to inform the experiences of heterosexual and gay and lesbian persons alike. Depending on the specific interpersonal and cultural scenarios that predicate the inherent ideologies of social institutions (e.g., universities), individuals may attempt to either conform to or challenge the noted tenets of hetero- and/ or homonormativity for various reasons. The next section speaks to this.

## CHOOSING TO ASSIMILATE OR TRANSGRESS NORMATIVITIES ON UNIVERSITY CAMPUSES

A number of recent studies commented on the prevailing influence of heteronormativity and homophobia on university campuses (Batten et al., 2018; R. Evans et al., 2017; Keenan, 2014; Marzetti, 2018). In particular, verbal harassment and threats of physical violence appear to be common for gay and lesbian students (Bhana, 2014; Francis, 2017b). Two forms of homophobia are worth noting in this regard: *institutional* and *internalized* homophobia. In terms of the former, A. H. Butler (2007, p. 72) noted that institutional homophobia refers to "the multiple levels . . . of oppression and discrimination gay and lesbian youth may experience as they interact and interface with various South African social institutions, at group, family, community and social levels." The agonizing experience of being considered different, accompanied by continuous verbal and physical abuse, may lead students to experience what is referred to as internalized homophobia. This results in self-hatred, self-devaluation, acting out, loneliness, isolation, self-destructiveness, aggression, a decline in academic performance, and inclinations towards suicide (Blackburn & McCready, 2009; A. H. Butler et al., 2003; Furr et al., 2001; Kosciw et al., 2008; Nel et al., 2007). Such discrimination results because of the supposed inability of gay and lesbian persons to conform to the principles of heteronormativity that consider heterosexuality as "pure" versus gay and lesbian identities as potentially "specialized, despised and punished" roles that deviate from the accepted sexual behavior (McIntosh, 1968, p. 184).

The South African Department of Education (2008) indicated that little continues to be done to address issues around heterosexism and homophobia in academic institutions. This claim was further supported by the *Report of the Ministerial Committee on Transformation and Social Cohesion and the Elimination of Discrimination in Public Higher Education Institutions.* The report states that "[in] the area of sexism and homophobia there are no higher academic institutions among those inspected that can assert to have completely resolved these concerns" (Department of Education, 2008, p. 46). However, the South African Department of Basic Education (2019) published full lesson plans for its comprehensive sexuality education (CSE) curriculum in November 2019, which envisaged learners being introduced to particular terminology, debates, and examples of themes

[274]   *Tshanduko Tshilongo and Jacques Rothmann*

related to gender and sexuality; references to sexual orientation at primary school level; high school foci include concepts such as "gay," "homosexual," and "sexual orientation" (Department of Basic Education, 2019). Such curriculum content is an attempt to counteract what Msibi (2016) referred to as "bitter knowledge." Based on his teaching queer material to pre-service teachers in South Africa, he argued that such knowledge reaffirms stereotyping gender and sexual identity, which may reinforce heteronormative and homophobic knowledge of students, incompatible with debates that favor sexual diversity. If left unchallenged, it may lead to violence, bigotry, and discrimination against LGBTIQ+ students. The discussion to follow echoes these sentiments on how the inclusion of topics about gender and sexual diversity in university courses may contribute to an increased sense of self-acceptance among gay and lesbian university students.

In support, Alvarez and Schneider's (2008) work claimed that universities tend to proclaim their promises to a diverse community of students, yet offer limited prospects for meaningful inclusion, a finding to which Allen et al. (2020) attested. Their findings echoed similar results from the present study on the need for safer spaces on a South African university campus (Tshilongo & Rothmann, 2019). Although observing the provisions of the South African Constitution that safeguard people, regardless of their sexual identity, only references to disability, gender, and race were included in the human rights policy and diversity statements of the university. According to Francis (2017b), the focus on race and gender, rather than sexual orientation, has also dominated the discussions on transformation, equity, and social and economic change in academic contexts. To address the LGBTIQ+ community's demands for access to academic inclusion and privilege, diversity initiatives are usually introduced by the institution with the "promise that with increased presence comes increased access," inclusion, and acceptance (Alvarez & Schneider, 2008, p. 73). N. J. Evans (2002) thus argued that university management is sensitized to the challenges faced by LGBTIQ+ students, which may result in the creation of positive and inclusive learning environments (D'Emilio, 1992; Ratts et al., 2013). Such attempts may be facilitated through the establishment of LGBTIQ+ student organizations and course curricula on gender and sexual diversity presented by openly gay and lesbian lecturers. The present study concurrently foregrounds the importance of these initiatives to contribute to a more inclusive campus culture.

Student organizations, as one example of the noted initiatives, seek to support and empower students by providing them and their heterosexual allies with information on themes such as "coming out," meeting with supportive faculty and staff members and teaching the students particular coping strategies when confronted with homophobia (Garcia-Alonso, 2004). Such support further manifests in what N. R. Evans (2002) termed the centralization of homosexual themes in lectures and course content. Such initiatives challenge and critically engage homophobic or heterosexist comments and behaviors expressed by other students. Grace (2017) argued that lecturers may also identify heteronormative assumptions in the course reading material and support gay and lesbian students' statements that relate to sexual orientation matters. As will be evident from the discussion to follow, participants advocated for such initiatives in order to curtail attempts at only foregrounding heterosexuality to the detriment of gay and lesbian voices.

Such an increase in visibility may, conversely, result in homophobia. It is worth citing Ghaziani's (2014) work on different eras related to gay and lesbian visibility. He differentiated between "the closet" (1869 to the early 1960s), "coming out" (late 1960s–1990s), and "postgay" eras (late 1990s to the present day). The first was characterized by gay and lesbian persons concealing their identities based on the fear of potential discrimination. The coming out era allowed a greater sense of gay pride and increased openness about one's sexuality. Therefore, notwithstanding the possibility of homophobia, this era encouraged increased visibility on the part of supposed sexual minorities that extended to the current postgay era (i.e., suggesting that gay men and lesbian women are adopting a so-called new gay paradigm). This paradigm is characterized by an increased tendency for gay and lesbian persons and subcultures to assimilate into mainstream heterosexual society in, among others, the United States, United Kingdom, Canada, and arguably South Africa (Rink, 2013). Ghaziani (2014, p. 33) attributed this to the lesbian and gay liberationist movements of the 1970s and 1980s in the United States and United Kingdom and similarly in South Africa (during the 1980s and 1990s). These movements fought for acknowledging LGBTIQ+ rights (e.g., the Stonewall riots in 1969 in New York), which encouraged and enabled gay and lesbian persons to "come out of the closet in large[r] numbers." Regardless of the potential redeeming features of increased visibility, recent studies contrariwise comment on the presence of homophobia in contemporary academic contexts. Drawing on data from a joint research project on "human rights literacy" (Roux & Du Preez, 2013), De Wet et al. (2016), and Rothmann and Simmonds (2015) explored the perceptions of fourth-year preservice teachers on homosexuality at South African universities. The studies concluded that the narratives of the respondents displayed a heteronormative bias that may aggravate discrimination and objectification toward visible gay and lesbian persons as the so-called other (Rothmann & Simmonds, 2015). The respondents objectified gay and lesbian individuals by referring to them as "it" and "they." Jagessar and Msibi's (2015) research emphasized how heterosexist regulation of gay, lesbian, and bisexual residency students by their heterosexual peers exacerbated the prevalence of homophobic violence (cf. Atkinson & De Palma, 2009). Such findings echo De Wet et al.'s (2016) research on how the visibility of counterheterosexual persons engender the preceding reference to a double-bind: Students know that the South African Constitution allows them to disclose their sexual orientation, but the incongruence between what the law offers and the actual treatment of gay and lesbian persons in civil society inhibits their freedom (cf. Allen et al., 2020).

## RESEARCH DESIGN AND METHODOLOGY

The general research objective for the current study focused on a qualitative exploration of the potential role of safe spaces on one of the campuses of a South African university. We included particular questions in the semistructured, open-ended interview schedule to contribute to the focus of the current chapter: These questions centered on *the visibility/invisibility of these lesbian and gay students on campus*; the importance they assigned to the *university management's provision of LGBTIQ+ student organizations on campus*; how they viewed the *inclusion of LGBTIQ+ topics in university courses*; and whether they had ever experienced *discrimination* on campus due to their sexual orientation.

In order to answer the noted questions, the study adopted social constructionism as an ontological approach and the epistemological approach of interpretivism—both associated with the central theoretical argument's queer theoretical focus (Bryman, 2016). This link relates to the social constructionist critique of these approaches of the supposed centrality of hetero- and homonormativity (Jackson & Scott, 2010). As evident from the preceding discussion, gender and sexuality are entrenched in and conveyed through these normative ideologies, through the different responses, values, expectations, roles, and responsibilities given to individuals and groups according to their gender and sexuality (J. L. Johnson et al., 2007). These approaches therefore postulate that the nature of our social (and sexual) realities are constantly constructed and reconstructed through interaction (Creswell & Creswell, 2018).

A qualitative research design provided an in-depth explanation of the gay and lesbian participants' subjective views of their lived experiences on campus. The objective of qualitative research centered on the accumulation of in-depth descriptions and the emphasis on the researcher's ability to understand, explain, and explore phenomena (Creswell & Creswell, 2018). The participants included 10 self-identified gay and 10 self-identified lesbian students registered as undergraduate or postgraduate students. The interviews comprised eight self-identified White, nine self-identified Black, and three self-identified colored participants.[2] Their faculties included engineering, law, arts, natural sciences, economic and management sciences, educational sciences, and health sciences. They were identified through nonprobability sampling methods of purposive and snowball sampling. The latter focused on identifying participants who may form part of what Browne (2005) and Rumens (2011), among others, considered to be a "hidden" group. The students' "hiddenness" was based on their potential fear of facing discrimination and prejudice if they were to disclose their gender and/or sexual identities. To redress this potential limitation, the participants who had already partaken in the study referred us to other members of the population with the relevant experience and knowledge related to the topic. Data were obtained by conversing with the participants using an interview schedule comprising three sections: the biographical and academic backgrounds and opinion-related questions (based on themes from the literature).

The interviews were transcribed and analyzed through thematic analysis (Braun & Clarke, 2006). Open and selective coding coded both existing themes and new themes from the data (as noted below). Ethical principles were adhered to by following the approved ethical clearance by the university's Faculty of Arts Ethics Committee, including voluntary participation, no physical or emotional harm to the participants, and the protection of the participants' identity. The present study was deemed potentially sensitive due to the focus on the students' sexual identities. As such, information on the protection of the participants' interests and well-being formed part of the Informed Consent Statement—with a particular emphasis on how we would observe the principles of anonymity, confidentiality, and privacy. Anonymity, also termed "pseudonymity," is a method used by the researcher "to protect the confidentiality of research participants 'through the use of pseudonyms applied to research participants, organisations and locations'" (Mukungu, 2017, pp. 2–3). Confidentiality, however, refers to private information about the research participants and settings that should not be attributed to a particular person when reporting the findings (Bryman, 2016). Participants of the present study were assigned pseudonyms at the beginning of the interview. Privacy was observed by refraining from any attempt to unnecessarily probe participants to elaborate on particular matters they deemed private or too sensitive to discuss (Creswell & Creswell, 2018).

## FINDINGS

This section speaks to the empirical findings that resulted from the semistructured interviews with the self-identified gay and lesbian students. Themes included the *negative experiences of the participants related to their sexuality on campus, how they sought to avoid potential discrimination*, and a choice to *assimilate* into either heteronormative or homonormative campus contexts to avoid public disclosure of their sexual orientation or attempted to *transgress* such "normativities" by critiquing its main tenets.

### Negative Experiences on Campus

Thirteen participants (six gay and seven lesbian) acknowledged that they faced *discrimination* on the university campus. Their experiences included bullying, isolation and/or loneliness, depression, declining academic performance, and suicidal thoughts. A gay student noted that owing to discrimination, he was verbally and socially bullied on campus; he was called names like "sister" as an attempt to "intimidate" him. He added:

> It is hurtful having to walk around campus that has people who, when they look at you, they see a bad person or a person who has no morals. And I don't think the very same people who destroy others' reputations are aware of the pain, the emotional and social damage they cause all because that person refuses to conform to their heterosexuality; their attitude and actions of discrimination towards me proves that they want me to change who and what I am so that I can be, as they call it, "normal" like them. (Enris, gay, educational studies)

Mxolisi, a student in economic and management sciences, had similar experiences, discovering that some people in class were gossiping about him. This accordingly had a negative impact on his academic performance. He stated: "Had I not got the help I needed, I would've failed some of my modules. . . . going to class had become a burden. I had moments when I would just feel a little sick and would miss the class because of feeling unsafe" (Mxolisi, gay, economic and management science). Alan, a White gay arts student, noted that such verbal abuse made him feel like a "nobody," and thus his academics "took a blow." He continued: "During initiations I would not be allowed to take part in the activities because I was gay and not man enough as they proclaimed; I would be called names such as 'sissy' and 'fag.' You think of yourself as unworthy of love and people bully you because you are gay" (Alan, gay, arts). Brenda, a Black lesbian student in economic and management sciences, shared a similar experience:

> The treatment is making me fail the one thing I came here to do, which is to study. . . . I believe that every person should get an education that is free from discrimination, harassments and any violence.

Bob similarly contemplated suicide because the pressure to "pass" as heterosexual became insurmountable. "Imagine having to deal with the fact that you are gay and you have to deal with being bullied, being isolated; the most important thing you came to university for, your academics, is taking a wrong turn" (Bob, gay, arts). Cyberbullying is another platform whereby students experience discrimination. Mario, a gay male student in natural sciences, noted that although one might not be directly bullied on social media, one is affected when fellow students post hurtful images online that discriminate against homosexual individuals. He recalled an image that read, "Gay is not okay" and "God hates fags" on a student's timeline. Precious, a White lesbian arts student, also recalled receiving an anonymous text: "Why are you trying to be like a man, can't you be woman enough?" The text made her feel unsafe and "scared" because she did not know what would happen to her the next day. Concurrently, these students tended to avoid overt disclosure of their sexual identity and decided to remain closeted. The reasons for this varied from fears of possible " stigmatisation" (Dee, lesbian, arts), "discrimination" (Larry, gay, arts) to how homosexuality is viewed by the wider campus community based on potential "stereotypes" (Enris, gay, educational sciences) assigned to sexual minorities. Alan, for example, described coming out as "nonideal" because it is not an easy process. This is because, once one is out of the closet, there is another world of discrimination that one has to face, which may seem "nice" when viewed from when a person is inside the closet; however, there is a possibility of "hostility" once the person is outside the closet. He noted: "It is this hostility that would make one want to go back into the closet."

## Avoiding Discrimination on Campus

The seven participants who had *not experienced discrimination* on campus noted that because of feelings of anxiety or fear, they opted to isolate themselves rather than openly disclose their sexual orientation to others.

Bradley expressed his fear of the unknown: "You might wake up tomorrow and find an anti-gay policy on campus" (Bradley, gay, law). A gay student, Larry, said: "I sometimes isolate myself from people because you never know when they may decide they don't want a gay friend, and that is a bit depressing." Santo, a gay engineering graduate, indicated that he had never experienced discrimination on campus since he did not pay much attention to discriminatory remarks. However, educationalist Enris stated: "When I walk . . . past a few people I feel as if I am too different and abnormal," but he believed that if one's support structure is "solid" one hardly notices people's opinions.

There were, however, positive experiences regardless of how they felt about themselves. Caroline attributed her view to her type of friends. She argued: "Campus is the best for me because my friends are so supportive and they are not prejudiced against any person of any kind" (Caroline, Black, lesbian, natural sciences). Santo attributed his positive experiences to the fact that he had "not really experienced any negativity. . . . It looks like a pretty welcoming campus and so far my friends have been great." Batso, a Black, lesbian, arts student, cited the lack of physical assaults as a source for her positivity but cautioned that she did not know what might happen in the future. To her, the fact that a historically religious campus allowed the establishment of LGBTIQ+ societies indicated progress. She believed the university was "becoming a place where gays and lesbians are recognised. . . . If the university consists of faculties such as Educational and Social Sciences that touch on issues concerning homosexuality, it means that the university is becoming modernised and not too traditional." Thinus (gay, arts) also noted that "knowledge is power," and the more informed people are, the more they are able to make informed decisions. Furthermore, participants indicated that these courses or the curricula that are inclusive of gay and lesbian topics have the potential to improve their outlook on the problems they face. Such courses, according to Zack (lesbian, education) and Thinus (gay, arts), may be of value to both gay and lesbian students and heterosexual students in terms of understanding the history of homosexuality. Using "correct terms," such as "gay or lesbian" instead of "faggot or dyke/lesbo" to describe sexual minorities, means that the more educated people and peers are about gay and lesbian lifestyles, the more they may become welcoming and accepting and potentially reducing prejudice and intolerance toward homosexuality in general. Dee, a faculty of arts student, stated: "For example in [arts], it is rare to hear anti-LGBT remarks in class because the course has topics and modules that incorporate gay and lesbian studies and the classroom and the department is much safer to go to; however, you can never say the same with engineering departments and theology."

Such initiatives therefore encouraged students to disclose their sexual orientation to others. Alan argued that students who hide their sexual orientation prefer wearing "face masks." As counterargument, Precious, a White arts student, stated: "I can never go through my life constantly changing who I am to please other people." Alan recalled that, although his family expressed disappointment when he came out of the closet, they never stopped supporting him; he became clear about who he was with them and never had to change his behavior around them, around his friends, and around campus. Alan and Precious's remarks encapsulated the divergent narratives of students who, regardless of studying *on the same campus*, expressed differential views relating to whether they wish to be more visible or invisible on campus. These experiences of students may therefore inform their choice to disclose their sexual orientation or remain closeted.

### Assimilation as Heteronormative or Homonormative

Having decided to remain closeted or to disclose their sexual orientation, the question of *hetero- or homonormative assimilation* arose during the interviews. Seven of ten gay and eight lesbian students deemed it significant to be part of existing *homosexual groups* on their campus owing to visibility and recognition. Three students expressed interesting insights. Larry (gay, arts) thought that being in a group catering for gay students' needs was "liberating," while Mario (gay, natural sciences) and Tshiamo (gay, arts) noted that being assimilated into a group was "cool" and a "great experience" since one has fun while bonding with other gay and lesbian students. According to Bob, a White, gay arts student, having gay and/ or lesbian friends at university was like having a "second family" that protected and supported you. Three of the male students emphasized that it was important to be part of a visible group on campus, being empowered to fight against marginalization and policies that govern the institution favoring the exclusion of sexual minorities. Enris noted: "It is important to be in a visible group on campus, especially if the group is a revolutionary movement to restructure or change policies to be inclusive" (Enris, gay, educational sciences). Lungile stated: "Being in a group of gays and lesbians is awesome; you know there is a group that is willing to voice out for you and support you in coming out of the closet" (Lungile, lesbian, health sciences).

Supporting this thought, Tshiamo offered:

> It is important to display characteristics associated with gay identity because it often works to your advantage; I am saying that I am comfortable with who I am, unlike those who do not display it, because they are afraid of adversity. (Tshiamo, gay, arts)

Bob argued: "I have always seen myself as flamboyant and I think that's what characterises my gay identity" (Bob, gay, arts). Mario mentioned that gay people come in different forms and "if I am more girly, I don't expect all gay men to be girly; some are conservative and not as outspoken. Therefore, if persons are comfortable with their appearance, they need to be accepted for who they are and want to be" (Mario, gay, natural sciences).

Three gay and two lesbian participants, however, did not assign importance to forming part of such visible groups on campus. Thinus attributed his view to the fact that he regarded it as unnecessary to make himself visible. He, however, acknowledged the positive aspects that may result from joining such groups, particularly for those students who are still in the closet (e.g., an "improved self-esteem and self-confidence"). Ellen (lesbian, educational sciences) and Thinus (gay, arts) viewed these groups as the "cause" of furthered segregation between heterosexuals and homosexuals; when one is seen in such a group, one tends to be treated differently by the overall campus community. Santo (gay, engineering) emphasized that visible gay groups sometimes lose their focus on being different, and they start to pursue equality with heterosexuals since *heterosexuality is regarded as normal*. Alan elaborated:

> Being in a visible group is like fighting to be like other people rather than embracing differences. . . . And trying to equalise myself with another person means that I regard how other people behave as normal [or] heterosexual and myself as abnormal, because I do not fit into the heterosexual category. (Alan, gay, arts)

Zack, a White lesbian student in education, mentioned that such groups are important for those who require more support in coming out and are still in the process of associating with people who only share the same experiences before associating with those who share similar interests, be it heterosexuals or homosexuals.

## DISCUSSION OF FINDINGS

It is important to note participants' positive experiences as well as look at the *challenges* they face on campus. Thirteen participants noted that they had faced some form of discrimination, which recalled findings from recent studies that asserted that LGBTIQ+ students were more likely than heterosexual students to feel lonely, depressed, and express sadness owing to the fear of disclosing their sexual orientation (i.e., examples of internalized homophobia) (Blackburn & McCready, 2009; A. H. Butler et al., 2003; Furr et al., 2001; Kosciw et al., 2008; Nel et al., 2007). Participants felt they experienced social and verbal bullying, such as overt verbal homophobia due to name-calling, resulting in depression and suicidal ideation by certain gay and lesbian students, experiences supported by Blackburn and McCready (2009), Kosciw et al. (2008), and Mudrey and Medina-Adams (2006). The narratives of those participants who expressed a sense of safety and nondiscrimination on campus recalled the recent work of Allen et al. (2020, p. 1076). Their research suggested that LGBTTIQA+[3] students can "simultaneously feel . . . safe and unsafe" on their campus, a finding to which Pryor (2018) attested. They attributed this to, among others, discrepancies in how the university's administrators supported students. On the one hand, students and staff were actively supported through the overt displays of rainbow stickers and posters advocating inclusivity. On the other hand, however, participants cited the "hollowness" of these gestures insofar as they, as LGBTTIQA students, had to take personal responsibility and potentially "'out' themselves" in order to report homophobic practices to management. In so doing, homophobia was posited as an individual *rather* than a structural problem (cf. Francis, 2017b; Lesch et al., 2017; Marston, 2015); Allen et al. (2020, p. 1087) therefore contended: "It is no wonder they [the students] felt 'safe but not safe' on campus" (Allen et al., 2020, p. 1087).

These findings further recall the work of De Wet et al. (2016) and Rothmann and Simmonds (2015), who attributed the prevalence of heterosexism and homophobia to the lack of congruence between the supposed acknowledgment of gender and sexual diversity in South African higher educational contexts and the actual enactment of formal policies to redress discrimination. This is exacerbated by staff and students' ignorance about the matter. Due to such ignorance, heterosexuality may be enforced through institutional traditions and cultures, echoed by our findings that universities tend to proclaim their promises to a diverse community of students, yet offer very limited prospects for meaningful inclusion (Tshilongo & Rothmann, 2019).

*Positive experiences* of students manifested in a number of subthemes. The first subtheme focused on the importance of *peer support* as a source for positive campus experience, echoed in Dietz's (1997) research. This implied that these students had never faced any physical or verbal assaults, and that the campus's progressive culture was evident through the opportunity to form gay and lesbian societies, attested by Garcia-Alonso (2004). C. O. Fox and Ore (2010) and Jackson and Scott (2010), among others, noted that one should be wary to assume that the creation of such separate (or exclusive) spaces and the student's individual agency indicated complete acceptance at a macro level of the country's larger cultural scenario. It may rather speak to the continuing efforts of sexual minorities to assimilate into either exclusively homonormative spaces or conform to the mainstream and "tolerant" heteronormative gendered and sexual context to avoid potential discrimination (Atkinson & De Palma, 2009). This recalls findings from Jagessar and Msibi's (2015) study indicating that LGB[4] residency students refrained from reporting homophobic acts directed at them owing to the ignorance of their residential managers. This recalls the work of Atkinson and De Palma (2009), who argued that other students provided "organised consent" since they considered the homophobia, as participants from their research indicated that the homophobia was "not that bad" (Jagessar & Msibi, 2015, p. 71). Lesch et al. (2017), for example, were of the opinion that university management should take the primary responsibility for safeguarding the rights of sexual minority students. Their study among same-sex student couples at a South African university indicated "that currently the local LGBT society carries the unfair and major burden of such social advocacy for LGBT issues, as well as offering support to LGBT students," as opposed to the university's management (Lesch et al., 2017, p. 144). In exercising their agency through, among others, joining LGBTIQ+ student organizations, students concurrently (although potentially unknowingly) enacted heteronormative and homonormative sexual identities, insofar as they may, as noted by Milani and Wolff (2015, p. 167), *"naturalise, normalise* and *legitimise* some expressions of same-sex desire, at the expense of others," thus assimilating into a "separate, private and non-political sexual culture" without critiquing the dominance of heteronormativity.

Students further attributed their positive experiences to the ability of *faculties to address issues concerning homosexuality.* These findings recall previous studies' emphasis on how the centralization of gay and lesbian students and themes in curricula may contribute to the "education *about* the others" (Kumashiro, 2002) in order "to bring visibility to ignored issues" (Msibi, 2015, p. 391; cf. Grace, 2017; McCormack, 2012), improve the academic performance of gay and lesbian students (Francis, 2013), and stimulate reciprocal discourse, inclusion and respect among all students (Gayle et al., 2013). N. J. Evans (2002) argued that such centralization is characterized by the inclusion of material that purposely centers on themes of homosexuality; thus, gay and lesbian students may experience the campus environment as more positive. According to Francis (2017b), if there is an exclusive emphasis on their negative experiences as gays and lesbians, they become labeled as powerless, negating any possible agency on their part. This agency exercised by participants, according to queer theorists, rejected what they call the "heterosexual matrix" (J. Butler, 1999) or what Ingraham (1996) typified as the "heterosexual imaginary," thus discarding the proposition of publicly presenting themselves according to what is considered appropriate heteronormatively or homonormatively.

The preceding views (whether in favor of or against compulsory heterosexual roles) challenge *and* uphold the centrality of heteronormativity insofar as these participants displayed liberationist and queer theoretical tendencies to challenge gender and sexual identity stereotypes and tended to also display assimilationist inclinations since they sought to emphasize "sameness" and association *with* heterosexuality and concurrently critique normative expectations (Van den Berg, 2016). Examples of how these students sought to reflect heteronormative principles included the performance of particular roles (cf. J. L. Johnson et al., 2007), therefore rendering the "other" types of experiences by "typical gay" men as abnormal. Such attempts notwithstanding, a liberationist tendency may, contradictorily, *both* transgress *and* reinforce heteronormativity, insofar as those who refuted heterosexual ideals through emphasizing their differences as opposed to similarities with heterosexuality, may risk further "othering" (cf. De Wet et al., 2016; Rothmann, 2016; Rothmann & Simmonds, 2015). Consider, for example, Plummer's (1998) reference to the fact that gay and lesbian persons may inadvertently render their identities "vulnerable," "privileged and sacred" since such an "ideological isolation may result in distinctions within and among members of the homosexual community themselves" (Rothmann, 2017, pp. 5–6). This results in what Plummer (1998, p. 85) considered to be "an ever increasing self-imposed segregation." Examples of such liberationist tendencies included the importance participants ascribed to constructing and enforcing specific spaces and policies, respectively, to protect gay and lesbian students on campus. This, according to them, potentially contributed to the affirmation of their identities; it challenged the system of "compulsory heterosexuality" (cf. Rich, 2004), restructured university policies toward being more inclusive (cf. Plummer, 2015), and encouraged sociopolitical engagement among the students (cf. Corrigan & Matthews, 2003).

This thought relates to whether participants assigned *importance to forming part of a LGBTIQ+ group.* Fifteen (15) participants regarded forming part of a visible group on campus as significant as it resulted in providing "comfort" and "safety and excitement" (Rankin, 2005), support (Payne & Smith, 2011; Rothmann, 2014), and understanding (Hind, 2004); "a second family" (Dietz, 1997); "visibility" (Weeks, 2007), a "sense of belonging," "embracing diversity" (National Consortium of Directors of Higher Education LGBT Resource Professionals, 2004); "networking" (N. J. Evans, 2002); "disclosure" of one's sexual identity to others like you (Nel et al., 2007); and "improved self-confidence" (McCormack, 2012) by positioning oneself "against heteronormativity" (D'Emilio, 1992). From the participants' narratives, corresponding with the preceding literature, being part of a group on campus impacted on their social lives. Although some participants had never been part of these groups while others had, they viewed affiliation with a group as important in their lives and in the lives of other gay and lesbian students, a thought evident in the work of Lee (2002). These findings echoed the precepts underlined by theorists and social scientists whose work recalled the principles of queer liberationists (Yep et al., 2003) dedicated to improving situations for gay and lesbian persons. Therefore, having a visible community and participating in such groups emphasized an organized assertion "against heteronormative ideologies" (Seidman, 2003, p. 65). With visibility, participants tended to support a queer liberationist's notion of exclusivity, which argued against hiding one's sexuality and gender expressions, but might have contradictorily upheld the principle of homosexual (or arguably, homonormative) difference, embracing homogeneity in homosexual circles, which may have reinforced a further binary between heteronormative standards of normality (Eide, 2010) and the supposed incurable and "exotic" homosexual subculture.

However, five participants noted that being part of a visible group was not necessarily significant, attributing these groups as being the "cause" for segregation and exacerbation of homophobia, attested by C. Fox (2007). Students might, unconsciously, uphold heteronormative precepts through their need for equality with heterosexual people, emphasizing principles associated with assimilation supporting gay and lesbian students deserving equal rights and acknowledgment (Robson, 2002). Proponents of queer theory critiqued this thought, referring to sexual minorities not merely being assimilated into an uncritical acceptance of heteronormative principles and ideologies (Epprecht, 2012; Francis, 2017b; Milani & Wolff, 2015). Plummer (2015, p. 121) contended that, from a queer theoretical perspective, "old radical languages of liberation, identity politics, rights and citizenship" should be critiqued and challenge such normalization.

## CONCLUSION

Evident from this discussion is that participants presumed their sexual and gender role identity performances were desirable and consistent *across* a continuum of human sexual identities. In critiquing essentialist views on homosexuality, participants emphasized the intersectional differences among gay and lesbian persons by emphasizing the varied ways whereby individuals construct, negotiate, and enact their identities.

The study consequently showed how students navigated a continuum of sexual fluidity that resulted in conforming to *heteronormativity* and/or *homonormativity* at one certain time or concurrently, depending on the particular context and motivation. This point notes that some students who did not conform to the predetermined gendered and sexual norms based on a cisgendered heteronormative system were likely to mask their sexual orientation and assimilate into the heterosexual campus culture to avoid discrimination, while others may have sought to highlight their inherent sexual differences to their heterosexual counterparts to critique and interrogate heterosexist binary logics foregrounding heteronormativity as the dominant gender and sexual arrangement. These findings emphasized the significant role of university management, academics, and LGBTIQ+ student organizations to acknowledge the inherent diversity among gay and lesbian students. This is imperative, as policies addressing the protection of the rights of the campus' gay and lesbian community should avoid implementing measures that homogenize the experiences of sexual minorities. Workshops, seminars, and colloquia should be encouraged, initiated, funded, and attended by representatives of, among others, the university management. This could address management's considering open and constructive debates on the lived experiences of gay and lesbian students as imperative, and that they would contribute to constructive and critical debates to identify practical measures for redressing the anxiety and fear of nonheterosexual persons. One should thus foreground the heterogeneity of the reflexive and individualized sexual identities of these students to facilitate the creation of a campus culture where they can continuously negotiate their choice to identify with principles associated with heterosexual, gay, and lesbian identities rather than an either–or approach.

## NOTES

1. We use the following terms and acronyms to denote sexual identity markers throughout the chapter: Gay and lesbian are used to refer to the participants of the present study who self-identified as such; the acronym LGBTIQ+ (lesbian, gay, bisexual, transgender, intersex, queer and questioning) is used to refer to the overarching acknowledgment of diverse gender and sexual identities in South African academic and legal institutions.
2. These students self-identified as "colored." Under Apartheid, the term was used to refer to mixed-race people that did not categorize as "white" or "black." Although the use of the term remains contentious today, some "multiracial" South Africans use the category. They attribute its use to them reclaiming a term that was previously used in a derogatory way (Erasmus, 2012).
3. Allen et al. (2020) used this acronym to refer to lesbian, gay, bisexual, transgender, Takatapui, intersex, queer, and asexual identities.
4. The LGB acronym was used by Jagessar and Msibi (2015) in their study, denoting their focus on self-identified lesbian, gay, and bisexual students.

## REFERENCES

Allen, L., Cowie, L., & Fenaughty, J. (2020). Safe but not safe: LGBTTIQA+ students' experiences of a university campus. *Higher Education Research & Development*, *39*(6), 1075–1090. https://doi.org/10.1080/07294360.2019.1706453

Alvarez, S. D., & Schneider, J. (2008). One college campus's need for a safe zone: A case study. *Journal of Gender Studies*, *17*(1), 71–74. https://doi.org/10.1080/09589230701838461

Asencio, M. (2011). "Locas," respect, and masculinity: Gender conformity in migrant Puerto Rican gay masculinities. *Gender & Society*, *25*(3), 335–354. https://doi.org/10.1177/0891243211409214

Atkinson, E., & De Palma, R. (2009). Un-believing the matrix: Queering consensual heteronormativity. *Gender and Education*, *21*(1), 17–29. https://doi.org/10.1080/09540250802213149

Batten, J., Ripley, M., Anderson, E., Batey, J., & White, A. (2018). Still an occupational hazard? The relationship between homophobia, heteronormativity, student learning and performance, and an openly gay university lecturer. *Teaching in Higher Education: Critical Perspectives*, *25*(2), 189–204. https://doi.org/10.1080/13562517.2018.1553031

Bhana, D. (2012). Understanding and addressing homophobia in schools: A view from teachers. *South African Journal of Education*, *32*(3), 307–318. https://doi.org/10.15700/saje.v32n3a659

Bhana, D. (2014). "Managing" the rights of gays and lesbians: Reflections from some South African secondary schools. *Education, Citizenship and Social Justice*, *9*(1), 67–80. https://doi.org/10.1177/1746197913497663

Blackburn, M. V., & McCready, L. T. (2009). Voices of queer youth in urban schools: Possibilities and limitations. *Theory into Practice*, *48*(3), 222–230. https://doi.org/10.1080/00405840902997485

Braun, V., & Clarke, V. (2006). Using thematic analysis in psychology. *Qualitative Research in Psychology, 3*(2), 77–101. https://doi.org/10.1191/1478088706 qp063oa

Brown, A., De Wet, A., & Van Wyk, E. (2018). Responding to sexual diversity in education. In A. De Wet (Ed.), *Diversity and difference in South African schools: An education law perspective* (pp. 119–145). Cape Town: Juta.

Brown, R. (2012). Corrective rape in South Africa: A continuing plight despite an international human rights response. *Annual Survey of International and Comparative Law, 18*, 45–66. https://digitalcommons.law.ggu.edu/annlsurvey/vol18/iss1/5/

Browne, K. (2005). Snowball sampling: Using social networks to reach non-heterosexual women. *International Journal of Social Research Methodology, 8*(1), 47–60. https://doi.org/10.1080/1364557032000081663

Bryman, A. (2016). *Social research methods*. Oxford University Press.

Butler, J. (1999). *Gender trouble: Feminism and the subversion of identity*. Routledge.

Butler, A. H. (2007). Navigating institutional homophobia. *Journal of Gay & Lesbian Social Services, 19*(1), 71–88. https://doi.org/10.1300/J041v19n01_05

Butler, A. H., Alpaslan, A. H., Strumpher, J., & Astbury, G. (2003). Gay and lesbian youth experiences of homophobia in South African secondary education. *Journal of Gay & Lesbian Issues in Education, 1*(2), 3–28. https://doi.org/10.1300/J367v01n02_02

Calhoun, C. (2008). In defence of same-sex marriage. In A. Soble & N. Power (Eds.), *The philosophy of sex: Contemporary readings* (5th ed., pp. 197–215). Rowman & Littlefield.

Corber, R. J., & Valocchi, S. (2003). *Queer studies: An interdisciplinary reader*. Blackwell.

Corrigan, P., & Matthews, A. (2003). Stigma and disclosure: Implications for coming out of the closet. *Journal of Mental Health, 12*(3), 235–248. https://doi.org/10.1080/0963823031000118221

Creswell, J. W., & Creswell, J. D. (2018). *Research design: Qualitative, quantitative, and mixed methods approaches* (5th ed.). Sage Publications.

Croce, M. (2015). Homonormative dynamics and the subversion of culture. *European Journal of Social Theory, 18*(1), 3–20. https://doi.org/10.1177/1368431014534349

D'Emilio, J. (1992). *Making trouble: Essays on gay history, politics, and the university*. Routledge.

Department of Basic Education. (2019). *Comprehensive sexuality education: Scripted lessons*. https://www.education.gov.za/Home/ComprehensiveSexualityEducation.aspx

Department of Education. (2008). *Report of the Ministerial Committee on Transformation and Social Cohesion and the Elimination of Discrimination in Public Higher Education Institutions*. Department of Education Printing Offices.

DePalma, R., & Francis, D. (2014). South African life orientation teachers: (Not) teaching about sexual diversity. *Journal of Homosexuality, 61*(12), 1687–1711. https://doi.org/10.1080/00918369.2014.951256

De Wet, A., Rothmann, J., & Simmonds, S. (2016). Human rights: Protecting sexual minorities or reinforcing the boundaries of "the closet"? *South African Review of Sociology, 47*(3), 85–109. https://doi.org/10.1080/21528586.2016.1163291

Dietz, T. J. (1997). The impact of membership in a support group for gay, lesbian, and bisexual students. *Journal of College Student Psychotherapy, 12*, 57–72.

Eaton, A. A., & Matamala, A. (2014). The relationship between heteronormative beliefs and verbal sexual coercion in college students. *Archives of Sexual Behavior, 43,* 1443–1457. https://doi.org/10.1007/s10508-014-0284-4

Eide, E. (2010). Strategic essentialism and ethnification. Hand in glove? *Nordicom Review, 31*(2), 63–78. https://doi.org/10.1515/nor-2017-0130

Epprecht, M. (2012). Sexual minorities, human rights and public health strategies in Africa. *African Affairs, 111*(443), 223–243. https://doi.org/10.1093/afraf/ads019

Erasmus, Z. (2012). Apartheid race categories: Daring to question their continued use. *Transformation: Critical Perspectives on Southern Africa, 79*(1), 1–11. doi:10.1353/trn.2012.0008

Eslen-Ziya, H., McGarry, A., Potgieter, C., & Reygan, F. C. (2015). *Equal but separate? LGBTI rights in contemporary South Africa. Discursive governance in politics, policy and the public.* Palgrave Macmillan.

Evans, N. J. (2002). The impact of an LGBT safe zone project on campus climate. *Journal of College Student Development, 43*(4), 522–539.

Evans, R., Nagoshi, C., Wheele, J., & Henderson, J. (2017). Voices from the stories untold: Lesbian, gay, bisexual, trans, and queer college students' experiences with campus climate. *Journal of Gay and Lesbian Social Services, 29*(4), 426–444. https://doi.org/10.1080/10538720.2018.1378144

Fox, C. (2007). From transaction to transformation: (En)countering white heteronormativity in "safe spaces." *College English, 69*(5), 496–511.

Fox, C. O., & Ore, R. E. (2010). (Un)covering normalized gender and race subjectivities in LGBT safe spaces. *Feminist Studies, 36*(3), 629–649.

Francis, D. (2013). "You know the homophobic stuff is not in me, like us, it's out there": Using participatory theatre to challenge heterosexism and heteronormativity in a South African school. *South African Journal of Education, 33*(4), 1–14. https://doi.org/10.15700/201412171338

Francis, D. (2017a). Homophobia and sexuality diversity in South African schools: A review. *Journal of LGBT Youth, 14*(4) 359–379. https://doi.org/10.1080/19361 653.2017.1326868

Francis, D. (2017b). *Troubling the teaching and learning of sexuality diversity in South African education.* Palgrave Macmillan.

Furr, S. R., Westefeld, J. S., McConnell, G. N., & Jenkins, J. M. (2001). Suicide and depression among college students: A decade later. *Professional Psychology: Research and Practice, 32*(1), 97–100. https://doi.org/10.1037/ 0735-7028.32.1.97

Garcia-Alonso, P. (2004). From surviving to thriving: An investigation of the utility of support groups designed to address the special needs of sexual minority youth in public high schools. Chicago: Loyola University.

Gayle, B. M., Cortez, D., & Preiss, R. W. (2013). Safe spaces, difficult dialogues, and critical thinking. *International Journal for the Scholarship of Teaching and Learning, 7*(2), 1–8. https://doi.org/10.20429/ijsotl.2013.070205

Ghaziani, A. (2014). *There goes the gayborhood?* Princeton University Press.

Grace, A. P. (2017). Two good gay teachers: Pioneering advocate-practitioners confronting homophobia in schooling in British Columbia, Canada. *Irish Educational Studies, 36*(1), 43–56. https://doi.org/10.1080/03323 315.2017.1289701

Hind, T. (2004). *Being real: Promoting the emotional health and mental well-being of lesbian, gay and bisexual young people accessing PACE youth work services.* London: Project for Advice Counselling and Education.

Ingraham, C. (1996). The heterosexual imaginary: Feminist sociology and theories of gender. In S. Seidman (Ed.), *Queer theory/sociology* (pp. 168–193). Blackwell Publishers.

Jackson, S., & Scott, S. (2010). *Theorizing sexuality*. McGraw Hill.

Jagessar, V., & Msibi, T. (2015). "It's not that bad": Homophobia in the residences of a university in KwaZulu-Natal, Durban, South Africa. *Agenda, 29*(1), 63–73. https://doi.org/10.1080/10130950.2015.1022984

Johnson, B. (2014). The need to prepare future teachers to understand and combat homophobia in schools. *South African Journal of Higher Education, 28*(5), 1249–1268. https://doi.org/10.20853/28-5-417

Johnson, J. L., Greaves, L., & Repta, R. (2007). *Better science with sex and gender: A primer for health research*. Women's Health Network.

Judge, M. (2017). *Blackwashing homophobia: Violence and the politics of sexuality, gender and race*. Routledge.

Keenan, M. (2014). *Coming out and fitting in: A qualitative exploration of lesbian, gay, bisexual, trans and queer students' university experiences*. Notthingham Trent University.

Kosciw, J. G., Diaz, E. M., & Gretak, E. A. (2008). *2007 National School Climate Survey: The experiences of lesbian, gay, bisexual, and transgender youth in our nation's schools*. GLSEN.

Kumashiro, K. (2002). *Troubling education: Queer activism and anti-oppressive pedagogy*. Routledge Falmer.

Lee, C. (2002). The impact of belonging to a high school gay/straight alliance. *High School Journal, 77*(1/2), 95–107. https://doi.org/10.1353/hsj.2002.0005

Lesch, E., Brits, S., & Naidoo, N. T. (2017). "Walking on eggshells not to offend people": Experiences of same-sex student couples at a South African university. *South African Journal of Higher Education, 31*(4), 127–149. https://doi.org/10.20853/31-4-893

Marston, K. (2015). Beyond bullying: The limitations of homophobic and transphobic bullying interventions for affirming lesbian, gay, bisexual and trans (LGBT) equality in education. *Pastoral Care Education, 33*(3), 161–168. https://doi.org/10.1080/02643944.2015.1074266

Marzetti, H. (2018). Proudly proactive: Celebrating and supporting LGBT+ students in Scotland. *Teaching in Higher Education, 23*(6), 701–717. https://doi.org/10.1080/13562517.2017.1414788

Matthyse, G. (2017). Heteronormative higher education: Challenging the status quo through LGBTIQ awareness-raising. *South African Journal of Higher Education, 31*(4), 112–126. https://doi.org/10.20853/31-4-890

McArthur, T. (2015). Homophobic violence in a Northern Cape school: Learners confront the issue. *Agenda, 29*(3), 53–59. https://doi.org/10.1080/10130 950.2015.1056587

McCormack, M. (2012). The positive experiences of openly gay, lesbian, bisexual and transgendered students in a Christian sixth form college. *Sociological Research Online, 17*(3), 1–27. https://doi.org/10.5153/sro.2461

McIntosh, M. (1968). The homosexual role. *Social Problems, 16*(2), 182–192. https://doi.org/10.2307/800003

Mendos, L. R. (2019). *State sponsored homophobia* (13th ed.). ILGA.

Milani, T. M., & Wolff, B. (2015). Queer skin, straight masks: Same-sex weddings and the discursive construction of identities and effects on a South African website. *Critical Arts, 29*(2), 165–182. https://doi.org/10.1080/02560046.2015.1039203

Msibi, T. (2012). "I'm used to it now": Experiences of homophobia among queer youth in South African township schools. *Gender and Education, 24*(5), 515–533. https://doi.org/10.1080/09540253.2011.645021

Msibi, T. (2014). *Is current theorising on same-sex sexuality relevant to the African context?* Pambazuka News.

Msibi, T. (2015). The teaching of sexual and gender diversity issues to pre-service teachers at the University of KwaZulu Natal: Lessons from student exam responses. *Alternation, 12*, 385–410.

Msibi, T. (2016). Bitter knowledge. In N. M. Rodriguez, W. J. Martino, J. C. Ingrey, & E. Brockenbrough (Eds.), *Critical concepts in queer studies and education: An international guide for the twenty-first century* (pp. 23–33). Palgrave Macmillan. https://doi.org/10.1057/978-1-137-55425-3_4

Mudrey, R., & Medina-Adams, A. (2006). Attitudes, perceptions, and knowledge of pre-service teachers regarding the educational isolation of sexual minority youth. *Journal of Homosexuality, 51*(4), 63–90. https://doi.org/10.1300/J082v5 1n04_04

Mukungu, K. (2017). "'How can you write about a person who does not exist?': Rethinking pseudonymity and informed consent in life history research. *Social Sciences, 6*(86), 1–9. https://doi.org/10.3390/socsci6030086

National Consortium of Higher Education LGBT Resource Professionals. (2005). http://www.lgbtcampus.org

Nel, J. A., Rich, E., & Joubert, K. D. (2007). Lifting the veil: Experiences of gay men in a therapy group. *South African Journal of Psychology, 37*(2), 284–306. https://doi.org/10.1177/008124630703700205

Payne, E. C., & Smith, M. (2011). The reduction of stigma in schools: A new professional development model for empowering educators to support LGBTQ students. *Journal of LGBT Youth, 8*(2), 174–200. https://doi.org/10.1080/19361 653.2011.563183

Plummer, K. (1998). Homosexual categories: Some research problems in the labelling perspective of homosexuality. In P.M. Nardi & B.E. Schneider (Eds.), *Social perspectives in lesbian and gay studies* (pp. 84–99). Routledge.

Plummer, K. (2015). *Cosmopolitan sexualities.* Polity Press.

Pryor, J. T. (2018). Visualizing queer spaces: LGBTQ students and the traditionally heterogendered institution. *Journal of LGBT Youth, 15*(1), 32–51. https://doi.org/10.1080/19361653.2017.1395307

Rankin, S. R. (2005). Campus climates for sexual minorities. *New Directions for Student Services, 111*, 17–23. https://doi.org/10.1002/ss.170

Ratts, M. J., Kaloper, M., McReady, C., Tighe, L., Butler, S. K., Dempsey, K., & McCullough, J. (2013). Safe space programs in K–12 schools: Creating a visible presence of LGBTQ allies. *Journal of LGBT Issues in Counseling, 7*(4), 387–404. https://doi.org/10.1080/15538605.2013.839344

Reddy, V. (2010). Identity, law, justice. Thinking about sexual rights and citizenship in postapartheid South Africa. *Perspectives, 4*(10), 18–23.

Rich, A. (2004). Reflections on "compulsory heterosexuality." *Journal of Women's History, 16*(1), 9–11. https://doi.org/10.1353/jowh.2004.0033

Richardson, D. (2012). Bordering theory. In D. Richardson, J. McLaughlin, & M. E. Casey (Eds.), *Intersections between feminist and queer theory* (pp. 19–37). Palgrave Macmillan.

Richardson, E. (2008). Using film to challenge heteronormativity: South African teachers "get real" in working with LGB youth. *Journal of LGBT Youth, 5*(2), 63–72. https://doi.org/10.1080/19361650802092416

Rink, B. M. (2013). Que(e)riyng Cape Town: Touring Africa's "gay capital" with the Pink Map. In J. Sarmento & E. Brito-Henriques (Eds.), *Tourism in the Global South: Heritages, identities and development* (pp. 65–90). Lisbon: Centre for Geographical Studies.

Robson, R. (2002). Assimilation, marriage, and lesbian liberation. *Temple Law Review, 75*(4), 710–820.

Rothmann, J. (2014). *(De)constructing the heterosexual/homosexual binary: The identity construction of gay male academics and students in South African tertiary education* [Unpublished doctoral dissertation]. North-West University.

Rothmann, J. (2016). The (de)professionalisation of the gay male academic identity: Locking the closet door on South African university campuses. *South African Review of Sociology, 47*(4), 40–59. https://doi.org/10.1080/21528 586.2016.1182444

Rothmann, J. (2017). The role of self-reflexivity on the part of gay male academics on South African university campuses. *Acta Academica, 49*(1), 1–31. https://doi. org/10.18820/24150479/aa49i1.4

Rothmann, J. (2018). A social constructionist approach to resilience for LGBTIQ+ academics and students in South African universities. *Transformation in Higher Education, 30*(0), 1–8. https://doi.org/10.4102/the.v3i0.34

Rothmann, J., & Simmonds, S. (2015). "Othering" non-normative sexualities through objectification of "the homosexual": Discursive discrimination by pre-service teachers. *Agenda, 29*(1), 116–126. https://doi.org/10.1080/10130 950.2015.1010288

Roux, C. D., & Du Preez, P. (2013). Human rights literacy: A quest for meaning. http://hreid-hrlit.blogspot.com/2013/04/Humanrightsliteracy-aquestformean ing-LiteraciesRhizomaticresearch.html

Rumens, N. (2011). *Queer company: The role and meaning of friendship in gay men's work lives*. Ashgate.

Seidman, S. (2002). *Beyond the closet: The transformation of gay and lesbian life*. Routledge.

Seidman, S. (2003). *The social construction of sexuality*. W. W. Norton and Company.

Smith, A. (2010). Queer theory and native studies: The heteronormativity of settler colonialism. *GLQ: A Journal of Lesbian and Gay Studies, 16*(1–2), 41–68. https:// doi.org/10.1215/10642684-2009-012

Smith, I., Oades, L. G., & McCarthy, G. (2012). Homophobia to heterosexism: Constructs in need of re-visitation. *Gay and Lesbian issues and Psychology Review, 8*(1), 34–44.

Tshilongo, T., & Rothmann, J. (2019). A sociological exploration of the need for safe spaces for lesbian and gay students on a South African university campus. *Transformation in Higher Education, 4*(0), a77. https://doi.org/10.4102/the. v4i0.77

Van den Berg, E. (2016). "The closet": A dangerous heteronormative space. *South African Review of Sociology, 47*(3), 25–43. https://doi.org/10.1080/21528 586.2016.1182445

Wailing, A., & Roffee, J.A. (2017). Knowing, performing and holding queerness: LGBTIQ+ student experiences in Australian tertiary education. *Sex Education, 17*(3), 302–318. https://doi.org/10.1080/14681811.2017.1294535

Warner, M. (1991). Fear of a queer planet. *Social Text*, *9*(14), 3–17.

Weeks, J. (2007). *The world we have won*. Routledge.

Yep, G. A., Lovaas, K. E., & Elia, J. P. (2003). A critical appraisal of assimilationist and radical ideologies underlying same-sex marriage in LGBT communities in the United States. *Journal of Homosexuality*, *45*(1), 45–64. https://doi.org/10.1300/J082v45n01_03

CHAPTER 15

# Norm-Critical Pedagogy as Femo- and Homonationalism

## Perspectives on Norm Critique in Swedish Research, Activism, and Educational Practice

EVA REIMERS

The school should actively and consciously promote the equal rights and opportunities of pupils, regardless of gender. The school also has a responsibility to combat gender patterns that limit the pupils' learning, choices and development. How the school organizes education, how pupils are treated and what demands and expectations are made of them all contribute to shaping their perceptions of what is female and what is male.

—Sverige, 2018

This citation from the Swedish National Curriculum can be read as a call for a queer pedagogy (Gowlett & Rasmussen, 2016; Rasmussen & Allen, 2014; Reimers, 2010; Sumara & Davis, 1999), that is, teaching practices that interrupt dominant gender and sexuality norms by stressing subjectivity as open, ambiguous, and contingent. The text states that the overarching goal for work with gender issues in education is to achieve gender equality. It articulates a binary understanding of gender by the usage of "girls and boys" and "female and male" and appeals

Eva Reimers, *Norm-Critical Pedagogy as Femo- and Homonationalism* In: *Queer Studies and Education*. Edited by: Nelson M. Rodriguez, Robert C. Mizzi, Louisa Allen, and Rob Cover, Oxford University Press.
© Oxford University Press 2023. DOI: 10.1093/oso/9780197687000.003.0016

against constraints of this dichotomy. Teachers shall "combat" the limitations of gender patterns. Reading this in line with Butler's claim (Butler, 1999, 2004) that stereotypical gender norms are inseparable from sexuality norms makes gender equality education based on the policy texts above into a queer project. In order to truly "combat gender patterns that limit the pupils' learning, choices and development," the school needs to queer notions of dichotomous stable gender and sexuality identities. Based on this, one of the questions that I want to raise in this chapter is whether the normalization of the norm-critical perspective is tantamount to a normalization of queerness and if this is even possible. A normalized queer—doesn't that contradict the very core of the notion of queerness?

This chapter begins with an investigation as to how the possibility of a queer gender and sexual education in Sweden (and other Nordic countries) has become formulated and normalized as "norm-critical pedagogy." This is followed by a theoretical section centered on the concepts norm critique, banal nationalism, and femo- and homonationalism. The third section presents some significant Nordic research about norm-critical education. I subsequently undertake an analysis of some possible effects of the normalization and naturalization of norm critique, focusing on how this phenomenon intersects with norms pertaining to nation and race (religion). The point of departure for the concluding discussion is the question whether it is possible or desirable to mainstream and normalize queer. Here, I stress the need for queering the depolitization of norm critique and homonationalism (in education).

## NORM-CRITICAL PEDAGOGY

In Sweden, the National Agency for Education promotes norm-critical pedagogy as both an approach for sex and relationship education and a tool to prevent bullying, harassment, and discrimination (Swedish National Agency for Education, 2013a, 2013b, 2013c). This has formed a market where nongovernmental organizations (NGOs) and educational entrepreneurs have become consultants and produced educational tools that convert norm-critical theory into exercises and teaching plans (Åkerlund, 2011; Brade, 2008; Bromseth & Darj, 2010). In this way, norm-critical pedagogy is now more or less mainstream in Swedish preschools and schools.

The aim of norm-critical teaching practices is to form awareness of the role of norms in shaping domination, subordination, inclusion, and exclusion. As described by Bengtsson and Bolander (2020), norm-critical pedagogy has a strong focus on language and is careful to name categories, identities, and practices as inclusively as possible, that is, avoiding gendered pronouns, and describing sexuality and gender in nonessential and nonheteronormative ways. The teachers are told not to presume that all students identify with hegemonic norms, including those related to gender, sexuality, ethnicity, and religion. Norm-critical pedagogy makes use of exercises interrogating values and norms in order to help students identify norms and their exclusionary effects. Differing from a pedagogy aiming to produce tolerance toward deviant identifications and practices, the focus is on the norm and what it produces rather than those who are excluded. A telling example of one of the first manuals in norm-critical pedagogy is *In the Eye of the Norm* (*I normens öga*) (Brade, 2008). The title alludes to the way in which norm-critical pedagogy aims to form awareness about exclusionary and marginalizing effects of norms, not the least among those who because of privileged positions are unaware of their privileges and how these affect others.

As a pedagogy, the norm-critical approach in education is a combination of critical pedagogy and queer pedagogy, much like the antioppressive pedagogy outlined by Kevin Kumashiro (2002). Rather than aiming for inclusion of the imagined other, Kumashiro argued for a pedagogy that scrutinizes and makes trouble with how different identity positions are victims of as well as agents for oppression. In order to make trouble with how education tends to reproduce hegemonic norms, he stressed the need to make students recognize how they in different ways are subjected to oppression. The point of departure for norm-critical pedagogy is a presumption that norms shape identities and lived experiences of groups and individuals, rewarding some expressions of gender and sexuality and simultaneously marginalizing or obfuscating others. To make more lives possible, norm-critical pedagogy troubles dominating regulative norms. It addresses norms that produce identity categories in terms of race, class, religion, and functionality, as well as other regulatory norms pertaining to economy, pedagogy, education, age, nation, politics, and so forth. It is thus an attempt to make use of an enlarged conception of intersectionality (Crenshaw, 1991), where all sorts of norms can be scrutinized. Consequently, the core of the norm-critical pedagogic approach is to map, trace, and make trouble for the way regulatory norms produce domination and subordination, making some lives not only more valuable but also more possible, than others.

## NORM-CRITICAL THEORY—AN EXPANDED APPLIANCE OF QUEER THEORY

Swedish researchers and educators have developed norm-critical theory in order to make visible and critically explore how different norms intersect in producing subordination, dominance, inclusion, and exclusion (Bromseth & Darj, 2010; Martinsson & Reimers, 2010; Martinsson et al., 2007). The advantage of the concept norm is that it is not limited to specific identity categories or social phenomena. Norms are everywhere and permeate everything. Norms constantly produce and are produced in processes of power, where some practices, ideas, and subjectivities are made normal, whereas others are made abnormal. Hereby, it is a concept that opens up opportunities for intersectional analyses of not only gender, sexuality, ableness, class, racialization, and age but also other norms, such as neoliberalism, capitalism, religion, education, and knowledge. The point of departure for norm-critical theory is queer theory and its emphasis on the ubiquitous materializations and effects of the heterosexual norm. In norm-critical theory, the interest is widened to focus on not only the heterosexual norm, but also the effects of all regulatory norms.

In putting queer and the concept heteronormativity to work in studies of education, it became apparent that gender and sexuality norms intersect with numerous other normative practices (Martinsson & Reimers, 2020; Martinsson et al., 2007; Reimers, 2007, 2014, 2017). The openness of the concept norm makes it possible to scrutinize how norms work together and what this produces. As a theoretical concept, "norm" draws on its colloquial usage, which encompasses both description and prescription. Even if there are many similarities between the concept norm and the concept discourse, they are not interchangeable. Where discourse emphasizes articulation and performance, norm more directly points to the regulative and disciplinary effects of notions, talk, policies, practices, and artifacts. Thus, it can effectively elucidate how power constantly permeates knowledge, representations, practices, and artifacts forming superiority and subordination.

Butler's theory on gender, performativity, and recognition is pivotal for norm-critical theory (Butler, 1999, 2004). Consequently, norms—regardless of what they point to—are understood as performative, unstable, diffused social constructions that exercise power in the way they are materialized and made significant in institutions, collectives, and individuals. Like Butler and queer theory, norm-critical theory stresses that constructions of any normality always encompass its outside. Articulations of norms always entail boundaries that produce the aberrant, strange, and divergent. Consequently, the most pertinent way to describe norm-critical theory is as an expanded and intersectional application of queer theory. Even if norms about gender and sexuality often are the point of departure for norm-critical studies, they are not necessarily in the forefront. Hereby, norm-critical theory combines and incorporates important observations and contributions from queer theory with contributions from critical race theory (Kumashiro, 2002; León Rosales, 2010); crip theory (Barden, 2018; Bylund, 2020a; McRuer, 2006); postcolonial theory (Mohanty, 1984, 2003); and critical theory in education (McLaren & Kincheloe, 2007). Thus, it is a theory that makes it possible to discern how norms intersect and work together and how this influences life possibilities of collectives and individuals. This has been important for elucidating how nationality, gender, and sexuality intersect in official and mundane procedures where some gender and sexual norms and practices become nationalized and thus perceived as significant for what constitutes the nation.

In order to focus on intersections of norms pertaining to gender and sexuality with norms about nationality, three other concepts and their ensuing theoretical approach are useful. These are "banal nationalism" (Billig, 1995), "homonationalism" (Puar, 2007), and "femonationalism" (Farris, 2017). Billig introduced the concept banal nationalism to critically elucidate and explore how taken-for-granted conceptions about the nation serve as taken-for-granted presumptions in mundane talk and practices, not the least in media and politics. Puar further develops this notion of nationalism by exploring how banal conceptions of the nation in the Global North demonstrate connections of sexuality, race, gender, nation, class, and ethnicity (Puar, 2007). The foundation for the concept homonationalism is the observation that sexuality has become increasingly used by Western countries to construct proper citizens as tolerant of LGBTQI+ subjects. In a similar way, Farris introduced femonationalism to highlight how gender equality values and politics are invoked in European nationalist and xenophobic discourses and rhetoric (Farris, 2017). In this chapter, femonationalism is used to describe how gender equality and feminism are understood and used as significant traits and values of a nation state. Femo- and homonationalism thus point to situations where self-identification in terms of gender equality, feminism, and tolerance towards LGBTQI+ persons produce nations and subjects in the Global South as the other, as non-White, homophobic, dangerously religious (often Muslim), patriarchal, and a threat to not only women and LGBTQI+ persons but also values such as freedom and democracy. Hereby, a self-perceived tolerance against "otherness" in terms of gender and sexuality serve as a resource and power in relation to xenophobia and racism, where non-European migrants are portrayed as threats against not only LGBTQI+ persons but also modernity and democracy.

## NORM-CRITICAL STUDIES OF EDUCATION

In this section, I give some examples of norm-critical educational research from Sweden and Norway. This is by no means a comprehensive review; rather, the aim is to demonstrate how norm-critical theory is put to use in the Nordic context. I do not claim that the conception of norm-critical theory is exclusive to Nordic educational research. Even if the concept norm critique is not mentioned, numerous studies from other contexts make use of the same or similar theorization of intersecting norms (e.g., Kumashiro, 2002; Renold & Allan, 2006; Renold & Epstein, 2010; Renold et al., 2015; Youdell, 2011).

One of the first elaborated presentations of norm-critical theory in relation to education was the introductory chapter of *Norm-Struggles: Sexualities in Contentions* (Martinsson & Reimers, 2010). Here, Martinsson and Reimers argued for the usefulness of the concept norm in order to explore how different norms simultaneously work in different directions. One example is how gender equality norms, on the one hand, subvert patriarchal norms and hierarchies, but on the other hand, reproduce heteronormative forces. Here, they stress norm-critical theory as a tool for scrutinizing the complexities and contingencies of how differing intersections of norms make way for different subjectivities, hierarchies, inclusions, and exclusions in various contexts. This, Martinsson and Reimers argued, makes norm performances—not the least in relation to gender and sexuality—an insecure and precarious matter. Furthermore, they pointed to the way norms are made possible and significant in how they are reiterated in connections between artifacts, technologies, bodies, and institutions. In relation to education, they argued for the need to both scrutinize and subvert norms in order to form educational practices that, in line with Biesta's ideas about subjectification (Biesta, 2006), make way for subjects who can imagine and contribute to a different societal order than the present one. In the same book, Nordberg et al. (2010) made use of this perspective to map how preschool children repeatedly contest heteronormative masculinity by performing alternative gender performances. One of their arguments was that a lot of the research on gender and education needs to make use of a more open conception of (gender) norms in order not to simply reproduce the hegemony of the binary heterosexual norm. One example is research on school performance, which often tends to homogenize boys and girls as under- or well achieving without recognizing that neither gender nor achievement are stable categories. In a study of heteronormativity in teacher education, Reimers (2007, 2010) elucidated how intersecting norms about gender, sexuality, race, religion, class, and education produce complex and frequently contradictory normative materializations about the relations between and significance of gender norms in schools. Based on interviews with self-identified hetero- and homosexual teachers, Lundgren (2010) demonstrated how the simultaneous articulation of teachers as role models and as homosexuals can go in differing directions. These articulations either produce a demand for lesbian and gay teachers to be closeted or a demand for the same teachers to be out and make use of their nonnormative sexual identification as a pedagogical resource (cf. Reimers, 2020). As closeted, LGBTQI+ teachers affirm dominant gender and sexuality norms, whereas as open, they not only disturb the hegemony but also open up for a wider specter of gender and sexuality identifications.

Two studies, one by Jonsson (2007) and one by Léon Rosales (2010), explore intersections of masculinity, race, education, and nation in schools with a high percentage of pupils with an immigrant background. Johnson's study explored how immigrant male stereotypes are constructed together with norms of sexuality and nationality. Léon Rosales's study focused on how these or similar identity positions intersect with discourse about success in relation to conceptions of the ideal pupil and the segregated urban landscape where the pupils are situated. Léon Rosales demonstrated how this facilitates and precludes differing life trajectories for these boys. Common to these two studies is how immigrant bodies in schools partake in constructions of what is understood as normative "Swedishness."

The way in which gender and sexuality norms operate in constructions of Norwegian national identity were explored by Mühleisen, Røthing, and Svendsen (Mühleisen, 2007; Mühleisen & Røthing, 2009; Mühleisen et al., 2012). Their analyses of migration policy documents, national curriculum, and textbooks disclosed how some sexual ideals and practices are constructed as desired and wholesome Norwegian sex and how this is done in relation to what then become old-fashioned, inappropriate, or offensive expressions of sexuality. This is especially explicit in textbooks, which largely present Norwegian sexuality in contrast to sexual norms and practices of "the other." Their analyses demonstrated Norwegian sexuality as signified by Whiteness, heterosexuality, gender equality, love, consent, and homotolerance (Røthing, 2008; Røthing & Svendsen, 2010, 2011). These are the same significant traits of Swedish sexuality as those identified by Reimers in the study of Swedish teacher education, mentioned above (Reimers, 2007, 2010).

In an ethnographic study of gender and social class among girls in upper secondary school, Ambjörnsson (2004) elucidated in detail how entanglements of gender, sexuality, class, and age are constructed and delimit and open up possibilities for different forms of agency. Another important norm-critical study of education is Bengtsson's (2013) study of intersections of gender and sexuality norms with age among children in Year 3 (9 years of age). The study elucidated the contradictory and fluid manner in which these norms are reiterated in talk and practice.

With its pronounced focus on a dominant norm and its effects, crip theory (McRuer, 2006) is in line with norm-critical theory. Christine Bylund is a crip theorist who contributes to both gender studies (Bylund, 2020a) and education science (Bylund, 2020b). Like norm-critical theory, crip theory focuses and scrutinizes a hegemonic norm—ableness—as a process and a socially constructed and powerful norm system, producing bodies and subjects as more or less intelligible. The aim of crip theory is to study the production of ableness, how it privileges some bodies and punishes others in terms of mobility, agency, access, and representation. Bylund painfully demonstrated how an ableist society often understands, and thereby deprives, dis/abled people of both gender and sexuality.

Recently, and in line with norm-critical theory, there have been several studies that use norm-critical theory to explore norm-critical pedagogy and how these practices not only make trouble for some norms (preferably gender and sexuality) but also reiterate and stabilize other norms. This is salient in Bengtsson and Bolander's (2020) study of norm-critical pedagogy in sexuality and relationship education in upper secondary education, where a majority of the students had migrated to Sweden or had parents who had migrated. The study revealed tensions between advocating certain values and simultaneously involving the students in norm-critical pedagogy. Bredström et al. (2019) developed this further by recognizing "the slippery line between *exposing* norms and *reinstating* them" (p. 547), not the least in situations where representatives of a White national majority use exercises and practices from norm-critical pedagogy in sex and relationship education for migrant students. They argued that norm-critical pedagogy reiterates a liberal conception of the individual (cf. Langmann & Månsson, 2016). The actual teaching thereby tends to ignore not only conflicting values based on culture and religion but also the cultural specificity of the values the teachers want to promote (gender equality, pleasure-oriented sexuality, an inclusive position on different sexualities). According to Bredström et al., the attempt to delink sexual values from specific cultures and base the teaching on universal values results in expressions of a Western European, or Swedish, viewpoint (cf. Bredström & Bolander,

2019). Their study, as well as an article by Langmann and Månsson (2016), can be seen as responses to the call from norm-critical theory of a never-ending process of norm critique, always ending the analysis by asking: "Now, what is now made into a norm?" (Martinsson & Reimers, 2020, p. 30). They thus stressed the importance of a continuous and self-reflexive norm critique.

## WHAT IS NOW MADE INTO A NORM? EMERGENT NORMS IN NORM-CRITICAL PEDAGOGY

Norm-critical theory and norm-critical pedagogy offer valuable tools to make visible, and make trouble for, domination, subordination, inclusion, and exclusion in everyday life in and outside educational institutions. This is why norm-critical pedagogy is promoted as the main tool for prevention of bullying, harassment, and discrimination in Swedish schools (Swedish National Agency of Education, 2013a, 2013b). However, by looking at practices of norm critique in education through the theoretical lenses of banal nationalism, homonationalism, and femonationalism, it becomes evident that there is a downside to these positive effects. In line with Røthing and Svendsen (2010, 2011), as well as Bredström et al. (2019), this section takes seriously the never-ending norm-critical question, "What becomes the norm now?," and addresses how norm-critical pedagogy and norm-critical theory, in some cases—and most likely unintentionally—reiterate a banal nationalism (Billig, 1995). This is a banal nationalism in the form of homonationalism (Puar, 2007) as well as femonationalism (Farris, 2017). These are postcolonial perspectives (Mohanty, 1984) that elucidate the significance of taking for granted the West as civilized, developed, and rational in contrast to the rest of the world as backward, disorganized, and irrational.

As civil servants, teachers in compulsory education represent the nation state. Articulations of norms in connection with teaching can thus be understood as practices of banal nationalism. With its roots in queer theory, the most frequent educational practices of norm critique are centered on gender and sexuality norms. When educational contexts elucidate discriminatory and marginalizing effects of patriarchal and heteronormative norms, these practices tend to reiterate and stabilize conceptions of a national gender-equal and LGBTQI+ friendly nation state. This produces homonationalism (Puar, 2007), a "we"—the feminist and homotolerant Swedes or Norwegians—in contrast to "them" (misogynist and homophobic people who do not really belong) (Reimers, 2017). When teachers and students self-evidently position themselves outside misogynistic and heteronormative practices and opinions, they not only perform femo- and homonationalism, but also obscure ongoing processes of "othering" in norm-critical classrooms. This is an othering produced by teachers and students who self-evidently position themselves outside of patriarchy and homophobia. Here, misogyny and homophobia emerge as anomalies, and persons (individuals and collectives) who adhere to those values appear as not only deviant but also foreigners. They are positioned outside the values and practices that signify the nation. The intersectional character of this process is not limited to gender and sexuality norms. It also includes and draws on norms about race, ethnicity, religion, and class (Reimers, 2017).

Nationalism, regardless whether it is banal nationalism, femonationalism, homonationalism, or right-wing nationalism, not only constitutes the nation as different in relation to other nation states but also as superior. Specific to femo- and homonationalism is that gender equality and attitudes toward LGBTQI+ persons are made into traits of the nation state. Conceptions about gender and LGBTQI+ persons set the nation apart from other nations, cultures, or religions. This is how it produces Sweden and Norway as gender-equal and homotolerant feminist nations in contrast to other places, nations, people, and religions that are homogenized as intolerant. This constructs incompatibility between feminism and homotolerance on the one hand and religiosity (not the least Islam) and non-Western heritage and culture on the other hand.

Swedish schools are contexts for iterations of banal nationalism (Billig, 1995). Teaching practices, rules, and regulations are articulated based on specific presumptions about perspectives, identities, behaviors, values, and beliefs as normal and self-evident in Sweden. This means that the aim to form a more inclusive school climate in relation to gender and sexuality collaterally forms an exclusive school climate in relation to race, ethnicity, culture, and religion (cf. Rasmussen, 2010), thus simply shifting around the boundaries and signifiers for inclusion and exclusion. The inclusion of differing gender performances and sexualities takes place at the expense of exclusion of certain racial, ethnic, and religious identifications. This is why norm-critical theory and pedagogy are never-ending endeavors and why using norm-critical perspectives needs to make use of intersectional approaches and not limit its interest to making trouble for gender and sexuality norms. Norm-critical studies of implementation of norm-critical pedagogy demonstrate the exclusionary force of banal nationalism in the form of femo- and homonationalism. Consequently, there is no endpoint for the use of norm-critical theory and pedagogy. There are no social spaces devoid of norms. Deconstruction of some norms thus entails (re)construction of other norms as a point of departure or as ensuing effects. To make schools and society inclusive and assertive of different identifications and subject positionings, it is imperative to question and disentangle networks of norms. There is a need to develop norm-critical theory and pedagogy in a double direction, asking questions about not only what norms produce but also how they are produced and what norms we as researchers and teachers produce in our norm-critical perspectives.

## THE (IM)POSSIBILITY OF HEGEMONIC NORM-CRITICAL THEORY AND PRACTICES

This chapter began with an account of official normalization of norm-critical theory and pedagogy in Swedish compulsory education. The national curriculum as well as policy documents describe norm-critical pedagogy as the preferred methodology for gender equality work as well as work to prevent discrimination, harassment, and bullying. In this final section, I discuss how this affects the subversive force of norm critique. As described previously in this chapter, norm-critical theory is an expansion of queer theory. At the core of queer theory is the objective to elucidate and make trouble for hegemonic gender and sexuality norms and thus subvert heteronormativity. Norm-critical theory recognizes that gender and sexuality norms always are articulated and made manifest together with other norms. In relation to queer theory, this section addresses whether it is possible for queer theory to remain queer when it is embraced by society and made hegemonic. What happens to norm-critical theory when norm-critical perspectives and pedagogies are represented and recommended as the norm for teaching? I argue that the effect is twofold and ambiguous.

On the one hand, normalization of queer and norm-critical theory in education possibly contributes to a greater awareness of delimiting norms of gender and sexuality and thus makes it possible for students and teachers to affirm and take on a wider range of gender and sexuality identifications. Teachers have become more conscious about how they address their students, what different practices presume and stabilize, and what normative assumptions their own performances presume and express. This norm-critical work goes beyond gender and sexuality norms. Teachers are increasingly aware of their own racialized and classed positions and how they affect their students. It is now apparent that Swedish secularism is based on a taken-for-granted Christian conception of religion, which forms an othering of other religions and religious affiliations (Reimers, 2019). The norms about ableness that are repeated in architecture and teaching

[306]  *Eva Reimers*

practices are made visible and subjected to more inclusive measures. Taken together, this points to many positive effects of norm-critical pedagogy.

On the other hand, the normalization of queer and norm-critical perspectives and practices is an apparent subversion of their disruptive power. How to perform gender, how to form life trajectories based on differing sexuality identifications, and how to address the place of religion in society, the superior position of Whiteness, and ableness as a powerful norm system are all political questions. Presenting norm-critical pedagogy as a preferred and nonproblematic way of addressing discrimination, marginalization, and bullying in schools in policy documents constitutes a depolitization of highly political issues. Scrutinizing and subverting these norms has wider implications than how students identify themselves and others and how to form an inclusive and benevolent school climate. As femo- and homonationalism disclose, these are norms at the core of the nation state. They concern who should count as a citizen, who should be listened to, and how legislation that secures the rights and obligations of all inhabitants should be formed. In that way, queer and norm-critical theory are sensitive and dangerous for the status quo and for all of those who benefit from the present hegemonies. So, unless queer and norm-critical theory and pedagogy retain their political force, it most likely will become yet another form of banal nationalism.

## REFERENCES

Åkerlund, C. (2011). *Bryt!: ett metodmaterial om normer i allmänhet och heteronormen i synnerhet* [Break!: A teaching tool to work with norms in general and specifically with the heteronorm] (3., [omarb.] uppl. / [redaktör: Carl Åkerlund]. ed.). Forum för levande historia: RFSL Ungdom.

Ambjörnsson, F. (2004). *I en klass för sig: genus, klass och sexualitet bland gymnasietjejer* [In a class of their own: Gender, class, and sexuality among upper secondary school girls]. Ordfront.

Barden, O. (2018). Crip times: Disability, globalisation, and resistance [Review of the book *Crip times: Disability, globalisation, and resistance*, by R. McRuer]. *Journal of Literary & Cultural Disability Studies, 12*(3), 379–387. https://doi.org/10.3828/jlcds.2018.30

Bengtsson, J. (2013). *Jag sa att jag älskade han men jag har redan sagt förlåt för det* [I said I loved him but I have already said I am sorry]. (3rd ed.). Linköpings universitet, Institutionen för samhälls-och välfärdsstudier.

Bengtsson, J., & Bolander, E. (2020). Strategies for inclusion and equality—"norm-critical" sex education in Sweden. *Sex Education, 20*(2), 154–169. https://doi.org/10.1080/14681811.2019.1634042

Biesta, G. (2006). *Beyond learning: Democratic education for a human future.* Paradigm Publishers.

Billig, M. (1995). *Banal nationalism*. Sage.

Brade, L. (2008). *I normens öga: metoder för en normbrytande undervisning* [In the eye of the norms: Methods for normbreaching teaching]. Friends.

Bredström, A., & Bolander, E. (2019). Beyond cultural racism: Challenges for an anti-racist sexual education for youth. In P. Aggleton, R. Cover, D. Leahy, D. Marshall, & M. L. Rasmussen (Eds.), *Youth, sexuality and sexual citizenship* (pp. 71–85). Routledge.

Bredström, A., Bolander, E., & Bengtsson, J. (2019). Norm-critical sex education in Sweden—Tensions within a progressive approach. In S. Lamb & J. Gilbert (Eds.), *The Cambridge handbook of sexual development: Childhood and adolescence* (pp. 537–558). Cambridge University Press.

Bromseth, J., & Darj, F. (2010). *Normkritisk pedagogik: makt, lärande och strategier för förändring* [Norm critical pedagogy: Powerlearning, and strategies for change]. Centrum för genusvetenskap, Uppsala universitet.

Butler, J. (1999). *Gender trouble: Feminism and the subversion of identity*. Routledge.

Butler, J. (2004). *Undoing gender*. Routledge.

Bylund, C. (2020a). Crip-femme-ininity. *Lambda Nordica, 25*(1), 31–37. https://doi.org/10.34041/ln.v25.609

Bylund, C. (2020b). Tio fingrar, tio tår och så ska man tåla ljusrörsljus: Funktionalitet och funktionsmaktsordningen [Ten fingers, ten toes and you have to stand fluorescent lighting: Functionality and the functionality order of power]. In L. Martinsson & E. Reimers (Eds.), *Skola i normer* [Schooling in norms] (Vol. 3, pp. 189–204). Gleerups.

Crenshaw, K. W. (1991). Mapping the margins: Intersectionality, identity politics, and violence against women of color. (Women of Color at the Center: Selections from the Third National Conference on Women of Color and the Law). *Stanford Law Review, 43*(6), 1299. https://doi.org/10.2307/1229039

Farris, S. R. (2017). *In the name of women's rights: The rise of femonationalism*. Duke University Press.

Gowlett, C., & Rasmussen, M. L. (2016). *The cultural politics of queer theory in education research*. Routledge.

Jonsson, R. (2007). *Blatte betyder kompis. Om maskulinitet och spark i en högstadieskola* [Blatte Means Friend : On Masculinity and Language in a Middle School]. Ordfront.

Kumashiro, K. K. (2002). *Troubling education: Queer activism and anti-oppressive pedagogy*. Routledge.

Langmann, E., & Månsson, N. (2016). Att vända blicken mot sig själv: En problematisering av den normkritiska pedagogiken [To turn the gaze to oneself: A problematization of norm critical pedagogy]. *Pedagogisk forskning i Sverige, 21*(1–2), 79–100.

León Rosales, R. (2010). *Vid framtidens hitersta gräns: om maskulina elevpositioner i en multietnisk skola* [At the closet border of the future: On masculine student positions in a multi-ethnic school]. Mångkulturellt centrum.

Lundgren, A.-S. (2010). Representing what? Aspects of the teacher's role in light of heteronormativity. In L. Martinsson & E. Reimers (Eds.), *Norm-struggles: Sexualities in contentions* (pp. 53–67). Cambridge Scholars.

Martinsson, L., & Reimers, E. (2010). *Norm-struggles: Sexualities in contentions*. Cambridge Scholars.

Martinsson, L., & Reimers, E. (2020). *Skola i normer* [Schooling in Norms] (Tredje upplagan ed.). Gleerups.

[308] *Eva Reimers*

Martinsson, L., Reimers, E., Reingardé, J., & Lundgren, A.-S. (2007). *Norms at work: Challenging homophobia and heteronormativity*. TRACE, RFSL.

McLaren, P., & Kincheloe, J. L. (2007). *Critical pedagogy: Where are we now?* Peter Lang.

McRuer, R. (2006). *Crip theory: Cultural signs of queerness and disability*. New York University Press.

Mohanty, C. T. (1984). Under Western eyes: Feminist scholarship and colonial discourses. *Boundary 2, 12*(3), 333–358.

Mohanty, C. T. (2003). "Under Western Eyes" revisited: Feminist solidarity through anticapitalist struggles. *Signs, 28*(2), 499–532. https://doi.org/10.1086/342914

Mühleisen, W. (2007). Mainstream sexualization and the potential for Nordic new feminism. *NORA—Nordic Journal of Feminist and Gender Research, 15*(2–3), 172–189. https://doi.org/10.1080/08038740701544058

Mühleisen, W., & Røthing, Å. (2009). *Norske sexualiteter* [Norwegian Sexualities]. Cappelen akademisk forlag.

Mühleisen, W., Røthing, Å., & Svendsen, S. H. B. (2012). Norwegian sexualities: Assimilation and exclusion in Norwegian immigration policy. *Sexualities, 15*(2), 139–155. https://doi.org/10.1177/1363460712436540

Nordberg, M., Saar, T., & Hellman, A. (2010). Deconstructing the "normal" boy: Heterosexuality and gender constructions in school and preschool. In L. Martinsson & E. Reimers (Eds.), *Norm-struggles: Sexualities in contentions* (pp. 29–52). Cambridge Scholars.

Puar, J. K. (2007). *Terrorist assemblages: Homonationalism in queer times*. Duke University Press.

Rasmussen, M. L. (2010). Secularism, religion and "progressive" sex education. *Sexualities, 13*(6), 699–712.

Rasmussen, M. L., & Allen, L. (2014). What can a concept do? Rethinking education's queer assemblages. *Discourse: Studies in the Cultural Politics of Education, 35*(3), 433–443. https://doi.org/10.1080/01596306.2014.888846

Reimers, E. (2007). Always somewhere else—Heteronormativity in Swedish teacher training. In L. Martinsson, E. Reimers, J. Reingardé, & A.-S. Lundgren (Eds.), *Norms at work: Challenging homophobia and heteronormativity* (pp. 54–68). TRACE, RFSL.

Reimers, E. (2010). Homotolerance or queer pedagogy? In L. Martinsson & E. Reimers (Eds.), *Norm-struggles: Sexualities in contentions* (pp. 14–28). Cambridge Scholars.

Reimers, E. (2014). Discourses of education and constitutions of class: Public discourses on education in Swedish PBS television. *Discourse: Studies in the Cultural Politics of Education, 35*(4), 540–553. https://doi.org/10.1080/01596 306.2013.871228

Reimers, E. (2017). Homonationalism in teacher education—Productions of schools as heteronormative national places. *Irish Educational Studies, 36*(1), 91–105. https://doi.org/10.1080/03323315.2017.1289703

Reimers, E. (2019). Secularism and religious traditions in non-confessional Swedish preschools: Entanglements of religion and cultural heritage. *British Journal of Religious Education, 42*(3), 275–284. https://doi.org/10.1080/01416 200.2019.1569501

Reimers, E. (2020). Disruptions of desexualized heteronormativity—Queer identification(s) as pedagogical resources. *Teaching Education, 31*(1), 112–125. https://doi.org/10.1080/10476210.2019.1708891

Renold, E., & Allan, A. (2006). Bright and beautiful: High achieving girls, ambivalent femininities, and the feminization of success in the primary school. *Discourse: Studies in the Cultural Politics of Education, 27*(4), 457–473. https://doi.org/10.1080/01596300600988606

Renold, E., & Epstein, D. (2010). Sexualities, schooling and schizoid agendas. In L. Martinsson & E. Reimers (Eds.), *Norm-struggles: Sexualities in contentions* (pp. 68–82). Cambridge Scholars.

Renold, E., Ringrose, J., & Egan, R. D. (2015). *Children, sexuality and sexualization.* Palgrave Macmillan.

Røthing, Å. (2008). Homotolerance and heteronormativity in Norwegian classrooms. *Gender and Education, 20*(3), 253–266. https://doi.org/10.1080/09540250802000405

Røthing, Å., & Svendsen, S. H. B. (2010). Homotolerance and heterosexuality as Norwegian values. *Journal of LGBT Youth, 7*(2), 147–166. https://doi.org/10.1080/19361651003799932

Røthing, Å., & Svendsen, S. H. B. (2011). Sexuality in Norwegian textbooks: Constructing and controlling ethnic borders? *Ethnic and Racial Studies, 34*(11), 1953–1973. https://doi.org/10.1080/01419870.2011.560275

Sumara, D., & Davis, B. (1999). Interrupting heteronormativity: Toward a queer curriculum theory. *Curriculum Inquiry, 29*(2), 191–208. https://doi.org/10.1111/0362-6784.00121

Sverige, S. (2018). *Curriculum for the compulsory school, preschool class and school-age education 2011: Revised 2018.* Skolverket.

Swedish National Agency of Education. (2013a). *Förskolans och skolans värdegrund: Förhållningssätt, verktyg och metoder* [The value foundation of the Swedish Preschool and School: Approaches, tools, and methods]. Swedish National Agency of Education.

Swedish National Agency of Education. (2013b). *Sex- och samlevnadsundervisning i grundskolans senare år: Jämställdhet, sexualitet och relationer i ämnesundervisningen. Årskurserna 7–9* [Sex and relationship education in the later years of compulsory school: Gender equality, sexualities, and relations in subject teaching]. Swedish National Agency of Education.

Swedish National Agency of Education. (2013c). *Sex-och samlevnadsundervisning i gymnasieskolan: Sexualitet, relationer och jämställdhet i de gymnasiegemensamma ämnena* [Sex and relationship education in upper secondary school: Sexuality, relations and gender equality in the common subjects]. Swedish National Agency of Education.

Youdell, D. (2011). *School trouble: Identity, power and politics in education.* Routledge.

# CHAPTER 16

# "The Only Orange Park Bench"

## Using Photo Elicitation to Explore Campus Experiences of LGBTIQA+ Students

JOHN FENAUGHTY, LUCY COWIE, AND LOUISA ALLEN

This chapter explores preliminary findings from an exploratory photo methods study with LGBTIQA+ students in an Aotearoa New Zealand university.[1] The aim was to examine these students' experiences of campus life, including barriers to safety, inclusion, and belonging. The campus where this research was conducted has received commendation for its progressive practices in relation to affirming and supporting LGBTIQA+ staff and students. Given this recognition, and research that increasingly documents the declining significance of homophobia in educational spaces, the study sought to determine if this campus could still be considered a cisheteronormative space.

To extend existing literature on heteronormativity in higher education, the current project experimentally employed photo methods. Photo methods have been recognized as a queer research method, with the capacity to uncover mundane and ignored lived experiences of daily life. In this study, they served to uncover lived experiences of contradiction for LGBTIQA+ students on campus. The image of a lone orange bench (when other benches were brown) on the outskirts of campus captured one of these contradictions. This photo was produced by a participant who declared campus was "friendly" and "welcoming," and that he did not

John Fenaughty, Lucy Cowie, and Louisa Allen, *"The Only Orange Park Bench"* In: *Queer Studies and Education*.
Edited by: Nelson M. Rodriguez, Robert C. Mizzi, Louisa Allen, and Rob Cover, Oxford University Press.
© Oxford University Press 2023. DOI: 10.1093/oso/9780197687000.003.0017

personally experience discrimination as a cisgendered gay man. However, when later talking about what the orange bench represented, he explained it was like "queer students"—"It should be celebrated for its uniqueness, but actually, it was really isolated and alone."

Findings demonstrated that homophobia (let alone transphobia and biphobia) have not been extinguished from this higher education institution (HEI). Participants noted an absence of blatant abuse and acknowledgment of LGBTIQA+ on campus in the form of "zero tolerance of discrimination" policy. However, their photos and narratives drew attention to cisheteronormativity's more nuanced forms. These manifested in an institutional culture of absence of nonbinary gender bathrooms and queer spaces for LGBTIQA+ students. Cisheteronormativity also inheres within the official process for addressing discrimination, which leaves this responsibility and burden to the person who experiences it. We argue that a broader definition of LGBTIQA+ discrimination is required, one that recognizes the nuances of its expressions beyond interpersonal relations and within less obvious institutional practices and material conditions.

## INTRODUCTION

Drawing on queer theory (Jagose, 1996), heteronormativity is defined as an organizing principle of social life that presumes desire, sexual practice, and identity are universally heterosexual (Warner, 1993). Concepts of ideal marriage, family, relationships, sexual practice, health, and friendship are influenced by this assumption (Kitzinger, 2005; McNeill, 2013). For instance, we often use "parents" interchangeably with "Mum and Dad." Similarly, cisnormativity is the idea that being cisgender is normal and acceptable, while being gender diverse is not (Pyne, 2011). Cisnormativity refers to the beliefs, practices, and structures that assume that one's gender identity will align with their [binary] biological sex assigned at birth. For instance, according to cisnormativity all people of a particular gender have a certain biology and set of experiences, making the terms man/male and woman/female interchangeable.

*Cisheteronormativity* refers to the beliefs, practices, and structures of cisnormativity *and* heteronormativity, which situate cisgender and heterosexual identity as natural, normal, and desirable and other sex, gender, and sexual expressions as unnatural, abnormal, and undesirable. While it can be argued the term *heteronormativity* already contains recognition of the problematics of an assumed alignment of biological sex and gender identity, the insertion of "cis" here gives emphasis to gender diversity politics

[312]   *Fenaughty et al.*

(Marzetti, 2018). Cisheteronormative assumptions are widely taken for granted and typically go unnoticed by most of society, but present barriers to acceptance and inclusion for queer and gender-diverse students (Lenskyj, 2013; Peel, 2001).

Cisheteronormative assumptions can mean the diversity of sexuality and gender is unrecognized or ignored at both individual and institutional levels (Lenskyj, 2013; Peel, 2001). At an individual level, those who identify as sex, gender, or sexually diverse can experience harassment, threats, abuse, and bullying based on ideas they are "unnatural" or "abnormal" (Fenaughty, 2019). As such, queer and gender-diverse people are more likely to experience negative health outcomes and be isolated in work and education settings (Wandrey et al., 2015). Institutional contexts such as universities, schools, hospitals, and government can perpetuate these normative ideas, scaffolding an environment that is potentially harmful for queer and gender-diverse individuals (Kitzinger, 2005; Willis, 2012).

The data we share in this chapter explored cisheteronormativity in the institutional context of a university campus. To date, a limited number of guides and "best practices" have been developed to encourage educational institutions, including HEIs, to become homophobia and transphobia-free (Equity Challenge Unit [ECU], 2010, 2012; National Union of Students [NUS], 2016; UNESCO [United Nations Educational, Scientific, and Cultural Organization], 2016). A common focus in such guides is recognizing and responding to cisheteronormative interpersonal harassment and bullying, usually by providing policy advice and guidance on bullying management and prevention. The focus on cisheteronormative bullying may well reflect the continued prevalence of such harassment on university campuses across the United Kingdom and the United States (Rankin, 2016; Tetreault et al., 2013; Yost & Gilmore, 2011). For nearly 30 years, research has indicated that homophobic bullying (D'Augelli, 1992) and then later transphobic bullying (Rankin, 2003) have been significant issues in a range of HEI contexts across the United States. A recent United States–based study reported queer and gender-diverse students continued to experience both verbal and physical abuse, typically from other students (Tetreault et al., 2013). Research in Aotearoa New Zealand where the current study was located is limited, but preliminary studies suggested similar patterns to the United States. For instance, in a survey with LGBTQIA+ students at the University of Otago, some reported fear for their safety, threats of having their identity exposed, and being denied opportunities, and many concealed their identities to reduce this harm (Treharne et al., 2016).

Concurrently, there is an emerging public and academic discourse of a posthomophobic world (Magrath, 2017; McCormack, 2012). In this contemporary utopia, homophobia is a thing of yesteryear. Increased knowledge about sex, gender, and sexuality, as well as exposure to sex, gender, and sexually diverse people and media figures, is suggested to underpin a decrease in ignorance and prejudice and therefore (cis)heteronormativity among young people (McCormack, 2012). In this frame, young people, particularly those that are in formal education, are unlikely to be homophobic (Ky Ng et al., 2017). Increasingly, there is a social expectation that the new generation of young people will be free of homophobia, especially in places of formal education.

Remaining skeptical about a "posthomophobia" world, some researchers understand cisheteronormativity is not only constituted in discrete one-on-one interactions between students in educational institutions (Marston, 2015). For instance, cisheteronormative discrimination infuses institutional culture via a plethora of routine processes and practices, including academic recordkeeping, misgendering of staff and students, cisheteronormative staff composition, lack of appropriate bathrooms and changing rooms, as well as exclusion and invisibility of LGBTIQA+ issues in the curriculum (Kosciw et al., 2009). Even when LGBTIQA+ and gender-diverse students are free of student-generated cisheteronormative oppressions, they may still experience transphobia and homophobia from staff and institutional practices (Marzetti, 2018). Such harassment may include "microaggressions," "brief and commonplace daily verbal, behavioural, or environmental indignities, whether intentional or unintentional, that communicate hostile, derogatory, or negative" (Sue et al., 2007, p. 271) slights and insults, which may see university students face insidious forms of discrimination (Roffee & Waling, 2016). These findings question whether homophobia has declined to the extent that it is no longer remarkable and, indeed, whether there are more nuanced manifestations of cisheteronormativity to be considered.

In response to growing recognition of other manifestations of cisheteronormativity, guidelines also emphasize the value in HEIs "raising visibility and demonstrating commitment to LGB equality" (ECU, 2010, p. 8), achieved through establishing information and support networks, ensuring representation of LGBTIQA+ people or issues in equity processes, posters, and other communication and marketing activities, including local pride events (and the like). The need to address discrimination in institutional residences and clubs and societies is also mentioned (ECU, 2010, 2012), along with appropriate practices for HEI sports groups (NUS, 2016). Some guidance also noted the need for HEIs to "develop the skills and confidence of teaching staff to appropriately and proportionately embed LGB equality in the curriculum" (ECU, 2012, p. 13).

Data for this chapter were generated from students in one social science faculty at a university in Aotearoa New Zealand. The university and faculty met the general guidelines detailed above, except that a *dedicated* homophobic/transphobic bullying policy had not yet been instituted. Instead, within the policy about discrimination and bullying and legalities, it noted: "The University has a particular commitment to ensuring safe, inclusive and equitable environment for the groups named in the equity policy, which include . . . lesbian, gay, bisexual, transgender, Intersex (LGBTI, and including people of diverse gender identities)" (reference withheld to protect institutional identity).[2]

This professed context of overt support for those who are sexually and gender diverse is opportune to explore whether homophobia (not withstanding transphobia and biphobia) is truly no longer an issue, especially in an HEI that broadly met the general "best practice" requirements and was populated with the brave new world of "informed" posthomophobia students. In this chapter, we highlight scenarios from two participants that offer rich understandings of nuances of cisheteronormativity on campus. The first scenario indicates how photo elicitation can be used by participants to identify contradictions in what institutional equity policy and process promises regarding cisheteronormativity, compared to what is actually enacted and experienced. The second scenario demonstrates the potential for photo elicitation to enable recognition of cisheteronormative phenomena that are tied to particular and everyday spaces of a university. Both scenarios demonstrate the potential photo elicitation provides for surfacing and critiquing cisheteronormative structures, spaces, and relations on a university campus.

## NOTES ON METHODOLOGY

To extend existing literature on cisheteronormativity in higher education, the current project experimentally employed photo methods (Prosser & Schwartz, 2006). Photo methods have been recognized as a *queer* research method (Allen, 2017) with the capacity to uncover mundane and ignored lived experiences of daily life. What makes photos "queer" in this study was not that they were taken by LGBTIQA+ participants. Rather, it was their capacity to capture elements of campus life that participants did not articulate verbally, but that seeped into photos anyway. In this vein, photo methods represent a disruption of conventional data methods like surveys, where the object of investigation and what it entails is known in advance.

The form of photo methods utilized was photo elicitation, initially developed by sociologist John Collier in the late 1950s (Collier & Collier, 1986). While photo elicitation is operationalized in diverse ways, fundamentally it "simply calls for photographs to be used in the interview process" (Torre & Murphy, 2015, p. 8). In our study, participants were encouraged to take 10 photographs using the camera on their digital phones. These photos were to illustrate their experiences of inclusion, exclusion, and feeling welcome or unwelcome as LGBTIQA+ students on campus. To increase participants' sense of agency over what could be photographed and how, they were assured that images could depict normal, everyday elements of being LGBTIQA+ on campus and did not need to be aesthetically "perfect."

Participants were typically given at least 1 week to take photographs, after which they participated in an individual semistructured interview with the second author. Lucy, who was also a student at this university (on another campus) shared commonalities with some participants as a queer, cisgender woman, a fact she explained at the interview outset. Research suggested that sharing a common identity can help participants feel they are in "safe hands," particularly when they identify with a marginalized group (Kanuha, 2000; Le Gallais, 2008). Interviews took between 40 and 104 minutes, with most lasting an hour. Photos were used to prompt discussion about experiences of being LGBTIQA+ on campus, offering rich detail about how cisheteronormativity manifested on campus.

Twelve students, ranging from 19 to 65 years, participated after seeing recruitment flyers in popular locations around campus (see Figure 16.1). Another recruitment method involved distributing study information to equity leaders on campus and through our own networks. We aimed to recruit a diverse sample of LGBTIQA+ students who had studied on campus as undergraduates or postgraduates for a minimum of 6 months within the last 2 years. These criteria ensured participants were familiar enough with campus life to participate fully in interviews. It was important to us, that people from a range of ethnicities, genders, and sexual orientations participated so that diverse perspectives and experiences could be taken into account. As such, we concluded recruitment once sufficient diversity in participants had been achieved.

The final sample comprised: three participants who identified as female; one as cisgender female; one as a cisgender woman; one as female/woman; one as woman/wāhine; two as male; one as trans male/male; one as nonbinary trans; and one as gender-fluid. In terms of sexuality, four participants identified as gay, one participant as bisexual, one as takatāpui,[3] one as pansexual, one as queer, one as queer/lesbian, one as lesbian and a bit asexual, one as lesbian/dyke, and one as bisexual although leaning

Figure 16.1 Recruitment flyer.

toward one sex more. With regard to ethnicity, six participants identified as New Zealand European or Pākehā (a Māori term for White settlers), one as Chinese, one as Chinese/Cantonese, one as Tongan, one as South Asian, and two as Māori/Pākehā). All but one participant were studying full time. Five participants were studying at the postgraduate level and seven at the undergraduate level.

Initially, narratives were analyzed using thematic analysis (Braun & Clarke, 2012) to generate common or notable themes that then were reported back to the senior leadership of the faculty for action. Resulting themes included microaggressions and other negative experiences; institutional barriers; surface-level support; a sense that other LGBTIQA+ people were worse off than them; loneliness; problems on student placements; lack of all-gender bathrooms; campus support available; and improvements that could be made. In this chapter we focus on photo elicitation as a queer *method* and present highlights from two scenarios. The scenarios were selected for their ability to demonstrate the potential for photo elicitation to open new ways in which researchers and participants can surface, identify, and trouble binaries and dominant norms.

**Scenario 1: Olivia**

The first scenario took a close reading of data around the apparent contradictions of "inclusive" university policy and practice in relation to interpersonal and institutional harassment and discrimination. Olivia was a cisgender Pākehā (New Zealand European) woman in her mid-20s who identified as queer/lesbian and had been studying at the postgraduate level for 1 year. She stated she volunteered because she felt isolated on campus because of her sexual orientation and wanted to support research that explored these experiences. Here, Olivia capitalized on the queer potential of photo methods by juxtaposing images to draw attention to contradictions apparent in university practices around inclusiveness.

OLIVIA: I took a photo . . . of the men's and women's bathrooms, and I . . . took this in context of some of the other pictures. . . . Picture number 5 which is about "Zero Tolerance for Discrimination" [see Figure 16.2] and those kind of university wide posters that they put up.

Number 5 [Figure 16.2] is like a poster . . . talking about zero tolerance for discrimination, and how the university stands beside their equity policies, and that kind of thing.

I . . . put these two photos together because . . . it's like clearly a policy decision that has been handed down . . . from the equity group and they have decided right a really good thing to do would be to put up some posters and . . . indicate to everyone . . . that we are trying to be inclusive to everyone, safe and inclusive and equitable as it says. But at the same time . . . there isn't really any information in that poster about . . . what you might do in a situation and I think . . . maybe . . . the posters are kind of targeted at a mainstream . . . notion of discrimination where there is like "a big bad person" who has "big bad beliefs" and they come along and "they beat you up for being queer" or "they say something overtly racist and

[318]  *Fenaughty et al.*

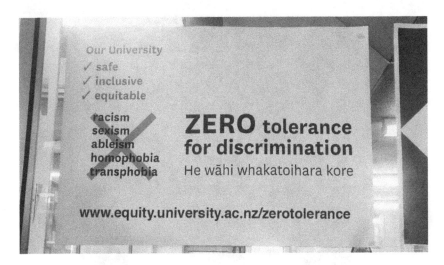

Figure 16.2 Zero tolerance for discrimination poster.

they keep going when you say it's racist, you know"? Like these kind of ideas that they're attacks and a thing that happens discretely... in one individual time and place, and they are quite vicious and violent and it is very clear to everyone involved that it's an instance of heterosexism or homophobia. And then you go along and you report someone and then they get banned from something, or you know, that kind of narrative.

So there was that, and it was nice to at least have this poster around, because at least... there is some acknowledgement of my whole life. But on the other hand, I had... picture Number 6 [see Figure 16.3] which is the picture of the... men's and women's bathrooms next door to each other.

So, I think that... there is some surface level acknowledgement that queerness exists and people can get isolated, or get bullied... that stuff can happen to people because of their identities and other people's lack of understanding. But then, the university doesn't actually have anything systematic in place to support that. Like there's still for example... just a standard bathroom... there wasn't any space... that I ever saw, of... a gender neutral bathroom or any acknowledgement that these gender roles are a bit whack.

I... put those two pictures together... [because] I think... as a society, we are at the level where people understand that it is not okay to say bad things about queer people. But people aren't yet at the level, and the university... is not at the level, of understanding what that actually means in practice and the structural kind of changes

**Figure 16.3** Cisheteronormative bathroom signs.

that need to happen. . . . The differences they actually need to make to things . . . [to] buildings and . . . policies and teaching practices and that kind of stuff. They are just like "oh well, there are some posters up and we clearly, we take a clear stance against them, but we are not really making steps towards changing it." You know, we haven't gone out of our way to make a new bathroom, we haven't gone out of our way to indicate that even the tiny little bits of intolerance, or, that saying "boys and girls" it's not okay . . . There is no leadership in that area.

I'm sure there are maybe individuals that are doing it, but it is not really about an individual thing, it is supposed to be structural, it is supposed to be something that all of the lecturers know about, all of the lecturers know not to say "boys and girls," or that there is a . . . gender neutral bathroom available. . . . Because you can have up posters about this, but if someone in my class . . . misgenders my partner . . . I am not going to go and tell someone higher up. But there should be understanding from other people, and understanding in that space, that actually that person is wrong rather, than me being a bit weird. . . .

LUCY: How does this make you feel?

OLIVIA: It just makes me feel like . . . we are not making as much progress as maybe I thought we were, coming from my bubble of like other queer people, other feminists, other super kind of activists on the button with lots of issues. We really try to make changes and push the university to have gender neutral spaces and . . . doing more with equity. . . . You just, you kind of feel resigned, you just feel like it is never going to get better, like there's no one there, and like it's just up to you to try and take your one class, when you get out to be a teacher, try to teach your one class at a time that there is more than just boys and girls in the world, or like boys don't have to wear black socks and girls don't have to wear white socks and gender doesn't matter that much, you know. Like it just feels like it is suddenly all up to me again, and not to just up to everyone and other people and like structural change and that the university should be taking more responsibility for this and it just makes me feel frustrated that no one's doing anything about it except me really.

Olivia juxtaposed an ostensibly "inclusive" image against one demonstrating exclusionary (gender) binaries present in the institution to open discussion about how harassment and discrimination were constructed in university policy and practice. This juxtaposition creates opportunities for reconsidering how cisheteronormativity, harassment, and discrimination were embedded in university practices despite its efforts to eradicate them. For instance, the zero-tolerance poster focuses on individual students, and potentially teaching staff, as the agents of harassment and discrimination. However, cisheteronormative discrimination is also apparent in the materiality of campus buildings that structure gender as a binary via the provision of toilets for those who are either male *or* female only. This practice denies the existence of gender-diverse students on campus and subsequently fails to value and respect their presence. By presenting these two photos together, Olivia constructed a powerful picture of contradiction in relation to institutional support for eradicating discrimination.

This juxtaposition also critiques "mainstream" notions of oppression and harassment, which do not account for microaggressions and isolation as significant experiences for LGBTQIA+ students. For instance, in relation to inclusion, Olivia noted the zero-tolerance poster was the only vector they saw the university proactively working in pursuit of inclusive practice. While the university said it has zero tolerance for discrimination, the posters themselves, if they are the primary mechanism for this, have very limited scope for capturing and addressing harassment and discrimination. This is not least in part because the posters constitute bullying, harassment, and discrimination as something that is implicitly experienced interpersonally as a discrete act (e.g., verbal abuse) that is clearly inappropriate (Allen, 2018; Formby, 2015). By drawing on human rights discourses that render campus inclusion and safety a matter of interpersonal action and neoliberal responsibility, these posters obscure features of harassment and discrimination embedded within institutional structures and culture (Marston, 2015).

Ironically, the visibility these posters afforded LGBTIQA+ students belies experiences of isolation and exclusion beyond those that are easily identifiable and occur interpersonally. In their crude focus on discrimination with a capital D, they missed the nuances of cisheteronormativity that occur when gender-neutral toilets are absent on campus. The bathroom issue is hardly a new topic for HEI contexts. Debates over the legal and social rights of transgender students have been marked by arguments over whether transgender people can use a bathroom in public environments that corresponds to their gender (Jereb, 2017). While the "bathroom debate" continues in legal, social, and media environments, research from the United States indicated that transgender students are often denied access to bathroom facilities at places of education, including HEIs (Seelman, 2016; Woodford et al., 2017). A lack of access to gender-neutral or single-stall bathrooms has been associated with transgender students feeling less safe on HEI campuses (Seelman, 2014).

In spite of the prominence of the bathroom debate also in New Zealand, and a relatively long-standing range of official policy urging schools to provide gender-affirming bathroom facilities (e.g., Ministry of Education, 2015, 2020a, 2020b), Olivia was left feeling "there is no one there" and it is "up to you" to agitate for inclusion and a discrimination-free university. On a surface level, the posters were valued for their explicit nod toward acknowledging and supporting queerness and gender diversity. However, when juxtaposed against existing material institutional discrimination, they offered a frustrating and demoralizing reminder of the more nuanced operation of cisheteronormativities that remained unaddressed.

[322]  *Fenaughty et al.*

The process highlighted by the posters for achieving inclusivity and equality was limited in its conceptualization of what counts as discrimination and how it might be effectively addressed. When the poster's advice for reporting discrimination in relation to homophobia and transphobia was followed (see web address on poster), several things became apparent. All the guidance was oriented toward interpersonal discrimination where students (and staff) are told, for example, they can claim "discrimination" in relation to "offensive comments" (author withheld). In this instance, the policy suggested the student directly addressed the discrimination (if they felt able to do so), and if not, recruited someone else to do this:

- If a complaint cannot be resolved by direct discussion, or an individual does not feel comfortable addressing the issue face to face or in writing, they should discuss the matter and seek guidance from an appropriate person
- For students this can be:
  - class representatives,
  - the Student Advocacy Network (University SA Student Advice Hub),
  - Student Information Centre,
  - academic head,
  - course convenor,
  - or the Proctor (author withheld)

This process was clearly oriented toward discrete incidents of discrimination that involved obviously prejudiced actions. It was also a process that was cisheteronormative. The impacted student was tasked with the labor of explaining either directly to the "perpetrator" (to use the language of the university harassment policy) why what was said was offensive, or they were forced to explain to one of the other named people, all of whom (other than the proctor presumably) may have had no understanding of these issues. In the absence of any student or staff training around what cisheteronormative discrimination can look like, the onus for identifying and addressing this discrimination was left to the person who experienced it.

Furthermore, this person was placed in the unenviable position of potentially prompting a disciplinary process for the "perpetrator," which required them to restate the offensive comments. Additionally, they then faced the possibility that in doing so they potentially criminalized a student or staff member who, perhaps due to a general "lack of understanding," may find themselves facing serious repercussions. Last, to make a formal complaint also required "outing" themselves across multiple levels of institutional hierarchy, including their head of school, faculty administrators, and the disciplinary committee.

The university policy on bullying, harassment and *discrimination* stated: "Allegations of bullying and/or harassment are serious matters and can potentially damage an individual's reputation. Intentionally false accusations of a *frivolous* or vexatious nature, or allegations that are found to be unsubstantiated will be viewed seriously and may result in the University taking disciplinary action against the complainant" (author withheld, emphasis added). Thus, in the absence of any shared dialogue or training around microaggressions, it would be a brave student who claimed, for instance, that their partner being misgendered in conversation was not a "frivolous" allegation. The point of microaggressions was that they were deemed completely "normal" within a cisheteronormative culture. This "normality" means within the boundaries of this policy statement that they would be difficult to construct as discrimination or harassment (let alone bullying).

Olivia used this poster to emphasize the ironic invisibility of queer and gender-diverse lives on campus. This poster and policy, while explicitly mentioning homophobia and transphobia, as well as inclusion, was really about capital "H" Homophobia and capital "T" Transphobia. That is, harassing actions that were clearly intentional, witnessed, and worthy of the sacrifice of the impacted student's time, current and/or future collegial relationships with staff or students, privacy, and the ability to "pass" as straight/cisgender. The inclusion promised to LGBTQIA+ students and staff by this poster was mitigated by Olivia's recognition that it was limited inclusion: the right not to be verbally or physically assaulted. It did not offer the right to be included and have one's identity respected through nuanced efforts to expose and address manifestations of prejudice and microaggressions as well as institutional discrimination.

### Scenario 2: Jack

Jack was a gay, cisgender, New Zealand European man in his mid-20s who had been studying at the postgraduate level for 2 years. He originally stated he did not want to participate in the study as he felt his campus experience was no different from if he was straight. However, after "digging deeper" into these experiences, he decided to take part.

LUCY: Shall we go through some of your photos?

JACK: This is kind of lame.... I have a story arc that comes with ... [the photos] and also a kind of metaphor behind the photos. ... So the metaphor is kind of small, so each one [photo] tells a story but when I did it, I wanted to do it ... as though the photos were like very harsh, not really well considered. So for example, you get like instead of nice, straight, very clear [photos] ... here [I'm] just kind of taking a quick photo and I wanted that to kind of reflect on the way that I feel the campus is ...

The extract above demonstrates how another participant used the opportunities afforded by photo elicitation to tell a story about his campus experience. Instead of producing a collection of discrete images, Jack used a series to create a spatial/temporal narrative detailing one possible account (or arc as he called it) of being gay on campus. He began by pointing out his sense of ambivalence around the topic due to his perception of lack of obvious negative experience on campus:

JACK: When you go to campus I find that, it's sort of just, you are just kind of like everybody else, in the sense you are not celebrated but you are also not like seen as any different. So, in a sense it is good because I noticed that I've just blended in and never felt either validated or invalidated. I'm just like everyone else.
LUCY: So, you quite like that, or, is it problematic in some way?
JACK: To be honest I like that because that is who I am, like I am gay and I'm quite out and I'm a little bit flamboyant and I am really proud to be a gay man, like I love the identity of that and being part of that culture. So, I always kind of feel like it doesn't mean anything different I guess, so it means something for me, but not in the sense of how I relate to anyone else or the community that I kind of get involved with. Like, yeah I don't feel like anyone treats me differently and I never connected with any of the queer communities when I was at [another university] campus.
LUCY: Okay, so it is kind of ... a non-issue?
JACK: Exactly, so ... in a sense I wouldn't feel any different and if I was straight I would have the exact same experiences.

Jack's narrative began with a sense of equality, that there was nothing unique about his experience, neither positive nor negative, especially given (as he noted later) his privilege in occupying a White cisgender gay male identity. However, he then described how the poster advertising the research sparked reflection on his experience of campus culture.

JACK: When I actually very first got your email . . . I hesitated initially to contact you. . . . The reason why is because in the poster it talks about barriers to inclusion . . . and my first thought was "oh well there was nothing really there, I haven't been welcomed or unwelcomed." . . . And so that was what got me thinking, and I was like . . . trying to dig into my own experiences a bit more . . . and I also . . . at the same time [it] is a bit of a reflection on how campus is, you know, it says it is friendly and welcoming, but you kind of dig a bit deeper and it's not. There is nothing there and it's, then you dig that little bit further and it's actually kind of yeah again, that invalidation.

As Jack presented his narrative, he did not have access to an obviously homophobic and cisheteronormative incident or phenomenon that he could easily claim as producing a barrier to his inclusion on campus. Instead, he reflected about the less tangible *omission* of validation, rather than the *addition* of discrimination. Rather than an external imposition of discrimination, he developed the idea of an internal sense of exclusion as precipitated by the general cisheteronormative milieu of the campus. To build on this idea he used a particular photo to conclude his narrative. Jack talked about walking out of the campus, past one of the last buildings on its far edge. He used the image of an orange bench (see Figure 16.4) to describe the feelings and experiences of potential others and himself on campus:

JACK: You have got all these seating areas throughout the main campus, you have even got the café, and as I was walking away there was just

Figure 16.4 The only orange bench.

this one single [seating area] and it is the only orange one that I found as well, and I just felt that was such a good message to leave that with. Like instead of being part of everyone else, instead of having that kind of shared, I feel like if you are someone that is LGBTQA+ on campus, you are just kind of the odd one out. Like it is something so beautiful, it is something that is really kind of makes you unique, it is something to really celebrate and instead, all we are doing is we are throwing it to the side and you are left alone, you are kind of isolated. There is not that validation and you are kind of sitting by yourself in a sense.

The difference in tone between the first and second part of Jack's interview demonstrated the ability of photo methods to open possibilities for reconfiguring participants' experiences and understandings. Until this point, Jack talked about how *other* "LGBTQIA+" people, rather than he himself, might be marginalized on campus. For instance, he highlighted the unacceptability of binary toilet facilities and lack of queer spaces, which have similarly been identified in other research as effacing queer, transgender, and nonbinary gender identities (Ingrey, 2018; Pryor, 2018). Jack also mentioned the lack of an obvious library presence around sex, gender, and sexual diversity, and the lack of queer spaces, all the while framing these issues as more pressing for others. However, the final image of the lone orange bench captures something Jack felt as a gay man ("being the odd one out"), but was not necessarily aware of or able to verbally articulate until he reflected on why he had taken this picture. The power of photo methods to act as a "can opener" for unacknowledged experiences and feelings is clearly seen here (Clark-Ibanez, 2004).

Jack's photo revealed something important about a seemingly welcoming and friendly campus culture where there was an apparent lack of obvious negative experiences for LGBTIQA+ students. Below this surface of "acceptability" continued to lie an unease for LGBTIQA+ students, that like the only orange bench, they did not "blend in" and were relegated to the literal margins of campus space. This feeling was communicated through institutional manifestations of cisheteronormativity that failed to provide material space for these students in the form of gender-neutral bathrooms, an obvious LGBTIQA+ library presence, and dedicated queer spaces for student study and recreation. Olivia and Jack's narratives made a similar point: Cisheteronormativity is not always "abusive," "violent," and "obvious" or occurring as discrete incidents of harassment at an interpersonal level. As these participants showed, cisheteronormativity had an insidious presence that was not always immediately discernible (even to those who are LGBTIQA+) and could be embedded in the institutional structures and material culture of HEIs.

## CONCLUSION

Findings from this study demonstrated that cisheterosexism was far from extinguished in this HEI. This is telling given that it largely met or exceeded "best practice" guidelines and had an active equity committee dedicated to addressing LGBTIQA+ inclusion, which included representation of the first and third authors. The scenarios selected in this chapter indicated that configurations of cisheteronormativity do not solely reside in obvious harassing actions of students. They can also be experienced in relation to seemingly supportive policy and practices underpinned by unacknowledged cisheteronormative assumptions and processes. Such experiences are more nuanced and less obvious forms of cisheteronormativity that form part of the mundane and everyday experience of campus life. Although less explicit than blatant forms of discrimination, these practices are nonetheless linked to feelings of isolation, exclusion, denigration, hypocrisy, and hopelessness for LGBTIQA+ participants.

This analysis implied HEIs need to consider whether simply having a dedicated "zero-tolerance" harassment policy that specifically mentions "homophobia" or "transphobia" is useful (or advisable) in the absence of acknowledging the limitations of this conceptualization of cisheteronormativity. A broader conceptualization of cisheteronormativity is required that understands this does not always manifest within interpersonal relations as blatant harassment or abuse. What this requires of HEIs is recognition of how their own (well-intentioned) policies and practices contain cisheteronormative assumptions. We suggest that recognizing this is a first step, and that providing training around what broader experiences of discrimination may look like for staff and students is another.

Some of these cisheteronormative assumptions underpin HEIs' advised reporting processes for such harassment. Rather than focusing solely on preventing and punishing homophobic and transphobic harassment, HEIs may be better off focusing on fostering inclusion and belonging at the levels of institutional practices and material culture. The powerful scenarios detailed here demonstrate that while ostensibly free of harassment, the experience on campus for some LGBTIQA+ students was far from celebrating difference and instead left them lonely, isolated, and frustrated through lack of perceived care. The findings emphasize that a better zero-tolerance

[328] *Fenaughty et al.*

policy might state "zero tolerance toward institutional exclusion and cisheteronormative privilege on campus."

## NOTES

1. This chapter draws on data published in an article in *Higher Education Research and Development*, February 2, 2020, copyright HERDSA. https://www.tandfonline.com/doi/full/10.1080/07294360.2019.1706453
2. We do not identify the institution in which this research took place as we do not wish to draw attention to it specifically. Our point is that cisheteronormativity is likely to operate in nuanced ways in all HEIs, including ostensibly LGBTIQA+ supportive campuses like this one.
3. A term reclaimed to include Aotearoa New Zealand's indigenous Māori who, from a Western worldview, may be framed as sex-, gender-, and sexually diverse, including whakawāhine (who might be seen by Westerners as trans women), tangata ira tāne (who a Western worldview might see as trans men), lesbian, gay, bisexual, transgender, intersex, and queer Māori (Kerekere, 2017).

## REFERENCES

Allen, L. (2017). *Schooling sexual cultures: Sexuality education and visual research.* Routledge.

Allen, L. (2018). Reconceptualising homophobia: By leaving "those kids" alone. *Discourse: Studies in the Cultural Politics of Education, 41*(3), 441–453. https://doi.org/10.1080/01596306.2018.1495617

Braun, V., & Clarke, V. (2012). Thematic analysis. In H. Cooper (Ed.), *The handbook of research methods in psychology.* American Psychological Association.

Clark-Ibanez, M. (2004). Framing the social world with photo-elicitation interviews. *American Behavioural Scientist, 47*(12), 1507–1527. https://doi.org/10.1177/0002764204266236

Collier, J., & Collier, M. (1986). *Visual anthropology: Photography as research method.* University of New Mexico Press.

D'Augelli, A. R. (1992). Lesbian and gay male undergraduates' experiences of harassment and fear on campus. *Journal of Interpersonal Violence, 7*(3), 383–395. https://doi.org/10.1177/088626092007003007

Equity Challenge Unit (ECU). (2010). Advancing LGB equality: Improving the experience of lesbian, gay and bisexual staff and students in higher education. https://www.advance-he.ac.uk/knowledge-hub/advancing-lgb-equality

Equity Challenge Unit (ECU). (2012). Delivering LGB equality: Making your college LGB-friendly. https://documents.advance-he.ac.uk/download/file/7873

Fenaughty, J. (2019). Developing resources to address homophobic and transphobic bullying: A framework incorporating co-design, critical pedagogies, and bullying research. *Sex Education, 19*(6), 627–643. https://doi.org/10.1080/14681811.2019.1579707

Formby, E. (2015). Limitations of focussing on homophobic, biphobic and transphobic "bullying" to understand and address LGBT young people's experiences within and beyond school. *Sex Education, 15*(6), 626–640. https://doi.org/10.1080/14681811.2015.1054024

Ingrey, J. (2018). Problematizing the cisgendering of school washroom space: Interrogating the politics of recognition of transgender and gender non-conforming youth. *Gender and Education, 30*(6), 774–789. https://doi.org/10.1080/09540253.2018.1483492

Jagose, A. (1996). *Queer theory: An introduction.* New York University Press.

Kanuha, V. K. (2000). "Being" native versus "going native": Conducting social work research as an insider. *Social Work, 45*(5), 439–447. https://doi.org/10.1093/sw/45.5.439

Kerekere, E. (2017). *Part of the whānau: The emergence of Takatāpui identity—he whāriki Takatāpui.* Victoria University of Wellington. http://researcharchive.vuw.ac.nz/handle/10063/6369

Kitzinger, C. (2005). Heteronormativity in action: Reproducing the heterosexual nuclear family in after-hours medical calls. *Social Problems, 52*(4), 477–498. https://doi.org/10.1525/sp.2005.52.4.477

Kosciw, J. G., Greytak, E. A., & Diaz, E. M. (2009). Who, what, where, when, and why: Demographic and ecological factors contributing to hostile school climate for lesbian, gay, bisexual, and transgender youth. *Journal of Youth and Adolescence, 38*(7), 976–988. https://doi.org/10.1007/s10964-009-9412-1

Ky Ng, C., Haines-Saah, R., Knight, R., Shoveller, J., & Johnson, J. (2017). "It's not my business": Exploring heteronormativity in young people's discourses about lesbian, gay, bisexual, transgender, and queer issues and their implications for youth health and wellbeing. *Health, 23*(1), 39–57. https://doi.org/10.1177/1363459317715776

Jereb, A. M. (2017). The bathroom right for transgender students and how the entire LGBT community can align to guarantee this. *Wake Forest Journal of Law & Policy, 7*(2), 585–606. https://heinonline.org/HOL/P?h=hein.journals/wfjlapo7&i=593

Le Gallais, T. (2008). Wherever I go there I am: Reflections on reflexivity and the research stance. *Reflective Practice, 9*(2), 145–155. https://doi.org/10.1080/14623940802005475

Lenskyj, H. J. (2013). Reflections on communication and sport on heteronormativity and gender identities. *Communication & Sport, 1*(1–2), 138–150. https://doi.org/10.1177/2167479512467327

Magrath, R. (2017). The intersection of race, religion and homophobia in British football. *International Review for Sociology of Sport, 52*(4), 411–429. https://doi.org/10.1177/1012690215597651

Marston, K. (2015). Beyond bullying: The limitations of homophobic and transphobic bullying interventions for affirming lesbian, gay, bisexual and trans (LGBT) equality in education. *Pastoral Care Education, 33*(3), 161–168. https://doi.org/10.1080/02643944.2015.1074266

Marzetti, H. (2018). Proudly proactive: Celebrating and supporting LGBT+ students in Scotland. *Teaching in Education, 23*(6), 701–717. https://doi.org/10.1080/13562517.2017.1414788

McCormack, M. (2012). *The declining significance of homophobia: How teenage boys are redefining masculinity and heterosexuality.* Oxford University Press.

McNeill, T. (2013). Sex education and the promotion of heteronormativity. *Sexualities*, *16*(7), 826–846. https://doi.org/10.1177/1363460713497216

Ministry of Education. (n.d.). Provide accessible, gender-neutral toilets. Inclusive Education. https://www.inclusive.tki.org.nz/guides/supporting-lgbtiqa-stude nts/provide-accessible-gender-neutral-toilets

Ministry of Education. (2015). *Bullying prevention and response: A guide for schools*. Ministry of Education. https://pb4l.tki.org.nz/content/download/261/1137/ file/Bullying%20prevention%20and%20response%20A%20guide%20for%20 schools.pdf

Ministry of Education. (2020a). *Relationships and sexuality education: A guide for teachers, leaders, and boards of trustees. Years 1–8*. Ministry of Education. https://hpe.tki.org.nz/assets/healthpe/pdfs/RSE+Guide+y1-8.pdf

Ministry of Education. (2020b). *Relationships and sexuality education: A guide for teachers, leaders, and boards of trustees. Years 9–13*. Ministry of Education. https://hpe.tki.org.nz/assets/healthpe/pdfs/RSE+Guide+y9-13.pdf

National Union of Students (NUS). (2016). Out in sport: LGBT students' experiences of sport. https://www.nusconnect.org.uk/resources/out-in-sport-lgbt-stude nts-experiences-of-sport-2012

Peel, E. (2001, October). Mundane heterosexism: Understanding incidents of the everyday. *Women's Studies International Forum, 24*(5), 541–554. https://doi.org/ 10.1016/S0277-5395(01)00194-7

Prosser, J., & Schwartz, D. (2006). Photographs within the sociological research process. In J. Prosser (Ed.), *Image-based research: A sourcebook for qualitative researchers* (pp. 115–130). RoutledgeFalmer.

Pryor, J. (2018). Visualizing queer spaces: LGBTQ students and the traditionally heterogendered institution. *Journal of LGBT Youth, 15*(1), 32–51. https://doi. org/10.1080/19361653.2017.1395307

Pyne, J. (2011). Unsuitable bodies: Trans people and cisnormativity in shelter services. *Canadian Social Work Review, 28*(1), 129–137. http://www.jstor.org/sta ble/41658838

Rankin, S. R. (2003). *Campus climate for gay, lesbian, bisexual, and transgender people: A national perspective*. National Gay and Lesbian Task Force Policy Institute.

Rankin, S. R. (2016). *Dartmouth College: Climate assessment for learning, living, and working*. Rankin and Associates. https://www.dartmouth.edu/oir/rankinandas sociatesfinalreport.pdf

Roffee, J. A., & Waling, A. (2016). Rethinking microaggressions and anti-social behaviour against LGBTIQ+ youth. *Safer Communities, 15*(4), 190–201. https:// doi.org/10.1108/SC-02-2016-0004

Seelman, K. L. (2014). Transgender individuals' access to college housing and bathrooms: Findings from the National Transgender Discrimination Survey. *Journal of Gay & Lesbian Social Services, 26*(2), 186–206. https://doi.org/ 10.1080/10538720.2014.891091

Seelman, K. L. (2016). Transgender adults' access to college bathrooms and housing and the relationship to suicidality. *Journal of Homosexuality, 63*(10), 1378–1399. https://doi.org/10.1080/00918369.2016.1157998

Sue, D. W., Capodilupo, C. M., Torino, G. C., Bucceri, J. M., Holder, A. M. B., Nadal, K. L., & Esquilin, M. (2007). Racial microaggressions in everyday life: Implications for clinical practice. *American Psychologist, 62*(4), 271–286. https://doi.org/10.1037/0003-066X.62.4.271

Tetreault, P. A., Fette, R., Meidlinger, P. C., & Hope, D. (2013). Perceptions of campus climate by sexual minorities. *Journal of Homosexuality*, *60*(7), 947–964. https://doi.org/10.1080/00918369.2013.774874

Torre, D., & Murphy, J. (2015). A different lens: Using photo-elicitation interviews in education research. *Education Policy Analysis Archives*, *23*(11), 1–23.

Treharne, G. J., Beres, M., Nicolson, M., Richardson, A., Ruzibiza, C., Graham, K., Briggs, H., & Ballantyne, N. (2016). Campus climate for students with diverse sexual orientations and/or gender identities at the University of Otago, Aotearoa New Zealand. Otago University Students' Association. https://ourarchive.otago.ac.nz/handle/10523/6950

UNESCO (United Nations Educational, Scientific, and Cultural Organization). (2016). Out in the open: Education sector responses to violence based on sexual orientation and gender identity/expression (summary report). http://unesdoc.unesco.org/images/0024/002447/244756e.pdf

Wandrey, R. L., Mosack, K. E., & Moore, E. M. (2015). Coming out to family and friends as bisexually identified young adult women: A discussion of homophobia, biphobia, and heteronormativity. *Journal of Bisexuality*, *15*(2), 204–229. https://doi.org/10.1080/15299716.2015.1018657

Warner, M. (1993). *Fear of a queer planet: Queer politics and social theory*. University of Minnesota Press.

Willis, P. (2012). Constructions of lesbian, gay, bisexual and queer identities among young people in contemporary Australia. *Culture, Health & Sexuality*, *14*(10), 1213–1227. https://doi.org/10.1080/13691058.2012.724087

Woodford, M. R., Joslin, J. Y., Pitcher, E. N., & Renn, K. A. (2017). A mixed-methods inquiry into trans* environmental microaggressions on college campuses: Experiences and outcomes. *Journal of Ethnic & Cultural Diversity in Social Work*, *26*(1-2), 95–111. https://doi.org/10.1080/15313204.2016.1263817

Yost, M. R., & Gilmore, S. (2011). Assessing LGBTQ campus climate and creating change. *Journal of Homosexuality*, *58*(9), 1330–1354. https://doi.org/10.1080/00918369.2011.605744

CHAPTER 17

# Trans Children in Primary Schools

## Thinking Queerly About Happiness and Time

AOIFE NEARY

Children are at once "dense figures of social anxiety and aspiration for the future" (Halberstam, 2018, p. 55). In primary schools, tropes of "childhood innocence" and discourses of "age appropriateness" are both produced by and productive of normative temporalities that plot gendered and heterosexualized timelines and pathways to adulthood for children (Davies & Robinson, 2010; DePalma & Atkinson, 2009; Robinson, 2012, 2013). Adults are affectively invested in such timelines and pathways of childhood development. However, such commitments come about through "the gauzy lens" of adulthood and can effectively invent ghostly childhoods that never were (Stockton, 2009). Halberstam (2005) pointed out that childhood should not be apprehended using adult logics of time and space that reproduce linear, chrononormative trajectories. Rather, as Hickey-Moody (2013) observed, childhood can be understood as occurring in multiple subjectivities and collective blocks, zigzagging across time.

Recent years have seen an increase in the visibility of very young trans and gender-diverse children in the public sphere (Price Minter, 2012), and Halberstam (2018) suggested that this "arrival" of trans and gender-diverse children "disrupts not only the meaning of the gendered body but our understanding of time, development and order itself" (p. 62). An emerging body of empirical research in primary school contexts has given particular attention to the everyday lives of trans and gender-diverse

Aoife Neary, *Trans Children in Primary Schools* In: *Queer Studies and Education*. Edited by: Nelson M. Rodriguez, Robert C. Mizzi, Louisa Allen, and Rob Cover, Oxford University Press. © Oxford University Press 2023.
DOI: 10.1093/oso/9780197687000.003.0018

children. Martino and Cumming-Potvin (2016) noted the potential in using queer- and trans-themed texts at school for attending to trans materialities, but were careful to underline how teacher subjectivities, knowledge, and positionalities are key mediating factors. Countering claims that children "are not ready" for such knowledge, Ryan et al. (2013) demonstrated how children productively learned to question restrictive social systems and think more inclusively in general. Payne and Smith (2014) outlined the fears and resistances of elementary school educators and how discourses of professional responsibility seek to "accommodate" trans children but are simultaneously invested in and constrained by the protection of normative understandings of childhood innocence. Other school leaders demonstrated more transgressive and transformative approaches in their attempts to make their primary schools more inclusive (Leonardi & Staley, 2018). My own research has explored the "messy and often incongruous terms through which gender is (re)produced" in primary schools (Neary, 2018, p. 445), also drawing attention to the complicated ways that trans children are at once violently impacted by and heavily invested in the workings of gender norms in primary schools (Neary, 2021).

Proceeding with the notion that *queer* is that which is unassimilable, destabilizing, and troubling of the totalizing logics underpinning normativity, this chapter builds on emerging research to think queerly about the everyday lives of trans children. Specifically, I employ theorizing on queer time and emotion to think through how the everyday experiences of trans children can help us to interrogate and reimagine the logics of gender normativity that are so embedded in education assemblages.

Thinking queerly about time involves an interrogation of the banal logics of time, facilitating alternative temporalities to emerge whereby futures can be imagined outside of normative social scripts. Thinking queerly about emotion reveals the ways that power and emotion are entangled, constructing cisheteronormative subjects, practices, discourses, and spaces but simultaneously enabling queer counterpublics and possibilities to emerge (Ahmed, 2004a, 2004b, 2006a, 2006b, 2008, 2010). The accounts drawn on in this chapter arose from a qualitative study conducted in partnership with the Transgender Equality Network of Ireland (TENI). Semistructured interviews were conducted with six educators and twelve parents of trans and gender-diverse children in primary schools. This study was rooted epistemologically by queer and trans studies theories of gender and, in particular, debates about normativity, materiality, and transgression (Butler, 1993, 2001, 2004; Halberstam, 2005, 2018). This chapter is underpinned by a commitment to thinking queerly about the architecture

[334] *Aoife Neary*

of gender (Enke, 2012; Halberstam, 2018; Mayo, 2017) while remaining led by the material dimensions of the lives of those who identify as trans (Mayo, 2017; Namaste, 2009) and the ways in which identities and gender norms are necessary for survival (Butler, 2004).

This chapter is organized in the following way: First, I lean on key theorists to articulate what thinking about time and emotion queerly might look like and the key questions that such theorizing raises for inquiring into the everyday lives of gender-nonconforming children and their parents. Illustrated by the accounts of parents, I go on then to explore how some became affectively invested in linear temporal paths to gender normativity while simultaneously being reflexively aware of the cruelty of their own fantasies and the fluidity of gender expression. These parents' accounts yielded a discussion of the ways in which happiness is bound up with gender normativity and what the concept of *happenstance*, instead of *happiness* (Ahmed, 2010), might offer for thinking anew about gender, childhood, and education.

## THINKING TIME QUEERLY

At the heart of modernism is a conceptualization of time as linear, sequential, stable, and passive (Lingard & Thompson, 2017). But many have pointed out how time works as "an invisible and silent relation of power" (Sharma, 2013, p. 315) in and through technologies such as clock time, biological time, and social time and via artifacts such as watches, time zones, calendars, timelines, and schedules (Leaton Gray, 2017). Much work on time has focused on how it is constructed according to the logics of capitalism, ensuring the organization of populations toward maximum productivity (Harvey, 1989; Thompson, 1967). Such articulations also bring together philosophical discussions about the connections between time and space. For example, echoing Marxist theory on the annihilation of space by time, Harvey's (1989) concept of "time-space compression" denotes how power works through the naturalization and presumption of time, inculcating "hidden rhythms" (Zerubavel, 1982), whereby institutional forces appear like somatic facts and go unnoticed by or "seem natural to those whom they privilege" (Freeman, 2010, p. 3).

But, some have pointed to the limitations of such analyses of time. In a critique of Harvey's (1989) analysis of time, Halberstam (2005) pointed out its failure to explicitly and adequately describe how time/space becomes naturalized toward normative and normalized ends and how hegemonic constructions of time are gendered and sexualized. Or, as Sharma (2013) put it, such an analysis fails to acknowledge that time is an "always-already intersecting form of social difference" (p. 317). For instance, biological, reproductive, and family time are "heteronormative time/space constructs" (Halberstam, 2005, p. 10). Sharma (2013, p. 315) argued that a truly critical inquiry into time—as relational, as multiple, and as an invisible vector of power—holds the potential to transform normative categories and practices.

For some queer theorists, thinking time queerly is to practice a nonteleological negativity. For example, Edelman's (2004) understanding of queer time necessitates refusing not only the structural repetition of "reproductive futurism" but also the entire architecture that would turn it into a "good." For Edelman, this included a refusal of redemptive "efforts to associate queerness with community, or a transformative future, or new forms of relationality" (Edelman, as cited in Dinshaw et al., 2007, p. 189). Others, such as Halberstam (2005), asserted that queer time involves "a counterintuitive critique, one that works against the grain of the true, the good, and the right but one that nonetheless refuses to make a new orthodoxy out of negativity" (Halberstam, as cited in Dinshaw et al., 2007, p. 194).

Fittingly, there is no consensus about how queer temporality is to be understood. Neither is thinking time queerly a guarantee of realizing "queer political projects" (Jagose, as cited in Dinshaw et al., 2007, p. 191). For example, a focus on the unevenness of time or being "out of time" is a logic also taken up by the evangelical Christian movement to tap into people's sense of being "out of step with contemporary mores" (Dinshaw et al., 2007, p. 190). Nevertheless, queer temporality allows considered attention to the specific entanglements of time with cisheteronormativity, the ways in which through everyday, banal logics of time, people become "bound to one another, engrouped, made to feel coherently collective" (Freeman, 2010, p. 3). Queer theorizing on time reveals how the state is invested in such temporal schema, marking out the boundaries of normativity and belonging in ways that are at once public and private, individual and social. Furthermore, in Halberstam's (2005) understanding, thinking time queerly facilitates an interrogation of the normative logics of time, facilitating alternative temporalities to emerge whereby futures can be imagined outside of normative social scripts prescribed by the "paradigmatic markers of life experience—namely, birth, marriage, reproduction, and death" (p. 2). Such thinking has particular resonances when it comes to thinking about the experiences of trans and gender-diverse children; children whose bodies and everyday lives are so very often discussed within and through narratives of time.

[336]   *Aoife Neary*

## THINKING EMOTIONS QUEERLY: HAPPINESS AS HAPPENSTANCE

Sarah Ahmed's (2000, 2004a, 2004b, 2008, 2010) work on emotion has explored how emotions function as affective economies moving and creating "the very effect of the surfaces or boundaries of bodies and worlds" (Ahmed, 2004b, p. 117). Power works through emotion, moving across bodies in spaces, orienting collectives toward normativity. Drawing on the concept of orientation and its denoting of the idea that consciousness is always directed toward an object, Ahmed (2006a, 2006b) developed a "queer phenomenology." Following Merleau-Ponty, Ahmed alerted us to how everyday life is full of queer moments; moments of disorientation which involve not only "the intellectual experience of disorder, but the vital experience of giddiness and nausea, which is the awareness of our own contingency and the horror with which it fills us" (Ahmed, 2006a, p. 544). Social collectives have vertical and horizontal lines that are "modes of following" such that these moments of "disorder" in the everyday are continuously righted, corrected, and overcome as "bodies are reoriented in the 'becoming vertical' of perspective" (Ahmed, 2006a, p. 544). In this way, bodies and collectives are oriented along (hetero)normative lines, correcting any queer moments or practices and ensuring that spaces are (re)oriented around the straight body. For her, there is also much promise in the "joy and excitement in the horror" of disorientation (Ahmed, 2006a, p. 544). Queer moments and practices can operate "out of line," producing a diagonal line "which cuts across 'slantwise' the vertical and horizontal lines . . . perhaps even challenging the 'becoming vertical' of ordinary perception" (Ahmed, 2006b, p. 107). As Ahmed (2004a) pointed out, "normativity is comfortable for those who can inhabit it . . . and comfort is very hard to notice when one experiences it" (p. 147). And so, paying attention, as she does, to the workings of emotion as part of a queer phenomenology reveals the ways that subjects, practices, discourses, and spaces become oriented toward cisheteronormativity. At the same time, echoing Halberstam's (2005) theorizing on time, such queer theorizing on emotion opens up the potentiality for queer counterpublics and possibilities to emerge.

Ahmed helped us to think about how objects accumulate affective value through emotions in ways that are inextricable from the logics of temporality. For Ahmed (2010), "feelings do not simply reside in subjects and then move outwards towards objects. Feelings are how objects create impressions in shared spaces of dwelling" (p. 14). For instance, Ahmed pointed out that happiness proffers itself as a promise, and our quest for happiness sends particular "happy objects" forth and maps out directions for us to follow toward this promise of happiness (Ahmed, 2010, p. 160). Such feelings, as directed toward objects in the present, "keep the past alive" while maintaining a sense of anticipation of what follows in the future, a future that never arrives (Ahmed, 2010, p. 181). Drawing on Bloch, Ahmed continued to explain how the future-oriented feeling of hope anticipates a happiness that is yet to come—"'an anticipatory consciousness'; we are aware of the 'not yet' in the unfolding of the present" (Bloch, as cited in Ahmed, 2010, p. 181) and how "we have a tendency to endure our struggles in the present by deferring our hope for happiness to some future point" (Ahmed, 2010, p. 183).

Here Ahmed powerfully drew our attention to the intense intertwining of emotions and temporality. Reading with Ahmed alongside Halberstam's (2018, p. 62) claim that the trans child disrupts "our understanding of time, development and order itself" begs close attention to the ways in which trans and gender-diverse children and their parents live and experience the entanglements of time and emotion. I suggest that such a reading facilitates thinking anew about how the architecture of gender governing childhood, "growing up," and primary schooling might be imagined otherwise.

## AFFECTIVE INVESTMENTS IN LINEAR TEMPORAL PATHS TO GENDER NORMATIVITY

Each of the parents in this study talked about how their child was gender nonconforming from as early as they could communicate. In navigating their everyday worlds, their child's gender expression was considerably different from what was typically expected of their birth-assigned gender. To their parents, it appeared that, at every turn, their child used the gendered artifacts and practices of their childhood (e.g., toys, clothes, TV programs, games, etc.) to "validate" their gender identity. Most children expressed discomfort and, in many cases, extreme upset at the gendered societal expectations associated with their assigned gender identity. Many children articulated negative feelings toward their bodies and expressed their gender identity through gestures, bodily comportment, and decisions about their hair. Paula's account provides an illustration of the extent of upset that several parents described:

> He was holding it together in school. And coming home and having these huge meltdowns. But he couldn't tell us why he didn't really know why. It was like the pressure cooker was maintaining itself in school and then when he came home the pressure cooker would blow. And he would get really distraught and just cry

and cry and cry. Sitting on my knee for an hour and a half bawling. (Paula, parent of Seán, age 10)

Understandably, these parents just wanted to ease the upset of their child: "I think we were feeling pressurised because of the distress Fred was under. . . . As a parent your instinct is to fix it" (Eavan, parent of Fred, age 8). They wanted to respond to their child and support them in whatever way they could to be happy: "I just wanted to make sure he was happy and sort this out for him" (Jane, parent of Justin, age 7).

This common desire for their child to be happy and to avoid distress had different manifestations for different children and their parents. The children's gender identity speech acts, along with their various other modes of expression, became the starting points for particular temporal pathways in childhood. Several parents' accounts outlined stories of vehement gender identity certainty, and there was a sense of happiness and ease associated with such discourses. For example, Richie displayed a sophisticated clarity in articulating his understanding of his gender identity:

I don't want to be identified as trans, I'm a boy. I'm not a trans, I'm a boy. . . . The only thing that is different about me to other boys is that I've got the wrong privates. I am a boy. I don't see the world through the eyes of a girl. I didn't use to be a girl and now I'm a boy, I'm not confused, I'm not a bit of both—I am a boy. (Sarah, parent of Richie, age 9)

Sarah reflected that Richie had previously been: "very anxious, very emotionally guarded. Very reticent very . . . very closed," but described how this new gender identity certainty and clarity of articulation was a turning point that brought a sense of ease and happiness to Richie and laid out a plan for Sarah to follow:

I think once he had made up his mind that he wanted to change his name and his gender pronouns . . . he wanted it done yesterday. And it was like he had suddenly seen the light. And it was literally like a light switch went on and . . . suddenly it was like the train had left the station. I couldn't catch up with him fast enough. . . . As far as he was concerned if we do this, everything else follows. Cos it falls into place. So he went to bed on a Monday night saying I don't want to be sad from now on. I need you to text everyone and tell them I'm a boy from now on. He got up the next morning, because I'm a boy I will go to the boy's school. I will make my communion. I will play on the boy's team. It was like everything fell in to place. . . . I suppose from there the bit for me was . . . to get all the supports and structures in place to catch up with that.

Here happiness was associated with a decision, a clear path that had fallen into place—a set of steps that could now be supported by Sarah.

Like some other children, Richie was also heavily invested in gender norms and gendered practices in order to assert and make clear to others his gender identity. In Richie's school, the practice of reentering the school after break involved the children forming gendered lines: boys' lines and girls' lines. In a supportive gesture, the teacher suggested that they would end this gendered practice, but Sarah described how Richie strongly resisted this:

> "Promise me you won't change the lines, there has to be a boy line I have to be in the boy line." . . . That was how he was going to . . . get his message, this is how he was going to say "you can't argue with this. This is the rules from above" and . . . changing the rules to muddy that water, he was absolutely . . . I mean he was, in a way . . . quite . . . empowered. At the time, he was like "Don't you dare!" He was quite primal. I think we're very clear on where we stand with this!

For Sarah and other parents in the study, the strength of certainty and clarity of the articulation of one gender identity on one side of the gender binary (using an "I am" statement) made their role as parent and their negotiations at school much easier than other parents. Their children's certainty and vehement clarity plotted a particular developmental temporal pathway that could be followed.

On the other hand, ambiguity in gender display was experienced as more difficult and was the source of much anxiety by other parents. One parent, Ailbhe (parent of Darren, age 6) was committed to a gender-fluid approach to parenting. In her interview, Ailbhe noted how researching trans children directed her to expect discourses of certainty from her child:

> Ailbhe: Darren was still only four. And it was around then when I was thinking . . . because, you know, he was expressing a lot at the time and he had said a couple of times . . . that he wished he was a girl and things like that. . . . And yet it's not the same as saying I *am* a girl. So I was quite puzzled by that. I was very at a loss. Really very at a loss. . . . And in a sense I was prepared for "Mummy I *am* a girl." Because that's what I found when I went looking for first-person accounts of parenting young trans children.
>
> Interviewer 2 (family support officer): And the same issue would arise when you've got adolescents who would be maybe entering puberty and making those kinds of statements and they see . . . they're

online. . . . "What should I be saying in order to get access?" . . . So, there's a whole different thing going on. When they're like three, four and five . . . it's a real basic level. . . . I don't know the answer and I've seen and heard both.

From her research, Ailbhe had expected Darren to use an "I am" statement about their gender identity and so was confused when he didn't. In their conversation here, both Ailbhe and the family support officer pointed to how discourses of gender stability and certainty can become understood as the gold star in practices of recognizing and affirming a child's gender identity. Their conversation alluded to how particular markers and indicators form what might be interpreted as a kind of diagnostic hierarchy for determining childhood gender identity. But in what ways do such frames hold open the potential for a diversity of gender identity expressions? Furthermore, as implied by the family support officer's statement above, many trans and gender-diverse teenagers feel pressure to report their lived experiences in particular ways that align with certain predefined, institutionalized criteria in order to have their personhood acknowledged and recognized. Such negotiations are inordinately difficult for many trans children. They also constrain the capaciousness of gender identities and the architecture of gender itself.

Ambiguities around gender identity were experienced as intensely difficult for Jason (age 5) and his family. Jason appeared to be clear about his gender identity, but various factors in his life, including the separation of his parents and their disagreement over dealing with Jason's gender identity expression, meant that he was being called Jason and Shauna in different contexts. His mother, Siobhán, explained how difficult this was:

I think she still struggles a bit socially because she doesn't properly fall in either group. . . . I would prefer if we could make a definite decision and move forward in a definite direction. . . . I think if we said: "OK, you're Jason in September" or whatever I think it would make the coming years a lot easier . . . I worry that if we go along like this the whole Shauna/Jason girl/boy thing . . . it's gonna become a bigger issue.

Here Siobhán worried about the ambiguity, about having two names and two genders and wishes for a "definite decision" and a clear temporal path in "a definite direction." In a slightly different but related vein, Helen's 12-year-old child, Kevin, said that while he identified as a boy, he is "not a typical boy." This worried Helen a lot and she said:

The bain of my life now is flower crowns (uber feminine paper or satin flowers on a hairband). He has at least three flower crowns. . . . I mean I'm there persuading members of my family [he's a boy]. . . . People are going to go [be confused]. . . . I have said you can wear what you like in the house. I have warned against wearing it out. For their safety, I said you cannot wear that and use the gent's toilet. You can't.

Helen's account here powerfully underscores the magnetic pull to comply with gender norms as a trans person and the risks that any kind of gender "uncertainty" or ambiguity poses—in terms of recognition, acceptance, and safety.

In each of the accounts above, parents were invested in the promise of happiness and avoidance of upset. The promise of such affects and avoidance of others oriented many parents along a linear teleological path and, in most cases, toward the promise of gender normativity. Deviations from typical gender norms and ambiguities around gender expression posed a threat to this pathway. Such orientations again raise further questions about the ways in which trans lives and bodies are apprehended through, and more intensely policed by, restrictive gender norms. Perhaps needless to say, this is not to question the gender identification process of trans or gender-diverse people or the individual choices that people make regarding expressing their gender identity. Rather, the point I want to make here is that the prevention of distress and upset and quest for their child to be happy induced parents' orientations toward a gender-normative display and gender "certainty" and stability. In other words, following Ahmed (2010), the promise of and hope for a future happiness drew close and oriented parents toward the object of the normatively gendered body, concealing what may be lost in such orientations.

## CRUEL FANTASIES OF THE FUTURE AND CAPACIOUSNESS OF THE PRESENT

While most parents were invested in the promise of happiness for their child, many also held an acute sense that the notion of a pathway to their child's future happiness as gender normative was a cruel fantasy. Furthermore, most parents continued to express feelings of sadness and anxiety about the uncertainty of their child's future. While much research with families of trans people outlines an "ambiguous loss" for their loved one's birth-assigned gender identity and grief for the gendered future that the child would now not have (Wahlig, 2015), most parents in this study

[342] *Aoife Neary*

described a disassociation with this kind of articulation of loss. Their child had taken them on a journey since birth, and, because of that, they didn't experience this kind of grief or loss. For example, Joni said:

> To me . . . I couldn't give a shit whether you're a girl or a boy, the heart of you is the same. You're my child and I love you. And I hear people talking about the grief of losing their son or daughter and I'm just like, "Okay, I get that's valid for you but it's just completely not an issue for me personally." (Joni, parent of Petra, age 6)

Instead, most parents orientated toward the future and, for many, a sense of sadness was strongly projected there. For example, Eavan (parent of Fred, age 8) reflected on the fantasy of a linear future toward gender normativity and the "realities of life":

> I think that we went through . . . not a grieving process for say the daughter that we thought we had . . . but I think a grieving . . . more a grieving for am . . . that life is going to be so much more difficult than it would have been if it was different. And, for us, I think that's where the sadness comes for me . . . not so much a loss but that the sadness around the realities of life. We had a meeting with Tavistock [U.K. company who have a satellite clinic in a Dublin hospital] during the summer and oh wow . . . that really came up for me just the sadness around the reality. . . . [Clinician] said to me: "There are no happy endings for Fred. Because he can never be who . . . never no matter what we do, no matter what he does, he will be a trans man, he won't just be a man." So there are no happy endings. And that hit me in the heart and I thought my heart was just going to break on the spot. Because I thought . . . fuck, we just want happy endings. . . . Can Fred reach the possible potential that is in him without being defined by this whole thing or is he limited because of being defined? And I find that really sad as well.

Eavan's quote reveals a sadness and loss related to the impossibility of ordinariness, of "just being a man." In Eavan's imagining of the future, time will not bring happiness; there are no happy endings because her son will always be a trans man, not a cisgender man. Following Schopenhauer, Ahmed (2010, p. 174) explained how "happiness always lies in the future, or else in the past, and the present may be compared to a small dark cloud which the wind drives over the sunny plain; before and behind it all is bright; only it itself always casts a shadow." Ahmed (2010, p. 178) invited us to see how this notion that "things 'will only get better' at some point that is always just 'over the horizon'" can be a way of avoiding the impact of suffering and function as a kind of coping strategy in the present. But equally, as illustrated by Eavan's account, pessimism can be a tactic of survival, an approach that expects the worst such that any positive experience is a pleasant and restoring surprise (Ahmed, 2010).

So, while the level of sophistication in articulating their gender identity expressions and articulations appeared to map some children's futures in particularly linear directions that promised happiness, all parents expressed significant fears and uncertainties about the future and what might lie ahead for their child. For example, Paula said:

> Now we're seeing the psychiatrist. . . . So she's preparing the treatment abroad forms and everything. We're only just starting. So all of this is all lovely and everything but when you have to start giving them puberty blockers, when you don't even want to give them too much Calpol [Paracetamol-based medicine] and then you've to give them this stuff . . . but . . . yeah . . . I'm afraid for that. Until he is a girl you can't . . . he's upset, he won't ever be a proper girl. It's very hard to just to see how his journey is going to go. So surgery . . . then relationships as well. I mean how do you . . . how do you . . . land that someone on somebody . . . by the way. It's a big one. (Paula, parent of Seán, age 10)

Echoing Eavan's previous account, the fantasy of the future linear path toward normativity is tempered again here by Paula's acknowledgment that her child, Seán, is strongly aware and upset that he will never "be a proper girl." Paula's worries about puberty blockers and hormone treatments were also echoed across the parents in this study. For example, Joni (parent of Petra, age 6) said: "But the thing that I find difficult and the bit that I think is a challenge is the idea that you know this might move down a road of needing to get medicalised and the life ahead is just so difficult for so many people in that situation and, as a mother, that's not something you would choose for your child and that frightens me." Similarly, Eavan (parent of Fred, age 8) said: "They only have kind of six years of data about the blockers and most of them are with kids that are older not with kids his age. And it's like bloody hell, like you're guinea pigs."

While parents articulated fears, worries, and future imaginaries of sadness about their children's futures, there were several examples of how children *themselves* were negotiating their present, everyday lives in ways that hold open the capaciousness of gender. For example, Anna explained how her child, Phil (age 8) constantly reminded her that the new name they have chosen is gender neutral, and that they are not making any definite decisions. There is also Darren (age 6), who explained his gender identity using the phrase "I am a boy who wears dresses." And then there is Kevin with his flower crown, who "turns around and says 'oh I could try on these dresses if I was taller' [and I'm going 'would you?!' Like I've not seen them in a dress since their communion and] . . . 'Mam I'm a boy I'm not your typical boy!"' (Helen, parent of Kevin, age 12). Such negotiations remind us of the complexity of gender and focus attention on the multiplicity and potential fluidity of the present, holding open possibilities and underlining the ambivalences and ambiguities of gender. Crucially, this complicated picture of gender is inclusive of the many trans children that have deeply embodied investments in a gender identity and associated gender norms dating back to as early as they could communicate.

## THE POTENTIAL OF HAPPENSTANCE IN REIMAGINING GENDER NORMATIVITY

Motivated by the avoidance of upset and distress of their child and a consciousness about the ways that ambiguities around gender are interpreted and approached in our social worlds, most parents became oriented toward linear pathways to gender normativity. For some, happiness hovered at a distance, at some point in the future, and was bound up with gender normativity. For others, the future was shrouded in a sense of unhappiness because of the uncertainties related to not only potentially medicalized pathways but also because of the idea that their child could never change their natal history and could never be "properly" their gender identity in the future. In this way, these parents' accounts alert us to how the feeling of happiness becomes bound to an essentialized gender-normative ideal. What might Ahmed's queer theorizing on how happiness operates offer here? Following Ahmed and Halberstam, how might these accounts from these parents about the everyday negotiations of their trans and gender-diverse children serve to disrupt normative logics of gender, time, and development so that alternatives might emerge?

In this vein, I turn to think about Ahmed's notion of "the freedom to be unhappy," in other words, "the freedom to live a life that deviates from the paths of happiness, wherever that deviation takes us" (Ahmed, 2010, p. 195). When Ahmed was talking about the freedom to be unhappy, she was not asserting that unhappiness becomes the endpoint. Rather, she said: "If we no longer assume happiness is our telos, unhappiness would register as more than what gets in the way." In this vision, unhappiness activates "a new political ontology," one that reveals how happiness—when considered as an endpoint—very often necessitates the concealment of suffering. This new political project advocated by Ahmed (2010) instead proceeded with a recognition of and attention to making visible the causes of unhappiness while also making peace with the notion of causing unhappiness, discomfort, and disruption. In challenging happiness, Ahmed (2010) also pointed us to the joy in deviating from the straight path and building solidarity on these grounds. Ahmed was suggesting that we should not direct our emotions toward the "objects of our cause," and in that way, this vision of happiness would become "alive to chance, to chance arrivals, to the perhaps of a happening . . . the happy future is the future of the perhaps" (Ahmed, 2010, p. 198). Noting how the "perhaps" and "happiness" share a "hap," Ahmed (2010, p. 219) asserted that we might commit to a version of happiness termed "happenstance." This would involve being open to the possibility of good and bad things happening. In this way of living, happiness would be one possibility among many possibilities, and if we "lighten the load of happiness," then new possibilities can emerge, and "we can value happiness for its precariousness, as something that comes and goes, as life does" (p. 219).

But what does the concept of happenstance offer for thinking through the accounts of these parents and their trans children? Of course, this thinking falls far short in alleviating the anxieties and utter distress experienced by many children and their families in navigating their everyday lives in this moment. And the intention of my line of discussion here is not to in any way detract from the lived realities of the ticking clock of puberty bringing with it physiological changes that betray many of these children's deeply embodied gender identities. Nor, of course, is it to suggest that trans children should somehow give up on joy or delight or contentment. But, arising from these parents' accounts, what I'm trying to think about in this chapter is how the concept of happiness is not neutral and how it becomes bound up in and attached to an essentialized version of gender normativity as a starting point for thinking about how it might become otherwise.

Parents' avoidance of sadness and upset and search for happiness as a presumed good oriented them toward the normatively gendered future body with a temporal pathway to get there. For some parents, this pathway was a relief. For others, this pathway revealed itself as a fantasy, as not achievable because of natal histories. But both articulations reference an endpoint ideal of gender normativity. These accounts powerfully draw attention to how gender uncertainties and ambiguities and bodies and lives that don't fit neatly into a binary are being righted and conditioned and oriented toward normativity in and through these affectively inflected temporal logics. Recalling Richie's "primal" investment in the boy and girl lines previously as a powerful symptom of an intensely gendered school system—Richie's happiness was dependent on standing in the boy line because this performative act affirmed his gender identity. But this deeply gendered system, quite literally, lays down the order through which children can be apprehended and recognized. In this way, these gendered systems and practices are creating rigidly gendered conditions of happiness. And so, could a politics of justice that is not reliant on future happiness but instead commits to past-present-future temporalities as "happenstance" help conjure imaginaries of alternative futures that are less plotted and more open to the capaciousness of gender? Might the gender-queer negotiations of children coupled with parents' reflexivity about the fantasy of "happy endings" be starting points for questioning and reconsidering the logics of gender and time in the everyday spaces of education? At the very least, the accounts presented in this chapter help us to ask the question: Through what everyday practices and moments are children's bodies and relations becoming oriented toward gender normativity as part of a tacit project of achieving "happiness"?

**REFERENCES**

Ahmed, S. (2000). Who knows? Knowing strangers and strangerness. *Australian Feminist Studies, 15*(31), 49–68. https://doi.org/10.1080/713611918

Ahmed, S. (2004a). Collective feelings: Or, the impressions left by others. *Theory, Culture & Society, 21*(2), 25–42. https://doi.org/10.1177/0263276404042133

Ahmed, S. (2004b). *The cultural politics of emotion*. Routledge.

Ahmed, S. (2006a). Orientations: Towards a queer phenomenology. *GLQ: A Journal of Lesbian and Gay Studies, 12*(4), 543–574. https://doi.org/10.1215/10642 684-2006-002

Ahmed, S. (2006b). *Queer phenomenology: Orientations, objects, others*. Duke University Press.

Ahmed, S. (2008). Sociable happiness. *Emotion, Space and Society, 1*(1), 10–13. https://doi.org/10.1016/j.emospa.2008.07.003

Ahmed, S. (2010). *The promise of happiness*. Duke University Press.

Butler, J. (1993). *Bodies that matter: On the discursive limits of "sex."* Routledge.

Butler, J. (2001). Doing justice to someone: Sex reassignment and allegories of transsexuality. *GLQ: A Journal of Lesbian and Gay Studies, 7*(4), 621–636. https://doi.org/10.1215/10642684-7-4-621

Butler, J. (2004). *Undoing gender*. Routledge.

Davies, C., & Robinson, K. (2010). Hatching babies and stork deliveries: Risk and regulation in the construction of children's sexual knowledge. *Contemporary Issues in Early Childhood, 11*(3), 249–262. https://doi.org/10.2304/ciec.2010.11.3.249

DePalma, R., & Atkinson, E. (2009). "No outsiders": Moving beyond a discourse of tolerance to challenge heteronormativity in primary schools. *British Educational Research Journal, 35*(6), 837–855. https://doi.org/10.1080/014119 20802688705

Dinshaw, C., Edelman, L., Ferguson, R. A., Freccero, C., Freeman, E., Halberstam, J., Jagose, A., Nealon, C., & Hoang, N. T. (2007). Theorizing queer temporalities: A roundtable discussion. *GLQ: A Journal of Lesbian and Gay Studies*, *13*(2–3), 177–195. https://doi.org/10.1215/10642684-2006-030

Edelman, L. (2004). *No future: Queer theory and the death drive*. Duke University Press.

Enke, F. (2012). *Transfeminist perspectives in and beyond trans and gender studies*. Temple University Press.

Freeman, E. (2010). *Time binds: Queer temporalities, queer histories*. Duke University Press.

Halberstam, J. (2005). *In a queer time and place: Trans bodies, subcultural lives*. New York University Press.

Halberstam, J. (2018). *Trans: A quick and quirky account of gender variability*. University of California Press.

Harvey, D. (1989). *The condition of postmodernity*. Blackwell.

Hickey-Moody, A. C. (2013). Deleuze's children. *Educational Philosophy and Theory*, *45*(3), 272–286. https://doi.org/10.1080/00131857.2012.741523

Leaton Gray, S. (2017). The social construction of time in contemporary education: Implications for technology, equality and Bernstein's "conditions for democracy." *British Journal of Sociology of Education*, *38*(1), 60–71. https://doi.org/10.1080/01425692.2016.1234366

Leonardi, B., & Staley, S. (2018). What's involved in "the work"? Understanding administrators' roles in bringing trans-affirming policies into practice. *Gender and Education*, *30*(6), 754–773. https://doi.org/10.1080/09540 253.2018.1455967

Lingard, B., & Thompson, G. (2017). *Doing time in the sociology of education*. Routledge.

Martino, W., & Cumming-Potvin, W. (2016). Teaching about sexual minorities and "princess boys": A queer and trans-infused approach to investigating LGBTQ-themed texts in the elementary school classroom. *Discourse: Studies in the Cultural Politics of Education*, *37*(6), 807–827. https://doi.org/10.1080/01596 306.2014.940239

Mayo, C. (2017). Queer and trans youth, relational subjectivity, and uncertain possibilities: Challenging research in complicated contexts. *Educational Researcher*, *46*(9), 530–538. https://doi.org/10.3102/0013189X17738737

Minter, S. P. (2012). Supporting trans children: New legal, social, and medical approaches. *Journal of Homosexuality*, *59*(3), 422–433. https://doi.org/10.1080/ 00918369.2012.653311

Namaste, V. (2009). Undoing theory: The "trans question" and the epistemic violence of Anglo-American feminist theory. *Hypatia*, *24*(3), 11–32. http://www.jstor. org/stable/20618162

Neary, A. (2018). New trans* visibilities: Working the limits and possibilities of gender at school. *Sex Education*, *18*(4), 435–448. https://doi.org/10.1080/14681 811.2017.1419950

Neary, A. (2021). Trans children and the necessity to complicate gender in primary schools. *Gender and Education*, *33*(8), 1073–1089. https://doi.org/10.1080/ 09540253.2021.1884200

Payne, E., & Smith, M. (2014). The big freak out: Educator fear in response to the presence of trans elementary school students. *Journal of Homosexuality*, *61*(3), 399–418. https://doi.org/10.1080/00918369.2013.842430

Robinson, K. H. (2012). "Difficult citizenship": The precarious relationships between childhood, sexuality and access to knowledge. *Sexualities*, *15*(3–4), 257–276. https://doi.org/10.1177/1363460712436469

Robinson, K. H. (2013). *Innocence, knowledge and the construction of childhood: The contradictory nature of sexuality and censorship in children's contemporary lives.* Routledge.

Ryan, C. L., Patraw, J. M., & Bednar, M. (2013). Discussing princess boys and pregnant men: Teaching about gender diversity and trans experiences within an elementary school curriculum. *Journal of LGBT Youth, 10*(1–2), 83–105. https://doi.org/10.1080/19361653.2012.718540

Sharma, S. (2013). Critical time. *Communication and Critical/Cultural Studies, 10*(2–3), 312–318. https://doi.org/10.1080/14791420.2013.812600

Stockton, K. B. (2009). *The queer child, or growing sideways in the twentieth century.* Duke University Press.

Thompson, E. P. (1967). Time, work-discipline, and industrial capitalism. *Past & Present, 38*(1), 56–97. https://doi.org/10.1093/past/38.1.56

Wahlig, J. L. (2015). Losing the child they thought they had: Therapeutic suggestions for an ambiguous loss perspective with parents of a trans child. *Journal of GLBT Family Studies, 11*(4), 305–326. https://doi.org/10.1080/15504 28X.2014.945676

Zerubavel, E. (1982). The standardization of time: A sociohistorical perspective. *American Journal of Sociology, 88*(1), 1–23. http://www.jstor.org/stable/2779401

# CHAPTER 18

# Queer Love and Education

## NELSON M. RODRIGUEZ AND WILLIAM F. PINAR

In an essay, "Queer Love," David M. Halperin (2019) pointed out that, unlike the category sex, queer theory has not engaged in much knowledge production about love. Indeed, as an object of queer critique or examination, love, it seems, has slipped under the queer radar. As Halperin explained:

> Queer theory has had something to say about sex, but until recently it has had almost nothing to say about love. Love has seemed too intimately bound up with institutions and discourses of the "normal," too deeply embedded in standard narratives of romance, to be available for "queering." Whereas sex, as queers know very well, is easy to stigmatize (or to celebrate) as kinky, transgressive, or perverse, love is typically represented as lying at the heart of normal life, thoroughly at home in conventional social structures such as marriage and the nuclear family. (p. 1)

In Halperin's highlighting of a lack of queer theoretical engagement with love, we see this as an invitation more generally to contribute queer analyses to the ever-expanding orbit of what constitutes queer's "proper objects"; or to say this in a slightly different way, we are reminded that maintaining queer's "openness and uncontainable aspects of queer commentary" (Somerville, 2020, p. 6) is critical to the furthering of queer knowledge production. In this way, as Rasmussen and Allen (2014) noted, queer "denotes a continuously changing assemblage of ideas that can

Nelson M. Rodriguez and William F. Pinar, *Queer Love and Education* In: *Queer Studies and Education.* Edited by: Nelson M. Rodriguez, Robert C. Mizzi, Louisa Allen, and Rob Cover, Oxford University Press. © Oxford University Press 2023.
DOI: 10.1093/oso/9780197687000.003.0019

mutate, renew, and be replaced" (p. 433). In addition, what we position as Halperin's invitation to think queerly about love also opens an opportunity, within the context and concerns of our chapter, not only to add to discourse production on queer love but also, more specifically, to generate discourse about queer love in education. Indeed, from critique to deployment, and all points in between and beyond, there is potentially much discourse to generate in reflecting on the theoretical, political, pedagogical, and methodological dimensions of queer love across any number of formal and informal contexts of education, including within discussions of curriculum and pedagogy, teaching and learning.

From this perspective, we situate our chapter as contributing to ongoing knowledge production on the topic of queer love through a set of critical analyses and reflections on its meanings and practices within education. More specifically, we examine recent work generated within the North American academic context on the concept of queer love, demonstrating, in part, that normativities and their repetitions encompass a range of practices. In light of these considerations, knowledge production across two narratives is presented: In the first section, "Queer Love and Sexuality Studies," Rodriguez draws on Halberstam's (2011) notion of queer failure, arguing that queer love can be formulated as a productive example of queer failure, thus offering ways of teaching and learning about something akin to what Foucault (2003) described as "subjugated knowledges" or "knowledges from below" (p. 7) within the context of the sexuality studies curriculum and classroom that can highlight and potentially disrupt how love and desire are oriented and configured temporally in heteronormative ways. In the second section, "Queer Love in the Curriculum," Pinar's narrative critically engages with Halperin's (2019) formulation of queer love, that is, with the repetitions of normative thought it potentially induces, by locating his reflections in relation to different moments in time related to (queer) knowledge production, queer history, as well as his own queer biography. The chapter concludes with a set of reflections on the generative possibilities of the concept of queer love.

## QUEER LOVE AND SEXUALITY STUDIES (RODRIGUEZ'S NARRATIVE)

My interest in exploring the notion of queer love in education stems from a broader pedagogical commitment in terms of utilizing critical concepts in the undergraduate sexuality studies classroom as a resource for analyzing and discussing with students forms of knowledge that might be viewed, without the use of such concepts, as frivolous, silly, or weird, thus being cast off as having little to offer in the way of advancing social justice. Halberstam (2011, p. 19) reminds us that "gender and sexuality are . . . too often dropped from most large-scale accounts of alternative worlds," so teaching and learning about forms of sexual knowledge, for instance, that are "obscure" may present even greater challenges in compelling students to view them as useful in terms of offering critiques of dominant ways of thinking and being. From this perspective, one of the things I've learned teaching sexuality studies is that when students have critical concepts to work with, silly objects, or things that seem strange, take on more political significance in highlighting the social construction of norms, including the construction of norms associated with heteronormativity. Teaching and learning about "peripheral knowledges," in other words, demonstrates not only the politics associated with the construction of dominant, hegemonic knowledge formations but also the potential "counterpolitics of the silly object" (Berlant, 1997, p. 12) in illuminating that "the social worlds that we inhabit . . . are not inevitable; they were not always bound to turn out this way, and what's more, in the process of producing this reality, many other realities, fields of knowledge, and ways of being have been discarded and, to cite Foucault . . . 'disqualified'" (Halberstam, 2011, pp. 8–9).

In my previous work (see Rodriguez, 2019), I utilized Foucault's (1997) concept of homosexual/queer ascesis to explore gay for pay—more specifically, to explore the praxis of friendship among straight-identified men who do gay for pay—as a technology of self-transformation, a queer ascesis that "constitutes an ongoing set of relations and practices with oneself in relation to others that subvert, or move beyond, *institutionalized* relations and modes of being" (Rodriguez, 2019, p. 141, original italics). Reading gay for pay, as well as texts (e.g., documentaries) about gay for pay, through the concept of queer ascesis has provided my students with the opportunity to move away from simply framing gay for pay as irrelevant knowledge to their own lives or as about men who are "really gay" but just can't admit it, to a much deeper and complicated conversation about the norms governing friendship, that is, about the ways in which norms govern the possibilities of the contours of friendship, including among men. Taking up gay for pay through the concept of queer ascesis has also provided my students with an example that can be read as moving beyond the paucity of institutionalized "readymade formulas" (Foucault, 1997, p. 137) of friendship to an understanding of friendship as an ongoing formation, a counterhegemonic set of practices to institutionalized relational codes that include "multiple intensities, variable colors, imperceptible movements, and changing

[352]   *Nelson M. Rodriguez and William F. Pinar*

forms" (Foucault, 1997, p. 137). In a similar way, I provide here a set of reflections on how the concept of queer love, or thinking queerly about love, might be leveraged as part of the sexuality studies curriculum to engage meaningfully with what Halberstam (2011, p. 16) referred to as "low theory" (more on this shortly)—that is, to engage with what might be framed as subjugated, "silly," or peripheral knowledge about (romantic) love to critically examine the institutionalization of heteronormative forms and timelines of love while exploring what might be formulated as noninstitutionalized forms of love, that is, what might be understood as queer love.

In a documentary, *Making the World's First Male Sex Doll* (Vice, 2016), one of the co-owners of Sinthetics, the Los Angeles–based company featured in the film that makes the doll, states: "I don't think the English language has enough words to describe love, enough words to describe affection, enough words to describe attraction." In noting the paucity of available language about love, I am reminded that love is a social construct representing a range of available ideas that change across space and time. What stories about love circulate at any given moment in time and place, and which of these narratives have become dominant in our imagination, making it difficult to "think love" otherwise? Following Lauren Berlant, Young (2017), for example, highlighted: "The romance plot that is so central to the ways we imagine love is only 'a particular version of the story of love' but one experienced as definitive and difficult to think beyond" (p. 198). What perspectives or concepts might be useful in further constructing ideas about love, thereby potentially broadening the grid of its intelligibility? Recently, within the North American academic context, scholarship on queer love, specifically by Halperin (2019) and by Young (2017), can be read as utilizing a queer perspective in the service of generating other vocabularies about love that might be useful in moving beyond the delimited ways that we can, in language, currently imagine it (i.e., theoretically and across lived experiences). Halperin's work on queer love is situated within the context of literary analysis while Young's is taken up across literary and cinematic texts that can be read as "queering" the conventional love narrative. In my own work here, I utilize some of Halperin's and Young's more general theoretical strokes or reflections about queer love to help inform my thinking about how queer love, formulated as queer failure, might serve as a critical lens for discussing with my students—by way of utilizing topics and texts in the sexuality studies classroom that might be written off as "silly" or unimportant—how love has been circumscribed around certain normative attachments (e.g., love between humans rather than between humans and dolls or, as I discuss in more detail below, between humans and balloons), as well as constructed around heteronormative timelines of "success" in relation to love, romance, and reproduction.

In "Queer Love," Halperin (2019) explained that "love's queerness has to do with those features of love that seem to resist sociality, that defy the form of the couple and other kinds of social bonds—such as love's random vagaries, its weird or unexpected intensities, its obscure objects, uncertain aims, unsystematic pleasures, and nonsensical desires" (p. 419). These different features of queer love suggest that something approximating so-called normal love (itself a construction) would include opposite features, such as straightforward (pun intended) or intelligible objects, certain or predictable aims, logical or common-sense desires, and more. In that queer love seems to fall outside of the "charmed circle" (Rubin, 1993) of love's "normal" features and attachments, one might consider it a form of "failed" love. Indeed, as Halperin noted, queer love is "love that is socially inapt, that threatens, rejects, ignores, or simply fails to correspond with established forms of social life" (2019, p. 397). Queer love, however, can be understood as "productive" failure, that is, formulated as a critical concept that might offer significant pedagogical pathways for exploring with students how various features associated with normal or normalized love are always constructed in relation to features of love that are otherized. Indeed, as an obvious example, heterosexual love as normal love has only made "sense" by constructing homosexual love as abnormal. In addition, however, to providing a critical optic on processes of normalization, queer love as queer failure might provide the conditions for imagining other, noninstitutionalized forms of love with greater or different rewards. In short, queer love as queer failure could allow us opportunities "to escape the punishing norms that discipline behavior and manage human development with the goal of delivering us from unruly childhoods to orderly and predictable adulthoods" (Halberstam, 2011, p. 3). In this way, knowledge production about queer love's failure can be viewed as contributing to discourses on "queer negativity," particularly discourses that frame queerness as a "horizon imbued with potentiality" (Muñoz, 2009, p. 1).

Regarding the production of discourses on queer negativity, of which queer failure is an example, Halberstam (IPAK Centar, 2014) explained his own work as "very deliberately setting out to name a subject position, a political agenda, and a form of critique that is radically dissenting, grounded in refusal, and explicitly queer." Indeed, in *The Queer Art of Failure*, Halberstam's (2011) conceptualization of queer failure functions as a language of critique and possibility, a counterhegemonic discourse that critically explores "ways of being and knowing that stand outside of conventional understandings of success" (p. 2), especially in relation to how success is often tied to "forms of reproductive maturity combined with wealth accumulation" (p. 2) within a heteronormative, capitalist society. In this way, Halberstam differentiates his own work on queer negativity from accounts, such as Edelman's (2004) "no future" formulation of queer negativity, that may be characterized as lacking or withdrawing from a transformative project. Halberstam examined the potential criticality that becomes accessible within "the queer art of failure" by turning to the "silly" archive of animated films because such an archive, as he explained, "allows me to make claims for alternatives that are markedly different from the claims that are made in relation to high cultural archives" (2011, p. 20). In a similar way, and for similar reasons, I'm interested in the critical perspectives that open up or become available about the social construction of "normal love" by taking up silly, weird, or discarded topics about love, that is, by examining texts that can be read as examples of queer love formulated as queer failure, that enable other, "queer," imaginaries about love to emerge. To cite Foucault (2003) again, it's these types of "knowledges from below" (p. 7), these "other" epistemologies that emerge across unusual or silly texts and, importantly, the critical reading practices they enable, that I take to mean what Halberstam (2011) referred to as "low theory . . . as a kind of theoretical model that flies below the radar, that is assembled from eccentric texts and examples and that refuses to confirm the hierarchies of knowing that maintain the high in high theory" (p. 16).

In an undergraduate course I regularly teach, "Introduction to Sexuality Studies," my students and I examine a broad range of written and visual texts with the general goal of exploring the notion of the social construction of sexuality, that is, the sociocultural and political dynamics related to sexuality. As part of the curriculum, we discuss various kink and fetish subcultures and practices. A number of years ago, while searching for new materials to add to the course, I stumbled across a documentary series produced by National Geographic, *Taboo* (Ives et al., 2012). The series, which is available for online streaming via Amazon's Prime Video platform, consists of several seasons and, within each season, multiple episodes. In Season 3, one of the episodes (Episode 10), "Strange Passions," features a segment about what the narrator of the segment described as "a subculture of balloon lovers known as 'Looners'" (Ives et al., 2012). The segment specifically highlighted the stories of two different looners. I was originally interested in this segment because, at the time, I had never heard of looners and wondered if my students had and what they would think about this subculture. Thus, I added this segment of the documentary to the kink and fetishes part of my syllabus and proceeded to discuss it with my students, primarily focusing in our discussions on the role of education in helping to reduce the stigma that some fetish communities or subcultures experience. Indeed, a part of the documentary that my students and I honed in on were the reflections offered by a sociology professor in the segment, who noted that: "People are afraid to be ostracized. They're afraid of discrimination and prejudice and there's also an internalized shame that a lot of people have because they've consistently been told there's something wrong with them for engaging in these behaviors" (Ives et al., 2012). Working toward collective understanding in the service of reducing stigmatization seemed like a laudable enough pedagogical goal, so at the time I left it at that. Several years passed before I showed the film again.

Recently, while rewatching the documentary on looners in preparing to show it again to my students, I was reading scholarship on the subject of queer love by Halperin (2019) and Young (2013, 2017). Around the same time, I was also rereading Halberstam's (2011) work on queer failure for research I was doing on another topic. As I watched again the specific segment about 27-year-old Dave Collins, one of the two looners featured in the documentary, I began to consider how his "strange passion" might be reformulated as queer love. After all, Collins himself used the word *love*, noting: "How I really feel about balloons, it's very passionate, very deep. I have this real, true love for them. . . . When you think about it in a real, true love sense, it really isn't a toy. I know I have nonsexual, romantic love for a balloon" (Ives et al., 2012). Appending the word *queer* to love to describe Collins' form of love makes more sense than describing it as a "strange passion" if we consider that a critical usage of queer denotes, to cite Warner's (1993) now-famous phrase, "resistance to regimes of the normal" (p. xxvi). Indeed, queer love seemed to me a more apt description of the kinds of hegemonic social forms of love that Collins's love was moving away from or beyond. In this way, Young (2017) explained: "Queer love is love that challenges (rather than ratifying) existing forms of sexual and social legitimacy—love that takes an unexpected or deviant form, that appears in unconventional contexts, that produces a shocking or scandalous outcome, that expresses itself in unacceptable ways, or that impels the lover to depart from feelings, social arrangements, or styles of life deemed normal" (p. 197). In other words, queer love can be understood as an example of queer failure, where failure constitutes a form of critical praxis—a critical pedagogy and epistemology that "lurks behind those activities that have been awarded the term failure" (Halberstam, 2011, p. 92), in this instance, a queer way of life (and "failed" form of love) that not only illuminates the construction of "regimes of the normal" around love, but also, potentially, in its very inventiveness, creates the conditions for continuing to imagine or live out queer(er) forms of love that exceed institutionalized forms, thus "inspire[ing], perhaps, an ethos of experimentation in art as much as in life" (Young, 2017, p. 209).

## QUEER LOVE IN THE CURRICULUM (PINAR'S NARRATIVE)

Sex is queer,[1] a matter of polymorphous perversity—as Freud knew a century ago[2]—but love not so much.[3] Like sexual desire it also is universal,[4] and like sexual desire it is experienced within and expressed to particular persons, with particular psyches, souls, and bodies, each of us embedded in specific cultures and historical situations. Like sexual desire, love can be experienced and expressed in what sometimes seems an infinity of ways, from tough to tender and all in-between points. Of course, the two merge—maybe especially in youth, ah romantic love—but for many men[5] not inevitably or always. Damon R. Young (2013, p. 15) allowed that: "There is a love, somehow distinct from and irreducible to sex and its figures."[6] Thankfully, as there are situations where sex and love ought not combine, as the incest taboo affirms. While God's love may be the archetype for many, for the secular parental love may be the source of any sense we have of love's unconditionality. While few parents avoid making their love on occasion conditional, few—one hopes—love only conditionally. Knowing that love is—ought to be—unconditional, even nontransactional, came from somewhere.

Sex can be casual, love never. Sex can be political; it can be a pastime, even an addiction. Even so, love is the more powerful—I know, that's claiming a lot given how horny the young ones can be. Love is what each of us not only wants but also must have. Yes, sex too, but one can survive without sex if need be. Love not. It's like oxygen for the heart. If one can control one's behavior, a sexless life is conceivable.[7] A loveless life is another matter. One can live without sex but not without love. Sex is worldly, love not necessarily. Love feels transcendent—God again—and can exist even when sex is prohibited. When the two are fused, fucking is out of this world.

Queer love in education brings me back to the incest taboo. In other eras—ah, the ancient Greeks, even in Foucault's time (although the backlash is well underway[8])—the strict separation of sex from teaching was not always obligatory. But in our prudish period, teachers—whatever their sexual identity—better keep their distance from kids of any age. The institution where I work calls it conflict of interest, a legalistic phrase and rightly so, as the consequences can quickly become legal. I keep my distance all right, keeping my office door open whenever (especially young male) students meet me there. Better to meet on Zoom, as even the homophobic appear to relax when I'm not actually there. (Yes, I've a specific student in mind.) As for love, that could be cool, as long as the noun isn't modified by "romantic" or "queer." Infamously, Freud thought that the "best teachers are the real homosexuals,"[9] an accusation obviously false empirically but in homosocial[10] terms a theoretical point well taken. In that homosocial sense, all men are gay (as my husband insists), a conclusion one might also reach from Simpson's insightful study of sport[11] or Herdt's study of the Sambia.[12]

In an essay on queer love David Halperin (2019) kept our minoritarian identity intact while mixing sex and love, not conflating them, but skipping from one to the other, on occasion subsuming the one within the other. "Passion, eroticism, love" were strung together by Halperin when love can lift us—especially queer teachers—above (or around) the first two (p. 399). The case can be made that love starts before sex,[13] learned as infants from our caretakers, often our mothers or another woman, although men are evidently increasingly involved. Halperin followed Foucault, determined to make what gay men experience as special and "new" somehow sidestepping institutional formations,[14] even asocial (after Bersani), always political (invoking Hocquenghem and Foucault).[15] Sex and love between men are special all right, but they are also special and "new" for straight, bisexual, and trans people. When Halperin (2019) wrote of "love's random vagaries, its weird or unexpected intensities, its obscure objects, uncertain aims, unsystematic pleasures, and nonsensical desires," surely he's thinking of sexual desire not love, as the former can be anonymous and with groups while with latter tends to be quite focused, even when it's love of country (p. 419). I'm in love with *you*. Pleasures follow, sexual and nonsexual. Sexual desire (of whatever stripe) doesn't always observe social niceties, but love can be quite observant of social forms, from holding hands to going to dinner with other couples, never mind marriage and raising children. Halperin (2019, p. 399) is wrong when he wrote "such love"—he's referencing queer love but he means gay male sexual desire—resists integration into "sanitized" society. That's precisely what has happened to us: thank god. Gay, lesbian, and trans couples are totally routine in several societies: That's how capitalism works; it incorporates anything subversive into commodities to be consumed. Capitalism compels obsession with the "new," including in academic life, evident when Halperin (2019)— still discussing Foucault—wrote "queer love entail[s] new modes of conduct" (p. 401). Really? Nothing could be more ancient than love and sex between men, as that Leviticus passage makes clear: After all, one doesn't prohibit what's not happening. Since time immemorial men have loved and had sex with each other, as they have loved and had sex with women and children. With sex, anatomy has everything to do with it, but with love not necessarily. Love does not always—again, often ought not (in the case of children—and students I say)—eroticize. Sex is socialized (e.g., compulsory heterosexuality), but love not so much. Love takes time, comes from the heart, is not necessarily an expression of desire. Falling in love is a romantic phenomenon, as much to do with desire as with love. Love is decentered and often unconditional. After 26 years—how long my husband and I have been together—sex and love can separate. The fact that love remains long after lust fades requires one to acknowledge the two were always at least a little distinct. Having slept with more fine-looking young men than I can count during my (earlier) gay life, I know—always knew—that lust was the consolation prize.[16] Love never is. There are guys you fuck, and guys you keep, that is, "keepers," and the two can be but are not always the same guys.

Yes, love between men (and between women and women, between men and women) is "intense" but not necessarily "uncodified" (Halperin, 2019, p. 400). We men know their "codes," part of the reason why love (and war) between men can be so easy: We often understand each other exactly. Not only "homosociality"[17] follows. None of this constitutes "counter-conduct" (Halperin, 2019, p. 400) except possibly when sexualized and then only to hypocrites and inhuman others (often trapped in institutionalized religions with their psychotic fundamentalisms). Homophobia is precisely that—fear of one's repressed homosexual desire—projected as a "threat" that gay men might find happiness and express their good fortune in public (Halperin, 2019, p. 403).[18] Halperin (2019, p. 404) thinks that unless marriage is queered it won't work for gay men, ignoring that marriage between a man and a woman doesn't work so well either, a fact many attempt to contradict by emphasizing ritual, roles, and tradition. Only strong socialization or commitment can contradict the tensions that can arise when two people—however much they love and/or sexually desire each other—try to make a life together. All the clichés about married life convey just how queer marriage is—never mind the divorce rate. Moreover, recall that men are involved in both gay and straight marriage. Many men can separate sex from love and notoriously do; gay marriages are hardly the only kind that can be "open." Men cheat on their wives constantly; I've slept with more than a few myself.

Halperin pronounced the "lonely, thankless, and inexpressible nature of love, whether romantic or parental" (2019, p. 408).[19] One may love alone but love's not lonely, as love is quite the companion in itself. Nor is love thankless; it is its own reward. Even when bottled up inside, it can, yes, exceed expression, certainly in words—I love you more than I can say—so one finds nonlinguistic and indirect ways to communicate, from keeping the ice tray filled for his cocktail hour to smiling at his then-inebriated efforts to be amusing. Such signs not only acknowledge the "poverty of expression" (Halperin, 2019, p. 413),[20] as my husband gets it. I can't imagine life without him.

Gay men, lesbians, transgender—queer (including straight and bisexual)—people remain at risk, even in the United States and Canada, but then so is everybody. Everyone will be as long as humanity is capable of inhumanity, something not so easily educated out of our makeup. Overall, at least in those two countries, queer people are no longer victims on a mass scale, no longer sexual renegades. As Damon R. Young (2013) noted: "Queer (or rather gay) love, then, has achieved visibility . . . at the paradoxical cost of its own absorption into a universal for which it now valiantly stands as an exemplary model" (p. 14).[21] Not sure how "valiant" our love is, but "absorbed" is surely right: Now we're in TV retirement ads for god's sake.[22] That's one price we pay for such "normalization"—sole possession of the term *queer*.[23] We're not so queer anymore. We never were, actually. That was what was mistaken about the appellation in the first place, that and the hatred behind it.[24] And "straight" people were never not queer. Given the down-low[25] and the too-often nasty politics of heterosexual relationships,[26] so-called straight people could be considered queerer than we are. Yes: "Love [is] something somehow distinct from sex, less punctual, less decisive, less insistent, more fragile, more difficult to figure, and more durational, if not enduring" (Young, 2013, p. 21).

We gay men don't own love. No one does. All of us—gay, straight, bisexual, transgender—seek someone to love. That same someone may be the same person we desire sexually, but not necessarily. "Queer love" in education? Keep it confined to the curriculum. Sit alongside Halperin: study poems lamenting and celebrating love in all its forms, including sexual ones. The distinctions and confluences between love and sexual desire? Clearly a topic for courses in philosophy, social studies, health. Its variability of feeling and expression? Enter anthropology and history. Science has to be in there somewhere—oh yes, that gay gene—but it is history[27] that strikes me as knowledge of most worth. Only then can students see how specific and universal love is.

## CONCLUDING THOUGHTS

The category queer, and more generally queer studies, continues to be productively deployed, that is, articulated to any number of other concepts, topics, bodies of knowledge, social, cultural, and political histories, national contexts, and more. In short, as a language of critique, as well as a language of hope and possibility, queer remains a "wild thing" (Halberstam, 2020), scattering promiscuously in numerous directions across a wide range of contexts while being picked up, however momentarily, as a critical resource for informing any number of projects committed to engaging with forms of queer critical praxis. In this way, as we highlighted at the start of our chapter, a "grounding" tenet of queer (studies) has been "not to presume ahead of time what methods or objects might constitute a queer project" (Somerville, 2020, p. 6), that is, not to delineate in advance queer's proper objects of study (Berlant & Warner, 1995). "Confluences" (Somerville, 2020, p. 7) between queer (studies) and various theoretical perspectives and concepts continue to expand or rework the terrain of "queer's proper objects" and attachments, resulting in the production of new knowledge formations, that is, the production of "distinct areas of inquiry in their own right" (Somerville, 2020, p. 7). McCann and Monaghan (2020) noted, for example, the vibrant knowledge production that's been generated by way of critical intersections

> between queer theory and Critical Race Studies which produced Black Queer Studies and queer analyses of race; queer theory's geopolitical turn, focused on issues including migration and diaspora; queer Indigenous studies; queer theory's ontological turn, focused on issues including materiality, affect, and a turn away from representation; intersections between Marxism and queer theory; and deployments of disability studies with queer theory. (p. 8)

Furthermore, as Amin (2020) explained, the concept queer is also being linked to or rooted in alternative founding genealogies of the field of queer theory/studies in ways that reveals not only "the element of chance that allowed certain theoretical schools to become central to the field" (p. 17), but also, for example, center, following Love's (2021) work, the "social scientific genealogy of queer theory," thus revealing "the field's occluded grounding in the critical humanities" (p. 23). In this regard, Amin (2020) further elaborated:

> Queer humanities scholarship is more likely to be classified as Queer Studies and as theory, whereas queer social science and historical scholarship is more likely to be classified as Sexuality or LGBT Studies and seen as contributing examples rather than theories. This disciplinary divide tends to reinforce the existing marginalization of work on the Asias, Latin America, and Africa in Queer Studies, given that much scholarship on sexuality in these areas is conducted within the social sciences, especially cultural anthropology. (p. 23)

We conclude with these reflections in order to highlight that the articulation of queer to that of the concept of love, and of queer love to that of education, can be understood as part of the broader contemporary theoretical, political, and pedagogical work demonstrating not only queer's ongoing myriad intersectional possibilities but also the epistemological insights that potentially become available in these intersections to unmoor the normalization of thinking about concepts like love in order to rethink and reuse them in vibrant, counterhegemonic ways, including within forms of queer critical praxis. From this perspective, as Halberstam (2011), following Gramsci, reminded us: "Queer studies offer us one method for imagining, not some fantasy of an elsewhere, but existing alternatives to hegemonic systems. What Gramsci terms 'common sense' depends heavily on the production of norms, and so the critique of dominant forms of common sense is also, in some sense, a critique of norms" (p. 89). In what ways have common sense discourses of love limited the range of intelligibility for how love might be thought or constructed otherwise; and how might the critical work of queer, particularly in its possible endless intersectional deployments, instigate new knowledge formations about queer love that radically reconfigure it as a transformative language and project across numerous contexts, including within educational theory and practice? This question at the very least suggests that the continued cultivation of queer imaginative thought might yield surprising and welcoming insights.

## NOTES

1. Referencing Sedgwick, Jagose (1996, p. 97) reminded that "despite its routine circulation as a descriptive term, queer can only be autodescriptive emphasizes the extent to which queer refers to self-identification rather than to empirical observations of other people's characteristics."
2. As my friend Peter Taubman (2011) reminded me when I shared with him the Halperin essay.
3. Damon R. Young (2017, p. 197) would seem to disagree, defining queer love as "love that is nonheterosexual or otherwise at odds with gendered norms," a conception that mixes sex and love, two phenomena that especially educators ought to keep apart. Young imagined love as even "queerer than sex" (2017, p. 198); later, he allowed that queer love is "not reducible to sexuality" (2017, p. 209).
4. No "liberal insistence," no "high-minded egalitarianism" (Young, 2013, p. 15), I am suggesting, just an empirical (for fundamentalists, an ugly and intolerable) fact. See also Young, 2017, p. 197; Ward, 2015, pp. 203–204.
5. There is no "monolithic male subject," Awkward (1995, p. 98) reminded.
6. Young is commenting on the question Luke asks Jon in *The Living End*.

7. Technically speaking, as sex goes on in the head maybe more than anywhere else. In that sense, even this old man remains sexually active.

8. https://medium.com/queertheory/foucaults-metoo-moment-a672a1d9a869

9. Quoted in Taubman, 2011, p. 4.

10. Sedgwick is the source here, for decades quoted widely to make a series of significant points about men and the often-convoluted character of their bonds with each other. "Within a patriarchal culture," Savran (1998, p. 186) pointed out, "the more intense male homosocial desire becomes, the more intensely male homosexual desire becomes stigmatized and proscribed. As Sedgwick emphasizes, this pattern has proven crucial at least since the early modern period for the maintenance of relations between men. . . . For Sedgwick, the vigilant policing of the male bond ensures that desire between men will rarely be directly expressed in (what passes for heterosexual) discourse. Rather, by means of an erotic triangle, male desire is mediated through the body of a woman whom two men profess to love." Some convert empirical fact into political potential; Derrick (1997, p. 223, n. 27) argued "that homosexuality disrupts the narcissism of male homosocial mirroring." Also citing Sedgwick, Stokes (2001, p. 18) addressed the racial nature of the homosocial bond: "White supremacy, then, can be usefully understood as a homosocial network that commodifies and appropriates the bodies of white women and black men in order to consolidate both whiteness and heterosexuality as governing ideologies, ever present abstractions, condensed forms of panic, and political structures," adding "that the homosocial may be a necessary component of any attempt to keep whiteness white, to keep whiteness pure."

11. Simpson (1994) studied much more than sport, but on that topic (and focused not on coaches but players): "Hugging, kissing, jumping on top of one another, delirious with pleasure, young men and old, express for a moment, within the sacred walls of the football ground, a love that is as exuberant and irrepressible as it is inconceivable outside those walls" (Simpson, 1994, p. 79).

12. Pinar, 2006, pp. 23–26.

13. They may start simultaneously, as Freud postulated: https://pubmed.ncbi.nlm.nih.gov/25988723/

14. Foucault was wrong when he wanted the love between men not to "resemble any of those already institutionalized" (quoted in Halperin, 2019, p. 400). Resemble these it does, made obvious by how easily (and often eagerly) gay men have slipped into institutionalized married life—never mind "tops" and "bottoms."

15. See Halperin, 2019 (p. 403, n. 14). Hocquenghem inspired my first foray into queer theory, celebrating anal eroticism while mocking the phallocentrism of macho-Marxists in my field (Pinar, 1983).

16. Young (2017, p. 200) also noted that love—as "attachment" (a rather vanilla term for love, no?)—cannot be "reduced" to lust.

17. And its "vexed relationship between the homosocial and the homosexual" (Savran, 1998, p. 73). Discussing the Beats—Burroughs, Ginsberg, Kerouac, and Cassady—Savran (1998, pp. 69–70) suggested that their "tangled and shifting homosocialities . . . not only challenge the normative male bonds of the [post–World War II] domestic revival but also dramatize a deep-seated disturbance in the relations between son and father, the subject and the Law, and the writer and the society in which he must reluctantly participate. Despite the fact that the first two figures were ostensibly homosexual and the latter two ostensibly

heterosexual, the complexity and intensity of their bonds attests to the difficulty in separating the homosexual from the homosocial."

18. Foucault seems Halperin's source here (see 2019, p. 403, n. 14). Genius that he was, even Foucault could not escape the historical moment he lived through. Neither can he—nor any of us—escape our own psychic situation. When Foucault found what to do the next morning an issue—even a political one (see that Note 14)—he was projecting. How about breakfast?

19. Halperin is here referencing Robert Hayden's poem, "Those Winter Sundays."

20. Yes, love can make us "illiterates" (Halperin, 2019, p. 416), a view disputed by Young, who asserted that "love is narrative" (2017, p. 198), but I say *all* of us, not just those who claim "queer." So-called "counter-love" (Halperin, 2019, p. 416)—by definition not love—seems grasping at straws.

21. Jane Ward (for one) declined, endorsing "defiant queer culture" (2015, p. 204). Good luck with that, Professor Ward.

22. It's summer 2021 as I write; on TV are TIAA (Teachers Insurance and Annuity Association) ads featuring an aging couple. So much for queer love being demarcated by temporality (Young, 2013, p. 15), specifically "no future."

23. Young (2017, p. 199) would seem to concur, observing that now that homosexuality is legally legitimate it is no longer queer.

24. Not only "behind" but "within" it, as homophobia internalized by those who identify as gay can be crippling. This is hardly the same as the violence—the murder—associated with *Brokeback Mountain*, but psychologically crippling all the same.

25. Ward (2015, p. 22, pp. 144–145) summarized succinctly the racialized as well as sexualized issues embedded in the term.

26. My husband and I just finished watching (yes, on Netflix) the first three seasons of *Virgin River*. No gay theme except indirectly: The unpleasantness of these heterosexual relationships—even between Mel and Jack—could turn anyone gay.

27. For years—when I was working on these topics (Pinar, 1998, 2001, 2006)—I subscribed to the *Journal of the History of Sexuality*, surely a central source for any curricular treatment of the subject: https://www.jstor.org/journal/jhistsexu

## REFERENCES

Amin, K. (2020). Genealogies of queer theory. In S. Somerville (Ed.), *The Cambridge companion to queer studies* (pp. 17–29). Cambridge University Press.

Awkward, M. (1995). *Negotiating difference: Race, gender, and the politics of positionality*. University of Chicago Press.

Berlant, L. (1997). *The queen of America goes to Washington City: Essays on sex and citizenship*. Duke University Press.

Berlant, L., & Warner, M. (1995). What does queer theory teach us about x? *PMLA, 110*(3), 343–349. http://www.jstor.org/stable/462930

Derrick, S. S. (1997). *Monumental anxieties: Homoerotic desire and feminine influence in nineteenth-century U.S. literature*. Rutgers University Press.

Edelman, L. (2004). *No future: Queer theory and the death drive*. Duke University Press.

Foucault, M. (1997). Friendship as a way of life. In P. Rabinow (Ed.), *Michel Foucault: Ethics, subjectivity, and truth* (pp. 135–140). Free Press.

Foucault, M. (2003). *Society must be defended: Lectures at the Collège de France, 1975–1976* (D. Macey, Trans.). Picador.

Halberstam, J. (2011). *The queer art of failure*. Duke University Press.

Halberstam, J. (2020). *Wild things: The disorder of desire*. Duke University Press.

Halperin, D. (2019). Queer love. *Critical Inquiry, 45*, 396–419. https://doi.org/10.1086/700993

IPAK Centar. (2014, September 5). *Jack Halberstam on queer failure, silly archives and the wild* [Video]. YouTube. https://www.youtube.com/watch?v=iKDEil7m1j8

Ives, M., Adair, J., Luscombe, J., Toni, B., Ulm, B., & Royle, D. (Producers). (2012). *Taboo season 3: Strange passions* [Video]. Amazon Prime Video. Amazon.com/primevideo

Jagose, A. (1996). *Queer theory: An introduction*. New York University Press.

Love, H. (2021). *Underdogs: Social deviance and queer theory*. University of Chicago Press.

McCann, H., & Monaghan, W. (2020). *Queer theory now: From foundations to futures*. Red Globe Press.

Muñoz, J. E. (2009). *Cruising utopia: The then and there of queer futurity*. New York University Press.

Pinar, W. F. (1983). Curriculum as gender text: Notes on reproduction, resistance, and male-male relations. *Journal of Curriculum Theorizing, 5*(1), 26–52.

Pinar, W. F. (Ed.). (1998). *Queer theory in education*. Lawrence Erlbaum Associates.

Pinar, W. F. (2001). *The gender of racial politics and violence in America: Lynching, prison rape, and the crisis of masculinity*. Peter Lang.

Pinar, W. F. (2006). *Race, religion and a curriculum of reparation*. Palgrave Macmillan.

Rasmussen, M. L., & Allen, L. (2014). What can a concept do? Rethinking education's queer assemblages. *Discourse: Studies in the Cultural Politics of Education, 35*(3), 433–443. https://doi.org/10.1080/01596306.2014.888846

Rodriguez, N. M. (2019). Michel Foucault and queer ascesis: Toward a pedagogy and politics of subversive friendships. In D. L. Carlson & N. M. Rodriguez (Eds.), *Michel Foucault and sexualities and genders in education: Friendship as ascesis* (pp. 139–153). Palgrave Macmillan. https://doi.org/10.1007/978-3-030-31737-9_10

Rubin, G. (1993). Thinking sex: Notes for a radical theory of the politics of sexuality. In H. Abelove, M. A. Barale, & D. M. Halperin (Eds.), *The lesbian and gay studies reader* (pp. 3–44). Routledge.

Savran, D. (1998). *Taking it like a man: White masculinity, masochism, and contemporary American culture*. Princeton University Press.

Simpson, M. (1994). *Male impersonators: Men performing masculinity*. Routledge.

Somerville, S. B. (2020). Introduction. In S. Somerville (Ed.), *The Cambridge companion to queer studies* (pp. 1–13). Cambridge University Press.

Stokes, M. (2001). *The color of sex: Whiteness, heterosexuality, and the fictions of White supremacy*. Duke University Press.

Taubman, P. M. (2011). *Disavowed knowledge: Psychoanalysis, education, and teaching*. Routledge.

Vice. (2016, October 20). *Making the world's first male sex doll* [Video]. YouTube. https://www.youtube.com/watch?v=GKFHZuCvvS4

Ward, J. (2015). *Not gay: Sex between straight white men*. New York University Press.

Warner, M. (1993). Introduction. In M. Warner (Ed.), *Fear of a queer planet: Queer politics and social theory* (pp. vii–xxxi). University of Minnesota Press.

Young, D. R. (2013). *The Living End*, or love without a future. In P. Demory & C. Pullen (Eds.), *Queer love in film and television: Critical essays* (pp. 13–22). Palgrave Macmillan.

Young, D. R. (2017). Queer love. In J. C. Nash (Ed.), *Gender: Love* (pp. 197–210). Macmillan Interdisciplinary Handbooks.

# INDEX

*For the benefit of digital users, indexed terms that span two pages (e.g., 52–53) may, on occasion, appear on only one of those pages.*

Tables and figures are indicated by *t* and *f* following the page number

abstinence only movement, 201–2
*Adventures of Priscilla, Queen of the Desert, The*, 243
Africa, "pro-family" countermovement in eastern and southern, 195–97, 212–13
   abstinence only movement, 201–2
   attacks on Comprehensive Sexuality Education, 203–6
   campaign to stop Comprehensive Sexuality Education, 206–10
   and geopoliticization of gender and sexuality, 210–11
   and need for Comprehensive Sexuality Education, 201–3
   research methodology, 199–201
   theoretical framework, 197–99
Ahmed, Sarah, 337–38, 343–44, 345–46
Amin, K., 361
Angeconeb, Garnet, 149–50
antidiscrimination paradigm, moving away from, 56–61
Aoteaora, New Zealand, 189–90
   characteristics of queer theory-informed practice in education, 184–86
   children's storytelling and support of children's narratives, 185–89
   deploying queer theory in education research, 176–80

development of early childhood education, 180–81
early childhood teaching in, 175–76
graduate education studies in, 68–72
heteronormativity, and early childhood education, 177–79
Maori culture and practices, 181–83
Ministry of Education Guidelines and suggested strategies, 188–89
queer-minded educational reform, 183–84
*See also* photo elicitation, and exploring campus experiences of LGBTQA+ students
aspiration, and graduate education, 71–72
assemblage, and German educational institutions, 81–95
   assemblage, definition and introduction of, 84–85
   education as an assemblage, 82–83
   and life course theory, 83–94
   social assemblage, 84–85, 88
assemblages, school sport and physical education, 218–20
AusQueerScreen study, 235–37
   *See also* LGBTQ film and television stories

banal nationalism, 300–1, 305
Berlant, L., 49

binaries, sexual and gender, 100

Black femininity
and nonsexual queerness, 32–33

*Black Skin, White Masks* (Fanon), 29–30, 31–32

Brazil, gender visibility and school marching bands, 156–59
and antioppressive practices, 170–71
disrupting gender roles, 164–67
diversity along Bolivian border, 161–64
gender expectations, 163
queer students and school safety, 161–63
reimagining identities, 160–61
social recognition from marching bands, 167–70

Brockenbrough, Edward, 83–84

business management education, 99–100
acknowledging queered failure, 105–6
exposing and challenging heteronormativity, 100
history of, 100–1
queered failure, 103–5
and queer pedagogy, 107–11
teaching evaluations, 107–9
women in, 101–2
workplace diversity and inclusivity, 108–9
workplace homophobia, 109

Butler, A. H., 274

Butler, Judith, 57–58, 60
gender performativity, 73–74
identity construction, 239–40
and norm-critical theory, 299–300
subjectivities, 178–79

Canadian Indian residential schools, decolonial analysis of photographs from, 138–39, 152–53
and decolonial queer theory, definitions and approaches, 139–42
decolonial queer theory and praxis, intersecting principles in, 140–41
gender binary dominance, 149–50
heteronormativity and gender regulation, 144–46

history of schools, 142–46
research process, 146–51
residual effects of school system, 143–44
resistance and refusal, 150–51
spatial dimensions of oppression, 148–49
Truth and Reconciliation Commission (TRC), 145–46
and Two-Spirit Indigenous people, 141–42

Care of Children Act of 2004, in New Zealand, 183–84

Carr, R., 36

Chancellor Hall, and Jamaican political elites, 37–39

Chapman, D. D., 102–3

"charmed circle," of sexuality, 119

children
and addressing homophobia in schools, 56–58
children's storytelling and support of children's narratives, 185–89
sexuality of, 52–56

children, gender-diverse
happenstance, and reimagining gender normativity, 345–47

children, gender-diverse and trans
ambiguities around gender identity, 341
emotions and temporality, 337–38
gender normativity, linear temporal paths to, 338–42
parents and children's fantasies of the future, 342–45
and temporality, 335–36
timelines and pathways of childhood development, 333–35

cisheteronormativity
cisheteronormative assumptions, 313
in context of university campus, 313, 314–15
definition of, 312–13

cisnormativity
definition of, 312

Civil Union Act of 2004, in New Zealand, 183–84

Collier, John, 316

colonial racialization, and "coding" of spaces, 31

Comprehensive Sexuality Education
(CSE), and "pro-family"
countermovement, 195–97, 212–13
abstinence only movement, 201–2
attacks on CSE in eastern and
southern Africa, 203–6
campaign to stop CSE, 206–10
and geopoliticization of gender and
sexuality, 210–11
need for CSE in southern and eastern
Africa, 201–3
research methodology, 199–201
theoretical framework, 197–99
CORE process and research
methodology, 120–24, 121t
create, 120–21
establish, 123–24
obtain, 122
reflect, 123
Crath, R., 31–32
Creed, Barbara, 237–38
Crenshaw, Kimberlé, 84
Cruz, C., 262–63
cultural pedagogies, and screen
media, 237–41
curriculum, and management
education, 107–11

dance, and physical education
pedagogy, 224
Davies, Bronwyn, 178–79
decolonial queer analysis, intersecting
principles in theory and
praxis, 140–41
decolonial queer analysis, of
photographs from Canadian
Indian residential schools, 138–
39, 152–53
decolonial queer theory, definitions
and approaches, 139–42
gender binary dominance, 149–50
heteronormativity and gender
regulation, 144–46
history of schools, 142–46
research process, 146–51
residual effects of school
system, 143–44
resistance and refusal, 150–51
spatial dimensions of
oppression, 148 49

Truth and Reconciliation Commission
(TRC), 145–46
and Two-Spirit Indigenous
people, 141–42
Deleuze, Gilles, 84–85
Diamond, L. M., 59
disidentification, 83–84
*Downriver*, 243–44
Dyer, H., 55

early childhood teaching, queer activism
and, 175–76, 189–90
characteristics of, 184–86
children's storytelling and support of
children's narratives, 185–89
deploying queer theory in education
research, 176–80
development of early childhood
education, 180–81
and heteronormativity, 177–79
New Zealand Ministry of Education
Guidelines and suggested
strategies, 188–89
queer-minded educational
reform, 183–84
re-forming queer, 181–83
Edelman, L., 336
educational research, queer of color
critique in, 254–56, 265–66
critique components, 258–59
fostering agency among queer
students of color, 263–64
implications for research, 264–65
queer theory, separatist *versus*
integrationist narrative, 256–58
research methodology, 260–61
resistance and agency among queer
youth, 261–63
scholarly body of critique, 259–60
*Epistemology of the Closet*
(Sedgwick), 257

failure, queer readings of, 71
*See also* queered failure, and
management education
faith schools
relationships and sex education (RSE),
guidance for, 51–52
families and parents
and sexuality of children, 53–56

*Index*  [369]

families and parents (*cont.*)
single parents and parental
binaries, 72–75
Fanon, Frantz, and zone of nonbeing,
29–33, 42–43
femininity
and nonsexual queerness, 32–33
femonationalism, 300–1, 305
Ferguson, Roderick A., 83–84, 258
film and television stories, 234–36, 251
*Adventures of Priscilla, Queen of the
Desert, The,* 243
AusQueerScreen study, 235–37
cultural pedagogies, 237–41
*Downriver,* 243–44
entertainment *versus*
information, 245–48
role models and representation
in, 248–51
screen production pedagogies, 242–45
Foucault, M., 178–79, 188–89, 223–24
fragmented citizenship, 86–87

gay and lesbian visibility, eras of, 276–77
Gedro, J., 102–3
gender
geopoliticization of, 210–11
school sport and physical education
assemblages, 218–20
and sexualities in physical
education, 221–22
gender, and parental constructs, 73–74
gender-diverse children, in primary
schools
ambiguities around gender
identity, 341
emotions and temporality, 337–38
gender normativity, linear temporal
paths to, 338–42
happenstance, and reimagining gender
normativity, 345–47
parents and children's fantasies of the
future, 342–45
and temporality, 335–36
timelines and pathways of childhood
development, 333–35
gender expectations, and school
marching bands, 163
gender normativity, linear temporal
paths to, 338–42

gender regulation, and
heteronormativity in Canadian
Indian residential schools, 144–
46, 149–50
gender roles, disrupting in school
marching bands, 164–67
gender visibility, and school marching
bands in Brazil, 156–59
antioppressive practices, 170–71
disrupting gender roles, 164–67
diversity along Bolivian border, 161–64
gender expectations, 163
reimagining identities, 160–61
social recognition from marching
bands, 167–70
geopoliticization, of gender and
sexuality, 210–11
Ghaziani, A, 276–77
Giddings, L., 102–3
Gilbert, Jen, 60
Giroux, Henry, 237–38
graduate education studies, queer theory
in, 65–66, 75–77
and aspiration, 71–72
doctoral education, case studies
of, 68–72
failure, queer readings of, 71
and gendered parental
constructs, 73–74
and gendered parental norms, 74–75
and parental binaries, 72–75
postgraduate education
research, 67–68
Grosfoguel, R., 31
Guattari, Fêlix, 84–85

Halberstam, J., 100, 104–5
*The Queer Art of Failure,* 354–55
temporality, 335–36
trans and gender-diverse
children, 333–34
Halperin, David M., 350–51, 354
Hames-Garcia, Michael, 257, 272
happenstance
happiness as, 337–38
role in reimagining gender
normativity, 345–47
heteronormativity
assimilation as
heteronormative, 282–83

critical engagement with, 1–4
definition of, 312
and early childhood
    education, 177–79
and gender regulation in Canadian
    Indian residential schools, 144–46
and management education, 100–3
queer theoretical critique of, 272–74
of schools as institutions, 49
heteronormativity, and German
    educational institutions, 81–95
fragmented citizenship, 86–87
"hidden" curriculum, 89–90
and life course analysis, 85–86
microaggressions, 92–94
shame, experiences of, 92
stigma consciousness, 91–92
theoretical approaches to
    understanding, 81–83
heterosexism, in higher
    education, 118–19
"hidden" curriculum, and German
    educational institutions, 89–90
higher education, personal and
    professional identity in, 115–16
and "charmed circle" of sexuality, 119
CORE process and research
    methodology, 120–24, 121t
experiences of professional
    identity, 124–26
implications for higher
    education, 133–34
intersecting identities, 127–29
queer experiences of
    professionalism, 118–24
research findings and
    discussion, 124–32
research methods, 119–24
social construction of
    identity, 116–18
higher education, using queer theory in,
    67–68, 75–77
and aspiration, 71–72
doctoral education, case studies
    of, 68–72
failure, queer readings of, 71
and gendered parental
    constructs, 73–74
and gendered parental norms, 74–75
and parental binaries, 72–75

homonationalism, 300–1, 305
homonormativity
assimilation as
    homonormative, 282–83
assimilationist *versus* queer
    liberationist perspective, 273
queer theoretical critique of, 272–74
homophobia
institutional *versus* internalized, 274
homophobia, addressing in
    schools, 56–61
human resource development, 99–111
exposing and challenging
    heteronormativity, 100, 102–3
workplace diversity and
    inclusivity, 108–9
workplace homophobia, 109

identity, personal and
    professional, 115–16
"charmed circle" of sexuality, 119
CORE process and research
    methodology, 120–24, 121t
experiences of professional
    identity, 124–26
implications for higher
    education, 133–34
intersecting identities, 127–29
queer experiences of
    professionalism, 118–24
research findings and
    discussion, 124–32
research methods, 119–24
separating identities, 129–34
social construction of, 116–18
identity, queer as, 67
indigenous populations, and Canadian
    Indian residential schools, 138–
    39, 152–53
decolonial queer theory, definitions
    and approaches, 139–42
decolonial queer theory and praxis,
    intersecting principles in, 140–41
gender binary dominance, 149–50
heteronormativity and gender
    regulation, 144–46
history of schools, 142–46
research process, 146–51
residual effects of school
    system, 143–44

*Index* [371]

indigenous populations, and Canadian Indian residential schools (*cont.*)
  resistance and refusal, 150–51
  spatial dimensions of oppression, 148–49
  Truth and Reconciliation Commission (TRC), 145–46
  and Two-Spirit Indigenous people, 141–42
International Olympic Committee, gender and sexuality assemblages, 218–20
intersectional identities, and resistance and agency among queer youth, 261–62
intersectionality
  definition and limitations, 84
  transgender migrants, 87–88, 90–91

Jagose, A., 139–40
Jamaica, and student housing at University of West Indies
  and articulation of national identity, 36–37
  Chancellor Hall, and Jamaican political elites, 37–39
  history of practices, 27–29
  Mary Seacole Hall, 39
  queer students, lived experiences of, 33–42
  Taylor Hall, 40
  UWI Security Act, and arrest and detention of students, 33–36
  and zones of nonbeing, 29–33
Johnson, K., 261–62
Johnson, L. P., 262–63

Kelly-Ware, J., 185–86
Kumashiro, K., 259–60

Lenskyj, H. J., 224–25
lesbian and gay visibility, eras of, 276–77
lesbian identity, and management education, 102–3
Lewis, R. A., 36
LGBTQA+ students, exploring campus experiences of, 311–12, 328–29
  cisheteronormativity, 312–13
  exclusion, photo portfolio and scenario, 324–28, 326f

inclusivity, photo portfolio and scenario, 318–24, 319f, 320f
  photo elicitation, definition of, 316
  posthomophobic world, discourse of, 313–14
  research participants and methodology, 315–18, 317f
LGBTQ film and television stories, 234–36, 251
  *Adventures of Priscilla, Queen of the Desert, The*, 243
  AusQueerScreen study, 235–37
  cultural pedagogies, 237–41
  *Downriver*, 243–44
  entertainment *versus* information, 245–48
  role models and representation in, 248–51
  screen production pedagogies, 242–45
LGBTQ youth, and queer of color critique in educational research, 254–56, 265–66
  critique components, 258–59
  fostering agency among queer students of color, 263–64
  implications for research, 264–65
  queer theory, separatist *versus* integrationist narrative, 256–58
  research methodology, 260–61
  resistance and agency among youth, 261–63
  scholarly body of critique, 259–60
life course theory, and German educational institutions, 83–94
Lugones, Maria, 210

*Making the World's First Male Sex Doll*, 353–54
management education, 99–111
  acknowledging queered failure, 105–6
  exposing and challenging heteronormativity, 100
  history of, 100–1
  queered failure, 103–5
  and queer pedagogy, 107–11
  teaching evaluations, 107–9
  women in, 101–2
  workplace diversity and inclusivity, 108–9
  workplace homophobia, 109

Manalansan, Martin, 83–84
marching bands, and social recognition
  in Brazil, 156–59
  diversity along Bolivian
    border, 161–64
  reimagining identities, 160–61
Martinsson, L., 301–2
Mary Seacole Hall, and student housing
  at University of West Indies, 39
McCann, H., 360–61
McQuarrie, F. A. E., 102–3
Meshoe, Kenneth, 207–8
microaggressions, and German
  educational institutions, 92–94
migrants, and heteronormativity in
  German schools, 81–83, 85–86
  and discourse around
    heteronormativity and transphobia
    in migrant communities, 90–91
Ministry of Education Guidelines, New
  Zealand, 188–89
Mizzi, Robert, 84–85
Monaghan, W., 360–61
Muñoz, José Esteban, 83–84, 104–5

Naidoo, Errol, 206–7
nationality and nationalism, norms
  regarding, 300–1
neoliberalism, cultural dimensions
  of, 13–15
New Zealand, Aoteaora, 189–90
  characteristics of queer
    theory-informed practice in
    education, 184–86
  children's storytelling and support of
    children's narratives, 185–89
  deploying queer theory in education
    research, 176–80
  development of early childhood
    education, 180–81
  early childhood teaching in, 175–76
  graduate education studies
    in, 68–72
  heteronormativity, and early
    childhood education, 177–79
  Maori culture and practices, 181–83
  Ministry of Education Guidelines and
    suggested strategies, 188–89
  queer-minded educational
    reform, 183–84

See also photo elicitation, and
  exploring campus experiences of
  LGBTQA+ students
nonsexual queerness, female body
  and, 32–33
normativities, assimilation or
  transgression of, 274–77
norm-critical pedagogy, 296–97
  emergent norms, 304–6
  and hegemonic norm-critical theory
    and practice, 306–7
  nationality and nationalism, norms
    regarding, 300–1
  norm-critical theory and queer theory,
    299–301
  practices and aims of, 297–98
Norm-Struggles (Martinsson &
  Reimers), 301–2
Norway, gender and sexuality norms, 302

Olympic Games, gender and sexuality
  assemblages, 218–20
oppression
  antioppressive practices, 170–71
  spatial dimensions of, 148–49

parasocial relationships, in screen
  media, 250
parental binaries, single parents
  and, 72–75
parents and families
  and sexuality of children, 53–56
Pereira, P, 141
personal and professional identity, in
  higher education, 115–16
  "charmed circle" of sexuality, 119
  CORE process and research
    methodology, 120–24, 121t
  experiences of professional
    identity, 124–26
  implications for higher
    education, 133–34
  intersecting identities, 127–29
  queer experiences of
    professionalism, 118–24
  research findings and
    discussion, 124–32
  research methods, 119–24
  separating identities, 129–34
  social construction of, 116–18

photo elicitation, and exploring campus experiences of LGBTQA+ students, 311–12, 328–29
cisheteronormativity, 312–13
definition of photo elicitation, 316
exclusion, participant portfolio and scenario, 324–28
exclusion, photo portfolio and scenario, 326f
inclusivity, participant portfolio and scenario, 318–24, 319f, 320f
posthomophobic world, discourse of, 313–14
research participants and methodology, 315–18, 317f
physical education, 217–18, 229–30
experience of diverse sexualities in, 225–26
and gender and sexuality assemblages, 218–20
genders and sexualities in, 221–22
narrative of diverse sexualities in, 226–29
progressive ways of viewing spaces in, 222–26
Pink, Sarah, 148
politics, queer as, 67
posthomophobic world, discourse of, 313–14
practice, queer as a, 67
Pringle, J., 102–3
"pro-family" countermovement in southern and eastern Africa, 195–97, 212–13
abstinence only movement, 201–2
attacks on Comprehensive Sexuality Education, 203–6
campaign to stop Comprehensive Sexuality Education, 206–10
and geopoliticization of gender and sexuality, 210–11
and need for Comprehensive Sexuality Education, 201–3
research methodology, 199–201
theoretical framework, 197–99
professional and personal identity, in higher education, 115–16
"charmed circle" of sexuality, 119
CORE process and research methodology, 120–24, 121t

experiences of professional identity, 124–26
implications for higher education, 133–34
intersecting identities, 127–29
queer experiences of professionalism, 118–24
research findings and discussion, 124–32
research methods, 119–24
separating identities, 129–34
social construction of, 116–18
professionalism, queer experiences of, 118–24

queer, categories of, 67
queer, definition of, 118
queer activism, and early childhood teaching, 175–76, 189–90
characteristics of, 184–86
children's storytelling and support of children's narratives, 185–89
deploying queer theory in research, 176–80
development of early childhood education, 180–81
and heteronormativity, 177–79
New Zealand Ministry of Education Guidelines and suggested strategies, 188–89
queer-minded educational reform, 183–84
re-forming queer, 181–83
Queer Art of Failure, The (Halberstam), 354–55
queered failure, and management education, 99–111
acknowledging queered failure, 105–6
exposing and challenging heteronormativity, 100, 103–5
history of management education, 100–1
and queer pedagogy, 107–11
teaching evaluations, 107–9
women in management education, 101–2
workplace diversity and inclusivity, 108–9
workplace homophobia, 109
queer love, and education, 350–51

queer love in the curriculum, 357–60
and sexuality studies, 351–57
queer negativity, discourse of, 104–5
queerness
nonsexual queerness, 32–33
systematic zoning of, 4–5
queer of color critique, in educational
research, 254–56, 265–66
critique components, 258–59
fostering agency among queer
students of color, 263–64
implications for research, 264–65
queer theory, separatist *versus*
integrationist narrative, 256–58
research methodology, 260–61
resistance and agency among queer
youth, 261–63
scholarly body of critique, 259–60
queer of color critique, in institutional
contexts, 83–94
fragmented citizenship, 86–87
"hidden" curriculum, 89–90
and life course analysis, 85–86
microaggressions, 92–94
shame, experiences of, 92
stigma consciousness, 91–92
queer pedagogy, and management
education, 107–11
queer theory
and childhood education
research, 176–80
critique of heteronormativity and
homonormativity, 272–74
cultural pedagogies and screen
media, 237–41
and norm-critical theory, 299–301
and queer sexuality education, 58–61
and relationships and sex education
(RSE), 47–49
separatist *versus* integrationist
narrative, 256–58
Quinn, Theresa, 261–62

racialization, and "coding" of spaces, 31
racism, and German educational
institutions, 81–95
fragmented citizenship, 86–87
"hidden" curriculum, 89–90
and life course analysis, 85–86
microaggressions, 92–94

shame, experiences of, 92
stigma consciousness, 91–92
theoretical approaches to
understanding, 81–83
Rasmussen, M. L., 160
Reimers, E., 301–2
relationships and sex education (RSE)
addressing homophobia, 56–58
policy and guidance for, 49–52
queer sexuality education, possibilities
for, 58–61
and queer theory, 47–49
and sexuality of children, 52–56
representation, in screen media, 248–51
Robinson, Margaret, 144–46
role models, in screen media, 248–51
Rosales, Léon, 302
Rubin, G. S., 119
Rubin, Gayle, 257

Salamon, G., 2
Sandlin, J. A., 119–20
school curriculum
addressing homophobia, 56–58
queer sexuality education, possibilities
for, 58–61
relationships and sex education
(RSE), 47–52
and sexuality of children, 52–56
schools. *See* heteronormativity, and
German educational institutions;
queer activism, and early childhood
teaching; social recognition, and
school marching bands in Brazil
school safety, and queer students in
Brazil, 161–63
school sport, 217–18, 229–30
and gender and sexuality
assemblages, 218–20
genders and sexualities in, 221–22
narrative of diverse sexualities
in, 226–29
progressive ways of viewing spaces
in, 222–26
Sedgwick, Eve Kosofsky, 48, 238–39, 257
sexuality
"charmed circle" of, 119
children's, 52–56
and gender in physical
education, 221–22

*Index* [375]

sexuality (*cont.*)
geopoliticization of, 210–11
queer love and sexuality
studies, 351–57
queer sexuality education, possibilities
for, 58–61
school sport and physical education
assemblages, 218–20
sexual minorities, intersection of
personal and professional
identities, 117–18
Sheller, M., 30
single parents, and parental
binaries, 72–75
social assemblage, 84–85, 88
social recognition
recognitive social justice, 179–80
social recognition, and school marching
bands in Brazil, 156–59, 167–70
antioppressive practices, 170–71
disrupting gender roles, 164–67
diversity along Bolivian
border, 161–64
gender expectations, 163
reimagining identities, 160–61
social recognition from marching
bands, 167–70
sole parents, and parental
binaries, 72–75
South Africa, campaign to stop
Comprehensive Sexuality Education
in, 206–8
South Africa, experiences of gay and
lesbian university students in, 270–
72, 288
assimilation as heteronormative or
homonormative, 282–83
avoiding discrimination on
campus, 280–82
inclusion, prospects for
meaningful, 275–76
negative campus
experiences, 279–80
normativities, assimilation or
transgression of, 274–77
research design and
methodology, 277–78
research findings, 279–83
research findings, discussion
of, 284–88

supportive student
organizations, 275–76
spaces, and resistance and agency among
queer youth, 262
spaces, gendering and sexualization
of, 4–5
Chancellor Hall, and Jamaican
political elites, 37–39
and Jamaican national identity, 36–37
and lived experiences of queer
students, 33–42
Mary Seacole Hall, 39
in physical education, 221–22
progressive ways of viewing
spaces in sport and physical
education, 222–26
and student housing, 27–29
Taylor Hall, 40
trans-identified students, arrest and
detention of, 33–36
and zones of nonbeing, 29–33, 42–43
*Speaking My Truth* (Angeconeb), 149–50
Spivak, G. C., 84–85
sports, 217–18, 229–30
and gender and sexuality
assemblages, 218–20
genders and sexualities in, 221–22
narrative of diverse sexualities
in, 226–29
progressive ways of viewing spaces
in, 222–26
stigma consciousness, 91–92
Stockton, Kathryn Bond, 53–54
student housing, and gendering and
sexualization of spaces
Chancellor Hall, and Jamaican
political elites, 37–39
history of practices, 27–29
and Jamaican national identity, 36–37
lived experiences of queer
students, 33–42
Mary Seacole Hall, 39
Taylor Hall, 40
trans-identified students, arrest and
detention of, 33–36
and zones of nonbeing, 29–33, 42–43
students, experiences of gay and lesbian,
270–72, 288
assimilation as heteronormative or
homonormative, 282–83

[376]   *Index*

avoiding discrimination on campus, 280–82

inclusion, prospects for meaningful, 275–76

negative campus experiences, 279–80

normativities, assimilation or transgression of, 274–77

research design and methodology, 277–78

research findings, 279–83

research findings, discussion of, 284–88

supportive student organizations, 275–76

*Sum of Us, The*, 249

Sweden, norm-critical pedagogy in, 296–97

emergent norms, 304–6

and hegemonic norm-critical theory and practice, 306–7

nationality and nationalism, norms regarding, 300–1

norm-critical studies of education, 301–4

norm-critical theory and queer theory, 299–301

practices and aims of, 297–98

Sykes, H., 221

Talburt, S., 160

Taylor Hall, and student housing at University of West Indies, 40

television and film stories, 234–36, 251

*Adventures of Priscilla, Queen of the Desert, The*, 243

AusQueerScreen study, 235–37

cultural pedagogies, 237–41

*Downriver*, 243–44

entertainment *versus* information, 245–48

role models and representation in, 248–51

screen production pedagogies, 242–45

temporality, and experiences of trans and gender-diverse children, 335–36

Terriquez, Veronica, 261–62

*Thinking Sex* (Rubin), 257

Thomson, R., 47–48

*Thousand Plateaus, A* (Deleuze & Guattari), 84–85

trans children, in primary schools

ambiguities around gender identity, 341

emotions and temporality, 337–38

gender normativity, linear temporal paths to, 338–42

happenstance, and reimagining gender normativity, 345–47

parents and children's fantasies of the future, 342–45

and temporality, 335–36

timelines and pathways of childhood development, 333–35

trans-identified students, arrest and detention at University of West Indies, 33–36

*Troubling Intersections of Race and Sexuality* (Kumashiro), 259–60

Truth and Reconciliation Commission (TRC), and Canadian Indian residential schools, 145–46

Two-Spirit Indigenous people, 141–42

undocuqueer youth, 261–62

university students, experiences of gay and lesbian, 270–72, 288

assimilation as heteronormative or homonormative, 282–83

avoiding discrimination on campus, 280–82

inclusion, prospects for meaningful, 275–76

negative campus experiences, 279–80

normativities, assimilation or transgression of, 274–77

research design and methodology, 277–78

research findings, 279–83

research findings, discussion of, 284–88

supportive student organizations, 275–76

U.S. Christian Right, and "pro-family" countermovement in southern and eastern Africa, 195–97, 212–13

abstinence only movement, 201–2

attacks on Comprehensive Sexuality Education, 203–6

*Index* [377]

U.S. Christian Right, and "pro-family" countermovement in southern and eastern Africa (*cont.*)
  campaign to stop Comprehensive Sexuality Education, 206–10
  and geopoliticization of gender and sexuality, 210–11
  and need for Comprehensive Sexuality Education, 201–3
  research methodology, 199–201
  theoretical framework, 197–99

victim paradigm, moving away from, 56–61
  and queer of color critique, 83–84
video making, and resistance and agency among queer youth, 262–63
visibility, eras of gay and lesbian, 276–77

Warner, M., 49
West Indies, University of
  Chancellor Hall, and Jamaican political elites, 37–39
  history of student housing practices, 27–29
  Mary Seacole Hall, 39
  queer students, lived experiences of, 33–42
  student housing, and zones of nonbeing, 29–33
  Taylor Hall, 40
  UWI Security Act, and arrest and detention of students, 33–36
Whittington, E., 47–48
Wickens, C. M., 119–20
women, in management education, 101–2
women of color (WOC) feminism, and queer of color critique in educational research, 258–59

workplace diversity and inclusivity, and management education, 108–9
workplace homophobia, and management education, 109
workplaces, personal and professional identity in, 115–16
  and "charmed circle" of sexuality, 119
  CORE process and research methodology, 120–24, 121t
  experiences of professional identity, 124–26
  implications for higher education, 133–34
  intersecting identities, 127–29
  queer experiences of professionalism, 118–24
  research findings and discussion, 124–32
  research methods, 119–24
  separating identities, 129–34
  social construction of identity, 116–18
writing clubs, afterschool, 262–63

youth, and queer of color critique in educational research, 254–56, 265–66
  critique components, 258–59
  fostering agency among queer students of color, 263–64
  implications for research, 264–65
  queer theory, separatist *versus* integrationist narrative, 256–58
  research methodology, 260–61
  resistance and agency among queer youth, 261–63
  scholarly body of critique, 259–60

Zambia, campaign to stop Comprehensive Sexuality Education in, 208–10